THE LAW UNDER THE SWASTIKA

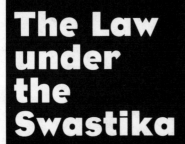

The Law under the Swastika

Studies on Legal History in Nazi Germany

Michael Stolleis

Translated by
THOMAS DUNLAP

Foreword by
MOSHE ZIMMERMANN

THE UNIVERSITY OF CHICAGO PRESS
Chicago & London

Michael Stolleis holds the chair in public law and early modern legal history at the Johann Wolfgang Goethe-Universitat, Frankfurt am Main. He is the author of *Geschichte des offentlichen Rechts in Deutschland* (2d edition 1992).

The University of Chicago Press, Chicago 60637
The University of Chicago Press, Ltd., London
© 1998 by The University of Chicago
All rights reserved. Published 1998
Printed in the United States of America

07 06 05 04 03 02 01 00 99 98   1 2 3 4 5

ISBN: 0-226-77525-9 (cloth)

Originally published in German as *Studien zur Rechtsgeschichte des Nationalsozialismus,* © Suhrkamp Verlag Frankfurt am Main 1994.

Library of Congress Cataloging-in-Publication Data

Stolleis, Michael, 1941–
    [Recht im Unrecht.   English]
    The law under the swastika : studies on legal history in Nazi Germany / Michael Stolleis ; translated by Thomas Dunlap ; foreword by Moshe Zimmermann.
        p.   cm.
    Includes bibliographical references and index.
    ISBN 0-226-77525-9 (cloth : alk. paper)
    1. Law—Germany—History. 2. National socialism. I. Title.
KK190.S7613   1998
349.43'09'043—dc21   97-36021
                                                   CIP

♾ The paper used in this publication meets the minimum requirements of the American National Standard for Information Sciences—Permanence of Paper for Printed Library Materials, ANSI Z39.48-1984.

CONTENTS

Only an extraterrestrial could describe an oxymoron like "justice in the Third Reich" in a responsible neutral manner. Otherwise, everything written on this matter can only be considered either an apology or an indictment, depending on the origin or approach of the author. Being of German origin or citizenship is sufficient to render an author a priori biased, even in his or her own eyes. This is precisely the case with Michael Stolleis, author of this collection of articles whose German title can be translated as *Justice within Injustice*. Stolleis feels he lacks "detached observation in dealing with National Socialism" because he is German and because he was shaped as a lawyer by the legal system and values of postwar Germany. Even the self-imposed commitment to neutralize the normative influence of these forces or to avoid "depicting the past in a distorted manner," earnestly pursued by the author, may not be considered satisfactory by all. Hence this additional introduction, written by one who, considered representative of the non-German view, belongs to the collective group of the victims of the National Socialist legal system.

Here a personal note is relevant: My father became a German citizen in 1929 according to the law and constitution of the Weimar Republic. Revoked by Nazi Germany in 1941 (three years after he had left for Palestine), his citizenship was not only eventually reinstated, consistent with the Basic Law of the Federal Republic of Germany, but also given to his son—again, consistent with the law of the Federal Republic. The irony of this personal connectedness to the legal framework of modern Germany helps explain the interest of an Israeli social historian in a topic that is usually outside his direct sphere of interest.

For a social historian as well as for the historian of mentality, it is specifically the philosophical debate about the quarrel between natural law and positive law that is central—a debate beyond the scope of the author's primary interest in this volume. After all, this is the debate that underlies the legal reckoning with the Third Reich. This explains the difficulty in choosing between the titles *Law (Justice) within Injustice (Recht im Unrecht)* and *Injustice within the Framework of Law (Unrecht im Recht)* for the German publication. In the German version the author cautiously opted for the first alternative. He considered the whole system unjust and thus referred to the lawmaking and legal procedure within this framework as a mere mechanism, without the spirit of justice. He did this undoubtedly because the system was an affront to natural rights and natural law. For those less cautious observers who respect positive law over natural law, the second alternative might have been as legitimate as the first: After all, the Weimar constitution, together with the traditional criminal and civil code, continued to exist in a modified way, enabling the traditional system to function under revolutionary and inhumane circumstances. Yes, the debate is essentially about natural vs. positive law.

However the interrelation between law and justice in the Nazi system is described, one conclusion becomes evident: Where the book of laws (among other things) is concerned, the Nazi revolution seems less radical by far than other revolutions, above all in comparison with the communist revolution. There is much continuity to be observed, leading from the Second German Reich (1871–1918), to the Weimar Republic (1918–1933), to the Third Reich (1933–1945), and then, surprisingly enough, to the postwar German republics, west and east.

Two factors explain this appearance of continuity. The first is the exclusion of specific segments of lawmaking and law enforcement (such as the concentration camps) from the main system. The second is the very gradual erosion in practice of rights that were formally valid, under pressure of both revolutionary ideology and the new apparatuses it created. Therefore, an important question must be asked: When did the legal system in Germany reach the point of no return and become a totally new one, creating a new system of (in)justice? Was that point already reached less than a month after Hitler's rise to power, when the "Emergency Regulations for the Defense of the People and the State" were promulgated (February 28, 1933) as a reaction to the Reichstag having been set on fire? Was it in March 1933, with the Enabling Law, practically uniting the executive and the legislature? Was it only later, with the laws establishing the authority of the Gestapo (February 10, 1936)? Or perhaps this point was never reached, and the system as a whole was more of a variation on the previous system than a break with it.

Whether we look at the essence of law, at the way the system functioned, or at the equilibrium between the different forces of law and law enforcement of the Third Reich, it becomes quite clear that the system of injustice was characteristic of this regime from the beginning. Even more, as Stolleis states very clearly, "it is a myth that some areas remained entirely untouched by the political claims of the system." This myth was nourished by cynical laymen who could argue, for instance, that the Weimar constitution was never formally abrogated. Yet it was not necessarily the influx of new laws, but rather the interpretation of law according to the maxims of *völkisch* (racist) thinking, adapted to the needs of *Volksgemeinschaft* (the people's community) and to "*völkisch* natural law," that made the difference—even if we agree with Stolleis that, strictly speaking, there was no real doctrine or legal philosophy of National Socialism.

The history of lawmaking concerning the Jews[1] provides not only a striking example of a focal area of legal activity of this revolutionary system, but also an illustration of the typical process of a "revolution by gradual small steps." The first anti-Jewish law (April 7, 1933), passed under the name "Law to Restore the Professional Civil Service," introduced racial anti-Jewish discrimination into the legal system. Yet because it was not totally implemented (Jews who had served at the front during World War I were exempted from it), the change at first did not seem too radical. Then, even the progression of laws and regulations leading up to the Nuremberg Laws (September 1935)—such as the "Law against the Disproportionately High Number of Jews Attending High Schools"—did not necessarily create the impression of a total break with the *Rechtsstaat*. There were Jews who were ready to accept even the Nuremberg Laws as a limited kind of regression rather than a total collapse of the system. Then the number of anti-Jewish laws and measures increased rapidly, and discrimination and persecution became more and more blatant. Still, because this took place within the framework of the law, a framework whose whole character underwent a transformation, changes within specific sectors (such as the "Jewish problem") could be conceived as normal. Even the harsh "Jewish laws" during the war could be considered "normal" by contemporaries, since the curtailing of rights and standard of living for the whole population became commonplace. The absurdity of this system became all the more apparent when the anti-Jewish lawmaking continued after October 1941, when Germany became practically free of Jews (*judenrein*). The law took an independent course, while its object— the Jews in this case—practically disappeared. This development turns any understanding of the concepts of 'law' and 'justice' on its head.

---

[1] Cf. Ingo von Münch, ed., *Gesetze des NS Staates* (Paderborn, 1994), 119–144; Joseph Walk, ed., *Das Sonderrecht für die Juden im NS Staat* (Heidelberg, 1995).

For any student of history, not only the history of law, three additional aspects of this history of "law under the swastika" need special attention.

First is the question of *singularity* and *historical approach*. Together with Stolleis, we may plead for the historization of National Socialism and its legal system, but not for the sake of relativization or apologetics. The question of "progress in legal history" in the era of National Socialism may provide us with an excellent test case. Social historians have been absorbed with the historization of National Socialist history at least since the *Historikerstreit* ten years ago.[2] Legal history makes no exception. Pointing to the Third Reich as a link in the development of social welfare, for example, has become a commonplace.[3] At the same time, it is obvious that attributing "modernization" to National Socialism is characteristic of the New Right in German historiography,[4] and therefore this approach should be dealt with very carefully. Thus, for example, Stolleis takes the party's "25 points program" very seriously, considering point 19 about the introduction of a German common law and its interpretation as an "incentive . . . to construct a new picture of Roman Law." In so doing he understands the "pressure of the *Zeitgeist*" or the political challenge presented by National Socialism as instrumental for the creation of "historiographical progress" or modern "scholarly response." We must not misunderstand this as an acceptance of the argumentation of the New Right.

Second is the attitude toward the *opposition* to National Socialism (*Widerstand*). If the National Socialist system was totally evil, then all legal procedure practiced by the Third Reich against any kind of opposition must be considered automatically unjust and therefore illegal, starting with the death sentences against thousands of common citizens who merely made pejorative remarks about the regime, and ending with activists engaging in conscious and political opposition, like the men of July 20, 1944, or the student White Rose group in Munich in 1943. Stolleis refers to the latter: In a film produced in 1982 about the White Rose, the producers directed public attention to the fact that the death sentence proclaimed by the special People's Court was still formally valid in Germany. The ensuing discussion revolved around

---

[2] Martin Broszat, "A Plea for the Historization of National Socialism," in Peter Baldwin, ed., *Reworking the Past* (Boston, 1990), 77–87.

[3] Hans G. Hockerts, "Bürgerliche Sozialreform nach 1945," in R. v. Bruch, ed., *Weder Kommunismus noch Kapitalismus* (Munich, 1985), 245–273.

[4] Rainer Zitelmann, "Die totalitäre Seite der Moderne," in Michael Prinz and Rainer Zitelmann, eds., *Nationalsozialismus und Modernisierung* (Darmstadt, 1994), 1–20; Z. Baumann, *Dialektik der Ordnung. Die Moderne und der Holocaust* (Frankfurt, 1992).

the question of whether sentences spoken within the framework of the then "valid law" should be accepted even today for that reason. Here we return to the basic question of whether it is right or even possible "to distinguish between 'normal' valid law from that [National Socialist] period, and 'law' that should be considered 'nonlaw' because it violated . . . natural law." Stolleis warns that the "layman's idea that legal norms . . . are invalid if they are felt to be unjust . . . is based on an unhistorical understanding of natural law." The modern social historian must react to this with some suspicion: The fallacies of historism are only too well known today, and for a historian to accept "historical understanding" as a moral absolution is one of historism's main fallacies. How far the fallacy and absurdity can go is demonstrated by another case: A Berlin court in 1955 still described an attempt against Hitler's life in 1938 as "attempted murder . . . because a deliberate plan to take a man's life was prepared"![5] Thus the court essentially left the 1939 sentence of the Nazi People's Court in force and rejected the elementary natural right to oppose a dictator, Hitler!

The problem, however, is clear: It is practically impossible to retroactively erase a whole system of law—a statement that also applies to the legal system of the GDR that ceased to exist in 1990. Therefore the next question, as to which parts of the legal complex should remain valid and which should not, inevitably leads to conflict and to much whitewashing of the evil system. It is precisely this combination of "normalcy" and evil that made it so difficult for contemporaries to grasp the unjust nature of the Nazi system. Likewise, ever since 1945 and still today, we find it difficult to decide what part, if any, of the National Socialist legal system can be accepted as "kosher" by us. From our perspective, the principle laid down by the Potsdam conference, according to which all Nazistic laws that provided Hitler's regime with a legal foundation must be abrogated, has to be considered not only naïve and undifferentiated, but also as a source of injustice and the failure of de-Nazification after 1945 because of this very naïveté.[6]

The problem does not end with the acceptance or rejection of laws and legal sentences. Much of the punishment against real or imagined opposition to the National Socialist system was imposed outside the framework of law—that is, in the concentration camps. That the inmates of the illegal system of the concentration camps were not automatically compensated after the end of the Third Reich, and that pensions of SS members usually exceed the monthly compensation paid

---

[5] Ingo Müller, *Furchtbare Juristen* (Munich, 1987), 287.
[6] Cf. Clemens Vollnhals, ed., *Entnazifizierung* (Munich, 1991).

to victims of the National Socialist system are well-known facts that illustrate the vagueness of the concepts of 'just' vs. 'unjust' within the framework of our discussion. In retrospect, even in these cases there is no sharp division between right and wrong, and even the distinction between regime and opposition does not provide us with a clear criterion for distinguishing 'just' from 'unjust.'

These examples lead us to the third point: the question of *continuity* from the Third Reich to the systems of postwar Germany. The Nuremberg Trials of 1946 were a legal act to punish and put an end to the entire National Socialist system. To ensure the effectiveness of the outcome, a parallel process of de-Nazification was launched. But it was the legal sector in particular that best demonstrated the shortcoming, if not the failure, of this process. It was impossible to find a formula by which a Nazi could be distinguished from a "non-Nazi," and therefore even Nazi judges, among other servants of the National Socialist system, could be reinstated in their jobs. In addition, the minds of the decisionmakers of the Allies in Germany were more preoccupied with the Cold War than with anything else. The four years of occupation introduced many new elements into the legal system of divided Germany, but the system and its participants remained very much the old ones. Stolleis states very clearly that there is little to say against those who accuse the judicial system of the Federal Republic of failure to deal with the Nazi judges on the level of criminal law, or of unwillingness to deal with these matters altogether. The fact that no Nazi judge was punished for his activity in the Third Reich is very revealing and throws the whole legal and judicial system of the Federal Republic into disrepute. Old Nazi judges covered up past crimes of members of their own guild or those of other Nazis, confirming the issues described at length in two popular books about this matter.[7] That jurists Wilhelm Stuckart and Hans Globke, instrumental in the implementation of the Nuremberg Laws, could become civil servants after 1949 (Globke became state secretary in Konrad Adenauer's *Kanzleramt*) is clear proof of the continuity from the Third Reich to the Federal Republic. The case of Professor Theodor Maunz, dealt with in one of Stolleis's chapters, is even more convincing: A pillar of Nazi law (professor of law in Freiburg from 1935), Maunz was a stalwart of postwar Germany's system of law, author of a popular textbook on German constitutional law, Bavarian minister of culture from 1957 to 1964. Though he lost his ministerial job because of his writings during the Third Reich, he remained an oracle of the German legal system until

---

[7] Jörg Friedrich, *Freispruch für die Nazi Justiz* (Reinbek, 1983); Müller, *Furchtbare Juristen.*

his death in 1993, when it was discovered that throughout that period he had served as an adviser to a neo-Nazi organization.

The paradox of continuity and ambiguity became apparent also in a parallel affair in the early 1960s. Theodor Oberländer, a minister in Adenauer's cabinet with a known Nazi past, used two lawyers, law commentators like Maunz during the Third Reich, to defend himself while maligning a member of the opposition, Carlo Schmid, as if his wartime activity had been no less prejudicial. The outcome of this lawsuit created the impression that everyone who lived through the Third Reich was in the same boat that should not be rocked retrospectively, because everyone was open to blackmail. Again, enmity and lack of criteria lead to the inability to distinguish between quantities of right and wrong in the Third Reich. Thus, personal continuity unavoidably also meant continuity in the spirit of the court, perhaps even in law and politics. This has cast a heavy shadow over the democratic, liberal image of postwar Germany.

But we should not deal with the legal sector as an isolated case. In many other sectors continuity was no less conspicuous. Just to mention one example: Robert Ritter, the expert par excellence on the "Gypsy question" of Nazi Germany, was consulted by the authorities of the Federal Republic as well.

If there is a lesson to be learned from this bizarre story of continuity, it is not how to find a sophisticated way to differentiate between 'just' and 'unjust' within the heritage of an evil regime. Rather, the lesson is that we must monitor the signs of evil and fight them before the evil regime is able to take power. This lesson should be known best to those of the legal profession.

—*Moshe Zimmermann*
Jerusalem

SOURCES

General Introduction	Revised version of the article "Nationalsozialistisches Recht," in A. Erler and E. Kaufmann, eds., *Handwörterbuch zur Deutschen Rechtsgeschichte*, vol. 20 (1981), cols. 873–892.
Chapter One	Essay in *NS-Recht in historischer Perspektive* (Munich and Vienna, 1982).
Chapter Two	Essay in M. Stolleis and D. Simon, eds., *Rechtsgeschichte im Nationalsozialismus. Beiträge zur Geschichte einer Disziplin* (Tübingen, 1989), 1–10.
Chapter Three	Essay in M. Stolleis and D. Simon, eds., *Rechtsgeschichte im Nationalsozialismus. Beiträge zur Geschichte einer Disziplin* (Tübingen, 1989), 177–197.
Chapter Four	*Vierteljahreshefte für Zeitgeschichte* (1972), 16–38.
Chapter Five	*Nihon University Comparative Law* 6 (1989): 11–28.
Chapter Six	Essay in K. Jeserich et al., eds., *Deutsche Verwaltungsgeschichte*, vol. 4, part 2 (1985), 707–721.
Chapter Seven	Essay in E. V. Heyen, ed., *Wissenschaft und Recht der Verwaltung seit dem Ancien Régime* (Frankfurt a. M., 1984), 147–162.
Chapter Eight	Essay in *Festschrift für Ch. F. Menger* (Cologne, 1985), 57–80.
Chapter Nine	Expanded version of two reviews, in *Geschichte in Wissenschaft und Unterricht*

Historical Introduction

The Judicial System and the Courts
in the Weimar Republic

The revolution of 1918 and the Constitution of 1919 (the so-called Weimar Constitution) transformed Germany from a monarchy into a republic. Germany became a democratic state with a strong presidency (modeled after the American presidency) and a chancellor at the head of a bicameral parliament (the Reichstag as the popularly elected lower house and the Reichsrat as the upper house representing the interests of the *Länder*, the states). The former *Länder* (Bavaria, Württemberg, Baden, Saxony, and especially Prussia) continued to exist, and together with the Reich they formed a federal state.

The structure of the legal system that had evolved between 1871 and 1918 was essentially retained. In Germany, as in France and Italy (and in contrast to the Anglo-American legal tradition), law codes have historically played a dominant role in the legal system. After the revolution of 1919, these law codes remained in force: the Civil Code of 1900, the Penal Code of 1871, and the Laws of Procedure. The function of the courts was merely to "apply" the rules laid down in the codes. The German legal system has significantly less judge-made or common law than the Anglo-American legal system.

The structure of the courts comprised three levels. The highest appellate court was the Reichsgericht (for civil matters and criminal cases, and after 1927 also for litigation involving labor law). At the middle level were the Oberlandesgerichte in the federal states. The lower courts for civil and criminal cases were the Amtsgerichte and Landgerichte, the local and regional courts. Specialized courts also existed for specific areas of the law, for example tax law (Reichsfinanzhof) and social law (Reichsversicherungsamt, Reichsversorgungsgericht). Beginning in the late nineteenth century, Verwaltungsgerichte (Administrative Courts) were set up to handle disputes between citizens and the state. Their function was to examine the lawfulness of administrative acts by the government with regard to its citizens. The most important of these courts was the Preußische Oberverwaltungsgericht in Berlin. At that time there was no supreme administrative court at the federal level. There was also no administrative court with comprehensive jurisdiction comparable to the U.S. Supreme Court or the modern-day German Bundesverfassungsgericht (Federal Constitutional Court). The powers of the Staatsgerichtshof, created after 1919, were limited.

Most of the judges who staffed the courts during the Weimar Republic had come to office before 1914. They were politically conservative and assumed a stance of "reserved loyalty" toward the republic. In political trials they were accused of rendering "class justice," and there was a good deal of truth to the charge.

The Nazi Era

The Nazi regime initially took over traditional law, the courts, and the judges en bloc. But already during the first months of 1933 there were dramatic and ominous signs that the regime was abandoning the traditional *Rechtsstaat,* the state based on the rule of law: Jewish judges, notaries, and lawyers were dismissed; criminal laws were stiffened; the principle "no punishment without law" was abolished; political enemies were sent to concentration camps. The mass killing of political rivals and others in June 1934 went unpunished; Hitler proclaimed a law that declared these murders "acts of national self-defense and as such lawful."

In the fall of 1933 the Reichsgericht acquitted several communist functionaries from involvement in the Reichstag fire for lack of evidence. In response, an angry Nazi government set up a Volksgerichtshof (the notorious People's Court) in April 1934 to deal with political cases and staffed it with National Socialists. The Volksgericht was essentially a revolutionary tribunal, a quasi-legal instrument of terror to persecute and intimidate political opponents of the regime. Between 1937 and 1944, it imposed the death penalty on 5,191 defendants.

As for the Verwaltungsgerichte, when they made occasional attempts to review measures taken by the Gestapo (Geheime Staatspolizei, the secret police), they were stripped of their jurisdiction in "political matters."

The other courts adapted to the new situation as well, occasionally adopting the new political language merely to hide behind it. Although the courts as a whole did not offer any significant resistance, it is not accurate to describe them collectively as "Hitler's willing instruments." The picture painted by scholarship is becoming increasingly differentiated and complex.

During the war, the judicial system was drastically curtailed. Stages of appeal were shortened or abolished. The younger judicial personnel were drafted into the military. Administrative jurisdiction ceased almost entirely. Paradoxically, the supreme administrative court, the Reichsverwaltungsgericht, was set up as late as 1941, though it failed to acquire any importance. The rest of the system was dominated by an increasingly harsh penal justice: External and internal pressure transformed it into a true instrument of terror during the war. However, since penal justice still failed to perform its tasks to the regime's satisfaction, Sondergerichte (special courts) were set up everywhere. During the war they dealt with everyday crime and at times imposed barbaric punishments. There were also the special courts of the military, so-called Wehrmachtjustiz (military justice), which tried to discipline the fighting troops with draconian punishments and thousands of death sentences. Finally, the darkest chapter of the judicial system was the execution, in particular by the SS (Schutzstaffel, "protective force"), of an untold number of people without trials and sentences.

The Postwar Period

After Germany's capitulation on May 8, 1945, the Allies assumed "supreme authority" and rebuilt the judicial system from the bottom up. In the process there were characteristic differences between the American, the British, and the French Zones. The Soviet Zone took a separate path altogether, under the domination of Josef Stalin.

The prevailing statutory law was "cleansed" of Nazi ideas and brought back. Judges were subjected to "de-Nazification" and rather generously restored to their positions. This explains a strong continuity in terms of personnel, which had unfortunate consequences for the prosecution of crimes from the Nazi era. The structure of the courts corresponded essentially to the model of the Weimar period. The Reichsgericht was renamed Bundesgerichtshof (Federal Supreme Court).

Two years after the creation of the Federal Republic of Germany in 1949, a new court was set up, the Bundesverfassungsgericht (Federal Constitutional Court). Its task is to translate the norms and values of the constitution into law. Like the U.S. Supreme Court, it is supposed to be the "guardian of the constitution." Its two panels (of eight judges each) have accomplished this task primarily by ruling on complaints of unconstitutionality brought by individual citizens. These complaints are very popular and have brought the court high renown.

After World War II, the Federal Republic made an energetic return to the *Rechtsstaat* and has sought to imbue the traditional—and fairly complicated—structure of the judicial system with a democratic spirit and values. Following the collapse of the political system in the German Democratic Republic in 1990–1991, the West German system was expanded to include the former East Germany.

The major issues debated today are whether the multi-layered legal protection provided by the German system is too slow and expensive, and how the traditional forms of legal protection can be adapted to the conditions of modern industrialized society.

General Introduction

Law and Despotism

It may seem paradoxical to speak of law and despotism in the same breath, for to do so raises the dilemma of the existence of "law" in a system that is on the whole "unlawful" and "unjust" or at least commits many unlawful acts. Using terminology familiar since Aristotle, we can phrase the statement as a question: How is it possible at all to speak of law under a tyranny? There are at least two answers.

The first is that no tyranny exercises power with perfect consistency. Even the worst regime has niches of order, remnants of law, islands of calm. There are always individuals who refuse to be completely compromised, who resist political pressure, and who behave "correctly," not only in their private affairs but also, and especially, in their official capacities. There are always areas of the law in which procedures continue to be "just" and "lawful." To be sure, the number of such areas will shrink the longer a despotic regime is in power and dissolves all norms, but some will remain, at least for a while. This answer presupposes two things: a concept of law that is material and substantive in content, and a system of values as the underpinning of that concept, whether or not it calls itself "natural law." In this case the law is either close to morality or merges with it. Only a norm of "good content" acquires the quality of "law." A person who kills a tyrant acts in accord with morality, and the deed is therefore not unlawful.

The second answer takes a formal starting point. It dispenses with a substantive distinction between law and nonlaw,[1] and describes as law anything that meets certain formal criteria. These criteria are determined by a given constitution. If the constitution has been reduced to the principle that the Führer's will is law and determines what is right and wrong, any expression of the state's will that is made with a claim to validity is law to the extent that it conforms to that will. This conception of the law is value-neutral and all-embracing. It excludes only those acts that fail to meet even the formal criteria, essentially only outright terror and arbitrary violence. Whatever else presents itself in the guise of a legal norm—possibly even the rules governing a concentration camp—is "law."[2] Consequently, a person who attempts to kill the tyrant is acting unlawfully, and if the attempt fails, he or she is "lawfully" sentenced and executed by the system. The fact that the individual acted in accord with morality, has a clear conscience, and is revered by posterity as a martyr is a second (moral) level that must be sharply distinguished from the law.

A third possible answer would be to deny that any of the acts of state that occurred in Germany between 1933 and 1945 had the quality of law. This position could be justified on the basis of natural law by maintaining that the regime was from the very outset incapable of rendering law and justice; it was, in the words of Augustine, a "gang of criminals." Alternatively, it could be justified on the basis of legal positivism, in which case it would have to start from the Enabling Act of March 24, 1933, arguing that since this act was invalid, all law that followed was also invalid. Both arguments run into problems, since the acts of state in question were, at least in part, voluntarily recognized as legal acts at home and abroad. In that sense, effective "law" was rendered in all areas of the law.

The essays on legal history collected in this volume do not, however, focus primarily on philosophical debates concerning whether law and morality are a single entity or separate entities, the quarrel between natural law and positive law, the question about the de facto validity of norms, or the difference between legality and legitimacy. On all these issues a legal historian will try to assume the stance of a detached observer, to avoid being drawn into the debate over the "correct" concept of law. By translating and interpreting texts, the legal historian seeks to observe how law functioned at various times, in different countries, and under different conditions. The approach is thus similar to that of an ethnologist, who seeks, through participatory observation, to decipher a cultural value system that is unfamiliar or appears familiar only by virtue of analogous elements. The debate about methodology in the humanities has repeatedly demonstrated that scholars who use this approach can deceive themselves about their perspective, that their memory can play tricks on them, that they misinterpret messages—in short, that they essentially produce a more or less subjective report that they try to present as the historical or ethnographic truth.

It is obvious what kind of difficulties work against a stance of detached observation in dealing with National Socialism and the law that was in force in Germany between January 30, 1933, and May 8, 1945. I am German; I grew up after 1945 in a peaceful and prosperous society and was neither directly nor indirectly a victim of that system. While I, like most people of my generation, do not have a sense of personal guilt, I do feel a sense of shared responsibility for that period and its crimes. Finally, I am a lawyer and thus have been shaped also by my study and practice of the prevailing system of law, a system to whose values I feel a strong personal attachment. These are the forces that have shaped my writing. Of course, my methodological conscience demands that I do whatever I can to neutralize their normative influences, to avoid perceiving or depicting the past in a distorted manner.

If we ask whether the first two answers I have sketched can be found in the corpus of National Socialist law, we encounter a complex situation. To begin with, there were important areas of the law that remained seemingly unchanged on the outside and functioned "normally," just as they had during the Weimar Republic. We know that the National Socialist regime took a strong interest in preserving the impression of "normality." Its rule was based essentially on its ability to gain the cooperation of the bourgeois economic elites and, above all, the civil servants and judges who were unhappy with the Weimar Republic. Those elites were largely nationalistic and antiparliamentarian in their thinking, but they also had a strong dislike of open terror. Before they could come to terms with the Nazi regime, they needed to be reassured that a "national *Rechtsstaat*" (state based on the rule of law) would now be set up, that everything would be done in accordance with the law, and that excesses would not be tolerated. This deceptive façade was completed by the ruling party's endorsement of a "positive Christianity" (point 24 of the party program). As far as the legal system was concerned, the initial strategy of the National Socialists was therefore to change only those elements that were indispensable to securing power and demarcating the main ideological positions. All other wishes for reform, it was said, could be fulfilled at some future time, after the "final victory." This was the approach the National Socialists took with respect to civil and criminal law: They preserved the façade of the "civil *Rechtsstaat*," did not overburden their own apparatus with overly ambitious reform plans, and in this way avoided scaring away the bourgeois elites. In the Academy for German Law these elites were given a platform where discussion could take place without pressure to translate anything into politics.

In this way the landscape of National Socialist law presented a very diverse picture. The statutory law that was in force during the Weimar

Republic was, in principle, taken over en bloc and continued to be valid unless it was superseded by new legislation. As far as legislation is concerned, we should rather speak of islands of "injustice" interspersed within a system that, on the whole, still functioned as "law." However, it is well known that this applies at most to the initial years of the regime. As the regime's output of laws continued, the *Reichsgesetzblatt* (the journal that published new laws) grew ever larger, and the ratio of traditional law to new law was progressively reversed and slowly changed to the detriment of the old order. The more secure the regime felt, the more openly it could jettison elements of the civil *Rechtsstaat*.

This development also changed the relationship between the "normative state" *(Normenstaat)* and the "prerogative state" *(Maßnahmestaat)*, first described by Ernst Fraenkel in his book *Der Doppelstaat* (*The Dual State* [1940]).[3] Fraenkel underscored the fact that "normality" and terror existed side by side, and he saw in this a structural principle of the National Socialist state. Whether the Nazi system would have had to retain a minimum of regularity in order to survive, or whether, failing that, it would have sunk into a chaos of rival power centers and become ungovernable even without the war, is not a question we can answer. But there is much to suggest that the relationship between norm and prerogative ("law" and "injustice") would not have remained stable. Instead, it would have continued to shift in one direction or another, and not necessarily in a self-destructive one. Authoritarian regimes, too, can develop forces that stabilize the system and generate a surprisingly long life span, as we now know from our experience with both Franco's Spain and the Soviet Union.

However, it is also characteristic of National Socialist law that the changes were only in part changes in legislation. While it is true that the "legislator"—a disparate conglomeration of lawmakers working side by side, including Hitler and the Reich Chancellery, ministries, the Party Chancellery, the SS, plenipotentiaries, and Gauleiter—produced a wealth of norms, the existing positive law was developed further on a day-to-day basis through a million individual decisions in the administration and the judicial system. What judges and administrative officials thought was right prevailed with the help of these decisions. Scholars have long since recognized that administrators and judges sometimes had no law to go on, sometimes gave a broad interpretation to the law (which was always in need of interpretation), and sometimes, in fact, "overtook" the law or raced ahead of it. Bernd Rüthers's book *Die unbegrenzte Auslegung* (The unrestrained interpretation of the law [1968]) called attention to this activity by the judges. More than two decades after the war, his work also refuted what the judiciary had long clung to as an exonerating thesis: namely, that the judicial system had, to a certain extent, become a victim of National Socialist laws because of the legal positivism so deeply ingrained in its representatives as a result of their legal training.[4]

By now it is widely held that the legal system that operated between 1933 and 1945 and claimed validity was a complex mix involving a judiciary and a bureaucracy that reacted quickly and legislative activity that progressed slowly. It is also clear that the various fields of the law and branches of the court system, in which the regime took varying degrees of interest, showed differing rates of change. However, it is a myth that some areas remained entirely untouched by the political claims of the system. Neither the frequently cited land register law, nor the social security or tax laws, nor the law concerning debts, property, family, and inheritance was in any way immune. Of course there were gradations of change. Areas that were highly technical and thoroughly standardized, and whose ability to function the regime was unable or unwilling to interfere with, were subjected to much less pressure.

II. The essays in this collection offer insights into only a few of all these areas, above all those of public law. It therefore seems appropriate to begin by making clear what is meant by "National Socialist law" and to provide an overview of it.[5]

The following can be described as "National Socialist law": (1) in the narrow sense, the law that was strongly influenced by National Socialist ideology (racial laws, marriage and family laws, the Hereditary Farm Law, labor law); (2) all the statutory and case law that was newly created under National Socialist rule and superseded the older legal order; (3) the entire legal order that was in force, practiced, and taught between 1933 and 1945. This threefold distinction was important to the legal regulations passed by the Allies to "liberate the German people from National Socialism and militarism,"[6] to the process of de-Nazification, to the continuing validity of law from the time before the convening of the Bundestag (Article 123 of the Basic Law), and to the rendering of legal decisions on the continuing validity of norms and legal relations from that time.[7] It also describes the stages of scholarly study of Nazi law. At first, as one would have expected, the focus was on the injustice and enormous suffering perpetrated by the system and on the legal norms that violated "fundamental principles of justice."[8] Subsequently the field of inquiry slowly broadened to include the remaining legislation, public administration, and the administration of justice, as well as the legal doctrine of National Socialism. Only very recently, in view of the continuing validity of norms taken over from the imperial period and the Weimar Republic, have scholars come to modify the overly simplistic epochal boundaries of 1933 and 1945, especially those scholars who take a subtler approach to questions concerning the continuity of the legal order of the Weimar Republic.

The goals, methodological principles, and style of the scholarly study of National Socialist law have also changed over time. The first years were dominated by eyewitness accounts,[9] bewildered helplessness, and affirmations of support for democracy and natural law.[10] Questions such as, How could this happen? and What now? were intended not so much to enhance scholarly understanding as to shape a political program.[11] Advocates of natural law fought legal positivism as the main culprit,[12] in the process often overlooking the fact that they were using the same arguments with which National Socialism itself had opposed positivism, though now under a different political banner. Similarly, some took methodological approaches that had been embarked upon after 1933: They propagated a new order of political values and recommended that these be implemented via the "breach points" *(Einbruchstellen)* of the general clauses.[13]

During the first years of the Federal Republic of Germany, the scholarly study of National Socialist law was overshadowed by other, more pressing tasks. Almost without exception, the law faculties and their legal historians shied away from the topic. The first surveys of the legal changes under National Socialism were still clearly subordinated to nonhistorical purposes that were pedagogical, apologetic, or political in nature, and they were of limited value. The perspective of "those who had been there" was narrowed down to a pattern of explanation that encompassed their own experiences. It took shape in the climate of a general "coming to terms with the past" *(Vergangenheitsbewältigung)* and involved a mixture of (a little) self-recrimination and (a lot of) self-justification, with the two motivations often difficult to tell apart. From both perspectives the National Socialist framework of power, together with its law, appeared to be a system of monolithic consistency, overpowering for victims and fellow travelers alike. The political situation of the Cold War also changed the way the past was perceived. Anti-Bolshevism proved a thread of continuity between National Socialism and the young Federal Republic. All this has been exhaustively discussed in the controversy over the various theories of totalitarianism and fascism.[14]

The domestic political consensus in the Federal Republic began to crack with the end of the Adenauer era. National Socialism was one of the controversial issues that were igniting a generational conflict.

The German Democratic Republic sought to capitalize on this for propaganda. Its *Brown Book* and *Gray Book* were distributed at universities in West Germany and widely read.[15] Beginning in 1965, in response to student initiatives, interdisciplinary lecture courses on National Socialism were organized at various universities.[16] They made important contributions also to the history of National Socialist law. Above all, however, they broke the taboo of a public discussion of the topic and gave impulse for further research.[17] A growing stream of specialized studies of National Socialist law appeared in their wake.[18] Most recently the topic has also been addressed in university histories.[19]

Though it is obvious that these first publications were connected with changes in domestic politics after 1965–1968, the growing number of sources and the increasing depth and subtlety of historical analysis developed a dynamic all their own. The professional standards applied to the quality of the scholarship rose, overly simplistic explanations and the political premises that had been dominant in the beginning lost their persuasive power. (However, that was true only in the Federal Republic. Corresponding scholarly work in the GDR lagged far behind in volume, despite the propaganda against the Federal Republic mentioned earlier; above all, it was to the very end strictly tied to political purposes and thus also qualitatively of limited value.)[20]

In this way the gaps in scholarship were slowly beginning to be filled in. It was now possible to present large syntheses of criminal law—which was particularly important in shaping National Socialist law—and the law of discrimination against minorities, which had attracted attention from the beginning.[21] Scholars looked at areas of the law that might seem somewhat remote, such as agrarian law,[22] tax law and economic law,[23] labor law and social law.[24] Some researchers reconstructed the activities of the National Socialist Lawyers' Association (NS-Rechtswahrerbund) and of the Academy for German Law,[25] while others wrote monumental studies analyzing individual courts and institutions and, in particular, judicial policy from the perspective of the Reich Ministry of Justice.[26] A collection of essays cast sidelights on "everyday justice."[27] The legal decisions of the Oberlandesgericht (Court of Appeals) in Celle came in for a thorough scrutiny,[28] as did the Special Court in Bremen[29] and the handling of Nazi crimes in terms of criminal law after 1945.[30] Eventually even lawyers themselves drew the attention of historians.[31]

Today, after two decades of wide-ranging scholarship, we are able to describe the most important fields of National

Socialist law with much greater precision. We can underpin such a description with a few basic characteristics of the legal situation at the time.

1. Regarding *constitutional law*, after January 30, 1933, Germany witnessed a transition from a parliamentary system (or what was left of it) to dictatorship in the space of a few months. The parties were dissolved through barely legalized terror and political pressure,[32] and the NSDAP (National Socialist German Workers' Party) was made the state party.[33] Intermediary powers and controls were abolished when the party staffed the most important executive posts (police power) with party functionaries, created a network of horizontal ties between the party and the state apparatus,[34] and refashioned the professional civil service into one that was cleansed of political enemies and victims of racial persecution and was duty-bound to the new state.[35] At the same time, however, these developments created the basis for new power struggles that continued to the end of the regime.

The *Gleichschaltung* (coordination)[36] of the states *(Länder)* put an end to federalism, in violation of the constitution.[37] The Reichsrat was abolished;[38] as the organ of the *Länder* in the legislative process, it had become as superfluous as the Reichstag, which, after the suppression of the KPD (Communist Party) and against the opposition of the SPD (Social Democratic Party), had acquiesced in its own emasculation through the Enabling Act.[39] Thereafter the Reichstag existed only as an organ of acclamation that could provide plebiscitary legitimacy and as a sounding board for declarations in foreign policy.[40] After the death of President Hindenburg, Hitler united in his person the offices of Reich President and Reich Chancellor.[41]

The principle of the separation of powers and the distinction between public and private law—including the liberty-securing guarantees of the liberal *Rechtsstaat*—were abolished, openly in part, and in part tacitly. Accordingly, the forms of free social organization—unions, professional organizations, associations, politically significant clubs—were either done away with or "coordinated." Only the churches were able to resist that development in the so-called *Kirchenkampf* (struggle between church and state), though they suffered heavy losses in charitable work and in the collection of donations. The process of formulating political objectives was progressively put under the control of the government, and the Reich Ministry for Public Enlightenment and Propaganda, set up in March 1933 and headed by Joseph Goebbels, took over the centralized regulation of language. The free press was eliminated[42] in accordance with Hitler's belief that freedom of the press was "objective lunacy."[43] Official supervision and control of art through the Reich Chamber of Culture was along much the same lines, if the remnant of artistic activity that had not emigrated and was not suppressed still deserved to be called art.

The result was a militarized and authoritarian centralized state that sought to gloss over the clash of competing interests with strident propaganda about a "communal way of thinking" *(Gemeinschaftsdenken)*.[44] Numerous power centers competed against one another within that state, though to the end they did so without posing a serious threat to the dominant position of the Führer.[45] A constitution in the usual sense no longer existed, even if the Weimar Constitution of the Reich was not formally abrogated. National Socialist legal literature did try to combine a few so-called "basic laws" into a constitution,[46] but this normative framework was not intended to impose any sort of self-restraint on the exercise of power. Rather, a lack of rules and a hostility to the law increasingly dominated the scene. Alongside the law there were "arbitrary measures" *(Maßnahmen)* and "Führer's orders," some of which were no longer even published. Areas in which the application of the law was "normal" stood alongside arbitrary terror.[47] The move to make the remaining normative guarantees of the law dependent on the concept of the "welfare of the national community," which could be defined however one wanted, was deliberately used by the regime as a way of generating fear. Step by step the "dual state" (E. Fraenkel) was turned into the "SS state" (E. Kogon). Acts of state bound by the law were replaced by a militaristic or pseudo-militaristic dynamism, which was driven by vague imperialistic goals and accompanied by increasing problems of self-regulation.

As was to be expected, constitutional scholars reacted in various ways to these developments.[48] Some had to flee (H. Kelsen, H. Heller, G. Leibholz, E. Kaufmann, H. Nawiasky), and the older generation withdrew (G. Anschütz, R. Thoma, H. Triepel, R. Smend). A few established scholars (C. Schmitt, O. Koellreutter, E. Tatarin-Tarnheyden, H. Gerber) and a whole series of younger university teachers (E. Forsthoff, E. R. Huber, G. A. Walz, Th. Maunz, R. Höhn, E. Küchenhoff, P. Ritterbusch) declared themselves in favor of National Socialism—whatever that may have meant concretely.[49] No significant works comparable to those of the 1920s were published on the theory of the state or constitutional law, with the possible exception of the summarizing and synthesizing book of Ernst Rudolf Huber, *Verfassungsrecht des Großdeutschen Reiches* (Constitutional law of the greater German Reich [1939]). In the end the voices that spoke about constitutional law fell silent. Those authors who did not stop publishing altogether chose innocuous topics in legal history, international law, and administrative law.

2. Closely linked with constitutional law were fundamental violations of the principle of equality through the *disenfranchisement of minorities*. This began when the regime revoked the citizenship of its opponents.[50] Soon after came the first discriminatory and persecutory measures against German (later also European) Jews, as well as against other political, religious, or racial minorities.[51] These measures intensified from a series of cunning and insidious acts of disenfranchisement and humiliation (confiscation of property, compulsory levies, "Aryanization" of businesses, forced adoption of the first names "Israel" and "Sarah" for Jews, wearing of the yellow star, and so forth) to a state-organized pogrom in 1938 (Kristallnacht) and the murder of millions in the extermination camps.[52] Until the gruesome final phase, in which disguise seemed superfluous, all discriminatory and disenfranchising measures were enacted within the forms of the law; they were published and commented on by jurists. The reasons hitherto given to explain at least the judiciary's role in the injustice—the anti-Semitism that pervaded bourgeois circles, the coming together of legal positivism and the "subservient German spirit," as well as the latent and common readiness of majorities to oppress minorities—shed only a partial light on the phenomenon.

3. In most of the traditional areas of the law, the National Socialists were initially confronted with the problem of having to govern with the existing law and judicial apparatus without any mature concepts of their own. One exception was the field of *agrarian policy*. Drawing on older theoreticians (G. Ruhland), they had already worked out a concept of state guidance with a corporative structure, price controls, and market guarantees.[53]

4. The *judicial system* was the target of the very first concrete actions. These actions were aimed at personnel policy and at providing guidance for the "cleansed" judges by educating them ideologically through "governing principles."[54] The principles laid down by the Reichsjuristenführer (leader of the jurists of the Reich), Hans Frank, on January 14, 1936, were the official line: "The basis for the interpretation of all legal sources is the National Socialist ideology, particularly as expressed in the party program and the Führer's statements. When it comes to those decisions by the Führer that are couched in the form of a law or a decree, a judge has no right of judicial review. A judge is also bound by other decisions of the Führer, insofar as they give unequivocal expression to the desire to establish a law."[55]

Both during the period of the seizure of power and during the war, interpreting the older law under the guidance of National Socialist ideology proved a superior approach than legislating new law. It was faster and more flexible, and in individual cases it could be more easily criticized and invalidated.[56] The regime evidently accepted the fact that the vague nature of "National Socialist ideology" in turn created some maneuvering room, which was used in various ways. Actual laws, by contrast, had to be measured against National Socialism's own claims. They also developed a certain binding effect that was bothersome to the new rulers.

Thus the move of turning the legal system into an instrument serving the goals set by the leadership ran on two tracks. Alongside hectic legislative activity that pushed "prerogative laws" increasingly into the foreground, it was above all "unrestrained interpretation," to use B. Rüthers's phrase, that changed the previous state of the law. The National Socialists, too, realized that it was to their advantage initially to take over the older legal system "en bloc, in order to wrench it out of the framework of the *Rechtsstaat* through decreed maxims of interpretation and general clauses."[57] Disregard of original legislative intent by ideologically guided judges became far more significant in the everyday legal life of National Socialism than injustice directly commanded by the lawmaker. And that is why the thesis disseminated in the 1950s— that the judiciary, because of its positivist orientation, had been helpless in the face of a legislator liberated from all constraints—contained only part of the truth, and why as a sweeping explanation it is downright misleading.[58] Already during the Weimar Republic, wide segments of the judiciary had chosen to oppose the democratically legitimized legislative body.[59] That is why the Nazis' call to "overcome narrow normatism" through legal interpretation—using the slogans "concrete thinking about order and organization," "will of the Führer," "needs of the *Volk* community," "common weal," "loyalty and faith," "immorality," or "healthy popular sentiment"—no longer posed any problems of method.

Little research has yet been done on the degree to which such an "ethnic-national natural law" was translated into practice, the affinity of various branches of the judiciary for taking this step or their relative immunity to it, and the tension between rhetorical effort and practical results (and here one can also find many highly praiseworthy cases of quiet and courageous resistance). And even though we now know much more about judicial policy on a ministerial level—thanks, above all, to Lothar Gruchmann's monumental study—it is on the whole still true, as Dieter Simon wrote two decades ago, that "we don't even have the basic outlines of a critical legal history of the Third Reich."[60]

The constitutional "coordination" of the states turned all existing *administration* into Reich administration. In 1939 the remnants of autonomous decisionmaking that the German Municipal Statute *(Deutsche Gemeindeordnung)* of January 30, 1935, had preserved for the municipalities were done away with.[61] However, federalism and the decentralization of administration returned in the rivalries of the Gauleiter and in the constant friction between the state and the party.[62] The overall picture is still unclear, since a good deal of source material has been lost and the material that still exists has been little studied. How local administrative practice developed, where the safeguards of a *Rechtsstaat* were preserved, and where the party's will abolished them: these are questions we can answer only for geographically and functionally circumscribed areas.[63]

Administrative law under National Socialism was characterized by the following developments: the end of the distinction developed by the *Rechtsstaat* between law, regulation, and individual act; the functional transformation of the norm from a barrier to administrative action to the given goal; the displacement of the notion of legality, now vilified as "liberal" or "positivist," by a material and ideologically charged concept of "rightfulness";[64] the curtailing of judicial review of "acts of political leadership" and discretionary political decisions; the elimination of personal right in public law and its replacement by the obligation of duty that was open to every kind of intervention and manipulation; the use of the notion of the common weal to abolish normative barriers and adapt the older administrative law to the "necessities of state."

The fate of *administrative jurisdiction* was closely tied to these dogmatic shifts. The administrative courts remained intact until after the beginning of the war. However, since they were considered "reactionary," in the sense of being part of the *Rechtsstaat,* they were progressively displaced from supervising administrative conduct.[65] This development began when the political police was exempted from supervision by the administrative courts (§ 7 of the Prussian Gestapo law of February 10, 1936, merely affirmed court decisions after 1933) and culminated when the competence of the courts was decisively curtailed during the war. The establishment of a Reich Administrative Court on April 4, 1941, by a decree of the Führer made no difference to the eventual irrelevance of administrative jurisdiction.[66] While the administration of justice differed a good deal among the various courts, the more important Higher Courts (the Oberverwaltungsgericht [Higher

Administrative Court] of Prussia, Saxony, and Thuringia, and the Verwaltungsgerichtshof [Higher Administrative Court] of Baden, Württemberg, and Bavaria) were able to preserve most of the constitutional foundations in the traditional areas of special administrative law (building law, trade and employment law, road law, energy and water law).[67]

5. In *civil law*, which largely retained its normative core, the balance shifted primarily through the administration of justice and jurisprudence.[68] The general clauses (paras. 138, 157, 226, and 826 of the Civil Code), against which the Nazis had warned,[69] were now recommended as "entry points" for National Socialist ideology. Emphasis on "communal thinking," the scaling back of rights in favor of duties,[70] the infusion of morality into the law, and its vulgarization: all this led to the loss of doctrinal rationality and legal certainty, as well as to the formation of new doctrinal forms. From 1937 on the Nazis talked about dismantling the Civil Code into individual laws and abolishing the general section (Reich Justice Ministry), and after 1939 they discussed the creation of a *Volksgesetzbuch* (people's law code), which reached the stage of a draft.[71]

Marriage law, family law, and *hereditary health law* underwent a special development that was, once again, driven by the legislator. The National Socialist state established its "public interest" in the policy of procreation through changes in the law of adoption, in the procedure of contesting legitimacy, in government loans to young married couples, and in child support. It pursued this further through the Law for the Prevention of Genetically Diseased Offspring of July 14, 1933; the so-called Blood Protection Law of September 15, 1935, forbidding marriage and sexual relations between Jews and non-Jews on the grounds that this constituted "racial pollution," outlawing the employment of non-Jewish domestic help by Jews, and barring Jews from flying the national colors; and the Marriage Law of July 27, 1938.[72]

Continuing an older, though now massively politicized, trend, *labor law* also drifted further away from the Civil Code. Following the breakup of the unions, the establishment of the German Labor Front, and the abolition of collective bargaining (replaced by "trustees of labor"), labor law was given a legal framework in the Law on the Organization of National Labor, promulgated on January 20, 1934, and modeled after the Italian *Carta del lavoro*. This law was flanked by the Law on Homeworking (Heimarbeitsgesetz, 1934), the Law on State Labor Service (Reichsarbeitsdienstgesetz, 1935), the Labor Organization (Arbeitsordnung, 1934/1938), and the Law for the Protection of Young People (Jugendschutzgesetz, 1938). Orienting employees and employers toward the "common benefit of the people and the state," interpreting the employer-employee relationship as a "communal relationship" infused with ethical meaning,[73] outlawing strikes, freezing wages, and abolishing the right to freely choose one's job during the war: all these steps came de facto at the expense of workers and employees. However, a propagandistic appreciation of workers, "Kraft durch Freude" (strength through joy)[74] events, and improved social security benefits compensated somewhat for these losses, at least on the subjective side; together with the overall system of centralized guidance, they prevented the outbreak of domestic unrest.[75]

6. Parallel to strengthening the position of employers in labor law (the "Führer principle"), the new leadership broadened the powers of management in *business law*. In the area of stock law this led to an increase in the authority of the board[76] and the state's right of intervention. In cartel law, as well, the state's abilities to intervene and direct developments were broadened.[77] The cartel court was abolished in 1938, and the cartels gradually turned into self-administering organs of the war economy working closely with the state.[78] In addition, the state took over the setting of price policy, at first gradually and then decisively with the outbreak of the war. It regulated foreign currency laws and used the foreign currency criminal laws as a variant of political criminal law (as the German Democratic Republic did later).[79] The other areas of business law and war economy law were also safeguarded through special penal laws.[80]

7. *Social law*, too, was affected by long-term structural changes and ideological influences. Public welfare on the whole was shunted aside as much as possible,[81] except for areas that could be used for propaganda and were looked after by the party's organizations. In 1935 the German Labor Front explained: "Until now, excessive amounts of money from the funds of the social administration and general welfare work have been spent on people who were hopelessly sick and unquestionably inferior." Accordingly, the Nazis tried to rid themselves of "useless" social welfare recipients through so-called "euthanasia actions" and deportations to concentration camps.

The economic upswing made it possible initially to restore the financial health of social security. By 1939 the number of insurance carriers had been reduced by 2,838 to 4,841. Various improved benefits were granted,[82] the pool of eligible recipients grew,[83] and in the area of accident insurance the state switched in 1942 from insuring businesses to insuring persons. However, the picture is complete only if we include the following facts: the destruction of self-government and the introduction of the Führer principle; the partial dismantling of social benefits; the retention of an increase in contributions during hard times; and the use of the assets of social security to finance the war.[84]

8. *Tax law* is an exemplary case for what I mentioned above as the ambivalent relationship between the seemingly apolitical, technical nature of an area of the law and its regulation through a superimposed general clause. The first paragraph of the Tax Amending Law of October 16, 1934, prescribed that the norms of tax law be interpreted in accord with "National Socialist ideology" (which was soon taken as the general principle of legal interpretation). This led to great difficulties for organizations the Nazis disliked (Jewish clubs of all kinds, hospitals, old age homes, ecclesiastical foundations, religious orders, and other ideologically colored institutions), most often through the denial of tax-exempt status. In addition, tax evasion was stylized into "treason against the national community." The decisions handed down by the Reich Fiscal Court *(Reichsfinanzhof)* played an important part in tightening the criteria of what constituted a tax offense and in actively interfering with Jewish clubs and the churches, in particular. This runs counter to a widely disseminated legend that the administration of tax law was purely professional.[85]

9. From the outset the National Socialists recognized the eminently political function of *criminal law* and acted accordingly. They used criminal law to intimidate opponents and suppress groups, to create fear even among their own supporters, and to create an attachment to the "national community" by criminalizing some visible victims (the so-called "November criminals," communists, Jews). Moreover, the Nazis had promised peace and order and "a ruthless battle against those who, by their activities, injure the general good" (point 18 of the party program). A "reform program" for criminal law did not exist in 1933, but there was a basic antiliberal and anti-individualistic attitude, which was shared in part by the legal literature on criminal law.[86]

Beginning with the police raids in the wake of the Reichstag Fire Decree of February 28, 1933, the Nazis erected on these foundations a system of penal control and oppression in which traditional criminal and trial law, gradually reshaped, played an important but not exclusive role. It was flanked by an expansive special criminal law,[87] by police law, and by the special powers granted to the party and the SS. A "special law" was in force in the conquered territories of the East, the sole purpose of which was the suppression of any hint of opposition.[88] To a large extent the Nazis did without a legal basis for their actions. The jurisdiction of regular and military courts over penal offenses committed by the civilian population was curtailed. Police courts-martial, SS courts, and executive acts without a legal foundation and based on "the necessities of state prevailing in the incorporated eastern territories" took the place of traditional justice.[89] Overall, criminal law and punishment "not only surrounded the dictatorial system with a protective wall by consistently pursuing the racial idea and the related destruction of supposedly inferior person, . . . it also caused incredible bloodshed."[90] Even if the Nazis implemented some points of the re- form discussion that had taken place during the Weimar Republic,[91] the primary trend was a movement away from the direction of reform initiated by Franz von Liszt and the elimination of the trial guarantees developed after the Enlightenment.

After 1933 the practice of criminal law and the writing about it were dominated by several developments. A crime was no longer seen as the violation of a legally protected interest but as a breach of duty, while punishment was meted out not to an offense but to a perpetra- tor's willingness to commit it. The strict typology of offenses was loos- ened through the introduction of new concepts that still needed to be fleshed out. The prohibition against the use of analogy was abolished, alternative punishment was permitted,[92] and retroactive force was in- troduced.[93] The range and severity of punishment was expanded, and the idea of deterrence and protection of the nation took precedence over rehabilitation. The procedural position of the prosecutor was strengthened, and the rights of defending lawyers were curtailed.[94] The appeal process was shortened. Special courts were introduced,[95] espe- cially the so-called People's Court *(Volksgerichtshof)*.[96] The powers of the police and the Gestapo were broadened. Finally, the principle of legality was formally abrogated.[97] The Nazis implemented these changes in part by passing specific laws,[98] in part by guiding the inter- pretation of existing law. Attempts to reform and codify substantive criminal law and trial law went no further than the draft stage, primar- ily, it would seem, because the leadership wanted to avoid committing itself in any way.

A topic unto itself is the controversial administration of justice by the Wehrmacht. Although no definitive verdict is possible at this time, the picture we get is at odds with the one painted by former military judges.[99] In recent years scholars have made major corrections.[100]

10. A survey of developments in the various areas of National So- cialist law makes it plain why there can be no real "legal doctrine" (legal philosophy, legal theory) of National Socialism. What prevailed from the whole range of legal philosophy before 1933 was chiefly con- servative Hegelianism (J. Binder, K. Larenz, E. R. Huber) and other variants of a neo-idealism that also picked up the threads of Johann

Fichte and Friedrich Schelling. Although "concrete thinking about order and organization" (C. Schmitt), the "jurisprudence of racial laws" (H. Nicolai), and "ethnic-national natural law" (H. H. Dietze) did not progress beyond vague sketches, by elevating brutal reality philosophically they rendered no small service to the system of power.[101]

Just as there was no separate "National Socialist history,"[102] a genuine "National Socialist legal history" was not able to develop either.[103] To be sure, a few legal historians professed their decided loyalty to National Socialism. However, it is more important to note the existence of a broad and very widespread affinity between the basic idealistic foundation of legal scholarship and the best face that National Socialist rule presented. The search for the working of "ideas" in historical material,[104] the attribution of specific ideas to specific peoples (such as community, honor, and "true" freedom to the Germans, self-interest and "false" freedom to the English, the Jews, and so on), notions about the decay and revival of such ideas, and the quest for the "eternal German spirit" that manifested itself in diverse forms: all this was easy to integrate into the pattern of National Socialist propaganda. Basic ideas of National Socialism and idealism above all set the Germanic branch of legal history on a voluntary or involuntary parallel track with Nazi ideology. After 1945, these interconnections were largely suppressed or denied. The branch of legal history that dealt with Roman law—because of its material, its international connections, and the fact that eminent scholars of the field were forced into emigration—proved much less susceptible to the influence of Nazi ideology.[105] Point 19 of the NSDAP party program—"We demand that Roman law, which serves a materialist world order, be replaced by German common law"—remained relatively insignificant. At best it reinforced the "crisis" that Paul Koschaker had diagnosed in that field of study.[106]

IV. If we return, following this cursory overview, to the history of scholarship, we note that the basic methodological problems were not really solved, and in all likelihood could not be solved. The stirring postwar questions, How could it happen? and How can we prevent something similar from happening again? continued to be unsettling because "jurists as such" were—and are—unable to answer them. Once the recommendations of natural law of the postwar period had lost their persuasive force and the modern theory of science had conveyed a basic awareness of methodology, the only thing left was recourse to a value-bound private morality, civic virtues, and democratic consciousness, and an appeal to the legal profession's sense of political responsibility.[107] Ingo Müller's popularly written book *Furcht-bare Juristen* (Terrible jurists: a title borrowed from Rolf Hochhuth) was published in 1987 and became a bestseller.[108] The simultaneous and unexpected eruption of the so-called *Historikerstreit* (historians' quarrel)[109] revealed how much the scholarly landscape had changed. This controversy revolved less around questions of fact than around issues of interpretation and evaluation. The most contentious issue was whether the historicization of the events of the Nazi era—which is no doubt an inevitable process—also entails strategies to relativize them and make them less burdensome. The *Historikerstreit* was essentially a moralistic-semantic debate. At the same time, however, it was also a struggle against the reappearance of nationalistic and apologetic positions. And seven years after the controversy we can say that it was not a struggle against imaginary dangers.

PART ONE

The Study of National Socialist Legal History

ONE

Biases and Value Judgments in the Study of National Socialist Legal History

Debates about scholarly methodology, like historical topics, experience trends and cycles. The intensity of these debates appears to be directly related to the uncertainties within the disciplines in which they are carried on or to the seriousness of challenges from the outside. As for legal history, it may indeed be true that such debates "have not played a significant role since the program of the historical school."[1] Still, they do fluctuate with the current of the times. For instance, the curriculum regulations of 1935, which threatened the position of Roman law, prompted broader methodological reflections,[2] and the end of the Nazi era—though not its beginning—led to several years of new methodological debates.

The postwar period was a time of deep insecurity and confusion. Historians and legal historians saw not only their methods but also the meaning of their work thrown into doubt. Faced with the "German catastrophe," Friedrich Meinecke brooded on the meaning of historical work beyond the "desacralized causal connection [*entgötterter Kausalzusammenhang*]."[3] Gerhard Dulckeit searched for the working of supra-temporal ideas in legal history,[4] and Heinrich Mitteis sought to demonstrate why "legal history was worth having."[5] Confronted with the abuse that idealism had suffered at the hand of Nazi propaganda, these scholars were trying to salvage their own methodology, which was based on idealism. They were trying to rebuild a humane image of man and were searching for an "idea of the law" in history that was "indestructible" in the face of all catastrophes.[6] As Mitteis said, "We invite legal history to appear before the forum of life, and ask it to prove that the fruits of its work can be directly translated into present values."[7]

Scholars pursued these goals on the basis of a more or less clearly formulated idealism and unbroken optimism about values, and they used a language that was only in part amenable to rational examination. In retrospect this may seem peculiar, as we might expect that the more obvious path would have been a return to the positions of Max Weber and of Viennese neo-positivism, an embrace of Western political thought and Anglo-Saxon analytical philosophy combined with a rejection of the traditions of German idealism. But such an expectation would amount to a complete misunderstanding of the intellectual situation of the postwar period.[8] Again and again one discovers that "in spite of catastrophes, rubble, and deepest degradation, the metaphors of late-idealistic ways of thinking continued unbroken. The longing for the 'good, beautiful, and true' had by no means died down; it was now given a defiant undertone of 'nevertheless.' The German spirit had been abused and dishonored, but not destroyed. People clung to the immortality of the classics."[9]

The methodological reflections of the first years after the war—in which, apart from Mitteis, Karl Siegfried Bader, Helmut Coing, Paul Koschaker, Hans Thieme, Theodor Viehweg, and Franz Wieacker were significantly involved[10]—soon subsided, once scholars, shaking off Nazi terminology,[11] had confirmed that the traditional methodological maxims were fundamentally sound. Only Wieacker remained restless, and he has continued to develop and change his position right down to the present.[12] The discipline of legal history as a whole—if I may speak in such broad terms—essentially continued as Mitteis had described: "With ever renewed joy of discovery it moved from one field of inquiry to the next, piling up its material into mountains of dizzying height and interpreting its sources thoroughly—though mostly in an unreflected manner—from the standpoint of a naive realism."[13] In all of this, one is tempted to add, the classificatory categories were derived from idealistic philosophy, especially of a Hegelian variety.

As a result, legal history was badly prepared for the methodological discussion that was carried on in all humanistic disciplines in the wake of the student movement of the late 1960s. The sudden calls for an "emancipatory legal history"[14] and a "materialist method,"[15] and the goal "of restoring in this field, as well, the necessary historical orientation of action through a materialist theory of history"[16] met with indignant opposition.

Legal historians could respond to these demands by maintaining that the best work in legal history had always used an approach that was now being called "materialist"—that is, it had included the social and economic conditions underlying the creation of legal norms. They could also argue that the "orientation toward action" (*Handlungsorien-*

tierung) that was being called for was nothing other than a new metaphysics of history. Replacing Hegel with Marx was *not* progress in terms of theory but the continued adherence to nineteenth-century categories of thinking.

Since that time, the question about the methods of legal history has advanced very little outside of Wieacker's studies.[17] The *Zeitschrift der Savigny-Stiftung für Rechtsgeschichte,* the leading journal in the field, has avoided methodological problems as studiously as it has avoided an examination of National Socialism and contemporary legal history. The *Zeitschrift für neuere Rechtsgeschichte,* which has been filling these gaps, began publication in 1979.[18]

II. Given this situation, remarks on the topic under discussion can only be preliminary and fragmentary. They are by no means intended to retrace the methodological debate from Leopold von Ranke and Johann Gustav Droysen up to the present by using National Socialism as an example. Rather, I will offer some observations drawn from my own legal scholarship. The point I will make is that a few special characteristics distinguish the literature on legal history under National Socialism as it has developed in the Federal Republic after 1945 from the rest of legal history.

1. Looking at the authors themselves, we note that a comparatively high percentage are former judges and administrative officials. Legal scholarship on topics ranging from antiquity to the nineteenth century has become fully professional—that is to say, it is pursued by scholars at universities, at non-university institutes, or in archives. By contrast, when it comes to the legal history of National Socialism, the debate has been joined by jurists and nonjurists who cannot be described as legal historians in the conventional sense. On the one hand, this enriches the debate, as it reduces scholarly isolation and can lead to fruitful contact with neighboring disciplines. On the other hand, there is greater danger of amateurism and subjectivity, since there is no guarantee that the sources will be selected and interpreted critically. In this way the boundary between analysis and self-portrayal becomes blurred, especially when the author is someone who worked in some capacity in the judicial apparatus of the Nazi state. Examples are the books of the former judges H. Schorn, H. Weinkauff, and O. P. Schweling.[19]

The study by Schweling, *Die deutsche Militärjustiz in der Zeit des Nationalsozialismus* (German military justice in the era of National Socialism [Marburg, 1977]), has become a virtually paradigmatic example of the dangers I have mentioned. The author himself had been a judge in the Air Force, and he was supported by the Vereinigung ehemaliger

Heeresrichter (Association of Former Military Judges) in gathering and selecting his material. The controversy between the author and the Munich Institute for Contemporary History over the publication of the manuscript—as well as the discussion about the value of the work, following its publication by Erich Schwinge after the author's death—revealed that some significant lines of battle had been drawn up: The Institute for Contemporary History, whose scholarly advisory board had recommended against publication, was opposed by former military judges and others who had been personally involved in the events, backed by articles in *Deutsche National-Zeitung* (a right-wing paper) and *Deutsche Wochenzeitung* (mouthpiece of the Nationaldemokratische Partei Deutschlands [NPD], a right-wing party).[20] This is not the place to analyze the positions that were staked out. However, the facts I have given already reveal how difficult it is for a consensus on the scholarly merit of a work to emerge if its author and his supporters are not professional historians, if they give free rein to their emotions and their overpowering interest in having the findings turn out a certain way, and if they are unable to see criticism of their method as anything but the result of political bias.

The starting point for understanding the "peculiarities" of legal scholarship on the Nazi era is thus a literary scenario in which historians and nonhistorians make statements about historical facts, with many of the nonhistorians having been active as jurists in the years 1933–1945. From a neutral point of view, the critical handling of the sources and the ideal of the greatest possible degree of scholarly objectivity are therefore compromised in a different way than in other fields of historical scholarship.

2. The emotional involvement of authors with their topic is not a problem unique to this field of research, though it surely occurs here with special intensity. National Socialism was not merely one dictatorship among many others, it has left its imprint on the psyche of several generations. If someone writes a book about the Nazi dictatorship, it can be assumed that he or she was in some way "affected" by it. This is as plainly true of émigrés as it is of those "who were there." And their children and grandchildren, too, cannot escape their own emotions.

However, authors have dealt with their feelings in a variety of ways. Some have expressed them openly, while others have sought to overcome them, allowing them to influence their scholarly work to varying degrees. In some cases, scholars who would have been perfectly suited for work on National Socialist law expressed their emotional relationship by their very silence on "the subject."

3. Another peculiarity of this field of historical scholarship is the political consequences of National Socialism, consequences that also influence the law that exists today. All those involved in scholarly work on Nazi law have been influenced, willingly or unwillingly, by the division of Germany that was caused by National Socialism and by the political premises, language rules, and tabooed thinking that have been internalized in West Germany and East Germany in different ways. We can take for granted that this has profound effects on how people deal with National Socialism.

An all-German discussion of National Socialism, let alone of the specific topic of National Socialist law, is obviously not taking place. The few legal historians of the former German Democratic Republic who have remained in contact with their western colleagues belong to the older generation, which, like the older generation in western Germany, has studiously avoided the topic.

4. This brings us to the fourth point: the generational problem. Not only does it play a role in the emotional weight that is given to the topic, it also exerts an influence on scholarship that is difficult to grasp and rarely articulated in public. Since many professors themselves are uncomfortable dealing with the Nazi era, whether because of personal involvement or out of consideration for colleagues or teachers, it is likely that they have not exactly encouraged students who have wanted to work in this field, and they may even have prevented them from doing so. In this way the understandable reluctance of scholars who were themselves involved in the events has influenced at least the next generation of students.

It strikes me as revealing that all the dissertations and *Habilitation* theses that have been written in the Federal Republic on the topic of National Socialist law were, as far as I know, supervised by professors who had not been involved with National Socialism in any way. It is also plausible to assume that an attempt to write a *Habilitation* thesis on this topic before 1965 would have run into great difficulties. In any case, nobody made such an effort, which in itself is quite revealing. Only the interdisciplinary lecture courses that were organized during the late 1960s in response to student pressure[21] removed a certain fear to enter on a discussion of this topic.

███ The points mentioned so far—the reticence of academic legal history and the prominent presence of former judges among those who have written on Nazi legal history, the inescapable emotionalization of the topic, the division of Germany and its political consequences, and the generational problem within the field—form the background to some widely used ways of talking about the subject that reflect many of the problems that beset the study of Nazi law.

To begin with, one often hears that "it is too soon to speak about National Socialism."[22] Others argue, conversely, that it is already too late to do so, at least for the younger generation, since "only someone who lived through that time can understand it." Other common refrains are these:

—"Only a jurist can speak competently about National Socialist law."
—"A study of the National Socialist period must be approached differently from a study of the legal ideas of the Carolingians."[23]
—"When it comes to rendering judgment on this period, everybody is affected and compelled to take a personal stand. More so than anywhere else, history must here be understood as the teacher of the present."[24]

The biases and value judgments contained in these statements spring from a common intent: they all seek in some way to guide research on National Socialism or on the law under National Socialism. A reductionism takes place, based always on a certain notion of how research should be conducted and who should do it. The last quotation begins by positing the inevitability of a personal stance. It then sets up a goal of historical work, that of teaching the present, which makes other goals secondary or excludes them altogether. This move, too, is reductionist.

Evidently all these biases and value judgments have their own historical and group-specific contexts. If one uses the tools of theory to discuss the "truth" or "falsehood" of these statements detached from their context, the result will be essentially a contribution to the methodology of legal history that uses these biases and value judgments as an example. By contrast, if one includes the context to examine when and with what intent these formulations were used, one's interest is "historical." In that case the discussion seeks to explain certain typical patterns of behavior on the part of (legal) historians of the postwar period and how they affected scholarship. That is precisely what the following remarks seek to do.

It is too soon to speak about National Socialism. The unforeseen changes it has set in motion in the world, and the catastrophe that befell large parts of Europe, and especially Germany, through World War II, have stirred up emotions that make an objective judgment difficult . . . That is why scholarship should refrain from making laudatory or damning judgments. Establishing the proper relationship between accomplishments and idealistic goals, on the one hand, and crimes and guilt, on the other, is a task that demands a detached judgment that has not been attained, and perhaps cannot be attained at this time.[25]

This position was formulated in 1951 by one of the scholarly protagonists of Nazi criminal law, G. Dahm. Considering that the author was personally involved in the events he is talking about and was writing only a few years after the end of the Nazi era, it is understandable why he would say this. This attitude was in fact widespread during the first years of the postwar period among scholars and the general public. By expecting a calm and detached judgment "sine ira et studio" at some later time, it kept open the possibility of a positive assessment of National Socialism in the future. At the same time it criticized the prevailing and unambiguously negative judgments of the Nazi era, which, as Dahm put it, amounted to an "excessive rejection and disparagement of the historical forces . . . that determined the fate of Germany between 1933 and 1945."

The further time moves on and the more sober historical scholarship shows that the time is now ripe for an assessment of the phenomenon of National Socialism, the more difficult it is to maintain the defensive strategy that tells historians that it is "too soon." We can see this, for example, in Robert Scheyhing, who justified leaving National Socialism out of his constitutional history of Germany, published in 1968, by arguing that the competence of a historian has reached its limits when it comes to the Nazi period. Those limits are reached, he argued, when the most recent past affects the present to such an extent that distance from the topic is lost, particularly if the present conceives of itself as a world consciously and deliberately opposed to the past: "The examination of legal history therefore should not take the period of Nazi rule in Germany into consideration. Today that period belongs more properly to the domain of the philosopher and legal philosopher than that of the historian."[26]

To be sure, experience has taught us that a certain distance in time and certain factual preconditions are necessary to attain higher levels of objectivity. The more the period under discussion was racked by ideological battles whose reverberations are still felt by the historian, the longer the interval of time that must elapse. This applies in a very high degree to National Socialism. Both the Federal Republic and the German Democratic Republic were founded and legitimated as different "historical answers" to National Socialism, and both demanded from their citizens the political rejection of "fascism." With regard to factual preconditions, we could mention especially the accessibility of sources and the normative guarantee that scholars are free to pursue their work and actually do so.

Fourteen years after Dahm's work, the exclusion of National Socialism from legal and constitutional history is—with all due respect to the problem of "proximity"—obviously no longer tenable. National Socialism has become "historical," with all the consequences this entails for the historical disciplines, including legal history. It is no longer possible to hand the topic over to philosophy or legal dogmatics. Numerous historical works on Nazi law have de facto cut the ground from under the defensive argument that it is "too soon."

The second refrain, that *only someone who lived in that time can form a judgment about it*,[27] is always used by the older generation against the younger one, with the former invoking direct experience against "knowledge acquired by reading." Nothing about this argument makes it unique to National Socialism. It is found anytime someone who "was there" wants his or her "authentic interpretation" to prevail against others. The discussion about judging people's behavior during the Nazi period has been carried on in this vein not only between former National Socialists and their children, but also between old and young communists, social democrats, and Christians, and between parents and children. The use of this argument will continue for as long as there are people who "were there."

It is undeniable that people who observed and/or participated in and helped shape a historical event are more informed about things they knew firsthand than someone who seeks to reconstruct a complex chain of events by interpreting what are for the most part written sources. It is also true that documents alone have limited evidentiary value in dictatorships and in the age of the telephone.[28] Still, the potential for errors that arises from the privileged position of the observer or actor is obvious. People who are directly involved frequently write interesting diaries and memoirs, but experience has shown that they cannot simultaneously be their own detached historian. The deeply human wish to cast the past and one's own accomplishments in a positive light invariably clashes with the demand for an objective account and assessment. We can study this phenomenon in many writers of memoirs, from Otto von Bismarck, Winston Churchill, and Charles de Gaulle to Heinrich Brüning, Konrad Adenauer, and Carlo Schmid.

If one believes that historical writing is more than a collection of reports of personal experience, the thesis that only someone who experienced a historical era can speak about it competently, taken to its logical extreme, would lead to the end of historiography as such.

Only a lawyer can speak competently about National Socialist law. Even in its more cautious formulation—that only the legal historian is in a position to answer the specifically judicial questions about the circumstances of the legal system under National Socialism—this thesis is rarely stated so explicitly. Nevertheless, the scholarship on National Socialist law is—with a few notable exceptions—the monopoly of lawyers. Historians, moreover, seem to accept this monopoly. For example, Helmut Krausnick said, in the introduction to the first volume of the series *Die deutsche Justiz und der Nationalsozialismus* (The German judicial system and National Socialism): "The nature of the topic (!) is such that its scholarly treatment devolved for the most part upon jurists."[29]

If the meaning or actual effect of this thesis is that nobody "from the outside" should judge the role of jurists in the Nazi state—that "misconduct" will be sanctioned internally, as it were, and good conduct rewarded internally—it is completely unacceptable. The historical examination of a specific segment of society under National Socialism cannot be monopolized by the scholarly discipline most directly concerned. Legal history—in formal terms the field most appropriate for dealing with the topic of Nazi law—is part of general historical studies, irrespective of the position it occupies in the training of jurists, a position that has no compelling theoretical justification (but is a sensible one).[30] For that reason all historical disciplines are in some way responsible for the study of Nazi law. Legal jargon and the difficulty of translating theoretical problems into everyday language pose no fundamental obstacles.

In general, the thesis is therefore understood in a milder form, for instance, in the sense that jurists have a professional advantage in mastering the terminology and grasping the specifically "legal" questions. Whether this is sufficient to constitute a separate field of research called "legal history" remains an open question. Here I am concerned with the consequences that flow from the jurists' monopoly as revealed by studies on Nazi law written by jurists. In my view those consequences have been largely negative, unless the legal competence of the authors was balanced by a corresponding historical view.

1. Jurists unconsciously, and in keeping with the maxims of their training, proceed from the existing law, from which they derive their guiding perspectives and criteria of evaluation. For example, Rudolf Echterhölter, in his study of public law under National Socialism, arranged the material in accordance with "the constitutional value judgments and principles that have crystallized today, precisely after the experiences under National Socialism. The material has been arranged around them even if corresponding principles were not yet present in the Weimar constitution, and the administration of justice under discussion therefore did not, from the perspective of the time, concern itself explicitly with questions of constitutional law."[31]

This approach is unhistorical and goes against the generally accepted methodological principle that a period must be measured by its own premises and its documents made comprehensible within their own context. The Basic Law, conceived as a political response to the experiences under National Socialism, cannot be the "correct" historical yardstick with which to measure National Socialism.

2. Jurists have a habit of letting themselves be guided by models of causality and fault derived from criminal and civil law. The narrowing of causation and fault—in the sense of a subjective allocation of responsibility—that is peculiar to legal thinking excludes entire causal chains that could be of interest to historians. Examples of this are not only the above-mentioned books by Schorn, Weinkauff, and Echterhölter, but especially Schweling's work on military justice. The guiding question for each author was whether the jurists in question were "guilty" because their decisions reveal the presence of "National Socialist ideas." To that end they drew up groups that bear an ominous resemblance to the categories used on de-Nazification questionnaires.[32]

Similarly, Echterhölter's study ignores all those "parts of public law that offered few footholds for National Socialist ideas."[33] This means that broad areas of public law are passed over in silence and that the relationship between these areas and those that did offer "footholds" remains unclear.

An impartial historical examination of Nazi law, one that is also not influenced by the legal perspective after 1945, must free itself from such categories of guilt and from the fixation on politically interesting points in order to reach a balanced overall picture.

3. It is typical of jurists that they are systematically trained to ignore, suppress, or dismiss extralegal motivations. They learn to frame situations to let the "legal question" come to the fore. This technique has its own good reasons in a state under the rule of law, and it is also founded on the division of labor in solving social conflicts. However, if applied to historical situations, it has a distorting effect: for what matters in these situations are, not least, the "extrajuridical" motivations, and our interest lies in the way the law is interwoven with the totality of its social determining factors. Jurists, accustomed to regarding all this as legally irrelevant, will find it difficult to let their perspective embrace not merely what is "legally relevant" but the totality of historical conditions.

As a result, legal works generally accentuate the normative scaffolding of events under discussion, a scaffolding that can be found in law gazettes and compendia of legal decisions. The reality that leads up to these norms, carries them, and is shaped by them is often reduced to a few general remarks, since the study of the law provides hardly any systematic guidance on how to come to grips with it.

4. In some cases the perspective is distorted not so much by an exclusive concern with the normative facts as by the elimination of entire procedural steps. For instance, it seems characteristic of historical accounts written by judges that they pay little attention, when it comes to criminal law proceedings, to police investigations (or the activities of the Gestapo) and the way in which sentences were carried out. Instead, they focus on the field of work concerned with rendering decision, the very field that is assigned to them also under existing law. In addition, they are accustomed to describing events from the perspective of decisionmakers, not the perspective of those at the receiving end of their justice. As officials in service to the judicial apparatus, they are hardly willing to take a detached view of how the entire judicial apparatus operated and functioned as a pillar of the National Socialist system. Here, too, the individual would be asked to assume a dual role—that of acting within the system and that of describing the system from outside with some claim to objectivity. Experience has shown us that such a dual role is more than most people can manage.

5. Jurists, unlike historians, have traditionally been raised with the belief that the law in its entirety forms a "system," and that it must therefore in principle be possible to describe and reconstruct it free of inconsistencies and contradictions. This makes it very tempting to find a system even where reality was chaotic. Just as jurists are ready, within the existing law, to take seriously the charge that something is contrary to the system, they will be inclined to interpret National Socialism, too, as a "system," in any case as an "unjust system." Consequently they will smooth out contradictions that historians could describe without scruples; to the jurists, these contradiction are primarily an annoyance. The effect of this will be particularly evident in an account of a dictatorship like National Socialism, where the lack of a system was an inherent feature of the system.

"A study of the Nazi period must be approached differently from a study of the legal ideas of the Carolingians."[34] This view is widely held, but it means different things depending on the context in which it is expressed. It is obvious that the nature of Nazi sources demands different methods (examination of files, interviews), but this does not pose a fundamental problem. A study of National Socialism, like a study of the Carolingians, is essentially concerned with interpreting the written evidence of a period.

More often than not this view means that National Socialism represents such a singular historical phenomenon that the historian's conventional methods have failed to come to grips with it. The intention of a person who uses the argument in this sense could be to demonize National Socialism, in the face of which historical science must capitulate as before an unsolvable mystery. It could also be to point out that public language and reality were separated by a particularly wide abyss under National Socialism.[35] Consequently a study in the field of Nazi law can be criticized for discussing National Socialist legal theory on the level purely of the history of ideas, without regard for the gap that separates this kind of writing from legal reality.

In most cases, though, something else is meant when works on the Nazi period are grouped together as a special genre of historiography. The historian is expected to take a "partial" or "personal stance," as H. Hattenhauer has put it, and these works are supposed to show a particular pedagogical essence: "More so than anywhere else, history must here be understood as the teacher of the present."[36] The concern is therefore not with research methods that are different in principle, but with the result of the historical interpretation and its application to the present. Evidently a treatment of the topic "National Socialism" that avoids a pedagogical application and is coolly detached is felt to be disquieting and perhaps even politically unacceptable. Behind this lies the emotional pressure and the political desire that a regime like that of the Nazis should never repeat itself. Essentially this is all about the objectivity of historical description, about the hoped-for effect of political education. Hattenhauer therefore speaks pejoratively of "supposed objectivity and impartiality," which, he fears, could render the overall picture "too conciliatory."[37] What seems to motivate him in all this is a concern for the democratic education of the next generation. And that is why he also demands that the discipline of history be intensely related to the present and express a clear preference for democracy.

This is perhaps the most popular demand that is made of history: it should prove its social utility, it should take its obligation of "political pedagogy" (Th. Mommsen) seriously and convey "lessons" from the past. Those who make this argument often point out that the representatives of the historical science are, after all, also supported by taxpayers' money. In this sense the Germanist Peter Wapnewski hopes that history will be useful "as the substructure of the present . . . as a chance to understand the present from the past and to surmise the future: if it can be that, history is the most honorable defense against the seduction through sloganlike illusions and penetrating ideologies, against the suggestive force of the terrible promise of salvation." The writer Hermann

Glaser adds that such an understanding of history "would be particularly welcome at this time."[38] An almost universal popular opinion demands not only that the present take its orientation from the past, but also that history take its orientation from the present: "The only way to do history meaningfully is to analyze it in order to learn from it for taking action today."[39] Even historians themselves for the most part agree, often tacitly, that the discipline of history, by throwing light on the past, should also illuminate the present. We are told that historians of the modern period, in particular, must not dodge "the obligation to find an explanation and to prevent a repetition of what has happened, an obligation which National Socialism has imposed on the German people before the entire world."[40]

In the honorable quarrel over the function of history—from Cicero's phrase "historia magistra vitae" to Nietzsche's reflections "On the Advantages and Disadvantages of History for Life" to Jean Jaurès's call to take from history not only the ashes but also the fire—this argument amounts to a revival of the pedagogically inspired position of Enlightenment historiography. Ranke's demand that events "should be recounted for the most objective possible examination with no regard for the likes or dislikes of the day," which stands at the beginning of modern historiography, was formulated at the time as an antithesis to this Enlightenment position.[41]

Current opinion, however, seeks neither to worship an unbroken Enlightenment optimism, "to teach the world for the benefit of future years," nor to identify with Ranke's naive confidence that it is indeed possible to show "how it actually was." The philosophical foundation of German post-Kantian idealism, which forms the basis also of the Marxist variations on the philosophy of history, no longer holds up. Of course, that is recognized more clearly outside Germany. At the same time Ranke's ideal of objectivity, in spite of being reformulated by Max Weber's "freedom from values," has been frequently attacked, in part "unmasked" as a bourgeois front for concrete interests, in part smiled at as mistaken by those who are sure of their mission and subjectivity. Most scholars, however, seek to combine "objectivity," on the one hand, with "usefulness for the present," on the other. There is a desire to recognize and utilize, in the words of Jürgen Habermas, the "historian's interests in understanding action-guiding self-conception"[42] without letting history become the servant of predetermined political understanding. There is a desire not to be on the sidelines in the debates of the day, to guide present action as an expert on the past, or even—in a version of secularized priesthood—to impart "orientation" to those who, in the historian's opinion, lack it. However, and this is the critical point, the conveyance of this "action-guiding self-conception" is to be given an aura of "objective scholarship." In this way the lessons of history lose their character as the historian's personal opinion and move into the realm of scholarly truth.

Some historians, in contrast, continue to hold to the separation of subject and object, and deny that it is possible to derive "ought" from past "is."[43] From this follows a rejection of the notion that the writing of history should be duty-bound by the present, even if the desire to do so springs from the best intentions of political pedagogy. Historians who take this position have, in a sense, lowered their expectations to the outside world; at most they promise that their discipline could prepare and support normative statements and strengthen their plausibility. Arguments that history should provide orientation for action find their "rational core" (D. Simon) in this reduced formulation, and to that extent a discussion about the pedagogical purpose of the study of history also seems meaningful. However, as long as historical scholarship does not violate its methodological principle that the blending of descriptive and prescriptive statements is unacceptable, one must not expect it to provide obligatory and binding lessons.

The price that exponents of this position pay is this: they cannot insist on their social utility as emphatically as can the majority of their colleagues. Moreover, they cannot participate in the politics of the day by assuming the superior air of the scholar; instead, they must use the usual methods of persuasion that are available to every citizen.

Legal historians who share this position, and I count myself among them, thus do not study Nazi law because of the positive results it may have for current law or the younger generation. They do not want to discover "the idea of law in history" or commit themselves from the outset to the "necessity" of historical processes of development, nor are they interested in contributing anything to the theory of current law, no matter how useful a side effect this may be. Precisely the act of breaking the link between legal history and the philosophy of current law has led to new findings, in the sense of a greater approximation to individual historical reality, for "a text of legal revelation cannot at the same time be the object of historical understanding."[44] The goal of a legal history emancipated from the claims of current law and politics is therefore to offer the most comprehensive, nondogmatic, and impartial illumination possible of normative historical structures.

The question to what end this illumination is pursued can be answered only by each person for him- or herself and on the basis of value decisions that are analytically irreducible. These value decisions can be based on the "historicity of our own existence"; on the need for "man's self-reassurance about his own 'constituent elements' of human existence, which he can grasp directly and which are self-discerning";[45] on the desire "to know how our troubles are related to the past . . . to see the line along which we may progress towards the solution of what we feel, and what we choose, to be our main tasks";[46] on a Christian decision of faith;[47] or on "curiosity" (which is perhaps only a way of putting an arbitrary end to the search for reasons we can articulate). In each and every case, the answer is left to the individual scholar. The methods used, however, do not change with the answer.

Legal History during the Nazi Period: Outlines of a Scholarly Field

No period of German history has been as intensely illuminated as the notorious years of Nazi rule between 1933 and 1945. All branches of history in Germany and abroad have studied National Socialism, preserving and uncovering a range of material so vast it can no longer be absorbed by any one person. And the output is continuing with undiminished vigor: new books, essay collections, and articles are published almost every day. In future historical scholarship, too, the Nazi era will be a "past that will not pass." Especially if it is true, as some have argued, that the real process of a thorough "historicization" of National Socialism has only just begun.

Scholarship on National Socialism from 1945 to today has by no means developed at an even pace. There have been phases of stagnation as well as "waves" and fashionable topics. That pattern reflects the interplay between the process of understanding and the various conditions that form the external framework of inquiry, an interplay that determines the history of every field of scholarship. Scholars themselves with their own private histories, the political and social context in which they move, and above all the chronological distance from the events have led to a constant renewal and transformation of scholarly interests and topics, of the kind of questions asked and the methodological approaches used.

All this holds true also for legal history. Beginning in about 1965, and with a noticeable lag behind the general historical sciences, it began to attract attention with contributions of its own. Scholars in this field, as well, are not as free as they themselves sometimes think when it comes to determining topics, formulating hypotheses, and selecting methodological approaches. Although it is true that scholars make their decisions as individuals, from a greater distance one can also see that they show a relatively uniform behavior as a group, and this allows us to make general observations. For example, we note that in the first decades after 1945, the representatives of legal history at German universities did not speak about Nazi law and Nazi crimes or about the role of legal history during the Nazi era. While other disciplines took at least the first steps toward an accounting of their past,[1] legal historians remained virtually silent. The first pertinent article appeared in the venerable *Savigny-Zeitschrift für Rechtsgeschichte* in 1986,[2] and not until the Twenty-seventh Conference of German Legal Historians in Bielefeld in 1988 was there a session with four brief papers on Nazi law.[3]

There are reasons for this silence up to about 1965. Some legal historians, almost without exception scholars of Roman law,[4] had been forced to emigrate. It is readily understandable that these scholars could not or would not participate in elucidating the story of their own suffering by studying Nazi legal history. Another group of scholars, primarily students of Germanic law and constitutional historians (H. Meyer, K. A. Eckhardt, H. F. Feine, G. K. Schmelzeisen, W. Ebel, K. G. Hugelmann, E. R. Huber, G. Dulckeit, E. Schönbauer, and others), had become involved with the regime—some blatantly, others less so—and they kept quiet. Nobody could seriously expect that these scholars would now take an active role in analyzing their own mistakes.

However, the majority of legal historians, who had remained in Germany and had neither offered resistance nor compromised themselves significantly, could have focused their scholarly attention on National Socialism or at least openly rethought the role of their own discipline—or so one might have thought in retrospect. But such expectations, occasionally voiced by the younger generation, were very unrealistic. Several taboos stood in the way.

1. Legal history was used to studying older law. Traditionally, the focus of research in Roman law was on antiquity and the Middle Ages, with a gradual shift into the period of the *usus modernus* and pandectics. In Germanic law the focus was on the early and high Middle Ages, also with a gradual shift into the modern period. The science of Roman law had broadened into "ancient legal history" and had joined up with the science of Germanic law to form the field of the "history of civil law in the modern period." Similarly, Germanic law and public law came together in the "constitutional history of the modern period." After 1945 there was more than enough work in these fields, and all scholars gladly returned to their specialties as soon as conditions permitted. There was no concept of a "contemporary legal history" analogous to the field of "contemporary history."[5]

2. There were understandable inhibitions. We can understand why Georg Dahm, in the 1951 revised edition of his book *Deutsches Recht*

(German law), cut the passages on Nazi law that had appeared in the 1944 edition and declared that "it is too soon to speak about National Socialism."[6] However, it is more difficult to grasp why Robert Scheyhing, who was untouched by National Socialism, maintained as late as 1968 that "an examination from the perspective of legal history must not take into consideration the period of National Socialist rule in Germany, a period that belongs more to philosophers and legal theorists than to historians."[7] It is equally difficult to fathom why Klaus Kröger's book on modern constitutional history ends with 1933; the author argues that the traditional line of development of the German constitution was ruptured in 1933, making it unnecessary to carry the discussion further.[8] And Knut Wolfgang Nörr concludes his account of the "civil law of the Weimar Republic" by vigorously rejecting any ideas about legal continuity, which, he believes, have "infected" even some legal historians. Given the destruction of the *Rechtsstaat* by National Socialism, he goes on to ask whether we "might not be better advised to regard the Third Reich as essentially a space *devoid of law*."[9]

3. Additional obstacles to an examination of the role of legal history under National Socialism were deference to colleagues and the widespread human desire to deal with unpleasant topics only as much as is absolutely necessary. As a result there was only one brief debate on methodology in the years between 1947 and 1952. Heinrich Mitteis emphasized the "existential value *[Lebenswert]* of legal history"[10] within the framework of an idealistic program related to the present; Gerhard Dulckeit, who accorded Hegel central prominence much more openly than Mitteis, did much the same.[11] Karl Siegfried Bader, Helmut Coing, Hans Thieme, and Franz Wieacker joined this debate, though without saying much about National Socialism.[12] Only Paul Koschaker, who already in 1938 had spoken courageously about the "crisis of Roman law," dealt straightforwardly with National Socialism and its tendencies that were hostile to Roman law.[13] Afterward, however, the interest in methodological questions waned again. The initial impetus that Koschaker had given to a discussion on the topic of "legal history under National Socialism" went nowhere.

A generational succession occurred around 1965—when the so-called "Adenauer era" and the economic miracle came to an end, when the first spectacular cases of ministers and top officials with a Nazi past came to light and the Auschwitz trial was taking place in Frankfurt, when students at the universities were growing restless and the first interdisciplinary courses were organized.[14] Not until this time was legal history asked about its own past during the National Socialist period. Bernd Rüthers published his book *Die unbegrenzte Auslegung*.

Zum Wandel der Privatrechtsordnung im Nationalsozialismus (The unrestrained interpretation of the law: On the transformation of private law under National Socialism [1968]), and Dieter Schwab spoke on legal history at an interdisciplinary course in Gießen.[15] Other contributions followed,[16] and slowly the outlines of a large and neglected area of scholarship emerged behind the first sketches.

What were the intellectual conditions under which the academic representatives of legal history entered the year 1933? How did the discipline react to "enticement and coercion"?[17] What impulses came from scholarship within legal history? How did the relationship to international scholarship change? What special accomplishments or "errors" can we take note of? Finally, how did the experiences of the Nazi period affect the new beginning of legal history after 1945? Was there in fact a "new beginning," or was there quiet continuity under the new banner of liberty?

Answers to these questions would require extensive analysis of published works, large-scale studies of the scholars active in the field, and a comprehensive review of the history of the discipline at the universities. These studies, in turn, would have to be embedded within the broader history of scholarship; as far as Germany is concerned, they would also have to take into account the lines of tradition stretching back to imperial Germany[18] and the cultural and political conditions of the Weimar Republic. An important role would have to be assigned to the characteristically German distinction between scholars of Roman law (Romanists) and scholars of Germanic law (Germanists). This distinction not only concerned the topics of scholarly work, but also affected the "atmosphere" and "feel" of the disciplines. As a generalization one could say that the representatives of Roman law were far more international and multilingual, and more deeply rooted in the world of liberal-humanistic education, the latter in part due to a higher proportion of Jewish scholars. The broadening of the field of Roman law into "ancient legal history" (L. Mitteis, L. Wenger) in the 1920s precluded a narrow nationalistic perspective.[19]

By contrast, the basic approach of the Germanists was national. Hans Planitz, for example, put it this way: "He who has a penchant for following the trail of the fathers, and who immerses himself lovingly in the Germanic pre-history, its life and law, will find in it the one thing he is really looking for: himself, his own nature . . . This inner way of seeking the unadulterated Germanic folkdom in history and showing the living working of German law in the past is the task of the legal historian."[20]

Regardless of whether the "national approach" had an upper-middle-class liberal, a German national, or an ethnic anti-Semitic slant, it was typically concerned with the problem of drawing lines of demarcation to the outside and discovering "its essence." It is obvious that the Germanists were far more susceptible to the conglomeration of emotionally charged words that was made up of ethnic-national, corporatist, authoritarian, and totalitarian elements and was establishing itself as the ideology of the state. Romanists saw a warning light in point 19 of the Nazi party program (which called for the replacement of Roman law by "German common law") and therefore had to be at least professionally suspicious of the new regime. Germanists, by contrast, saw the Third Reich as the fulfillment of their frequently expressed longing for a revitalization of the national community and "Führerdom," of the cooperative idea, as well as of the organic structuring of the totality of the nation and the ethnic-national character of the law. Fears of modern civilization and cultural criticism obviously merged here with a neo-Romantic idealization of pre-industrial conditions, with anti-Semitism, and with a corresponding mania for Germanic things.

However, below the political and cultural choices, which can be read at the surface level, there were also differences of basic philosophical orientation. Among legal historians that orientation typically finds its way into scholarship in a rather veiled fashion. One reason why it is difficult to decipher is that it is often an eclectic concoction of "everyday philosophies." The Romanists, with their scholarly methodology focused on philology and interpretation, strike us as more sober and less speculative than the Germanists. The predominance in their discipline of topics dealing with the history of theoretical concepts in civil law may have reinforced this difference. The Germanists showed a more pronounced penchant for exerting political influence on the present, a tendency that was already visible in the nineteenth century. They also seemed to agree that the purpose of legal history was to derive from the historical material certain eternal "ideas," which were then frequently applied to the situation of the day, often in bold speculative moves.[21]

The legacy of German idealistic philosophy that was in this way projected into legal scholarship, or tacitly presupposed, played a major role in making National Socialism appear attractive. Anyone who accepted the proposition that one could assign to specific peoples certain "innate" ideas underlying their legal thinking had to set out "in search of the German essence" (Cl. v. Schwerin): "Finding the way back to the spirit of German law is the most sacred duty, back to the ideas that underlie the law, ideas that cannot be lost as long as there are Germanic peoples."[22]

This attitude called upon the legal scholar as an expert to provide building blocks for the renewal of the law: "An immeasurable treasure of ancient and inherited Nordic wisdom has been passed down to us in the older Germanic legal sources. We can draw from them the great ideal of justice, the Germanic criteria of justice, and the great formative ideas that constantly recur as leitmotifs in all parts of German law."[23]

Since this treasure had supposedly been squandered in the course of history, and had been further diminished by the "national tragedy" of the reception of Roman law, the task at hand was to reassemble this treasure and resume the struggle against the reception of Roman law. A doctrine of national spirit *(Volksgeist)*—far removed from Savigny's ideas, narrow-mindedly conceived, ethnically trivialized,[24] and usually transmitted in the line from Georg Beseler to Otto von Gierke[25]—was now made available to the party ideologues, who hammered it into the simplest propaganda slogans.[26] At the same time, professors of legal history took over, to a greater or lesser degree, key words from the Nazi vocabulary, either out of genuine conviction and the desire to distinguish themselves for the task of "legal renewal" or as a form of camouflage. The fact that even a few Romanists were involved (H. Lange, G. Dulckeit, E. Schönbauer) merely shows how powerful was the tornado that swept up all public language.

Once we have noted "affinities" in language and way of thought, we are also able to recognize—beyond the superficial attribution of guilt in the postwar period—that the educated middle class and the National Socialist regime were dependent on each other. Broad sectors of the middle class felt that the overthrow of the self-paralyzing Weimar party-state and the transition to an authoritarian national regime was liberating. The driving forces behind this were deep-seated fears of "Bolshevism" and social degradation, as well as a longing for leadership in a society that seemed chaotic and threatening. The Nazi regime, for its part, could not govern without middle-class intelligence and capable personnel in the administration, the judiciary, and the educational system. The result was a partial symbiosis. The events over the following years—the Röhm murders in 1934, the struggle against the churches after 1934, the anti-Jewish pogrom of 1938, the outbreak of the war in 1939, the "euthanasia" program in 1940–1941, the murder of the Jews, the resistance movement—slowly broke down this symbiosis. In the end the middle class realized with resignation not only that its fundamental ideals had been eroded, but also that it had played its part in maintaining the façade of "normality" that was so important to the regime.

The Germanists among the legal historians also had to admit that they had hailed this regime as an emanation of the eternal German spirit and the historical fulfillment of the primeval German will, in the hope that they would in return be entrusted with important tasks of legal policy. One example of this was Justus Wilhelm Hedemann's passionate support for the "People's Law Code" *(Volksgesetzbuch)*,[27] a support that was all but blind to reality.

The question of how we should assess the scholarly output in the field of legal history during this confusing period has no simple answers. To be sure, hardly ever has so much pompous nonsense been said and written by scholars in so short a period as was the case specifically in the years 1933–1935. It was "an agitated time."[28] On the other hand, it is undeniable that—precisely within the framework of that "normality"—scholarship in legal history marched on undeterred by the political circumstances. However, between the extremes of empty rhetoric and nonpolitical expertise there was a third group of writers. These were the scholars who had not relinquished their claim to pure scholarship, but who reacted consciously to the political oscillations of the time and—either in agreement or in dissent—imparted to their work the particular accent it would not have had in other circumstances. Is it therefore possible to say that apart from emphatic agreement, accommodation, and quiet nonpolitical industry, there were also genuine "advances" in scholarship? Advances that were stimulated by the prevailing ideology and the greater distancing from the results of nineteenth-century scholarship it entailed? Did the field of legal history, as well, experience a "modernization" that was initiated by National Socialism?[29]

Finally, the scholarly topic I have outlined here also includes the situation of legal history after 1945. By that time the discipline had lost many of its best minds in the fields of Roman and canon law, and international contacts had been severed and had to be laboriously reestablished. In the Soviet occupation zone, later the GDR, legal history found itself in an unfavorable political climate and was all but suppressed in its "bourgeois" form.[30] In West Germany we can speak of continuity in spite of the rapid disappearance of a certain kind of Nazi vocabulary and the replacement of the Germanic-German idea of "ethnic-national community" *(Volksgemeinschaft)* with the idea of "freedom."[31] After all, for more than a decade a priori ideas from transcendental philosophy—now for the most part couched in terms of

Christianity and natural law—prevailed, and they continued to direct the task of legal history toward finding certain guiding ideas within the historical material and bringing them to light. The field of Germanic law, in particular, recovered after a brief period of uncertainty. The *Savigny-Zeitschrift für Rechtsgeschichte,* arguably the most important journal in German legal history, soon reappeared with an unchanged makeup and with Heinrich Mitteis at the editorial helm. Looking back over the first hundred years of this journal in 1961, Hans Thieme felt he could write: "The fact that Mitteis was able to reconnect with the past *without a break* may be seen as a sign of inner health."[32] And Adalbert Erler added in 1988: "It is conservatism— in the spirit of which the science of legal history is pursued—that accomplished such miracles—though 'thrones may break asunder and kingdoms shatter.'"[33]

THREE

Was There "Progress in Legal History" during the Nazi Period?

One observation about the development of historical scholarship has been confirmed many times over: New historical insights depend not only on improvements in the available sources and the skill and industry of the scholars who interpret them, but also on changes in the political situation as it is experienced by scholars. Whether the new insights as such deserve to be called "progress" and in what sense we can even speak of "progress" in the historical disciplines are important questions. We can leave them unanswered for now, as long as we agree not to impart to the word *progress* the meaning of something absolute and quantifiable, and to see it instead as a positive assessment by a given community of scholars who have agreed that a more recent interpretation comes closer to the "historical truth" than an older one and therefore represents a relative improvement.

It is in this sense that legal historians during the era of National Socialism advanced theses which, despite their obvious connection to the circumstances of the time, were recognized as "progress" after 1945 as well.

However, mentioning National Socialism and "progress" in one breath—progress in the sense of the elimination of outmoded social structures and a burst of technological innovation—was tabooed after 1945, at least as long as some apologists tried to combine the horrors of the regime with its reduction of unemployment, the construction of the Autobahns, the development of the people's radio receiver, the creation of the Volkswagen, and the provision of Winter Relief into some kind of overall balance sheet. It was not until the 1960s that sociologists pointed out the kind of modernizing function National Socialism had played for the society and economy of the Federal Republic through the destruction of traditional loyalties and values, the propaganda of the "national community," and the ravages of war and the misery of refugees.[1] Even if scholars, somewhat at a loss, called it "pseudo-modernization" on the grounds that National Socialism was reactionary and supposedly incapable of building lasting structures, the fact itself was recognized. And this offered a starting point for conceptualizing National Socialism itself as a crisis phenomenon of industrial society, as the dead end, so to speak, during a period of stress in the process of modernization.[2]

These questions, which have been discussed in the historical profession, form the backdrop to a similar problematic issue in the history of legal scholarship: The impact of the Nazi era freed up certain traditional topics of legal history by breaking the spell of the nineteenth century that had bound them. Those topics included the alleged *individualism of Roman law*, the historical aspects of the *separation of public and private law*, and questions about the meaning and extent of the *reception of Roman law* in the late Middle Ages and the early modern period.

▐▐▄ When German legal historians began their lectures in the summer semester of 1933, there were already signs that the change of government on January 30, 1933, was unlike any previous one. Jewish colleagues no longer appeared at some of the faculty meetings and their lectures were canceled, heated discussions took place in university committees, new rectors had been appointed and gave speeches reflecting the new spirit of the time, the Nazi party became a noisy presence at the universities, and every scholar was wondering what all this meant for himself and his work.[3]

Those swept up by the rising tide of anti-Semitism did not have to worry about such things; for them the only real question was when to leave and where to go. All other scholars who remained in their positions could wait and see, and they intended to do just that.[4] It was still unclear what effect the political changes would have on research and teaching in their fields. In particular, point 19 of the Nazi party program ("We demand that Roman law, which serves a materialist world order, be replaced by German common law"),[5] which struck experts as bizarre, hung as a vague threat over the fields of "history of Roman law" and "Roman private law," with scholars unable to decide just how seriously to take it.

The fact that the legal historian Karl August Eckhardt (1901–1979)[6] had become a department head in the Reich Ministry for Science, Education, and People's Education seemed to be a favorable sign for legal history. Then on July 22, 1934, the new regulations on legal training went into effect.[7] The new rules emphasized the historical element of legal education by requiring that students should "acquire an overview of the entire intellectual life of the nation, as one should expect from an educated German man. This includes knowledge of German history and the history of peoples who have had a favorable influence on the cultural development of the German *Volk*, in particular the history of the Greeks and Romans" (par. 4).

The obligatory historical part of the examination that was introduced at the same time was intended to give students a chance "to demonstrate their understanding of the interconnections in the history of the German people" (par. 13, sec. 5). Of course, the possibility of testing Roman law in the *Referendar* examination[8] was dropped, and with it a protective barrier that until then had more or less concealed the looming "crisis of Roman law."

The League of National Socialist German Jurists[9] invited legal scholars to a meeting on December 20 and 21, 1934, to discuss the draft of a curriculum plan that was to go into effect a month later, on January 18, 1935. Siegfried Reicke (1897–1972) spoke at this meeting about legal history, Hans Kreller (1887–1958) about Roman law.[10] Eckhardt gave a summary talk on the study of jurisprudence.[11] The meeting reaffirmed that the overall official line was not unfavorable to legal history. It was repeatedly emphasized that the educated "German man"—women students were thus by definition excluded from the study of the law—had to know something about Roman history, and consequently German jurists had to know something about the history of Roman law.[12] Even a quote from *Mein Kampf* proved helpful: as Hitler had put it, "especially in historical instruction we must not be deterred from the study of antiquity. Roman history correctly conceived in extremely broad outlines is and remains the best mentor, not only for today, but probably for all time. The Hellenic ideal of culture should also remain preserved for us in its exemplary beauty."[13]

With the first round against point 19 of the party program apparently won, interest now shifted to the concrete shape these plans would take for teaching at the universities. The new curriculum combined the older courses on German private law and Roman private law into "History of Private Law in the Modern Period." This was a modernizing step many felt was long overdue.[14] It combined two courses that dated back to the creation of the Civil Code in 1900 and had become so isolated as to have virtually no function at all. It expressed in words the "reconciliation" *(Überwindung)* of the Romanist-Germanist dichotomy, and it served to lighten the curriculum as a whole by combining two courses into one. At the same time "Roman" private law had been cleverly made to disappear, so it would no longer offend party comrades who had no expertise in this field.[15] Much the same happened to "History of Roman Law," which, as W. Kunkel later said, "was now tolerated under the lightly veiled neo-classical term 'History of Ancient Law.'"[16]

Still, the questions concerning the future status of ancient (specifically Roman) legal history, the extent to which it would be taught and how it would be taught, and the international connections of the discipline were still unresolved. The discipline remained under threat, having already been very seriously affected by the expulsion of Jewish scholars.[17] The number of hours in the curriculum was cut back,[18] the number of students dropped, the humanistic educational canon unraveled with increasing speed in a hostile environment. The Nazi party, insofar as it even took an interest in the content of what was studied, continued to regard Roman law with suspicion after the Curriculum Regulations of 1935, seeing it as "Jewified" and as the stronghold of everything the Nazis opposed: individualism, formalism, liberalism, "bookish wisdom," and "hair-splitting sophistry."[19] Roman law became the "foreign" per se;[20] it was regarded as the "strongly orientalized law of a degenerate mixed European-Asiatic population, a law of the ruthless large-scale capitalist exploitation of one's fellow man."[21]

More important still than the situation created by such phrase-mongering and the deterioration of the external context was the "crisis of Roman law" itself. This crisis had been talked about ever since the Civil Code had gone into effect.[22] Freed from the dogmatism of the current civil law, legal history had begun to see itself increasingly as a purely historical field, and, as Franz Wieacker put it in 1939, it had gone on an "Alexander campaign" to Egypt and the Orient to conquer new fields.[23] Much of what had been, until the nineteenth century, part of the foundation of the dogma of Roman law now fell prey to historical criticism, as the study of interpolations undermined a "thousand-year-old faith in the sources."

The price for this "progress" of historical understanding was that the place of legal history within legal education became uncertain. With the usefulness of legal history for the prevailing law becoming increasingly doubtful—especially at a time when the faith in finding certain truth through deductive-conceptual methods was wavering, and high priority was being given to the idea of practical purpose and the analysis of interests—all that remained was the educational value of a legal history that was seen as "antipandectistic" (Wieacker). In Wieacker's eyes, it had lost its role as the "preparatory school *[Vorschule]* of civil law."[24]

The majority of legal historians, however, thought differently. Paul

Koschaker (1879–1951) had published his work *Die Krise des römischen Rechts und die romanistische Rechtswissenschaft* (The crisis of Roman law and Romanistic jurisprudence) through the Academy for German Law, incidentally without being a member of the academy.[25] He saw the neo-humanist separation of prevailing law and legal history as the greatest danger, the true cause of the crisis, indeed as the departure of legal history from a centuries-old tradition.[26] In 1947 he noted that National Socialism had not caused the crisis of Roman law, it had only made it visible and more acute; the real problem lay in the historicization of legal history. His response was to pursue a kind of dual strategy. The neo-humanistic, strictly historical study of the sources should continue, but "in addition" a renewed connection between legal history and the theory of civil law should be sought.[27] As Koschacker had put it in 1938, the Romanist should "present Roman law with the Corpus Juris in one hand and the Civil Code in the other."[28]

The problems arising from this dual strategy were discussed in the 1950s but soon put aside again.[29] The crisis was not resolved, and to this day little has changed about the hidden division of legal historians into "neo-humanists" and "neo-pandectists." Some historians are still looking for a concept that unites legal history and the dogmatics of civil law "on a new level of the history of science," in the words of G. Dilcher—notwithstanding all indications that the formulation of historical questions is distorted by references to normative application.[30] At the same time, the diagnosis of crisis is confirmed by the fact that in 1987 D. Simon could speak about a "continuous loss of substance" in legal history at German universities and draw no voice of disagreement.[31]

Even if Simon's diagnosis reveals a continuity of the problem, the situation today is fundamentally different from that after 1933. When Koschaker, Wieacker, Erich Genzmer, Max Kaser, Hans Kreller, Ernst Schönbauer, Jürgen von Kempski, and others were discussing the contemporary value of Roman law between 1933 and 1944, they were trying to ward off an acute danger.[32] Point 19 of the party program, despite its absurd content, was a very real threat. "The German study of Roman law," Kreller argued, "must therefore demonstrate that it can continue on the current path without ending up in opposition to this plank of the program, indeed, that by doing so it can in fact contribute to its implementation."[33] In this situation every argument for the defense was welcome. For instance, once Hitler and Mussolini had formed the Berlin-Rome axis, scholars liked to point out the Indo-Germanic blood kinship between the Romans and the Germanic peoples, long invoked in ethnic-nationalistic writings.[34] Defenders also emphasized the danger of international isolation, pointed out that Roman law was intensively cultivated among all cultured nations, even the Japanese, and said in 1936—the year of the Berlin Olympics—that Germany could not afford *not* to participate "in these Olympics" of Romanistic scholarship.[35] Others explained that it was perfectly possible to separate the good, ancient Roman and classical law from later, corrupted layers. Moreover, Kreller argued, the point was not the content of Roman law, but the introductory technique of legal work, and even if it was all about content, one could still work on it "in the spirit of a national-conscious German science."[36]

This amassing of arguments and the indifference toward the contradictions they harbored reveal how strongly scholars felt the outside pressure. It seems that all Romanists had agreed to form one great coalition to defend their discipline. Welcome reinforcement came from the few colleagues who had come out in favor of the regime: Heinrich Lange, for example, who had let himself be carried away into making less than honorable attacks on Fritz Schulz;[37] or Ernst Schönbauer (1885–1966), dean in Vienna and later rector at the university and "hereditary farmer" *(Erbhofbauer)*, whose support for National Socialism was beyond question, which is precisely what allowed him to stand up for Roman law and play a kind of protective role.[38]

Roman Law as a "Communal Order" (Gemeinschaftsordnung)

Schönbauer's name is also linked with the first larger attempt to defend Roman law against the well-known accusation of individualism or the lack of communal bonds *(Gemeinschaftsgebundenheit)*. One way to do so was to follow the old theory of the decline of the Roman world and retrace the story of Roman law from the good old agricultural order via the republic, the principate, and the "Syrian-Jewish-Byzantine" decay all the way to the study of the Pandects in the nineteenth century. In this way scholars could at least save classical Roman law as having been "community bound."[39] This was the usual approach: It made sense historically, was supported by popular and nationalistic writings, and even met with approval from Germanist colleagues.

However, a second defensive strategy that now appeared seemed more effective, since it reopened the entire debate on a fundamental level and sought to prove that the clichés about Roman law were false. Scholars using this approach rejected the charge of individualism in general and pointed to the manifold ethical and transpersonal bonds that had accompanied the Roman legal order as a kind of parallel normative system. For example, Fritz Schulz (1879–1957), in his lectures on the principles of Roman law,[40] singled out the Romans' attachment to tradition, their patriotism and sense of freedom, their concepts of *auctoritas* and *fides*,[41] and emphasized the communal bonds of property. In this way he drew a picture of classical Roman law that clearly contradicted National Socialist propaganda, and this also prompted Heinrich Lange's protest against Schulz.[42] By declaring, for example, that the so-called Roman individualism was a myth[43] and pointing out that none of the legal institutions and instruments of modern capitalism—land annuity bonds, negotiable instruments, stocks, letters of exchange, capitalist trading companies, mortgages as capital investments, direct proxy[44]—was derived from Roman law, Schulz cut the ground from under point 19 of the party program. Lange sensed this when he argued that "Schulz was gently showing the claws of opposition under the velvet glove of scholarly objectivity."[45] In the epilogue of his book, Schulz revealed that he was fully aware of how his theses related to contemporary events: "A new experience of the state and politics also lets us experience the Roman world and its law anew and shows us many things in a new and clearer light."[46] This might have been a *captatio benevolentiae*, an attempt, perhaps, to escape the imminent expulsion. It was, at any rate, an attempt undertaken with the intent of lending support to Roman law in a changed political landscape by underlining its imperial traits and communal values.

In any case, this appeared to be the right defensive strategy against the pressure coming from the Nazis. Schönbauer, in his lecture "The Communal Element in the Structure of the Roman Legal Order," delivered in 1936 at the Fifth Conference of Legal Historians in Tübingen,[47] staked out this very approach by endowing Roman law with all the characteristics that had hitherto been ascribed to Germanic-German law: community-relatedness, an orientation to the whole, subordination of self-interest, the absence of basic rights inimical to the community, the idea of the Führer, and a consciousness of race reflected in the fact "that the Romans usually integrated conquered territories politically but not by blood. The excess of national strength went afield in a 'sacred spring' to establish an outpost of the homeland."[48]

However, this vigorous defense of Roman law—after the motto "the Romans, too, were Aryans"[49]—apparently went too far in the eyes of the Germanists. In the discussion following Schönbauer's talk, Claudius von Schwerin emphasized that the Germanic tradition was "sufficient for us" (!). In a later article he reiterated that the attempt to prove that certain fundamental ideas of Germanic law existed also in Roman law could only lead to distortions.[50]

Three years after the legal historians' conference, Max Kaser published his short monograph *Römisches Recht als Gemeinschaftsordnung* (Roman law as communal order).[51] Gently distancing himself from his countryman Schönbauer, Kaser maintained that Schönbauer, "full of glowing passion for the political greatness of the Roman world," had undertaken a "first and very useful excursion" to free Roman law from the charge of irresponsible and unfettered individualism. But since it had been only an "excursion," Kaser would now take a more thorough approach "to answer the question about the communal value of Roman law on the basis of its levels of development in antiquity and from a historical perspective that has been purified by our national experience."[52] He proceeded to do this step by step. In the early period we find *gens, curia,* and *tribus* as "associations of blood and soil"; the "Führer position of the king" and the concomitant duty of loyalty and allegiance; and *mos maiorum* as the "categorical imperative of the common good." Then came the separation of law and mores, with the latter, as an uncodified social conscience, counterbalancing, reinforcing, but also softening the harshness of the law. The transition to the principate was, of course, accompanied by a loosening of the mores. Self-interest and the abuse of power appeared on the scene: "Individualism replaced community."[53] Although Augustus succeeded once more in stopping the evil through education, inner recovery, racial protection, and moral austerity, things went downhill after his death: "The general process of dissolution had undermined not only the racial existence of the Roman people but also the sense of community."[54] What was handed down as Roman law in the following centuries was therefore only its shell, not its essence. Hence the nineteenth century, with its individualism and liberalism, had, so to speak, presented "un-Roman" Roman law. Kaser therefore exhorted his readers at the end to despise, not Roman law, "but only its modern distortion and the *Zeitgeist* that pressed it into service in this form."[55]

What interests us in this monograph are not those elements that were conditioned by the time and that neither Kaser nor his students would care to emphasize today: the nationalistic and racial tones, the emotional embrace of community, and talk of the "evil of individualism." We are, instead, interested in those elements underneath this veneer that strike us as "progress" even today. For Kaser, like Schulz, did in fact offer a clearer view of Roman law and Roman mores, a view that was apparently possible only when the political context had changed and the nineteenth century itself receded into history. Beginning at the turn of the century, the nineteenth century had been vigorously attacked in all areas of intellectual history. Legal history was no exception, even though it owed so much to the nineteenth century. As the distance from the study of the Pandects grew, scholars gradually realized that it was conditioned by its time and had been cast into a liberal mold, underneath which the historical substance had to be rediscovered.[56] Today it is well recognized that Schulz's and Kaser's observations that there was a correspondence between law and mores, and that the application of the law depended on unwritten social constraints, are historically "correct" and were new insights in the 1940s. While it is obvious that such a "more accurate" view could arise only at a certain distance from the nineteenth century, its politics and economic system, we need to formulate the phenomenon even more clearly: Only Nazi propaganda against Roman law, which had derived its distorted materialist-liberal picture of that law from the nineteenth century, on the one hand, and anti-individualist Nazi propaganda about the unity of law and mores, of the individual and the community, on the other, gave legal historians the incentive to construct a new picture of Roman law. In this way, the pressures of the *Zeitgeist,* the defense of the scholarly discipline of Roman law, and historiographical progress could merge.

IV. The Distinction between Public and Private Law

We have another example of this mechanism of political challenge and scholarly response: how legal historians assessed the famous continental separation of the legal order into public and private law. Studies over the last few decades have demonstrated that the categorical (a priori) dualism of the law as an idea was foreign to German jurisprudence up to the end of the eighteenth century.[57] Only after 1800 did idealistic philosophy and political and economic liberalism work hand in hand to effect a fundamental separation of state and society, of public and private law, and to enshrine them as categories of supposedly eternal value. The notion of a dichotomy— if not philosophically "necessary," yet irrevocable in practical terms— saturated the legal order throughout the nineteenth century. Ulpian's formula of the *duae positiones* (*Digest* 1.1.1.2) supplied the venerable principle of categorization. Even when liberalism had passed its zenith in 1878 and found itself on the defensive with regard to the interventionist state,[58] this dichotomy was retained as an intellectual construct. The new labor and social law, the war administration law, the social tenancy laws, and the business law of the 1920s barely encroached upon this dogma. Even textbooks from the end of the Weimar period gave no indication of serious doubts about this legal dualism.

Only National Socialism made an official and emphatic break with nineteenth-century currents of tradition, proclaiming a new unity of the legal order and declaring that the separation of state and society was as outmoded as the basic rights of the citizen. Residues of privacy were to be dissolved, society was to be integrated into the state and the state into the "movement." Legal literature after 1933 was in agreement that the old antagonism between public and private law had now been "overcome."[59] No other maxim was as widely accepted as this one.

Legal historians who addressed this question after 1933 started from various points of departure. Scholars who spoke as Germanists had it fairly easy. For instance, in 1935 Herbert Meyer hailed the end of the separation of public and private law as the restoration of a legal unity that had always existed in Germanic-German law, blaming the reception of Roman law and nineteenth-century liberalism for the fact that this pernicious separation had established itself in the first place.[60] The Romanist who tried to declare that this separation was scientifically untenable, indeed philosophically "nonexistent," and who tried to protect his own discipline by seeking to prove that Roman law was not to blame for the historically undeniable fact of this separation, faced certain difficulties. He had to classify Ulpian's statement as a product of late Roman decay in order to dismiss it. This was Gerhard Dulckeit's approach.[61] Dulckeit sought to prove that classical Roman law had still been dominated by the idea of unity, whereas Ulpian's dichotomy, interpreted as an indication of the weakness of the state, originated "only in the period of political and cultural decadence in late antiquity."[62] This move saved the period when Rome was a powerful state and the notion of the "unity of the legal order" (K. Engisch), and it was now easy to relate them to the present and to the "transcendence of the liberal ideology of separation."

Here, too, we see what seems at first glance to be a confusing picture—namely, that the practical and ideological destruction of liberalism by an authoritarian way of thinking that had become virulent after the turn of the century and culminated in National Socialism was able to give legal history the impulse it needed to see an old problem in a new light. The Nazi state accelerated an existing current—the rejection of the ideas of 1789—and drove it to the point of crisis, in the process bringing into view the historicization of the nineteenth century that had long since begun. In doing so the Nazi state also allowed scholars to distance themselves from the traditional notion that the separation into public and private law was an indispensable and "essential" characteristic of any highly evolved legal order. It was now easier for legal historians to perceive and express something they had, in essence, long since known or could have known by looking at the legal culture of the Anglo-Saxon world: This dichotomy of the law was nothing more than the unstable product of specific historical circumstances. Moreover, it became clear, in terms of the politics of scholarship, why the nineteenth century had had such an interest in portraying this dichotomy as timeless, superimposing it on Roman law as though the kind of separation of state and society that prevailed in nineteenth-century central Europe had existed in the Roman Empire. In this regard the National Socialist period produced "progress" as earlier defined: a persuasive historiographical insight that outlasted the fall of the National Socialist state.

V. The Reception of Roman Law

The reception of Roman law is the third and last example for the thesis that legal history, under the conditions of the Nazi state, was particularly disposed toward insights that had to arise from the growing distance from the nineteenth century.

It is not necessary to describe the long history of the discussion on Roman law from the seventeenth to the twentieth century. Peter Bender, in his Ph.D. dissertation at the University of Freiburg, presented an abundance of material and devoted a separate chapter to statements from the Nazi era.[63] Everything that authors such as Hans Frank, Helmut Nicolai, Wilhelm Stuckart, Roland Freisler, Rudolf Walter Darré, Johann von Leers, or Alfred Rosenberg wrote about the reception of Roman law was drawn from the Germanistic literature since Georg Beseler, which had by then been infused with a national-Romantic and anti-Semitic language. A brief monograph from 1913 reveals that even an emphatic approval of the Civil Code could be combined with this kind of language: "The legal force of Italian law [welsche Recht], which had always remained foreign to the spirit of the German people and for centuries had forced Germanic consciousness under the Caudine yoke of black-haired Roman tyranny, was destroyed by the Civil Code."[64]

The "Rembrandt-German" Julius Langbehn, Oswald Spengler,[65] Houston Steward Chamberlain,[66] and, finally, Moeller van den Bruck[67] were the authorities on the issue. Their voices were little challenged, since the university publications in the 1930s sounded the same basic tune that the reception of Roman law was a "national misfortune." What professors such as Herbert Meyer, Walther Merk, Gustav Klemens Schmelzeisen, or Walther Schönfeld said differed little in substance, and sometimes they said it less elegantly: The received Roman law was alien from the people, selfish, individualistic, liberal, commercial, rational, a dead letter—and certainly "un-German."

Romanists responded with the standard arguments we have already encountered. First of all they pointed out how different the various periods of Roman law had been. That explains why Wieacker said in 1941 that it was a great merit of "legal-political writing," in particular, that an understanding of the various periods of Roman law had entered into general consciousness.[68]

The second argument, and certainly a valid point, was that it was by no means Roman law itself that had been received, but medieval "Roman-Italian" law (G. Dahm). What was taught in Bologna had been, so to speak, an *arteigen* (true to type) product of the empire grown from two related roots.

The third argument maintained that the much quoted defensive reactions against the learned doctors in the sixteenth century had not been protests against Roman law, but rather protests against individuals and the social conditions they legitimated.

The fourth argument was the most important one. It maintained that the reception process involved not so much the content of Roman law as a new way of thinking. The most important characteristics of the reception and the period following it had been the establishment of the legal system on a written basis, university training, specialized terminology, and methodology—in short, the process of turning the law into a science *(Verwissenschaftlichung)*.

We must leave open the details of how this new interpretation of the reception process arose, and who—beginning in the late nineteenth century—prepared the ground for it. Max Weber's interpretation of Western rationalizing processes undoubtedly played a role, as did the scholarship of Georg Simmel, Werner Sombart, and Karl Mannheim. Within the discipline of legal history, the university course on the history of private law in the modern period had a stimulating effect, in part by providing an impulse for the editing of sources and by giving rise to studies like those by Woldemar Engelmann, Helmut Coing, Friedrich Schaffstein, and Karl Michaelis.[69]

The question of who was the first to use the term *Verwissenschaftlichung* cannot be resolved here. In all likelihood a discussion was carried on within the inner circles of the former Kiel School, for besides Michaelis and Schaffstein, it was above all Georg Dahm and Franz Wieacker who developed the basic idea. Dahm wrote in 1942 that the essence of the reception was methodological; the thesis that "the reception of the foreign law had destroyed or permanently damaged the

order of the German nation represents an unacceptable simplification,"
for one must not "blame the reception of Roman law for the destruction and disruption national life suffered in the nineteenth and twentieth centuries." Moreover, the polemics against Roman law were a
"petty bourgeois narrowing of the field of vision . . . which regards
any reception of foreign cultural traditions as a disaster."[70]

At around the same time the word *Verwissenschaftlichung* appeared
in the writings of Wieacker. Beginning in about 1942, we can trace in
his articles how he developed the basic idea, until he was able to present
it to a larger audience in the first edition of his *Privatrechtsgeschichte
der Neuzeit* (History of private law in the modern era [1952]).[71] In 1944
he argued that one could characterize the reception "as a *Verwissenschaftlichung* and rationalization of German law."[72] The essence of
reception was not the "adoption of a law foreign in content": "We
must look for the good and evil of this reception neither in the 'foreignization' of the substance nor in the growing pains of an impetuous
Verwissenschaftlichung, but rather in this *Verwissenschaftlichung* itself."[73]

Verwissenschaftlichung, the process of turning jurisprudence into a
science, Wieacker maintained, also contained the key to the connection
between reception and the development of the modern state.

The thesis that the reception of Roman law was not a "foreignization" of German law but part of the modern processes of rationalization
became a widely accepted topos in postwar legal history. This was so
not only because of its inherent scholarly persuasive power, but also
because of the collapse of the nationalistic world view in Germany and
the embrace—encouraged by all political camps—of Europe and its
intellectual traditions. The title of Koschaker's 1947 book, *Europa und
das römische Recht* (Europe and Roman law), expressed that mood exactly.[74]

I have recalled the formative period of the thesis that the reception
of Roman law constituted a process that turned jurisprudence into a
science because this example, too, demonstrates how scholarly "progress" can take place under political pressure. The emphasis on the
methodological side of reception was surely an insight derived from
scholarship itself. Moreover, in terms of the history of the discipline,
it was also time to recognize that the interpretation of the reception
process as "foreignization" was a national-Romantic myth created in
the nineteenth century to make a distinction between content and
method, accentuate the European aspect of reception and its connection to the modern rationalizing process, and highlight the social and
administrative side of the process that made the modern state a state of
laws. At the same time, this view clearly offered a defensive strategy—

welcome at the time—of highlighting value-neutral methodology instead of the incriminated content of the law.

What Dahm and Wieacker wrote in 1942 and 1944 could no longer be reconciled with the party's propaganda concerning point 19 of the party program. In 1942 Wieacker also complained emphatically that the common opinion about the reception of Roman law was still not taking into consideration "the revolutionary changes in the most recent insights, methods, and opinions in legal history."[75] To be sure, the party's propaganda against Roman law had fallen silent during the war, the discipline had recovered its self-confidence, and its language was becoming freer again. Now, moreover, during a time of great danger, the European connections came into view again with greater clarity.[76]

The Study of Germanic Law

VI. It is probably no coincidence that these examples of advances in legal history come from the fields of Roman law and the private law of the modern period. Here the conflict was focused, here the "crisis" had been smoldering since the turn of the century, here the changes in the curriculum plan of 1935 and the broad antiliberal current of the time—which was necessarily also a current hostile to Roman law—had the most marked effect. These factors provided a stimulus for subjecting to critical analysis the notion of "liberal" Roman law, the "transcended" separation of public and private law, and the notion that the reception of Roman law had been a "national disaster," and refuting them with sound scholarship. I think scholars today would agree that the results of these efforts can be called "progress" and have retained their importance over and above the tactical concerns that were also on the minds of legal historians at the time.

A look at the field of Germanic law[77] provides negative proof. After 1933 legal historians of Germanic law could feel the wind blowing their way. Especially since the political thinking of most of them was probably predominantly German-national, they often drew inspiration from the national version of the youth movement,[78] and they demonstrated by their choice of topics that they moved overwhelmingly along the paths charted by scholars from Beseler to Otto von Gierke, Amira, Brunner, and Schröder.[79] The Germanists now felt validated and encouraged, even if they objected to this or that manifestation of the Nazi state. Herbert Meyer (1875–1941), for instance, was later described by his former student Krahwinkel as one of those "Germanic enthusiasts who believed the appearance of the Third Reich would finally bring them the recognition they were hoping for."[80] In 1948 Hans

Thieme said in a self-critical reflection: "We were tempted more than the Romanists, who were from the beginning sulking on the sidelines."[81] He had good reason to say, somewhat apologetically, that experts know "our writings also contain some things we now wish had remained unwritten."[82]

The study of Germanic law was not suppressed in the Nazi state, it was—much worse—hardly taken note of.[83] It played no role of any significance either in the application of the law or in legal policy.[84] When a National Socialist Amtsgericht (district court) judge invoked historical arguments in an effort to replace monogamous marriage with concubinage, he became the laughingstock of his colleagues, even of those who agreed with him politically.[85] On the whole Hitler's saying set the tone: "These professors and ignoramuses with their Nordic myths mean nothing to us."[86]

Of course, one must beware of claiming that none of the literary creations of legal historians had any political effect. Scholarly writings share the responsibility for the overall intellectual climate in which political processes take place, especially in countries with a traditional orientation toward and faith in science and scholarship, as was true of Germany. In the case of National Socialism, we must add the fact that one of the most important Germanists, Karl August Eckhardt, was closely connected with Heinrich Himmler. As a result, Germanic scholarship (in the SS research and teaching society Ahnenerbe) and research into Germanic tribal legal codes developed a relationship to the death machinery of the SS similar to those of anthropology and "racial science" (Rassenlehre).[87] Certainly, Eckhardt's calls for the "elimination of degenerates" (by which he meant homosexuals) did not, in the strict sense, cause the internment of homosexuals in concentration camps, but the policy of "elimination" that was practiced did rest on a foundation of approval by the bourgeois elites. Without this approval, which was continuously percolating out through published opinions, the regime would undoubtedly have developed differently; at the very least it would have concealed its actions even better than it did. The reality of protests from the churches in the case of the "euthanasia" campaign has shown that this subterranean contact between the rulers and the ruled did function.

Still, "normal" Germanic scholarship existed on the sidelines more or less ignored, neither threatened nor courted in any special way. As a discipline it had no cause to undertake fundamental reflections on where it stood. Heinrich Mitteis confirmed this in 1947 when he said that legal history—from his perspective, the Germanic branch—"has not yet become a problem unto itself; it has behaved with greater indifference toward methodological questions than other fields of the humanities."[88] If this assessment is on the whole true—leaving aside individual studies of great merit—one likely reason is that Germanists did not feel the challenge that was directed at Romanists. Scholars of Germanic law, among whom the old battle lines of the nineteenth century were still in place, even if in a muted and "enlightened" form, had no reason to be particularly annoyed with the Nazi state, especially if they were able to continue their research in peace. There was, in any case, no talk about a "crisis" in Germanic legal history.[89] Herein lies the reason why we cannot speak of epochal "advances" in this field, despite the assiduous broadening of the available sources, despite penetrating studies on the Middle Ages, and despite the continuation of legal archaeology and the study of legal folk traditions.[90] The only work with a new perspective and deep resonance that was published during these years, Otto Brunner's *Land und Herrschaft*,[91] came as a challenge from outside the field.

FOUR

Community and National Community *(Volksgemeinschaft)*: Reflections on Legal Terminology under National Socialism

In 1934 Ernst Forsthoff wrote: "Every intellectual-political epoch develops a language appropriate to its thought. A political way of thinking reveals its superiority most clearly through its ability to establish its terminology as universally valid and accepted as a matter of course."[1]

If we examine legal terminology between 1933 and 1945 from this point of view, we note two things: a quick penetration of new National Socialist terms into the old conceptual world and a remarkable resistance to all attempts at innovation. The contradiction between these two observations is more apparent than real, and it is revealing in two ways. First, experience has shown that the quarrel over language is usually a reflection of struggles over ideas and real interests. By examining the development of certain terms, their use within the language, their frequency, and the contexts in which they are embedded, we can gain insights into their underlying ideology.[2]

Second, a legal-historical analysis of the terms used in legal texts between 1933 and 1945 is indispensable for the self-conception of jurisprudence today, which uses these or similar terms every day without being aware of their historical use and semantic associations. All this becomes especially apparent with the term *community (Gemeinschaft)*. After 1945 it played an important role in the field of labor law, which preserved a National Socialist tradition of community metaphors and blended it with the structurally similar social doctrine of the church, especially when it came to the question of the legal qualifications of contracts of employment. Sometimes employment was described as a community of personal law, sometimes as a community-establishing contract or a contract with communal elements.[3]

In the constitutional law of the Federal Republic, as well, the term *community* appears in a variety of contexts. For instance, the Federal Administrative Court (Bundesverwaltungsgericht) drew on the so-called "community clause" in interpreting the limits inherent in the basic rights. This clause maintains that a basic right cannot be invoked "if, by doing so, protected legal interests necessary for the existence of the community are endangered."[4] In another decision by the Federal Administrative Court, the "idea of community" was first read into the Basic Law and then used as the basis for a legal argument. This is the crucial passage:

> The meaning of the idea of community, as well, which has found expression in the basic principles of the social *Rechtsstaat* (arts. 20 and 28) and in the social embeddedness of property (art. 14, sec. 2), does not exhaust itself in the provision of material benefits. Rather, it demands that those who participate in the community be recognized as the bearers of their own rights who in principle are equal before the law (see also article 3), and that no essential segment of the people in this community be without rights with respect to its existence.[5]

The "idea of community" is invoked most frequently in interpreting the clause of the Basic Law that obliges the right of property to take the common weal into consideration (art. 14, sec. 2). A modern commentator has actually called this article "the bridge to communal thinking."[6] For now we shall leave open the question of what is meant by the term *community* that is used in such different contexts. The mere fact that it is used unabashedly justifies an examination of its history. The following account will look first at the general trend that sought to make the idea of community the foundation of a National Socialist jurisprudence (I). Next it will indicate the consequences of this idea in different areas of the law (II), particularly in constitutional law (III, IV). Finally, it will examine the function and consequences of the idea of community in the National Socialist state (V).

I. Legal discussions after 1933 were dominated—apart from the eradication of all liberal, individualistic, and democratic thinking—by the struggle against the nineteenth-century system of legal concepts.[7] That struggle was driven by claims that the existing system was alien to the nation and of un-German, Roman abstractness, that it had prevented "real" decisions, that law and ethics had become dissociated, and so on. A completely new system of law was therefore necessary. One way to restructure the law was to introduce new terms and either stop using old terms or reinterpret them. As B. Rüthers has shown,[8] reinterpretation proved a far more effective method for implementing the ideological change than the introduction of new terms and concepts. Still, from the beginning the National Socialists placed great stock in the introduction of new terms in all spheres of life as a symbol of the "new thinking."[9] In legal terminology two contradictory tendencies emerged in the process, tendencies that reflected the revolutionary and the conservative-authoritarian components of National Socialism itself. Younger, politicized scholars pushed for the introduction of the new terminology while at the same time fending off attempts at formulating definitions, on the grounds that they wanted to keep the legal order "fluid" and open to future political decisions. Jurists who were well versed in so-called conceptual jurisprudence (usually the older ones) were dubious about attempts to establish the terms *nation, Führer, clan, honor, blood and soil, Weltanschauung, race, community,* and *national community* as "legal concepts." This generational conflict, fanned by the revolutionary arrogance of many young scholars, complicated the already existing political and scholarly differences.

The term *community* or *national community* assumed a prominent place in the discussion. It predated National Socialism as the favorite term of philosophical irrationalism and political conservatism, which seized upon it beginning with the programs of the youth movement and especially the "communal experience" of August 1914 and the quickly mystified "battlefront community." "The idea of a communal culture," according to Gustav Radbruch, "emerged first of all from the youth movement—next to Socialism the strongest intellectual movement of our day. Unlike the uproar of earlier generations of young people, this revolt of youth is not a call for freedom, but rather the opposite: a renunciation of the excesses of individualism and an embrace of community—that is, the longing for new bonds, bonds of custom, style, culture, of camaraderie, Führerdom, and obedience *[Gefolgschaft].*"[10]

Karl Sontheimer has called the concept of community "one of the magic words of the Weimar period."[11] He is right, for the idea of community was already invoked before 1933 in countless publications that were in part ethnic-nationalistic or socialist in content, in part religious or philosophical. Radbruch, a contemporary of keen mind and balanced judgment, noted that "new words are gaining an increasingly deep and warm resonance, above all the word 'community.'"[12] Both Catholic social doctrine[13] and Protestant ethics[14] used this originally sociological term.[15] Because it was employed primarily in an antirationalistic and antidemocratic sense, it was almost inevitable that the term would also appear in the vocabulary of National Socialist propaganda, from where it made its way into legal terminology after 1933. From that point on, hardly any author forgot to point to the "now prevailing idea of community" and to draw from it the legal consequences for whatever problem was under discussion. Hans Frank, Reich Minister and President of the Academy for German Law, said in 1934: "We start from the law of the community, and this communal law is the real inner reversal of our legal point of view and our legal system."[16] This programmatic declaration became a topos of legal argumentation, as the titles of relevant books and articles show.[17] And in the language of legislation after 1933 there appeared—alongside older terms, such as *common weal, common welfare, common interest, well-being of the people, common benefit, the best for all*[18]—new creations, such as *national community, community of national comrades, business community, traffic community, household community, air raid protection community, physical education community*. Among the new terms, *national community* topped the list in frequency of use.[19]

A first overview of legislation and the professional literature reveals that the term *community* and its specialized derivations were used in such multifarious ways as to raise legitimate doubts whether we can even associate them with a specific meaning derived from the word itself. Philosophical, sociological, religious,[20] legal, and propagandistic contexts imparted all kinds of nuances to the term *community* and turned it into a dubious tool for jurists at the time. E. R. Huber, for instance, warned of the danger that the term "could degenerate into an abstract commonplace because of its frequent and undifferentiated use."[21] C. H. Ule spoke in a similar vein: "The concept of the 'concretely visible community' has become a true slogan. It is not possible to associate a sensible meaning with it, since there are no 'abstract communities' and a community itself can never become 'visible'."[22]

However, these concerns involved more than the term *community*, which had already been talked to death in the books and journalism of the Weimar period. Another issue was the admission of propagandistic phrases into legal terminology—a practice that was in general frowned upon. As a consequence of this phenomenon, the lines between the application of the law and legal policy became blurred. Terms from the *Kampfzeit* ("time of struggle," referring to the early days of the Nazi movement in Munich), "which expressed the feeling of dissatisfaction with the existing situation, but are not yet symbols of realities that have already been achieved,"[23] created a sense of terminological uncertainty in many jurists. For instance, as early as 1934, H. Helfritz voiced this criticism: "We are currently living in a confusion of legal terms that couldn't conceivably be any worse for the field." Further, "it is simply unacceptable that propaganda expressions are taken into the field uncritically, and that scholarly terms are given a different content than previously to make them serviceable to propaganda."[24]

Difficulties of this kind, which a legal system with traditional usages of long standing tends to encounter when the political foundation changes through revolutionary upheaval, occurred in all fields of the law under National Socialism. Before discussing the introduction of the concept of community into constitutional law, I shall at least indicate the repercussions of communal thinking for other fields of the law. My comments will be sketchy, their purpose being to make clear that this was not a question limited to constitutional law, but a problem basic to the entire legal order.

Since the goal in all areas of the law was to refashion the foundation, the core ideas were very simple, but the implications for any particular problem were complicated. For it was not always the case—and this seems to have been a typical feature—that the consequences were also "community related." Rather, in many instances the old solutions, discredited as liberal, were retained in the new dress of communal thinking. That was especially so with authors who adopted the topos of communal law outwardly while in reality advocating the preservation of the old legal order. But even among authors who were emphatically looking for new solutions in line with National Socialist thinking, the traditional legal system sometimes won out, thanks to its resilience as the *ratio scripta*.

Whenever "communal thinking" was mentioned in the literature, a few emotion-laden and vague ideas made their appearance. For the moment we may summarize them as follows: After the victory of National Socialism, the German people are no longer split into different groups, such as classes, confessions, or rulers and ruled. Instead, they form a community organically structured into subcommunities. The state, as the instrument of leadership, must serve this community. The law, as part of order to be developed out of the "essence" of the community, is articulated by the leadership. The opposition between public and private law, between the individual and the state, is dialectically "transcended" in communal law. Since trust prevails in the community, the call for supervision of the leadership is a breach of trust. The community does not discuss, it marches.

Wolfgang Siebert's call for a struggle "to loosen and transform concepts and doctrines which, because of their abstract and normative content, are obstacles to the penetration of the communal idea and to the concrete orders that are based on it,"[25] was not limited to civil law in the narrower sense. Just as the community sought to embrace all national comrades and all spheres of life with its totalitarian claim, the liberation from abstract-universal concepts was thought of as "total." These concepts were to be replaced by "reality-related ideas *[Sinngebilde]*" (K. Larenz).[26]

The speed with which the concept of community pervaded different areas of the law varied. Experts also held divergent opinions on which area was further along in the process. There was consensus, however, that within civil law, *property law* had most thoroughly absorbed the communal idea. As evidence jurists listed, among others, the Hereditary Farm Law of September 29, 1933; the law limiting the rights of neighbors with regard to businesses that were particularly important to the strengthening of the nation (promulgated on December 13, 1933);[27] the law regulating the land needs of the authorities (promulgated March 29, 1935); the real estate law of June 26, 1936; and the legislation on tenant law.

These and other laws created what were in part extensive restrictions on the law of private property in favor of the "community." In particular, the state's obligation to pay compensation was limited with the argument that the right of compensation had already been "inherently" curtailed for an individual through the bonds of community.[28]

The communal idea seemed more difficult to establish in the *law of obligations*. Still in 1936 W. Herschel noted that "the idea of community is making advances in the area of the existing law of obligations."[29] H. Stoll, for instance, whose background was in the school of *Interessenjurisprudenz*, sought new "community related" solutions.[30] However, Stoll was essentially activating ideas that had previously been represented in the concepts "good faith" and "common decency." These maintained that the subjective rights granted by the law could not be exercised without restraint but had to respect an inherent limit that was drawn either by the debt relationship itself or by the public interest. In setting that limit, jurists now drew increasingly on the "needs of the national community." Some even characterized the debt relationship as a "community relationship" with elements of public law obligations. Stoll, however, did not go that far. While he did pay wordy reverence to the idea of community, he did *not* elevate the relationship between debtor and creditor to a community relationship.[31] Here as elsewhere, we see that theorists, because of the inertia of the material they were dealing with, for the most part had to refrain from entirely new conceptualizations and content themselves with a rhetorical shift of accent.

The introduction of the idea of community occasionally led to strange results in some areas of civil law. For instance, in *compensation law* Rothe criticized the "unwillingness to accept a misfortune that simply happened, and the desperate effort to compensate oneself at the expense of others."[32] Consideration for the idea of community, he felt, should reduce suits for damages, since the filing of an unjustified suit was an offense against the national community.

H. Roquette's work in *landlord and tenant law* was more solidly grounded. He noted three new ethical ideas in this area of the law (those of community, duty, and welfare) and sought to deduce legal consequences from them—a procedure that is also methodologically revealing for its matter-of-fact conjoining of ethical and legal argumentation.[33] The idea of community, Roquette maintained, abolished the tensions between tenant and landlord, for the house community comprised both parties and called for cooperation based on mutual trust. In this respect the invocation of a higher community, in which ethical obligations were to tie the hands of economic adversaries, turned out to be an appeal for harmony. Roquette admitted that the main value of the idea of community lay in the ethical directive that the national community should avoid internal conflicts as far as possible.

This tendency emerged even more clearly in the area of *labor law*. One of the core questions in this area, especially in the theoretical discussion of jurisprudence, was the continuing applicability of paragraphs 611 and following of the Civil Code, which, after the promulgation in 1934 of the Law on the Organization of National Labor (AOG),[34] could at best claim limited validity. The regulation of the employer-employee relationship in these paragraphs (contract of employment) had been regarded as unsatisfactory long before 1933, since it did not do justice to the importance of labor law, either linguistically or in terms of content. The development away from the Civil Code was strongly supported after 1933 by the Reich Labor Court and jurisprudence. Some jurists even believed they could dispense with the legal figure of the contract, since labor law was beginning to show increasingly strong traits of public law under the reign of the idea of community.[35] Following the victory of the idea of the (national) community, so the argument ran, the old conflicts between employers and employees were abolished in the factory (or plant) community and the national community. Both parties were obligated to work together in the business community for the welfare of the national community; the class struggle had thus been ended. One cliché in legal argumentation in labor law was the "renunciation of the individualistic attitude and the change to a communal attitude in the relationship between the manager and the factory personnel."[36]

The factory community as "an association of social law determined by the common purpose of the enterprise and the benefit of the nation and the state (§ 1 AOG)"[37] thus pushed increasingly to the fore as a legal point of reference. In a phrase borrowed from Carl Schmitt, it was frequently described as a "concrete order" from which the new law flowed.[38] Even more evident here than in landlord and tenant law is the desire to pacify society internally by bringing competing interests together into "communities," thereby placing at the state's disposal the energies that had hitherto been tied up in domestic politics. Thus wage freezes, the outlawing of strikes, and a drastic curtailment of freedom of movement were direct devices for taming class struggle, while Kraft durch Freude outings and a general mystification of labor were indirect ones. The bourgeoisie's understandable desire to get relief from the pressure exerted on it by the workers was complemented by the state's interest in domestic peace. In the process the idea of community became one of the primary means of giving ideological backing to direct interference in the right to strike and freedom of movement, and the suppression of wage demands. An intensive communal education was to make this idea so strong that the state could do without external methods of compulsion. However, the authorities were realistic enough to include "relapses into the old spirit of self-interest and mistrust . . . especially on the question of pay" into their calculations.[39]

All advances in the sphere of social policy that were achieved after 1945 cannot conceal the fact that this National Socialist pattern also underlies the currently prevailing interpretation of the employer-employee relationship as a community relationship that obligates the employer to show "solicitude" *(Fürsorge)* and the employee to show "loyalty." The same holds true for equating the desire of employers for consistent wages and the prevention of strikes with the "common good." It has been widely maintained that the interpretation of the employer-employee relationship as a community relationship represents progress on the theoretical level. However, in my view, P. Schwerdtner has convincingly demonstrated that it is in fact a relapse into communal relationships that are bound to persons, compared to which the contract based on the law of obligations (despite the dangers for the weaker party) represented a liberation of the individual. Of course, to speak of progress or relapse in this sphere presupposes an a priori decision to regard the liberation of human beings from personal and material bonds as something valuable. National Socialist jurists and their successors in the field of labor law, however, made an a priori decision that was exactly the opposite.

It is widely known that the ideology of community and race had substantial influence on National Socialist *marriage law*. In accordance with the goal of "increasing and preserving the species and the race,"[40] breeding was the dominant idea. The propagation of children became "a duty toward the true idea of kinship and the idea of community."[41] These principles were embodied in the marriage law of 1938. Rüthers, in his 1970 study, compiled the effects of this law on the administration of justice in the courts of the Reich.[42] His comparison of the decisions rendered by the Reichsgericht and the Federal High Court (Bundesgerichtshof) revealed that nearly identical argumentation led to different outcomes. The Reichsgericht, with the help of the argument that marriage was to serve the national community, developed a "moderate readiness to grant divorces"[43]—that is, marriages of no use to the national community were dissolved fairly quickly. By contrast, the Bundesgerichtshof, which also argued that the ethical order of marriage served the meaningful structure of a higher whole to which individuals had to subordinate themselves,[44] reached the opposite decision— namely, that marriage was fundamentally indissoluble. We have here an obvious example of how ideological a priori decisions can be retroactively endowed with a semblance of rationality with the help of techniques of legal argumentation.

As for the changes the idea of community brought with it in economic legislation, in particular cartel and energy law, all I can do here is refer readers to the relevant literature.[45] The same goes for copyright law and commercial legal protection (patent law and laws on competition, trademark law, and design law).[46] Some of the changes implemented were reforms long demanded and long overdue, which the parliaments of the Weimar era had not been able to accomplish. The idea that the rights of the individual had to be restricted in favor of the "community" established itself more or less strongly in all these areas of the law. If we examine this shift from the perspective of the dichotomy between private law and public law, we note an increasing expansion of the sphere of public law. And it must be strongly emphasized that this occurred without regard to ideological positions both before and after National Socialism, as Franz Wieacker has shown, for example, in the area of land law.[47] The rapid growth of technology in all spheres of life, the rise in population, and the reconstruction that the states of postwar Europe had to accomplish were probably the main reasons behind this development.

The idea that the national community, as the highest interest protected by the law, had priority of protection was also behind the drive to transform *criminal law*. The rights of an individual involved in a criminal case and the idea of rehabilitation vanished almost completely before the call for "elimination" and "deterrence." The common refrain was that the "community-forming power of criminal law"[48] could manifest itself only if one eliminated the incorrigible and deterred potential criminals, deterrence having become "respectable" again.[49]

At first National Socialist criminal jurists limited themselves to "emphasizing" the communal idea, which in this field of the law entailed tougher penalties, a shift from the culpability of an act to the culpability of the criminal will, the introduction of new offenses,[50] the admission of legal analogy to the defendant's disadvantage, and the elimination of the defendant's procedural rights. The existing dogmatic devices were retained. However, it soon became clear that a consistent implementation of the communal idea also called for the development of new concepts. We encounter a first attempt at restating the existing system in the work of G. Dahm.[51] He made a fundamental distinction between treason and crime: "Treason destroys the community and dissolves the order. Treason dishonors the guilty person and expels him from the community . . . The case is different with the criminal. He remains subject to the law. His deed violates the order, but it still leaves open the possibility for the perpetrator to restore his relationship to the community. . . . Penal law ends where a relationship to the community is absent, where no order is involved."[52] This distinction corresponded to the penalties suggested by Dahm: ostracism for the traitor who had broken the bond between self and community, punishment for the criminal.

Our survey of the effects of the communal idea in these different legal fields has shown that we are dealing with a basic ideological concept, and that the speed and effectiveness of its implementation varied with the special circumstances in a given field. More successful than the attempt to introduce the concept of community as a new term in the legal language was the method of merely setting it up as an ethical principle and using the tried and tested interpretive aids to derive new, "community related" meanings from the old, unchanged texts. It is not surprising that this realization has led to a loss of trust in the traditional, quasi-logical interpretive procedures of jurisprudence. The survey has further refuted once and for all the view—still widespread today—that there are nonpolitical fields of the law, by showing that the entire legal order was distorted under National Socialism. Naturally, this dependence of the legal order and its conceptual system on the political base manifested itself most glaringly in *constitutional law*, to which our analysis now shifts. As E. R. Huber wrote: "In constitutional law, in particular, the basic political currents of the reality of the state are most clearly visible, and it is here that the old formal-logical and normative thinking will most readily be overcome by political communal thinking."[53]

In 1933 constitutional theory, following a period of intense debate in the Weimar Republic,[54] stood at the threshold of a new development whose contours nobody could divine. The prospects for new concepts in constitutional law thus seemed particularly promising. The basic discussion about the pros and cons of the parliamentary system was cut off. Those who continued to speak out in writing saw themselves directed to *commentary* on the transformation of the entire structure of the state, and to efforts at drawing theoretical distinctions between the concepts of state and national community, nation and "movement," party law, Reich law, and so on. After what has already been said, it is hardly surprising that the idea of community took a prominent place in these discussions. The following questions became relevant: Is "community" usable only as a sociological or also as a legal concept? Does the word have a content that is verifiable in a legal sense? Can the concept of community, in particular, replace the traditional notion of the state as a legal entity, or should "communal thinking" find use only as an interpretive aid?[55]

Reinhard Höhn, who had developed his ideas of community as a constitutional theorist of the Jungdeutscher Orden (Order of Young Germans, a conservative bourgeois group)[56] by positing an antithesis between bourgeois-constitutional democracy and "true Germanic democracy,"[57] switched to the National Socialist camp in 1933 and became the champion of the communal idea in constitutional law. In so doing he resumed what Otto von Gierke, as early as 1902 in a completely different historical situation, had bemoaned as the "war of annihilation against the concept of the personality of the state *[Staatspersönlichkeit].*"[58] Höhn's arguments with Wilhelm Merk, Ernst Rudolf Huber, and Otto Koellreutter are characteristic of the difficulties posed by the concept of community, and of the state of constitutional theory as such. As Hans Frank put it, constitutional theory should no longer be seen as a science "of the relations between citizens endowed with subjective public rights, on the one hand, and representatives of the state burdened with corresponding obligations, on the other. Rather, it must be seen as a theory of order based on the personal element of a nation's loyalty in following the leader it has legitimated."[59]

Höhn opposed everything he thought he could identify as "liberal thinking," and in this he was right in line with the usual polemics against individualism and liberalism: "What needs to be done in constitutional law is to point out the individualistic aspect in all innovations, to clearly bring out the opposing position, and thereby promote the whole."[60] Liberalism, individualism, and the traditional doctrine of constitutional law saturated by these ideas, became his sworn enemy, which had to be fought everywhere, but especially in the concepts of the "legal community" and of the "state and the public corporation as legal persons." He therefore saw it as his main task to establish "community" and "national community" as basic concepts of constitutional theory, to "positivize" them, and thereby to eliminate from constitutional theory the now superfluous notion of public law as a legal person. Höhn summarized it this way: "The place of the principle of individualism has today been taken by a different principle, that of community. The foundation and cornerstone of constitutional law is no longer the legal person of the state; rather, the national community is the new starting point . . . The state as a legal person and the concept of community are mutually exclusive."[61]

These thoughts were by no means limited to Höhn. Th. Maunz, F. W. Jerusalem (whose assistant Höhn had been), and G. Küchenhoff also advocated them in similar form.[62] However, Höhn's debate with the literature on constitutional law shows he believed that he represented the communal idea in a particularly pure and consistent form.[63] It is not surprising that in the process he lumped older authors like G. Jellinek, Kelsen, Heller, O. Mayer, and Anschütz together into the liberal-individualistic camp. But even authors who, he conceded, were already showing "communal" feeling, such as E. R. Huber, O. Koellreutter, K. Bilfinger, A. Köttgen, H. Gerber, U. Scheuner, and E. Tatarin-Tarnheyden, did not escape the charge that they wanted to cling to the basis of individualism, thereby misjudging or at least weakening the importance of the communal idea for the new constitutional law. The final verdict of this criticism was this: "The prevailing constitutional theory has been unable to this very day to break with the concept of the state as a legal person. Though it no longer emphasizes this concept, as it still did during Jellinek's time, it has always retained it, and it forms the basis of its dogma."[64]

Höhn's criticism of constitutional theory was, in turn, the substratum of common clichés in the current of antidemocratic thinking. The crass antitheses between "liberal" and "authoritarian" and between "individualistic thinking" and "communal thinking," on which this current was based, were derived from a literary tradition whose arguments and effects were already outlined in historical and sociological books.[65] Projected into the legal reform and propaganda literature, these antitheses read as follows: German (Germanic, Nordic, Aryan) thinking is organic, concrete, close to the people and true to life, oriented toward the "whole," unifying, dynamic, synthetic, related to values and community. The opposite of this is "Roman-Jewish" thinking, characterized as liberal, rationalistic, positivistic, abstract-conceptual, individualistic, materialistic, rigid, constructed, alien to life and the people, analytic, nihilistic, corrupting, and so on. Typical of this approach, which bestowed negative attributes on the concept of the state and positive attributes on the concept of community, is a passage from an essay by Heinrich Lange:

> Anyone who sharply juxtaposes that which separates our legal sensibility from Roman legal thinking will arrive at the following conclusion: Roman legal thought is individualistic and materialistic, the state is the absolute external apparatus of power; German legal feeling is directed toward connectedness *[Bindung]*, toward the community, which is the order of communal life composed of the various groups. The Roman divides the world into persona and res, starkly juxtaposing master and object; for the German the antagonisms *[Gegensätze]* disappear in service to the great tasks and values of the nation.[66]

The state, discredited as an "apparatus," thus became the evil principle under whose rule a "genuine" national community could not be realized. As long as the antidemocratic movement before 1933 meant the despised Weimar state when it said "state," the attacks on the concept of the state were driven by this negative feeling. After 1933, when the state and the national community had become identical, at least in theory, the attacks against the state become less intense.[67] After 1933 the debate, now largely an academic one, revolved only around the theoretical ranking of the concepts of state and (national) community within the National Socialist theory of the state.

One of the arguments used in this debate was that Hitler himself had said the state was no end in itself but only the means to preserve and advance the nation.[68] Höhn invoked it to criticize Huber's thesis that only the state made the natural nation into a "political nation."[69] Here, Höhn argued, one could still see, shining through, the individualistic juxtaposition of a state capable of acting and the nation incapable of acting. This dualism was wrong, he maintained, because it did not correspond to National Socialist reality, which had already implemented the concept of community in its law.

It is true that the terms *community* and *national community* were used with increasing frequency in legislation after 1933. As I have indicated earlier,[70] the term *national community* saw an almost inflationary expansion in usage. The following examples show that these phrases had two functions: to appeal to the conscience of the individual and/or to serve as the basis for encroachment upon his or her rights.

—In accordance with § 24 AOG, expert witnesses had to swear not to pursue any special interest and to serve only the welfare of the "national community."[71]

—One precondition for obtaining a government loan for young married couples was that the marriage was in "the interest of the national community."[72]

—According to § 2 of the Law on the Hitler Youth, the entire German youth was to be educated "for service to the nation and the national community."[73]

—According to § 15 of the Reich Notary Law, notaries had to exercise their office "for the benefit of the national community."[74]

—The public prosecutor could intervene in civil legal matters in order to put forward "the position of the national community."[75]

By contrast, the word *community* appeared much more rarely in legislation. In many instances it was used merely to stand for *national community*—for example, in § 10 AOG, which speaks of the "community of all national comrades"—or it served to designate smaller communities, as in the disciplinary laws of the Reich Labor Service[76] or in traffic regulations, which were supposed to establish the "true community of all drivers and pedestrians."[77] The term *community* was not used at all in legislation in the sense we are interested in. Instead, when the intent was to describe the all-encompassing community, the term *national community* usually took its place. For instance, when Roland Freisler and Höhn argued that the concept of community had already made its way into *legislation,* they were forced to draw on relatively insignificant evidence: the preamble to the German Communal Regulations of January 30, 1935; the task of Reich Agriculture, described as "beneficial to the community"; the saying "common interest before self-interest"; the first three paragraphs of the AOG; paragraphs 1 and following of the German Civil Service Law; and the ordinance of the Reich Treasurer of the Nazi party of March 29, 1935, which spoke of the "National Socialist community."[78] These examples, which were unable to support the authors' thesis, at least show how indiscriminate this method of furnishing proof was, and how unclear was the supposed "meaning" of *community.*

IV. Höhn's efforts to replace the legal person of the state with the concept of community were opposed especially by Wilhelm Merk and Otto Koellreutter. As early as 1935 Merk noted that Höhn's attempt had failed, that he had prematurely cheered the "fall" of the legal person of the state.[79] Merk argued that it had not been made sufficiently clear what liberalism actually was, and that the terms *community* and *leadership,* which were borrowed from the military sphere, were not usable in the legal context. Citing many examples from constitutional and administrative law, he demonstrated that the concept of the state as a legal person continued to be indispensable—for instance, as an intellectual point of reference in civil service and police law, in finance law, and in citizenship law, as well as in the legal understanding of the Reich's foreign relations.[80] The critical voices of Helfritz, H. Reuss, Jerusalem, and G. Neesze in opposition to Höhn were convincingly summarized or anticipated by Merk, who argued that the concept of the state as a legal person—along with the consequences that flowed from it (the sovereignty of the state, hierarchical relationships in administrative law, the position of the head of state as an institution)—had not been abolished by the National Socialist revolution. For theoretical reasons the legal person of the state was indispensable also in the future.[81]

Koellreutter concurred with this conclusion. In numerous argumentative writings, replete with attacks against Forsthoff, Höhn, Maunz, C. Schmitt, Jerusalem, and J. Heckel, he tried to draw the picture of an authoritarian state in which the two principles that the administration adhered to laws and that courts provided legal protection were, admittedly, restricted but nevertheless preserved. During the final phase of National Socialism he realized ever more clearly that this was not the state he had called for in the 1930s and which he initially saw realized under National Socialism. In his later essays he pointed more and more frequently to other countries under authoritarian rule—such as Japan and Italy—in which the protection of individual rights had not vanished, and he warned of the danger of dehumanization and the fall of European culture.[82] This view also underlies his rejection of the concept of community. His argument that one could not get "a legal grasp" on the term[83] and that "certainty" came for now only from the concept of the legal person reflected—apart from theoretical concerns—his anxiety to preserve traditional ordering elements, which he saw endangered by a concept of community that was infinitely malleable.

Despite his early praise of Höhn for having refuted the legal person of the state,[84] Huber too could not bring himself to give up the concept of the state. In his eyes, the change brought about by National Socialism was primarily the abolition of the gulf between state and society, a process that did not make the state disappear within the national community but actually strengthened it. As Huber saw it, the state made the natural nation into a "political" nation. In the process, nation and state became an "inseparable" entity, the state being the "higher communal order" or "lasting political form." Beginning in 1939 he suggested the term *Reich* for the state and *state organization* for its

technical apparatus (administrative and military).[85] Huber's opposition
to premature ideas about identity and the "indiscriminate generalization of certain political constitutional principles, above all the community principle and the Führer principle, and their abstract transfer to
organizational forms of communal law," could well be seen as a response to Höhn.[86] Later, in 1941, Huber spelled it out more clearly:
"The task confronting German political theory is not to polemicize
against the state, but to absorb all elements of statehood into the concept of the Reich."[87] Huber now saw the notion of the Reich as the
central concept in which the opposition between the concepts of community and state could be dialectically resolved.

As the totalitarian traits of National Socialism, beginning in 1938,
asserted themselves increasingly over its authoritarian traits, the initially lively debate over the idea of community became less and less
relevant. The so-called "war against the person of the state"[88] was quietly abandoned. That explains how A. Köttgen in 1945, in response
to the question whether the Reich as a legal person had still been the
employer of the civil servants, could rightly note that the criticism of
the central concept of the person of the state had exerted no significant
influence on legislation.[89] The West German Federal Constitutional
Court (Bundesverfassungsgericht) did accept this argument in the controversy over whether civil servant status had continued after April 8,
1945. However, it dismissed it as irrelevant, precisely because it was
concerned to show that the formally continuing relationship of the civil
servant to the legal person of the state had been essentially changed,
so that it was not possible to speak of continuity after this date. The
series of "131 decisions" by the Federal Constitutional Court, and the
emotional debate they triggered,[90] illuminates once more in retrospect
this distortion of traditional concepts, such as "the state as legal person" and "professional civil service."

That the discussion over the concept of community largely died
down after 1938[91] was hardly because the question of legal terminology
was seen as having been resolved—on the contrary. But the quarrel
over terms seemed increasingly meaningless in view of the massive
inroads into the remnants of the *Rechtsstaat* by the Nazi party and the
SS. Koellreutter, for example, spoke out against the admissibility of
secret laws; against the leveling of the difference between constitutional
law, laws, and decrees;[92] and against the dualism of party law and state
law.[93] The fact that many scholars turned from constitutional law to
less risky historical topics or issues of international law emphasizes
how jurists had essentially realized that neither the category of community nor any other category was suitable for explaining, let alone influ-

encing, the phenomenon of the totalitarian state. As Hitler explained, "The health of the German nation is more important than the letter of the law."[94]

V. We can name several, mutually interconnected, reasons why the term *(national) community* posed difficulties within the traditional legal system. Probably the most evident reason was that the term could take on all kinds of meaning, a characteristic that the many attempts at defining it could not eliminate. The language of these attempts reveals that their purpose was not to grasp reality with the greatest possible precision, but to establish a metaphysical superstructure. Here, for example, is how Ritterbusch described the relationship between *Weltanschauung* and national community:

> The totality of our being, which is taking shape in this movement and developing into the essential reality of our existence, is the holistic community of the race-specific *[artgebunden]* nation. The National Socialist movement is the becoming-of-the-nation *[Volkswerdung]*, and this becoming is nothing other than the fulfilling realization of the truth and reality of our selves. The lasting becoming-of-the-nation fulfills the law of our reality and truth, for only the whole is true and real, and only the nation is the wholeness and therefore the truth and reality of our selves.[95]

As long as the definitions were developed descriptively from the concept itself—for instance, through recourse to the "essence" of the community—they merely reproduced the views of those doing the defining. Their informational value was virtually nil. Let us look at three examples:

> Höhn: "In the community the individual completely casts off his individual personality, he no longer feels as an individual person, he merges with the community spirit and acts out of the community spirit. He becomes the bearer of this spirit and is now ready to make sacrifices, even if his individual interests are thereby severely damaged."[96]
> C. Dernedde: "Belonging to a community means participating with other people in a shared world of values. In all members a highest value must be recognized as the universally binding law and made the starting point of individual and social action."[97]
> Larenz: "Being a member of a community does not mean being the bearer of abstract qualities common to all. Instead, it means that a person, with his individual nature, is woven into a larger whole that is also individual in nature."[98]

We could multiply such examples at will from the literature of all legal fields. All descriptions of what "community" is had certain characteristic traits: acknowledgment of an absolutely binding—though, paradoxically, never precisely defined—value system, the claim of exclusivity with regard to those who were not included in the community, and, finally, the suppression of "community-harming" opposition, that is, the subordination of the individual to the whole, which was said to represent the truth in the Hegelian sense.[99]

Other than by force, this subordination could be effected only by transfiguring external compulsion into supposed voluntarism. That is why National Socialist literature affirmed time and again that the subordination of the individual to the (national) community was not an act of external compulsion; instead, individuals were following the reawakened call of the blood, which was urging them toward community. Hence the literature spoke repeatedly of the community that was "ordered" and "charged" by blood; the element establishing community was "blood, not some abstraction."[100]

Moreover, the corollary to community, the idea of the person, was not to be understood as the individualistic counterpart to community. Instead, a person, too, should regard him- or herself merely as a member of the whole, whose rights—without a need to emphasize this explicitly—were "inherently" limited by the interests of the community.[101]

The propagandistic creation of an "inner" compulsion toward community thus complemented the external compulsion of the state's instruments of power. The pressure that was exerted on "honor and conscience," as a more sublimated instrument of rule, had the advantage of working indirectly and therefore being more difficult to recognize. The intentions of those who propagated the national community were to create a soldierly war community that had abolished or suppressed its internal contradictions in order to heighten its effectiveness on the battlefield. Those contradictions included the distinction between private and public law—that is, the dualism of state and society, and the principle of the separation of powers. If these were abolished, the protection of individual liberty also became meaningless, for in the total community, in which rulers and ruled are identical, a violation of the sphere of private liberty can no longer occur. Höhn logically concluded that a legal dispute between the individual and the administration no longer made sense.[102]

As a result, anyone who—like Koellreutter—wanted to preserve a minimum of legal protection against encroachments by the state could be defamed as a "liberal reactionary." Individuals who insisted on their "rights" showed by this very act that they had not yet fully grasped the idea of community. Likewise, efforts to circumscribe the concept of community through definitions could be interpreted as inner reservations toward the community, since the latter by its "nature" did not know any boundaries.

By analogy to the military Führer-follower model, a community no longer needed any supervision of the rulers. Distrust of the leadership was replaced by trust, the separation of powers by the consolidation of state power in one hand. The following passage from a speech by Freisler illustrates the consequences for the law of this kind of thinking:

> We Germans march in columns. As soldiers we look forward. And there we see one person: our leader. Wherever he points we march. And wherever he points he always marches first, ahead of us. That is in keeping with our German nature. In the face of this all the "constitutional law" of the past has blown away like chaff in the wind:
>
> The separation of powers; supervision of the leadership by the led; protection of personal rights by courts; a state based on the rule of law, which nobody wanted less than the organs of justice themselves, that is to say, the review of true acts of leadership to determine whether they are in formal compliance with the law; constraints on the vanguard and limitations on their instruments of leadership; the rule of numbers over will, of anonymous numbers, that is, of irresponsibility.
>
> All this—once carefully hedged about in constitutions with legal guarantees—has now been swept away.[103]

This kind of communal thinking was incompatible with a legal system that regarded as its cornerstones the legally enforceable subjective right of the individual and the concept of the state as a legal person. The terminological difficulties that arose from this incompatibility are only the reflections of a larger conflict that was by no means resolved when National Socialism came to an end. They reveal the discrepancies between the traditional *Rechtsstaat* and the totalitarian state contemptuous of the law, as well as the vagueness of National Socialist "ideology." For instance, it remained unclear whether *community*, in keeping with the idea of race, meant all "Aryan" people without regard for national boundaries, or whether it meant the "political nation." The invocations of "common blood" seem to point to the first possibility, talk about the national community more to the second. Finally, the terminological difficulties reveal the predicament of a jurisprudence that was accustomed to circumscribe concepts and piece them together into a system, but was now confronted with a government that openly dismissed intellectual systematics, definitions, and boundaries as a nuisance to its freedom of action.

We have seen how the concept of community was invoked to dialectically abolish social contradictions first of all in the realm of language.[104] For the most part these were contradictions of an economic nature, for instance, between seller and buyer, tenant and landlord, and other partners in debt relationships; between employer and employee; between neighbors; between public authorities and private property owners; and so on. In constitutional law economic contradictions (classes), old historical contradictions (confessions), and hierarchical contradictions (rulers, subjects) were presented as having been abolished in the concepts "community" and "Reich," though in reality they had by no means been done away with. The establishment of a comprehensive police system and a network of informants and spies turned the concept of community into a mere phrase, unmasking it as the core of an ideology of power.

However, it would be wrong to deduce from this a fundamental affinity between communal thinking and totalitarian forms of rule. Given that in every form of government, including democracy, a few exercise rule over many and a permanent need exists for overcoming social tensions, the communal idea time and again offers itself as a way of abolishing these tensions on a higher, seemingly impartial level. As a component of a social metaphysics, the concept of community is a cross between empiricism and value judgment. As such it serves to rebuff individual demands, to resolve conflicts from the standpoint of the "interest of the community," and to make the moral appeal to individuals to identify their own interests with those of the state.

PART TWO

Legal Theory
and Practice

In the Belly of the Beast: Constitutional Legal Theory *(Staatsrechtslehre)*[1] under National Socialism

During the first half of the twentieth century German constitutional theory kept up with the transition from a constitutional monarchy to a democratic republic, from a republic to a one-party dictatorship, and from a dictatorship back to a democratic republic. The theory of administrative law had to adjust to the transformation of the liberal constitutional state into a social interventionist state. Twice it had to provide commentary on the so-called "war administration law," and it accompanied the citizens from the age of the stagecoach to the age of the airplane and the computer.

These revolutions and developments posed a great intellectual and scholarly challenge. At the same time they harbored considerable dangers, for a science that proves utterly adaptable and malleable must develop doubts about its own character as a science, and its representatives must ask themselves whether they are capable of coping psychologically with these shifting identities. An urgent question therefore arose: what could preserve the continuity of constitutional theory behind these changing façades and impart stability to it?

This question is of more than historical interest. The political culture of Germany is to a large degree shaped by constitutional theory, by the Federal Constitutional Court and its decisions, and by public discussion of constitutional issues. Nearly all the arguments that are used today date to a period before the Federal Republic, to the empire of 1870 and especially to the Weimar Republic.

In the interest of contemporary political culture, one should therefore ask how constitutional theory weathered these upheavals. How did professors of constitutional and administrative law handle their arguments, and how did they—as politically involved, intelligent, and sensitive people (a general presupposition we shall make)—react to such political upheavals?

Scholars themselves have not contributed much to answering this question. The Association of Constitutional Lawyers did not meet between 1933 and 1949, and it could therefore feel somewhat relieved of the burden of having to subject its own past to critical scrutiny. It was apparently enough to single out a few "black sheep" (Carl Schmitt, Ernst Rudolf Huber, Otto Koellreutter, Reinhard Höhn). Beyond that, the attitude was that anybody who had not been "excessively" National Socialist, who had merely commented on the prevailing law, could soon return, perhaps clutching a democratic textbook on constitutional theory under his arm. In fact, after 1950 it was considered "tactless" to speak about Nazi constitutional law and the involvement of specific individuals. By doing so one ran the danger of insulting a colleague or teacher; moreover, the interpretation of West Germany's Basic Law provided enough work.

However, during recent years there have been growing signs of a less restrained language and a less biased treatment of the subject. We are currently witnessing for the first time a true "historicization" of National Socialism. During the so-called *Historikerstreit,* some expressed the concern that a purely historical (amoral) examination could lead to a dangerous minimizing of what happened. Opposing voices emphasized that the blending of historical and moral questions that had always been practiced in the past must finally be transcended in favor of "professional" historiography.

As far as constitutional and administrative legal theory are concerned, until now scholars have indeed been in the habit of working with standardized labels. All too often the history of the discipline amounted merely to classifying people as "good" and "evil," as Nazis and non-Nazis. This was the perspective of de-Nazification and the postwar criminal trials, a perspective that continued to resonate. However, this is now beginning to change. There is a growing number of studies that take a broader perspective, that analyze without moralizing and thus work "historically" in the classic sense. This essay is an attempt at an interim assessment in that direction.

The seemingly stable and unchallenged starting point of constitutional theory as a "science" is the constitutional positivism founded by Carl Friedrich von Gerber and Paul Laband between 1855 and 1875. It appropriated the designation "scientific" and became the yardstick of constitutional law that was practiced in a scientific manner. It was not a political theory but a methodologically justified narrowing of the perspective of judicial theory to the positive constitutional law of the Reich; of course, it did presuppose political agreement with the establishment of the Reich. In this context scholars concurred with the "content" of positive law. That which was legal also appeared to be legitimate. The task of legal science was to extract the basic ideas contained in the positive law and to work them into a coherent conceptual system.

I will not pursue the political choices behind this façade, nor the attractive questions concerning the origins of the "constructive method" from civil law that was used in this process. What interests us is when and where the first cracks appeared in this seemingly solid structure. There are four clues:

1. Around the turn of the century, so-called "sociological sciences of the state" (Ludwig Gumplowicz, Gustav Ratzenhofer, Franz Oppenheimer, Anton Menger) arose "at the margins" of the discipline. Suddenly there was a resurgence of the demand for an empirical understanding of the state instead of mere legal construction (Conrad Bornhak). Romanticism's organological theory of the state, long since believed to be dead, experienced a revival, and handbooks of "general theory of the state," of which there had been none in thirty years, suddenly reappeared around 1900 (Richard Schmidt, G. Jellinek).

2. Shortly before World War I the so-called *Freirechtsschule* (H. Kantorowicz, E. Fuchs, E. Stampe, E. Ehrlich) voiced doubts about the model of how law was produced, spoke about the "public harmfulness of constructive jurisprudence," and tried to once again give the judge greater latitude in interpreting the law. The classic model of logical syllogism was thus beginning to waver, and the first voices were heard that based the legitimacy of judges' decisions no longer on their content and derivation from the law, but on what was authorized by the state (Carl Schmitt).

3. The positive constitutional law of the Bismarckian Constitution of 1871 also proved inadequate, so jurists began to think about *Constitutional Amendment and Constitutional Change* (Georg Jellinek, 1906) and *Unwritten Constitutional Law in the Monarchical Federal State* (Rudolf Smend, 1916).

4. The basic debate over legal philosophy in the general theory of the state came to life, and the paths diverged: On the one hand, positivism intensified in unison with the neo-Kantianism of the turn of the century (H. Cohen, P. Natorp, Hans Kelsen); on the other hand, the opposing camp saw a massive politicization and ethicization of the law, almost exclusively in an antidemocratic direction (Erich Kaufmann, *Das Wesen des Völkerrechts und die Clausula rebus sic stantibus* [The nature of international law and the Clausula rebus sic stantibus, 1911]).

The empirical and political elements of constitutional law, pushed aside since 1870, had thus reappeared before World War I. Since one could not simply return to the pre-positivist blending of legal and nonlegal elements, theorists helped themselves by doubling their perspective. Accordingly, Georg Jellinek's *Allgemeine Staatslehre* (General theory of the state [1900]), "the most perfect summation of the nineteenth-century theory of the state," as Kelsen would later say, split into two parts: a legal (normative) and a sociological (empirical) concept of the state. This move took into account how the empirical sciences were clamoring for recognition, and at the same time it preserved the purity of the legal province. Of course, this created epistemological contradictions, and it became clear that Jellinek had based his empirical assumptions, as well, on an idealistic metaphysics of history.

Hans Kelsen (1881–1973), in particular, exposed these shortcomings in his keen and penetrating writings. He demanded a clearer separation of 'is' and 'ought', of normative and empirical statements, and the expulsion of ethics, politics, and metaphysics from jurisprudence. Through his writings from 1911 on, he led constitutional theory into a fundamental discussion of legal theory. Before 1919 this discussion was carried on in academic circles, but during the turbulent 1920s it broadened and became strident—with anti-Semitic overtones. For instance, the so-called Vienna School of constitutional law clashed with the "prevailing opinion" in Germany philosophically as well as politically.

What was this "prevailing opinion"? If we take, for example, the eighty-four names on the 1922 membership list of the Association of Constitutional Lawyers, we can, by greatly simplifying, form a few groups:[2]

1. Initially, the proponents of classic constitutional positivism were still dominant. They accepted the new republic and its constitution, not exactly enthusiastically, but loyally, because in keeping with the doctrine of the "law-creating power of the successful revolution," it was incontestable in terms of positive law. These were the "rational republicans" *(Vernunftrepublikaner)* of constitutional theory, all of them older men, and they tried to preserve the links to earlier constitutional theory. Typical of this group were Richard Thoma, Heinrich Triepel, and Gerhard Anschütz, who were among the most respected theorists of public law during the Weimar era and later kept their distance from National Socialism.

2. Alongside these jurists, special methodological and political groups increasingly emerged. Taking methodology first, we would probably have to mention Erich Kaufmann as the first "antipositivist

opponent." His *Kritik der neukantischen Rechtsphilosophie* (Critique of neo-Kantian legal philosophy [1921]), "a first-rate polemical work,"[3] and his talk on the principle of equality at the 1926 Meeting of Constitutional Theorists[4] were the first affirmations of a material idea of law *above* positive law, of a renunciation of rationalism and relativism of values—in political terms, the renunciation of parliamentary democracy.

The idea propagated by Kaufmann and others, such as Günter Holstein (who died early)—namely, a change toward "humanistic methodology"—was picked up by Rudolf Smend, who worked it into a theory on the basis of Theodor Litt's philosophy of culture. In 1928 Smend published his famous book *Verfassung und Verfassungsrecht* (Constitution and constitutional law), which sought to apply the sociological concept of 'integration' to the political process. The book's theory of integration, which resonates to this day—I mention his students Ulrich Scheuner, Konrad Hesse, Wilhelm Hennis, Horst Ehmke, and Peter von Oertzen--was from the beginning surrounded by a twilight of deliberate vagueness. Constantly moving back and forth between descriptive and normative statements, it was searching for a dialectical solution to the tension between the individual and the community. By linking the quality of a state to a polity's capacity for integration, the theory could brand the Weimar state as a nonstate because it was incapable of integration. And that is precisely how it was understood in the political landscape of 1928.

However, with Kaufmann, Holstein, and Smend, we already find ourselves in the center of the opposition movement against the prevailing constitutional positivism. The only point on which they agreed was their opposition to its methodology. "Without a doubt," Smend wrote in 1973, looking back, "opinions diverged thereafter. But how the members grouped themselves numerically after that is impossible to say. And in any case, [Hans] Nawiasky was right to protest in 1927 that one couldn't speak so readily about a prevailing doctrine in the first place."[5]

Still, between 1926 and 1929 it became clear that this group, because it rejected the methodological foundations from the imperial era and distrusted the formal understanding of democracy, contained at least the potential of becoming the prevailing opinion in the future. With the exception of Hermann Heller,[6] who could be included in this group methodologically but who, as a Social Democrat, was at the other end of the political spectrum, the "antipositivists" were conservative in the sense that they suffered from the humiliation of the Versailles Treaty, rejected the party system, and sought to establish a powerful national state and abolish class warfare in a national community. They were no longer monarchists, not yet fascists, though no more than lukewarm republicans; they were members of the middle class who were unhappy with the situation under the Weimar regime.

3. A third group is characterized not so much by methodological subtleties as by its clear political opposition to the republic.[7] While the majority of constitutional theorists and teachers pursued their political inclinations covertly, in keeping with the ideal of a nonpolitical science of constitutional law, some actively fought against the republic from the lectern. Oddities like the denigration of the national flag as "black, red, mustard" or "black, red, brass" (the actual colors were black, red, gold) or an antirepublican inaugural speech in verse pointed the way.

The group of active opponents of the republic included Otto Koell-reutter.[8] In an expert opinion on the unconstitutionality of the Communist Party (KPD) and the Nazi party, he came to the conclusion that both parties wanted to destroy the existing order, but that only the KPD was unconstitutional since the Nazis were pursuing a legitimate goal, the national power state.

Others—among them some legal historians and legal philosophers—drafted new ideas: for E. Tatarin-Tarnheyden[9] and H. Herrfahrdt,[10] a future authoritarian corporate state; for J. Binder,[11] an authoritarian state based on Hegel and Fichte; for Hans Gerber,[12] Walther Merk, and others, a Germanic Führer-state with folk law and vigorous leadership. All these variants had in common their fundamental antidemocratic features, their rejection of Marxism, and their philosophical attachment to nineteenth-century German idealism.

4. Finally, a fourth group formed during the last years of the republic and saw itself as the group of the "young rightists." There were many contacts with the so-called TAT circle (H. Zehrer) and the Order of Young Germans. Philosophically, they were "legal Hegelians," such as K. Larenz,[13] F. Brunstäd, and Gerhard Dulckeit, or they cultivated a kind of heroic decisionism in the sense of Ernst Jünger. Some of them soon joined National Socialism as staunch supporters; Ernst Rudolf Huber,[14] Ernst Forsthoff,[15] and Reinhard Höhn[16] were among this group. This, more than anywhere else, is also where we should place the ambiguously multifaceted Carl Schmitt: clearly above average in eloquence, education, and intelligence, he sought to deal the weakened republic the final, deliberate blows. The man who had still worked with Chancellor Franz von Papen and General Kurt von Schleicher in the fall of 1932 became, the following January, the first prominent constitutional theorist to make himself available to the National Socialists.[17]

If we survey these individuals once more, it becomes clear how difficult it is to assign them to one group or another. Positivist methodology did not always go along with approval for the republic, but frequently it did. Hostility toward positivism often converged with hostility toward the republic, though it could also be grounded in a conception of natural law, derived, for instance, from Catholic social doctrine. The only Social Democrat among the constitutional theorists, Hermann Heller,[18] was not a "positivist." He combined a strong social-science orientation with elements of philosophical idealism, and politically he, like Kelsen, was an unequivocal and impressive defender of parliamentary democracy.

However, the example of Hermann Heller is by no means intended to suggest that the methodological and political positions could be combined at will. In actual fact, from about 1925 on there was a main current that combined various streams: the right-leaning political orientation of the bourgeoisie in the crises of the republic, all variants of philosophical irrationalism, the longing for "leadership" and "community," and the basic anti-Enlightenment mood of these years. This current went along with a move—fed by the war experience of 1914—toward "national community," which people sought out as an island of salvation, as it were, in the sea of class warfare. The solid structures of this national community were looked for in new "orders," corporate models, and in imitation of the Reich President's quasi-dictatorial powers.

Negatively, this meant a rejection of the so-called corrupting *(zersetzendes)* intellect, contempt for supposedly "flat" rational and utilitarian arguments, a rejection of parliamentarianism and parties with their compromises and inability to engage in the "vigorous" politics people were longing for. Within a period of a few years appeared a spate of books, such as Moeller van den Bruck's *Drittes Reich* (Third Reich [1923]), Othmar Spann's *Wahrer Staat* (The true state [1921]), Edgar Jung's *Die Herrschaft der Minderwertigen* (The rule of the inferior [1927]), Ernst Jünger's *Der Arbeiter* (The worker [1928]), the Balthic enthusiast Krannhals's *Organische Weltbild* (The organic view of the world [1925]), and Carl Schmitt's destructive analyses of the "state of parliamentarianism in terms of the history of ideas" (1923). Constitutional theory inevitably was affected by this. In fact, for the most part it was found on one side of the barricades, with the republic on the other.

We could elucidate the authoritarian and irrational trend in the thought of the period, which was on the whole very unfavorable to the republic, in the field of constitutional theory by looking at individual themes. For example, one could think of the revival of the doctrine of the purpose of state *(Staatszweck)*, which positivism had once declared finished and "unjuristic."[19]

A second example would be the question, hotly contested in the Weimar Republic, of whether a judge had the authority to declare a legal norm unconstitutional (the so-called right of judicial review). This is a good example because it allows us to observe in a very graphic way how scholarly opinion wavered in the political current of the time and eventually came down on the antiparliamentary side: After 1925 more and more constitutional theorists argued that a judge was permitted to suspend parliamentary law.[20]

A third example would be the deliberate widening of the Reich President's dictatorial powers on the basis of Article 48 of the Weimar Constitution. The methodological tools of supra-positive justifications of a "national emergency" that were created in the process were undoubtedly useful in the transition to the National Socialist system. And when it was said in the *Reichsgesetzblatt* of 1934 that the Röhm murders had been legal as a form of "national self-defense," constitutional theory had neither the will nor the actual ability to lodge a collective protest.[21]

More important than these examples, however, are the reasons that led German constitutional theorists to abandon the republic so easily, to consider the *Rechtsstaat* something that could be so readily dispensed with, and to elevate the executive in such a metaphysical way. In part they are identical with the known reasons for the failure of the republic as such; after all, constitutional theory is not a separate province of intellectual life. But there are a few specific characteristics of German state thinking that imparted an added impulse to the general trend.

In Germany, thinking about the state has always been done from the perspective of administration. The great theorists (V. L. von Seckendorff, G. H. G. von Justi, R. von Mohl, L. von Stein, and R. von Gneist) devoted themselves to administration, and we look in vain for classic state thinkers like Hobbes and Locke, Montesquieu and Rousseau. As a result, in Germany the executive got a traditional head start over the other branches of government. Parliamentarianism arrived late, and it has retained certain weaknesses down to this day. The hour of need is in Germany the hour of the executive. The Bismarckian constitutional conflict (1862–1866) showed this just as clearly as did Bismarck's later toying with and threats of a "plan for a coup d'état." It is also revealed by the way in which Article 48 of the Weimar Constitution was handled. In crises, parliamentary formulation of political objectives and judicial control are seen as inconvenient obstacles.

I consider this intellectual tradition—fundamentally different from that in England, for instance—a crucial factor in assessing German domestic politics in the twentieth century. A second essential characteristic of German state thinking is, in my view, its strong metaphysical foundation. The differences with Western rationalism, utilitarianism, and pragmatism reach far back into history. In Germany we find a decidedly Christian understanding of officeholding and service, a relationship to authority shaped by ethics. In the philosophy of German idealism this idea was retained in a secular form, and in the philosophical discussion of the 1920s we encounter the same problem: on one side, tendencies toward a relativism of values, liberalism, and parliamentary democracy, especially in Hans Kelsen; on the other side, idealistic philosophy (with its variants guided by Fichte, Schelling, and Hegel) with its belief in "eternal truths" and in the state as a "moral idea." From this point of view the state is not an emergency shelter created by human beings, not a rational contract, but a supra-human being in service to which the individual finds fulfillment.

Kelsen felt very clearly how the two sides were weighted. In 1932 he noted with resignation that

> today it goes without saying . . . in the circles of constitutional theorists and sociologists to speak of democracy only with words of contempt. It is considered modern to hail dictatorship—directly or indirectly— as the dawn of a new era. And this change in "scientific" attitude goes hand in hand with a switch in philosophical positions: away from the clarity of empirical-critical rationalism, the spiritual home of democracy, now decried as shallowness, and back to the darkness of metaphysics, which is taken for profundity, to the cult of nebulous irrationalism, this very atmosphere in which since time immemorial the various forms of autocracy have flourished best. That is the slogan of today.[22]

IV. Autocracy was indeed at the door. The suspension of the most important basic rights,[23] a large wave of arrests and emigration, the Enabling Act,[24] and the breakup of the parties and unions: in the space of only a few weeks, from January to May 1933, all this swept over a Germany that was dazed in part by jubilation and in part by fear.

Soon it became clear that for the second time in the twentieth century German constitutional law had been deprived of its foundation in positive law. The wide-ranging discussion about the continuing validity of the Weimar Constitution after 1933[25] revolved around a pseudo-problem and concealed the true positional struggles. In actuality, now that there was no doubt that parliamentary democracy and the "so-called civil constitutional state" *(bürgerlicher Rechtsstaat)*, to use the words of Carl Schmitt, no longer existed, political life found itself at square one. For instance, in 1933 Ulrich Scheuner said that "numerous concepts and principles of the earlier period, the right of parliaments and the parties, the principle of separation of powers, the idea of basic rights, and so forth, have been stripped of their meaning by the new organization."[26] Not only that, it was unclear, and became ever more so, whether it would even be possible to arrive at a consolidated state of political life that would be amenable to legal treatment. Constitutional theorists became increasingly aware that general constitutional theory and constitutional law now dealt only with fragments of their former subject matter and for the rest were confronted with an amorphous exercise of power devoid of rules. As basic constitutional norms turned into something arbitrary, there seemed to be less point in dealing with them in a scientific manner. The National Socialist camp had derisive comments about this development: "Just as the old state will not return, the old constitutional theory will cease to have any meaning. It is equally useless, however, to write learned treatises about the nature of the new state—here, too, the pens are scribbling in vain. Today only one person knows what the new structure of the state will look like after ten years, the Führer, and he won't allow himself to be influenced in this knowledge by any writers, no matter how learned."[27]

Thus, the majority of constitutional theorists were confronted in the spring of 1933 with the question of how to respond to these developments.[28] Only a few, among them Otto Koellreutter, had already declared themselves in favor of National Socialism. Now the others had to put their cards on the table. Emigration was unavoidable for democrats or Social Democrats like Kelsen and Heller, especially since both were of Jewish descent. Heller died in Madrid shortly after leaving Germany. Kelsen, vilified in Prague in 1936 by nationalistic students of his own student Fritz Sander, escaped to Geneva. Erich Kaufmann withdrew to Berlin and did not emigrate until 1938; Gerhard Leibholz and Hans Nawiasky left the same year. A politically upright young scholar like Ernst Friesenhahn broke with his teacher Carl Schmitt, resisted later blandishments, and existed in a quiet corner, so to speak, with a lectureship and a law practice. Representatives of the older generation, such as Gerhard Anschütz, Conrad Bornhak, Rudolf von Laun, Richard Schmidt, Paul Schoen, Rudolf Smend, Richard Thoma, and Heinrich Triepel, opted for retirement (if they were not already retired). Some kept to themselves indignantly, others resignedly: They published little or turned to harmless topics, often historical topics or ones dealing with international law.

Schmitt and Koellreutter were the most prominent among the renowned scholars who professed themselves followers of National Socialism. At first the new rulers noted Schmitt's National Socialist conversion[29] with considerable gratitude: after all, he was a "leading figure," a sharp critic of parliamentarianism, an advocate of the dictatorship of the Reich President, of the sovereign "order-creating decision," and of the existential distinction between friend and foe. Hermann Göring rewarded him with the title of a Prussian councilor of state *(Staatsrat)*. There followed membership in the Academy for German Law, appointment as director of the University Teachers' Group of the League of National Socialist German Jurists, and the job of editor of the leading law journal, the *Deutsche Juristen-Zeitung*. Schmitt in turn expressed his thanks with the infamous article "Der Führer schützt das Recht" (The Führer protects the law),[30] which gave constitutional absolution to the Röhm murders. Later, when he was in trouble, he also engaged in anti-Semitic propaganda, which will forever cast a dark shadow on his name.[31]

Koellreutter, clearly inferior to Carl Schmitt in intellectual agility and eloquence, had been a supporter of National Socialism from the elections in September 1930. He was among those German Nationals who were now looking forward to the establishment of the "national constitutional state." It was with this in mind that he wrote, as early as 1933, the first National Socialist constitutional theory, an outline of National Socialist constitutional law in 1935, and a textbook of administrative law in 1936.[32]

However, the true core of the new National Socialist theory of constitutional and administrative law was formed by the group of professors who in 1933 almost simultaneously moved into professorial positions that had become vacant and who were initially clear supporters of the new system. It included Ernst Rudolf Huber[33] and Ernst Forsthoff,[34] Gustav Adolf Walz,[35] Herbert Krüger,[36] Theodor Maunz,[37] and at the fringes—even if always cautiously tempered—Ulrich Scheuner.[38] Paul Ritterbusch[39] and Reinhard Höhn[40] soon made a name for themselves as decidedly radical National Socialists. Höhn had come from the Order of Young Germans and now switched over to the SS. There were hardly any authors who came directly from work in the party and could have made themselves heard. At most one could mention Helmut Nicolai,[41] author of *Rassengesetzliche Rechtslehre* (Legal theory of racial laws) and a booklet entitled *Der Staat im nationalsozialistischen Weltbild* (The state in National Socialist ideology [1933]).

These individuals, united only by their clear commitment to National Socialism, represented a great variety of approaches. Some were working up suggestions by Schmitt on the basis of right-wing Hegelianism; others came from Smend's theory of integration; still others combined a rather simplistic legal positivism with the prevailing propaganda slogans of "national community" and "leadership," "authority downward, responsibility upward," "common good before individual good," and so on. The unanimous opinion was that the National Socialist state was in no way comparable to the liberal state; rather, it was, as people now said, the living form of the nation, in the last analysis only an instrument to preserve the nation (Hitler, Rosenberg).

Considering the diversity of the constitutional theorists in Germany in terms of their intellectual profile, their goals, their identification with National Socialism, and—not least—their very different proximity to power, it is not surprising that we cannot find an internally coherent "National Socialist theory of the state." Given that the structure of National Socialist constitutional law (if one even wants to speak of such a thing) was fluid, its intellectual superstructure was correspondingly unstable.

Constructing something like a "system" out of the countless statements on the theory of the state is therefore a rather pointless exercise. The quest for a system seems to me a wrong approach to begin with, since no system existed and none was supposed to. Where decision-making power is concentrated in a mystically transfigured person, any kind of system would merely have the effect of creating obligations and commitments, which is precisely what the rulers do not want. At the level of constitutional law, to overstate it somewhat, political life was dominated by the struggle for power and the authoritative decision that was revocable at will. At the same time, however—and this is what makes such a state schizophrenic—adherence to the rules could certainly be demanded and implemented at the level of day-to-day administrative decisions, violations of the law could be reprimanded, and even a certain measure of legal protection could be preserved. This explains why certain spheres of administrative law—for instance, the nonpolitical parts of tax law, the law of eminent domain, commercial law, and so on—were able to maintain legal procedures virtually untouched from beginning to end of the Nazi regime.[42]

We thus find in the legal journals of the Nazi era a colorful mix of irrational fantasies,[43] self-debasing declarations of submission, and traditional dogmatic jurisprudence with a ready (positivist) acceptance of the new legal order. This mix reflects the actual situation, the intersecting currents that were shaped above all by a progressive loss of power on the part of those groups that were interested in a traditionally "functioning" executive and were intent on preserving minimal standards of a constitutional state. The well-known antagonism within the regime—"Gau chiefs[44] vs. traditional administration," "Gestapo vs. criminal justice in general," "the wishes of the party vs. administrative law"—reappear here, this time in the garb of legal debates.

In this convoluted process constitutional theory responded to the various phases in the development of the regime.[45] In 1933–1934 it supported the coalition of German Nationals and National Socialists, it accompanied the consolidation and expansion of the Führer-state until 1938, and thereafter it fell into a telling silence. Except for Huber's *Verfassungsrecht des Großdeutschen Reiches* (Constitutional law of the Greater German Reich [1939]), nothing of importance was written after that time. The retreat into the harmless fields of international law, legal history, administrative theory, and general political science began. There was neither a debate about basic questions of constitutional law nor fundamental methodological reflection. Another "general theory of the state" did not appear: Writing it probably seemed either too risky or simply pointless.

The balance sheet at the end is depressing. A theory of constitutional and administrative law that would have deserved the name of a scholarly field no longer existed. Its death throes had begun with the silent acceptance of the legal justification of the Röhm murders. Incidentally, the Association of Constitutional Lawyers ceased its activity at the same time. The National Socialist state had no need for a theory of constitutional and administrative law. Hitler didn't think much of professors. Most jurists were late in accepting the bitter realization that they were dispensable, and some never did.

We look in vain, however, for the members of the Association of Constitutional Lawyers in the circles of active resistance. Officers, clergy, students, and workers were represented, but as far as we know not a single professor of constitutional and administrative law. Perhaps this is merely a coincidence. Perhaps it does say something about a stratum of scholars who were closer to power than others, and who were especially familiar with how to relativize the criteria for 'good' and 'evil'.

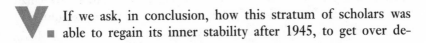 If we ask, in conclusion, how this stratum of scholars was able to regain its inner stability after 1945, to get over de-

Nazification, to reoccupy chairs, to write democratic textbooks and commentaries, and to preach to young jurists the paean on the constitutional state,[46] we get into difficult psychological and historical issues and circumstances.

Before one deplores these developments with moral outrage, one should investigate the political causes and determine in each case where there is continuity in terms of personnel and ideas. Here I can only sketch a few lines:

1. The Association of Constitutional Lawyers, which had ceased its activity in 1933, was reestablished on October 21, 1949. Its honorary President and President by seniority, Richard Thoma, was probably a bit too hymnal when he said that the association could "now reemerge . . . with its head held high."[47]

The makeup of the association (eighty-two members) had changed in an interesting way. Forty members had died since 1933. Some who were clearly compromised by their Nazi past had left (Schmitt, Koellreutter, Huber, Höhn). Kelsen had remained in the United States, other emigrants had returned (Erich Kaufmann, Gerhard Leibholz, Wilhelm Hoegner, Hans Nawiasky), and some important democrats had newly joined (Wolfgang Abendroth, Hermann L. Brill, Carlo Schmid). With a total membership of eighty-five professors (today nearly four hundred), this was on the whole quite a substantial change.

2. Of course, the professors of constitutional and administrative law, like all other Germans in the western occupation zones, became caught up in the equally well-intentioned and ineffective machinery of "de-Nazification"—a process that strengthened the feeling of togetherness and the unwillingness to expose black sheep in one's own ranks. In the end, the solidarity of the professional elite, a solidarity that has also been observed in other homogeneous groups, transcended any political differences.

3. Another characteristic feature of the years after 1945 was that the psychological disposition to let the past be past was particularly strong. Those who concentrated on the task of reconstruction, on the day-to-day questions concerning the constitutions of the federal states, and on the creation of the Basic Law could not at the same time confront and come to terms with the past. By turning to the new one could combine the useful with the pleasant. In short, those "former ones" who gave signs that they were willing to cooperate under democratic conditions were accepted. Hence there was neither a revolutionary upheaval through an across-the-board dismissal of all those who had taught between 1933 and 1945 (this would have been a gross injustice) nor a detailed stocktaking. For about twenty years the difficult ques-

tions were passed over in the belief that everything would work itself out in due course.

But that hope was illusory. The repressed past came back. The Federal Constitutional Court caused the first shock by declaring that all National Socialist civil service positions had terminated on May 8, 1945.[48] The protests of the professors of constitutional law were to no avail. The second shock began in 1965 when it turned out that the ghosts of the past were not dead, they had merely been silenced. Cases of ex-Nazis in important positions were uncovered in rapid succession: Th. Maunz, M. Oberländer, H. Globke, K. G. Kiesinger, H. Filbinger, and more. They did serious damage to the political culture of the Federal Republic by shaking the trust especially of the younger generation and by lending weight to the suspicion that formerly active National Socialists could rise to eminent positions in the Federal Republic, while those on the left of the political spectrum were mercilessly punished both socially and professionally.

More than sixty years separate us from the beginnings of the National Socialist state. From a longer historical perspective, that is not much. The past is alive and we run into it every day, if only we look and listen attentively. As professors in Germany, we should *accept it and come to terms with it as our own past*. I mean this "coming to terms" also in a psychoanalytical sense: If we ever want to attain a political culture and constitutional theory that are practiced as something self-evident and are tranquil internally, we cannot do it by looking away and suppressing the past, or by making sweeping accusations. We can achieve it only by analyzing, patiently and precisely, the reasons behind the events of the past.

SIX

The Science of
Administrative Law under
National Socialism

The "Revolution" of 1933

The science of administrative law was still reeling from the encroachments on administrative law by the Brüning and Papen
governments[1] when it was forced to come to terms with the consequences of the collapse of the Weimar state and the *Machtergreifung*
(seizure of power) by the National Socialists.[2] The representatives of
public law—that is, those who did not emigrate[3] and who did not give
up teaching or were not forced to give it up[4]—grappled with the new
situation in very different ways.

On the surface we find the often described mood of 1933, which
vacillated between enthusiasm and anxious skepticism. Many elated
outlines of the "new foundation of administrative law" were published.[5] This was stocktaking of the first hour, an attempt to get even
with "liberalism, positivism, normativism," with the liberal *Rechtsstaat*
and the binding force of the law, with basic rights and subjective-public
rights. At the same time it was also an embrace of Führerdom and
loyalty, of "political" and "dynamic" administration, of community
and national community as the bedrock and final goal of all individual
rights and all administrative activity.[6] Much was still up in the air
during this first phase, which lasted from January 1933 to about the
summer of 1934. Still dominant was the hope that the regime, after
overcoming the revolutionary phase of transition, would set up a "national *Rechtsstaat*."[7] When Hans Frank began a much cited speech by
saying, "The state of Adolf Hitler is a *Rechtsstaat*,"[8] he triggered a
lively debate about the concept of the *Rechtsstaat*.[9] In this debate,
some—such as H. Frick, Helmut Nicolai, Koellreutter, and Frank—
sought to preserve certain elements of the *Rechtsstaat*, while others—
such as Reinhard Höhn, Roland Freisler, and Wilhelm Stuckart—de-
tected in this attempt bureaucratic thinking and remnants of liberalism.

To that extent the debate over the *Rechtsstaat* was symptomatic of the coming clashes.

At this point it was still not clear exactly where the battle lines were forming. There were authors who, after a quick embrace of the "new Reich," retreated again. Others jettisoned their prior credo of administrative law, fearful that developments might "pass them by."[10] Still others, motivated by idealistic enthusiasm for the façade of values erected by the National Socialists, made honest attempts to somehow reconcile the new guidelines with the traditional doctrines in administrative law. Frequently this led them to adopt National Socialist terminology on a superficial level, either as a form of camouflage or from the conviction that it would be enough to align liberal administrative law more strongly with "communal thinking," to emphasize "common good over self-interest," and to dismantle "liberal excesses."[11]

Ardent National Socialists, however, opposed these positions strenuously, branding them "liberal remnants" and rejecting compromises with the old thinking. In language filled with warlike images, they called for the expulsion and destruction of the "tenacious mass of tradition."[12] Traditionalists, meanwhile, argued that their position was by no means "individualistic" or "liberal" but precisely the one best suited to the new state.

Since it no longer seemed possible to profess open support for the principles of strict subordination to the law, the validity of basic rights, and the legal protection of the individual, authors worked with concealed arguments. "Legal security,"[13] the preservation of the laws "as the plan shaped by the Führer,"[14] and the preservation of administrative jurisdiction as a control inherent in the system should be guaranteed not for the sake of the individual but for the sake of the national community.[15] One should not overturn the concepts of the state and the corporate body,[16] merely revalue and redirect them while carefully preserving what was objectively necessary. The clashes between party and state,[17] between the prerogative state and the normative state,[18] between authoritarian and totalitarian currents[19] were here played out in the terminology of administrative law. As in other areas, they remained unresolved right up to the end of the regime. However, the front lines shifted in tandem with the developmental phases of the entire regime. The first phase of broad and often enthusiastic support (1933–1934) was followed by years of internal and external consolidation (1935–1938). In the doctrine of administrative law this caused some of the enthusiasts of the first hour to fall silent, but it also led to the emergence of a group of "leading National Socialist theorists of administrative law," and especially to the first handbooks that tried to digest the new legal situation.[20] After 1938 more moderate authors were heard once again more loudly alongside the voices directly beholden to the Nazis. The pressures of war brought a certain loosening, as a result of which themes that had already been declared "finished" in the euphoria of the first years reappeared in the discussion about administrative law.

Journals

Journals on public law continued to be a significant factor in shaping the scholarly discourse. As visible bastions of influence on the field, they immediately fell under the control of publishers regarded as reliable by the Nazi party.

1. In *Archiv des öffentlichen Rechts,* the founders Felix Stoerck and Paul Laband were no longer mentioned after 1934. Heinrich Triepel, Rudolf Smend, and Johannes Heckel left in 1935, Albrecht Mendelssohn-Bartholdy in 1934. Koellreutter, who had been co-publisher after 1921 and now, as a National Socialist, assumed a key post, was joined by Hans Gerber, Franz Albrecht Medicus, and Helmut Nicolai. Only a year later, after becoming involved in a conflict with the party as President of the administrative district of Magdeburg, Nicolai left.[21]

2. Parallel developments took place at the *Preußisches Verwaltungsblatt / Reichsverwaltungsblatt* (1879–1943) and the *Verwaltungsarchiv.* Heinrich Lindenau, Gerhard Lassar, and Hans Peters left as early as the end of April 1933; Georg Kaisenberg followed in October. The new editors, Adolf Mirow, Heinrich Lammers, Koellreutter, Hans Pfundtner, Medicus, and Nicolai, guaranteed close adherence to the party line. Here, too, Nicolai made only a guest appearance, remaining until February 1935.[22] In the *Verwaltungsarchiv,* Erich Kaufmann was pushed out, along with Lassar, Peters, and Lindenau. Their place was taken by the same editors who now ran the *Reichsverwaltungsblatt.*

3. The *Bayerische Verwaltungsblätter,* under the new name *Deutsche Verwaltungsblätter* (1934–1937), retained Ottmar Kollmann, who had been acting editor since 1925.[23] However, orthodox National Socialists, such as Walther Sommer, appeared in its circle of "contributors."[24]

4. *Deutsche Verwaltung,* a continuation (from 1923) of the *Mitteilungen des Reichsverbandes der akademischen Finanz- und Zollbeamten,* was for all intents and purposes a new National Socialist journal for Nazi propaganda in administrative law. It was the mouthpiece of the group "guardians of administrative law" (Verwaltungsrechtswahrer, the terminology used after 1939) in the National Socialist Lawyers'

Association. As Nicolai explained its purpose in the foreword: "It is meant for leisure hours, for deeper reflection . . . for politics, for world view . . . Administrative jurisprudence proper shall be left to the existing journals."

However, as in other areas of the law, a process of consolidation began. In 1938 *Deutsche Verwaltung* was expanded into the central organ of administrative law. It took over *Reich und Länder* as well as *Deutsche Verwaltungsblätter* (the old Bavarian *Blätter für administrative Praxis*), and after 1939 the *Württembergische Zeitschrift für Verwaltung und Verwaltungsrechtspflege* (in existence since 1908). From 1935 onward Staatssekretär Wilhelm Stuckart was the editor.[25] He had replaced Nicolai, Frank's close collaborator.

5. Next to these central organs, the journals for state administrative law lost in importance. Those not absorbed into the journals *Deutsche Verwaltung* (Bavaria, Württemberg) or *Reichsverwaltungsblatt* (Prussia) were little more than official information bulletins (*Sächsisches Verwaltungsblatt* [1921–1943], *Zeitschrift für badische Verwaltung und Verwaltungsrechtspflege* [1869–1940]).

6. We should also mention, as new National Socialist journals in the narrower sense, *Zeitschrift der Akademie für Deutsches Recht* and its *Jahrbuch*, as well as the journal *Reich-Volksordnung-Lebensraum*. While the *Zeitschrift der Akademie* functioned as a connecting link between traditional scholarship and a National Socialism of the Frank type and carried few topics on administrative law, *Reich-Volksordnung-Lebensraum* was started up as a forum for geopolitics and administrative law with an unequivocal National Socialist staff and approach. It was here, among other places, that the planned "governmental reorganization of the East" was prepared in the media.[26]

The Debate over Administrative Law: An Outline

The generally accepted starting point for all reflections on administrative law after 1933 was the presumption that there existed a deep inner chasm between the liberal past and the authoritarian present. A "revaluation of all values" seemed to be under way. The national community was to take the place of the totality of state citizens, "community" was to replace the concept of the state, and the place of the individual was to be determined primarily by duties, not by rights.[27]

Writers accordingly attempted to formulate the purpose of administration no longer in negative terms—as governmental activity other than legislation and the administration of justice—but as an activity ultimately oriented toward fulfilling the communal purposes of the "totality of the nation."[28] Utility for the "whole" became the dominant purpose and the new center of gravity for thinking about administrative law: the preservation of legal boundaries and the protection of basic rights and of subjective-public rights, as well as the supervision of administration by independent judges, were no longer ends in themselves but means. At best, they could be defended by showing that the goals of the national community would be more readily attained by preserving them than by not preserving them. For many, the use of an idealistic vocabulary *(community, wholeness, organism, essence, living forces of volkdom, concrete order)* concealed the totalitarian character of the new concepts of law. Because everything was destined to serve as the means to the "common good," which was actualized by the will of the leaders, administrative law and the science of administrative law lost their autonomous character. "Not only constitutional law, but administrative law, too, must vanish, because the state and the age from which administration has until now drawn its norms have vanished."[29] Or more directly still: "A healthy administration has nothing at all to do with paragraphs."[30] If administration became the "creative act of the leadership," then administrative law would tend to become merely a collection of inconvenient formalities that one used either because one had not yet "overcome" the remnants of bourgeois thinking, or because modern mass administration apparently could not get by without such formalities.[31]

This already hints at the dilemma in the discussion over the ways in which administration was bound by the law. Those authors who insisted on the continuing validity of the postulate that administration was bound by the law had to admit that the political and constitutional-legal situation of the nineteenth century, which had brought forth this idea, no longer existed. The dualism of bourgeois society and a monarchically directed executive had dissolved. The ideology of the "national community" tolerated no dualisms, no distrust of state authority, and no insistence that acts of intervention have a basis in law. At the same time, however, most authors tried to partially preserve this principle, though not by using the classic justification of the rights of the citizen, which can only be infringed upon "legally," but by invoking the supposed will of the leadership and the benefits the national community would derive from an administration operating in accordance with rules.[32] "Administration, as bureaucratic administration, is bound to laws and general rules. Only in this state can it show the advantages that make it indispensable in a modern mass state: precision of implementation, predictability, and steadiness in accomplishing the tasks entrusted to it."[33] This position was weak, however, and could be under-cut at any time by an alteration of the political premises.

The question was further complicated by the fact that the regime demanded a twofold approach when it came to the binding force of the law. As a matter of principle, administrative law from the period before 1933 was to be examined for its compatibility with a National Socialist ideology that was wisely left undefined. The new leaders rec-ommended that these older norms be ignored or reinterpreted, and they rewarded such moves as "creative" acts. At the same time, newly established National Socialist administrative law was enforced by in-sisting that the law was strictly binding. Both approaches were pursued side by side, though in the early years the antipositivist circumvention of the older law was far more important.[34] Administrative law played a pioneering role in this process: It encouraged the executive and the judiciary, to the extent that they were still hesitating, to "loosen the binding force of the law,"[35] and it demonstrated through individual examples, in particular the general clauses,[36] how practical results could be achieved by invoking the supra-positive will of the Führer, National Socialist ideology, or the benefit to the national community.

The conflict over the survival of subjective-public rights developed along much the same lines.[37] As the cornerstone of liberal administra-tive law, subjective-public rights drew a lot of interest, and Theodor Maunz was soon able to assert that the "scholarly attack launched against subjective-public right concentrically from all sides" had been successful.[38] The place of subjective-public rights was now taken by the "subordination of the person within the community"—that is, in-dividual will and interest were formed into the will and interest of the totality, the *status negativus* was dissolved. What remained was the attachment of the individual to "concrete communities" and the "whole." The individual had obligations as a citizen of the Reich, as a person who owed military and labor service, as a civil servant, a property owner, a factory manager, a follower *(Gefolgschaftsmitglied)*, or a lawyer *(Rechtswahrer)*, while rights against the state were theoreti-cally abolished, though this did not mean that they disappeared.

It was only logical that the discussion about the continuation of administrative jurisdiction began soon after the debate over adminis-trative law. The task of administrative jurisdiction was now to "secure the legal position of the national comrade,"[39] not for the sake of the comrade, but for the sake of the totality. And it went without saying that "the administration of administrative law can never block or im-pede the decisions of the Führer."[40] The autonomous space left to the individual had become—concurrent with the collapse of the idea of legal protection—a concession by the community that could be further restricted at any time. It was only inside this argumentative framework that the advocates of administrative jurisdiction could champion its preservation.[41] Here, especially, we find much tactical lip service to the system combined with a skillful defense of administrative jurisdiction, which on the whole was able to preserve a more liberal line than other jurisdictions.[42]

A second, more intensive, phase of this discussion took shape during the war, when administrative jurisdiction came under strong pressure in the wake of the regime's general measures for more simplification and savings.[43] The fact that the regime eventually established the Reich Administrative Court, which had already been provided for in the Weimar Constitution,[44] and that a man contemptuous of administrative law was allowed to function as its President for a brief period[45] is one of the contradictions that shaped the National Socialist system.

To summarize our observations to this point: Individual rights were replaced by collective duties, the binding force of the law and the protection provided by subjective-public right were destroyed, equality before the law came to an end, and a formal, predictable legal order was abrogated by a "prerogative state" that was sinking ever more deeply into chaos and thinking only along utilitarian lines. The balance sheet for the science of administrative law during these years thus appears wholly negative, for it contributed in essential ways to these developments. Those university professors, administrative officials, and judges who published and were permitted to publish—we are hardly in a position to judge the others—relativized and devalued the guiding principles of administrative law as they had developed from Otto Mayer to Walter Jellinek. The polemics against liberalism, individualism, and positivism paved the way for the subordination of administrative law to political purposes and the decisions of the political leaders.

Our perspective shifts, however, if we move beyond the framework of liberalism vs. collectivism[46] and ask another question: whether the tools offered by the theory of administrative law after 1933 were better suited than the liberal administrative law of the 1920s for grasping certain phenomena typical of the modern interventionist and mass administrative state. We have already noted that the textbook theory of administrative law and administrative reality at the end of the Weimar Republic had fallen into a certain state of dissonance. The administrative law of public welfare was being neglected, expanding administrative fields (public commercial law, social law) were barely taken note of, and the dichotomy of state and society on which the theory rested was no longer in accord with the reality of the active interventionist state that intermingled state and society.

In this situation, the politically motivated, radical break with liberal administrative law after 1933 also had an innovative effect.[47] It accelerated the transformation of administrative law that was already in the air. After the legal barriers had been lowered, administrative reality and political purposes flowed in unimpeded. It became clear that the notion of sovereign "intervention" was no longer sufficient to grasp the main task of administration: "A broad segment of administration serves no other purpose, first of all, than to secure the prerequisites of life for the German people in a very elementary sense."[48] Ernst Forsthoff, following Karl Jaspers,[49] called this *Daseinsfürsorge* (1935) or *Daseinsvorsorge*[50] (both terms mean "providing for and securing existence"), and here he touched on a central issue. In this way the social importance of the administrative law of public welfare and the need for "participation" by the individual entered into the theory of administrative law.[51] Once the constitutional question had been entrusted to the decision of the Führer and was no longer subject to scholarly discussion,[52] the interest of many theorists of public law shifted to administrative law and administrative theory. Perhaps this, as well as the attempt to keep the party "out of normal administration,"[53] contributed to a sharper accentuation of *Daseinsvorsorge*.

The break with liberal administrative law in scholarship and the Nazi state's claim to unlimited authority also moved administrative planning to the fore.[54] Job creation and rearmament, access to raw materials, and the fundamentals of food supply *(Reichsnährstand)*, as well as the management of supplies and production in wartime, made the plan into the most important instrument of the Nazi leadership: "The Führer plans, the administrative apparatus implements the plan."[55] Concerns about a "planned economy" on the Soviet model that are so common in the literature of the period were intended, on one level, to ward off tendencies of a "German socialism" in that direction.[56] At the same time they also reflected reality: The type of planning preferred in the National Socialist state was a form of guidance and control,[57] but it did not infringe upon private property. To that extent it was relatively easy for postwar thinking about administrative law to quietly integrate the preliminary work that had been done under National Socialism on the legal concept of the "plan."[58]

In the stage that the discussion over administrative law had reached by the end of the Nazi system—marked, for instance, by the third edition of Arnold Köttgen's *Deutsche Verwaltung* (German administration [1944])—the question about legal form, having become unimportant, receded into the background. The legal form proved to be arbitrary and interchangeable. And since it was no longer tied to a liberal conception of the state and legal protection, it no longer served any function. Instead, administrative purposes moved to the fore: They shaped the development of the system, and it appeared they might be able to become the new starting point for an anti-individualist theory of administrative law. The classic administrative purpose of intervention to ward off danger and organize things was now joined by notions of guidance and service. Later, under entirely transformed circumstances, Peter Badura picked up the thread of this fundamental reorientation of administration: "A consistent replacement of the systems-idea of the liberal constitutional state by that of the social constitutional state would have to develop the theory of administration on the basis of administrative purposes that cannot be reduced further: warding off danger, levying taxes, providing services and guidance."[59]

Finally, the retreat of legal form and legal protection in the Nazi state also devalued the theoretical intellectual accomplishment of the liberal doctrine of administrative law. The original impulse to develop a general part of administrative law (meaning its more abstract norms) came from the idea of a uniform, predictable, and controllable exercise of executive power. Where the "well-ordered constitutional state" (in the phrase of O. Mayer) was dissolving, the general part had no function.[60] This strengthened the tendency to seek footholds in specific areas and to establish some kind of order. That is why Carl Schmitt's notion of "concrete orders" and the "concrete ordering and formative thinking" they entailed was so successful.[61] It legitimated the development of special, purpose-oriented spheres of power (army, SA, SS, enterprises, professional structures, labor service, special administrations). It supported the tendency toward the breaking of general, abstract rules—in fact, it endowed this process with a philosophical aura derived from Hegel. To be sure, it is possible to interpret this institutional "thinking in terms of order" as an attempt to counteract a totally disorderly decisionmaking process;[62] however, "will" and "formative act" remained decisive with regard to institutional and normative bonds and obligations. In the end, all outlines of orders drafted by theorists of administrative law and their attempts to oppose in writing the emerging chaos of competing fragments of administration were futile. All reflections on the relationship between administration and party, on professional ordering structures, on general and special administrations were several steps behind reality. Stable conditions could now be achieved only locally and for brief periods. The passage of time revealed that attempts at establishing a legal order were as futile in administrative law as they were in constitutional law.

IV. Textbooks of Administrative Law

Textbooks, too, reflect clearly how unstable and internally unsettled the overall situation of administrative law was. The attempts to force this fluid element into a "system" were not very promising: on the one hand, because the flood of legislation was unsystematic and guided not by ordering principles but by the prevailing rivalries and power struggles within the regime;[63] on the other, because administrative law in general had been devalued by being politicized and eliminated from professional training.[64] As the newly installed President of the Reich Administrative Court put it, "the less administrative law, the more room for the art of administration."[65]

Authors of textbooks of administrative law found very different ways to come to terms with the flood of norms and the politicization and degradation of administrative law. A few specialists in administrative law in Württemberg and Bavaria (Ludwig von Köhler, Wilhelm Hofacker, R. Nebinger, E. von Scheurl, Wilhelm Laforet, and others) merely covered the traditional stock of liberal administrative law with a verbal whitewash. They occasionally quoted *Mein Kampf* and avoided sensitive issues, such as the dualism of state and party. A good example of this approach is Ludwig von Köhler's *Grundlehren des Deutschen Verwaltungsrechts* (Principles of German administrative law [1935]).[66] He openly said that he was reluctant to change at his age and retained everything that the activists of Nazi administrative law rejected: the constitutional state in the liberal sense, subjective-public right and an independent administrative jurisdiction, the separation of powers, and the fundamental division between state and society.

Wilhelm Laforet took a similar approach in his textbook *Deutsches Verwaltungsrecht* (German administrative law [1937]).[67] He, too, retained the dichotomy of public and private law, the separation of powers (though now reduced to the organizational level), and the postulates of the *Rechtsstaat* and legal security. His rejection of subjective-public right seems superficial, as do the emphatically neutral passages on the "movement" and the "party." Both books thus outline the positions of conservative liberals who wanted a state that was strong but that acted within legal forms and who expected civil servants to adhere to the law and have a neutral "orientation toward the common good."[68]

A late example of an account that was at its core committed to traditional administrative law is Bodo Dennewitz's *Verwaltung und Verwal-*

tungsrecht (Administration and administrative law [1944]).[69] Only its title tried to accommodate the renaming, in 1935, of administrative law as administration; between the covers it was a pure textbook of administrative law. Dennewitz openly drew on Otto Mayer's work, and he maintained the separation between public and private law, the "technical organizational separation of powers," and the concept of subjective-public right. Though he adhered to the general doctrine of the binding character of National Socialist *Weltanschauung* through the interpretation of vague legal concepts and general clauses, he emphasized the technical functioning of administration over its ideological task. He himself noted a clear influence of praxis.[70]

In looking at these textbooks and outlines, however, we have only touched on the outer circle of books, which did not have much influence and cannot be considered as representative of National Socialist administrative law. The same goes for the study aids and manuals of administrative law.[71] We will not examine them here, but their influence on the broad mass of jurists should not be underestimated, because they offered the catchwords familiar to every jurist at the time in a form that was thoroughly adapted to public speech.

The inner circle of textbooks on administrative law was made up of the works of Koellreutter and Maunz, the volume edited by Frank, and the textbook by Köttgen. Koellreutter's book could have become the leading work after 1933, owing to the author's standing, but that did not happen.[72] When he wrote it, Koellreutter was without a doubt still a "follower" of the Nazis, loyal to the party line, and he tried to do justice to its claim of leadership with forceful phrases: "Administration is action *(Tat)*"[73] and "right goes before law."[74] Koellreutter's thinking was characterized by an orientation toward the politically defined communal purpose, a relativization of the boundary between public law and private law, the elevation of "common good before self-interest" to a source of law and a corrective of the legal order, and the proclaimed end of subjective-public right. The foundations of liberal administrative law visible beneath these notions were no longer sufficient to give Koellreutter's "national *Rechtsstaat*" any firm contours. They were not strong enough to resist the party's claim to unlimited authority. Only a few years later Koellreutter realized that the formula of the "national *Rechtsstaat*" was hardly more than the expression of self-deception by National Socialist jurists who had hoped to combine their political activism with the tradition of the *Rechtsstaat* they were familiar with.

Theodor Maunz's 1937 textbook *Verwaltung* (Administration) leads us into the heart of National Socialist administrative law.[75] His transformation from a positivist administrative jurist before 1933 to a champion of a "new administrative law" oriented toward "the Führer-idea, community, and national subordination" had been swift. Without being a student of Carl Schmitt, he immediately fell under the spell of "concrete order thinking" and proclaimed in numerous publications the end of subjective-public right, of the binding force of the law, and of the concept of the corporate body—in short, the end of all individualist liberal administrative law.[76] The task now was to "clear away" the "rubble" of that law. Maunz played a leading role in this process. He secured for "National Socialist thinking the scholarly starting positions of German administrative law"[77] and eventually "cast administrative law as such into doubt."[78] His textbook began by defining the new concept of administration as "the shaping of communal life by the work of agencies and special offices in accord with a plan devised by the Führer of the community in a given situation."[79] He then sketched the "bourgeois-constitutional administrative law" that needed to be overcome. Having prepared the ground, he went on to describe the organization of administration (state, party, and local government), its concrete activities (administrative acts and the administration of justice, the latter as part of administration, as well as police and administrative liability), and finally its instruments (officials, public property, eminent domain, coercion, and punishment). Within this self-contained concept, the book was really an outline, more committed to the grand perspective than to details, more interested in the new ideological orientation than in conveying information; the last point, incidentally, was also the opinion of reviewers at the time.[80]

In this sense Maunz worked also as a trendsetter for the official party anthology *Deutsches Verwaltungsrecht* (German administrative law [1937]), edited by Hans Frank, to which he contributed two introductory articles.[81] This anthology mirrored the divergent trends within the system. While one contributor, Höhn, declared administrative jurisdiction outmoded, others, such as Justus Danckwerts, defended it halfheartedly "for the time being"; while some, like Frick, advocated the unity of leadership and state power, others made a pointed distinction between leadership and administration, often doing so for a variety of reasons (to reduce the influence of the party or, as in Höhn's case, precisely to liberate leadership from bureaucratic impediments). Similar tensions can be made out in the effort to fix the place of self-government and to limit police tasks.[82] *Deutsches Verwaltungsrecht* vacillated between martial noise and internal uncertainty about how to go on, and it had a transitional character between traditional elements and a still nebulous "communal law." Its mixed panel included distinguished contributors who were more bourgeois–German National than National Socialist in their thinking, alongside SS jurists, such as Höhn and Werner Best. It was thus a particularly typical creation of those years. During a phase of consolidation by the regime, it marked a pause before the coming radicalization.

Probably the best contribution qualitatively to the textbook literature on administrative law under National Socialism was Arnold Köttgen's *Deutsche Verwaltung* (German administration [1936]).[83] He tried emphatically to "include administrative reality"[84] and at the same time to grasp administration and administrative law theoretically above the stream of continual changes to the law. This freed him of the need to engage in dogmatic discussions and give an account of the current legal situation in the various fields. Köttgen's work, particularly in its revised third edition of 1944,[85] was one of the last attempts to defend rationality and the administration's subordination to the law, to defend administrative law as an "ordering system" against the chaos of a disorderly exercise of power. It is a prime example of how defensive positions could be constructed by taking advantage of the smallest maneuvering room for argument and using unassailable National Socialist vocabulary.[86] At the same time, however, Köttgen's book shows that this was not necessarily tantamount to a return to the administrative law doctrine of the Weimar period. Köttgen had departed from that doctrine by familiarizing himself thoroughly with administrative reality and by expanding his perspective—clearly in correlation with Forsthoff—to embrace the new tasks of administration. To that extent one can say that he "made a significant contribution to overcoming administrative law positivism,"[87] while at the same time employing downright positivist arguments with regard to "an administration that was becoming totalitarian"[88] with the intent of slowing down the pace of change.

SEVEN

The "Revival of Administrative Studies" *(Verwaltungslehre)* under National Socialism

Complaints about the insignificance of administrative studies have accompanied virtually every step in the development of administrative law in Germany during the past century. In fact, Lorenz von Stein found no one to carry on his effort to arrest the disintegration of the political sciences with the help of a concept of administrative studies that was grounded in philosophy. Stein claimed to be dealing simultaneously with the totality of administration: its practical work and the legal form peculiar to it, its subordination to the constitution, and its society-shaping activity. Stein's modernism notwithstanding, this claim struck proponents of positivism as overblown and old-fashioned because of its ties to Hegel's philosophy, which had been declared "outmoded." To be sure, given Stein's standing in Vienna, his work had some influence in Austria,[1] where Karl-Theodor von Inama-Sternegg and Ludwig Gumplowicz taught administrative studies.[2] Still, Ferdinand Schmid was right when he said in 1909 that administrative studies had practically disappeared from German universities.[3]

Administrative studies saw itself supplanted by administrative law, which, from the time of Otto Mayer, was committed to the "legal method"[4] and which also began to assert itself at the universities from the 1880s on. The science of administration *(Polizeiwissenschaft)* had been given up: Its economic elements flowed into the disciplines of economics and finance, its social elements into statistics and social policy. As for the training of jurists, all that was left of administration was the "purely legal element." This was not an expression of, say, the intellectual obtuseness of the positivism of administrative law, as was occasionally argued later on; rather, it corresponded to the constitutional situation. The contents and purposes of administrative activity did not seem to pose much of a problem. What was of political and pedagogical interest was the legal form and the legal protection of the individual it provided. Administrative praxis and routine were learned in administration itself. Various attempts at reviving administrative studies[5] could not change the fact that it had "gone missing"[6] from university studies and scholarly literature before World War I. Attempts to find a place for administrative studies outside law faculties or to create research establishments for it outside the universities came to nothing.[7] Walter Jellinek saw administrative studies "at a dead end";[8] Walter Norden considered it a "violet blooming in secret."[9]

As negative as this picture of administrative studies might have appeared to contemporaries, it is important to understand what their gloomy assessments were referring to. In the first place they were talking about "administrative studies" in the curriculum of legal education, about the creation of suitable teaching materials, and corresponding material support for research. If one focused on these points, there were indeed few successes. But this was not the entire picture. Administrative studies had run into considerable turbulence after World War I. It was imperative to take note of the changes that had occurred. Empirical questions thrust themselves to the fore. Administration was rife with political tensions, something traditional civil servants sensed with indignation and irritation. Questions of administrative reform had to be resolved. Industrialization was proceeding apace, and with it the social issues and the problems of maintaining local government become more acute. Political crises, inflation, and unemployment jolted the republic.

It is true that the science of administrative law neither reacted to these challenges in its textbooks nor responded by creating a field of administrative studies. However, it did address the political and empirical problems in numerous monographs.[10] And it was much less traditionalist than the textbooks would suggest when it came to judges working outside the courts and engaging in teaching.

In the spring of 1933, shortly after the National Socialists had seized power, Norden published a short work with the title *Was bedeutet und wozu studiert man Verwaltungswissenschaft?* (What is administrative studies and what is the purpose of studying it?).[11] It was the culmination of efforts to "revive" administrative studies during the Weimar period and made a few half-hearted attempts to recommend the subject warmly to the new rulers. Norden tried to work out the independent task of an administrative theory of political science and to demarcate it from the former subdisciplines of *Polizeiwissenschaft* (economics, finance, statistics, social policy, political science). His goal was to find a place for it outside the law schools and within the general field of political science as an autonomous and "systematic empirical science"

(Seins-Wissenschaft) of administration. However, this work was neither a textbook nor an electrifying platform. It was the voice of an academic outsider and was drowned out by the tumult of the "national revolution." Before the year 1933 was over, Norden felt compelled to emigrate to Switzerland.

"The revival of healthy administrative studies is consistent with the political ideas of the new state."[12] This was the leitmotif of the first efforts after 1933 to pursue the implications of the so-called national revolution in the sphere of administrative law. Impulses from a variety of directions were behind the many calls in legal journals to make a fresh start, to "overcome" positivism, to restore the unity of theory and practice, and to recognize that the dogma of an apolitical administration was a form of ideology. To begin with, discomfort with the purely legal methodology of administrative law had been building up for quite some time, as early as the decade before World War I. There were repeated warnings that the historical foundations had to be taken into consideration, that thinking should reflect the administration's dependency on politics and the constitution, and that administrative reality should not be forgotten when formulating theoretical foundations. This unease grew stronger during the years of the Weimar Republic, because the gap between the basic theoretical principles imparted by administrative studies and administrative reality had widened. The war economy had created a host of public enterprises, and the state and the economy continued to cooperate after the war; a public commercial law was created. The services provided by the state continued to expand. A wave of incorporations beginning in 1920 created larger communal entities. Social legislation broadened during the first years of the republic (welfare, youth welfare, protection of children and young people, miners' insurance, unemployment insurance). The new discipline of labor law developed without regard for the conventional boundaries between civil law and public law. Ernst Forsthoff was right when he noted that the state, "by reorganizing the large banks; regulating the labor market, imports, and exports; acquiring foreign currency; providing countless subsidies; and taking individual measures and supportive actions, has entered as a participant directly into production and the turnover of goods. As a result, plant closings and a rise or decline in jobs can no longer be considered only a private piece of good luck or misfortune."[13]

In view of all this, it comes as no surprise that in 1933 many were hoping to resolve at a single stroke the problems in the training of jurists that had been created by these upheavals. The retrenchment of studies in positivist administrative law seemed to create room for the long overdue admission of administrative reality into the classroom.

A second—and, in the final analysis, politically stronger—motive was the hope that this would make it possible to bring administrative science more quickly and effectively into line with National Socialism. Many believed that opposing "liberal" ("bloodless," "ossified," "dead," "reactionary") administrative law with an administrative science as the theory of an active, creative, and political administration would furnish an instrument to oust outdated content in courses on administrative law and incorrigible dogmatists of traditional administrative law. From this perspective, administrative studies was the vehicle of National Socialist ideology within the field of administrative law.

Curriculum reform was also pursued along these lines. Its most visible result was changing the name of the fourth-semester course "Administrative Law" into "Administration."[14] The deletion of the word *law* was of considerable symbolic significance: It indicated that a liberal line committed to the legal protection of the individual had been deliberately broken. The change was to remind professors that their primary topics were not law and legal protection, but the purposes and instruments of an administration that was duty-bound to the new state.

However, it is possible that this renaming obstructed the formulation of an independent science of administration. Those professors who were not inclined to make major changes to begin with seemed to believe that the essential step had been taken by this change in name. Shielded by the new title, they could continue to present traditional administrative law. It no longer appeared necessary to offer separate courses in administrative studies alongside this course. To those professors who took the renaming seriously, and who included the new name in the titles of their textbooks,[15] curriculum reform offered an opportunity to become more open to administrative reality, to embrace the purposes of administration, and consequently to deal only secondarily with questions of legal forms and legal protection.

Given this starting position, it becomes clear why the effort to determine the relationship between administrative law and administrative studies was a political question on which those involved in the debate did not show their cards openly. Someone who clung to administrative law as the central subject matter could be an "incorrigible" in the Nazi sense, an administrative jurist of the older generation. However, he could also be a conservative loyal to the new regime, who adhered to the ideal of the "national *Rechtsstaat*" and sought to defend this state against "encroachments" and "arbitrary acts" on the part of the party. A similar motivational split existed among the proponents of an integration of administration and administrative law, who in turn could not entirely agree among themselves upon the proper path to take: an "integrated" science of administration or separate offerings of administrative law and administrative studies. The lines were further blurred by the fact that the proponents of administrative studies also had in their ranks authors who combined vagueness with all the more emphatic rhetoric. One example was the tirelessly publishing Otto Nass.[16] Finally, traditional university rivalries also came into play on the question of whether administrative studies should be considered part of a jurist's training or whether they should be affiliated with economics, political science, or perhaps even philosophy.

The many and varied statements about the "revival of administrative studies" during the first years of the regime[17] still shared some traits. They all rejected the model of the "legal method" that had held sway since Mayer. In so doing they implemented in administrative law the results of the so-called "quarrel over direction" in constitutional theory.[18] As it was, the old task of legal work, "to construct legal institutes, trace individual rules of law back to general concepts, and . . . deduce the implications arising from these concepts,"[19] had long since changed under the impact of teleological thinking. After a slight delay, the trend toward making constitutional interpretation open to political, social, philosophical, and historical considerations,[20] which had begun around 1926, took hold of administrative law as well. Calls to take "reality" or "life" into consideration were the order of the day, though at first the methodological questions of how to grasp "reality," what data to select, and, above all, how to translate them into normative principles were discussed hardly at all or in a noticeably vague fashion.

A second characteristic shared by all champions of administrative studies was the rejection of the image of an "apolitical" administration. That was the gist of Otto Koellreuter's programmatic essay "Das Wesen des 'Politischen' in der öffentlichen Verwaltung" (The nature of the 'political' in public administration).[21] It was simultaneously a declaration in favor of the Nazi state, which, as one could hear everywhere, would not allow administration to deviate from the new basic political course. Objectivity and political neutrality, the orientation of administration toward the "job" *(Sache)* and a "common good" divorced from political needs of the day, attitudes that the same authors had praised as late as 1932, were now declared to be out of date.

To be sure, approval of the new state cannot be reduced to a uniform pattern, for the intellectual and social currents of which National Socialism made political use were too varied. But it was precisely those slogans about the "national *Rechtsstaat*," about transcending the "jurist out of touch with reality" (Koellreutter), about including "life" and "reality" that allowed every person to believe that subjective ideas could be realized. Talk about the "political responsibility of work in administrative law"[22] therefore combined approval of the new state outwardly with the inner mental qualification that one really had one's own political ideas in mind. Differences of opinion reemerged as soon as the question of implementing the new political commitment of administration was posed in concrete terms. Orthodox party jurists, in an effort to promote the mobilization of the executive in keeping with National Socialist ideology, strenuously denied that there was any difference between administrative activity and the "movement." Others, while recognizing the political task of administration, sought to define lines of separation. For instance, Forsthoff emphasized the "essential difference" between bureaucratic administration and "dynamic leadership." Bureaucracy, he maintained, took care of everyday things, operated in accord with strict rules in the mass administration peculiar to it, and was supervisable from above and reliable from below. Leadership, by contrast, dealt with the political decisions that set the course. Forsthoff's express concern to protect the Nazi party from the humdrum of administrative service was in reality a defense of an administration guided by rules against the party's claims to power. The party, too, saw it that way, and its reaction to this work was accordingly negative.

The third common trait was a turn toward administrative realities, at least in the form of declared intent.[23] The underlying need was the same that had led to the break with legal positivism. The difference was that the issue here was not to broaden the maxims of interpretation but to close the gap between norm and administrative reality. This was the real starting point of an administrative science that sought to elucidate which rules administration actually followed, what laws guided the conduct of bureaucrats and their personnel, and how decisions were made and implemented "on the spot." However, material actually gathered from administrative praxis and available in readable form was sparse. Ernst von Harnack, a retired Regierungspräsident and a civil servant of the old school, offered such material "as a systematization of remembrances, experiences, and insights . . . put down in the form of memoirs by men in the administration."[24] Since his book did not affirm National Socialism politically, it met with virtually no response. In any case, to my knowledge no comprehensive empirical works on administration were written, aside from Harnack's book.

Hans Peters was therefore right when he said in 1936 that it was not possible at the time to fix the date for genuine courses in administrative studies and that a comprehensive training for administrative officials could not be accomplished at the universities.[25] There was little more than a call for administrative studies to try to "look into administrative practice"[26] as a way to develop scientific administrative studies. Such a field should integrate normative and empirical factors—though, as Arnold Köttgen warned, without letting this lead to the disintegration of administrative law into vague discussions about "concrete orders."[27] This shows that Köttgen, too, much like Forsthoff, fairly soon recognized the dangers that a dynamic and politicized concept of the law— even in the guise of the familiar demand for a revival of administrative studies—posed to legal security and the stability of the entire system.

In the meantime there was an effort to link up with other countries in administrative studies, and here the need for professional exchange went hand in hand with the regime's desire to be represented on the international stage. The International Institute for Administrative Studies, headquartered in Brussels, had organized a congress in Vienna in 1933. At that time "the German Reich declined to participate, for reasons that need no further explanation."[28] A German delegation was present at the subsequent congress in Warsaw in 1936 (it consisted of Ministerialrat Dr. Medicus, Professor Ritterbusch, Lord Mayor Dr. Weidemann, the President of the German League of Municipalities, Dr. Jeserich, and Ministerialdirektor Jäger for the National Socialist Lawyers' Association). A short time later, Undersecretary Wilhelm Stuckart announced that the German Reich would join the International Institute and that "a section would be set up in Germany . . . in the near future." As expected, Stuckart was made President of this section,[29] and he succeeded in having the next congress scheduled in Berlin for September 13–19, 1939. Various activities took place in the lead-up to this congress, among them an essay contest on the topic of "the pedagogical importance of administration," and a joint work on "contemporary foreign administrative law."[30] World War II broke out two weeks before the start of the congress.

Thereafter, international contacts were limited to states allied with the Axis powers. But contacts in the field of administrative law did not amount to much. No activities in administrative studies developed in the Academy for German Law, either under Carl Schmitt's chairmanship in the committee for administrative law or under that of his successor, Stuckart.[31] In 1942 Stuckart established an International Academy for Political and Administrative Sciences in Berlin, and Hans Frank founded an Institute for the Techniques of State in Munich before his dismissal as President of the academy and Reichsführer of the National Socialist Lawyers.[32] However, the goal of Frank's institute was not the study of "administrative technique" in the conventional sense, but the relationships between technology and the state. These international contacts and institutes produced no visible results during the war.

IV. In the meantime the debate over the state of administrative studies and its proper tasks had continued, becoming more vigorous in the lead-up to the 1939 congress. Peters felt provoked into a lengthy response by Nass's article charging that administrative studies had utterly failed.[33] He hinted that his own textbook on administrative science, long in planning, had been blocked by the National Socialist seizure of power. However, since the summer semester of 1933 he had been lecturing on administrative science, as had Kurt Jeserich and the lecturers at the academies of administration. He described his own view of the relationship among administrative law, administrative policy, and administrative studies as follows:

> Administration is the activity of the state or, in certain instances, of public associations, aimed at giving concrete shape to the purposes of the state. Independent initiative and judgment are typical of administration. Law, technology, medicine, biology, psychology, and so on, are means that administration uses to attain its goals . . . The essential task of administrative science is to describe administration in all its manifestations and components, to produce a systematic order, to clarify concepts, and to show causal connections and the reasons for their existence. Administrative law as a science of norms must clarify the rules by which administration should work, investigate their foundations, and resolve existing uncertainties through interpretation. Administrative policy as a science of values must study the suitability of individual administrative institutions, especially from the perspective of the basic ideas of the relevant political systems.[34]

In addition to these fundamental demarcations, which reappeared later in his 1949 textbook,[35] Peters outlined the chapter headings of his "Verwaltungslehre," a book that was not published in its planned form.

Gerhard Wacke's textbook on administrative studies suffered the same fate. It was scheduled to appear in 1941 in the Kohlhammer Verlag under the title "The Destiny and Task of Administrative Studies," but the relevant party office refused permission to print it. And since the manuscript was destroyed, it was not possible to publish it later, either. However, various articles indicate that what Wacke had in mind was not an integration of empirical and normative work as a simple "art of administration" that would discuss the means of administration, its instruments of leadership, its organization, and questions of personnel.[36] Wacke was too much a jurist to abandon the original guiding function of the law, and he was clearly on the side of an administration that was orderly and bound by the law. His retrospective in 1942 was sobering and contained some pointed comments. He noted that the hopes in 1933 for a revival of administrative studies had not been fulfilled: "The impulse of 1933 and a few symbolic acts as well as hopeful beginnings (for instance, the work of the Institute of Communal Science at the University of Berlin) could in no way keep pace with the headlong developments in all fields of administration."[37] By emphasizing the accomplishments in the fields before 1933, he was able to criticize the present and do justice to the past.

It is striking that the discussion about the training of administrative officials and the reform of the public law component in the legal curriculum intensified precisely during the war. One impetus came from the renewed debate about the legal curriculum in 1941 as efforts were under way to separate the training of administrative lawyers *(Rechtswahrer)* from the general training of jurists.[38] The controversies also reflected the general difficulties of an administration that was expanding rapidly and was embroiled in constant battles with the Nazi party and the SS. Given this background, the debate about training, documented chiefly in the 1942 issue of *Deutsche Verwaltung,*[39] took on different contours than it had in 1935, for example, when the new curriculum was introduced. Those who emphasized praxis over theory were now absolutely dominant. The crucial issue was who would eventually control the separate educational track for administrative officials. Grand designs and declarations of intent had given way to careful tactical maneuvering. Language, too, reflected the generally more sober atmosphere in a time of war.

Euphoric voices were heard more rarely. When W. Taeuber wrote in 1942 that "the historical moment has now come for newly establishing—in a sense, rediscovering—administrative studies," that jurisprudence had "finally entered onto the right path," that the ground was "prepared for the sowing of ideas from administrative studies," that legal positivism had been "transcended" and legal philosophy seemed "to be heading for a heyday,"[40] this merely proved how much he had lost touch with reality. The hope that administrative studies could become the main subject of the political sciences, on the basis of Nicolai Hartmann's "natural realism" and following in Stein's footsteps, was illusory. Wacke saw this much more clearly: "There is still no development of an administrative science proper—a science that has a comprehensive understanding of the overall situation of public administration also in terms of its political importance and its transformations, and could thus in turn provide the foundation for the future design of administration."[41]

V. Efforts after 1933 to bring about a "revival of administrative studies" had thus failed. This was reflected in the new curricula of legal studies in the fall of 1943,[42] which no longer contained a course with the title "Administration." Attempts to set up lasting and well-funded research institutes for administrative studies, to create a canon of basic knowledge, and to supply the necessary textbooks and study materials were equally unsuccessful.

However, in no way can one argue from these outcomes that attempts by the Nazis and the SS to politicize the administration had been successfully deflected, because some champions of administrative science did in fact wish to use it as a Trojan horse for precisely that purpose. Rather, the reasons for the lack of success are to be found both in the external circumstances and within the field itself.

Among external conditions we should include the shortness of time, the feverishness that was characteristic of all undertakings during the Third Reich, and war conditions that were generally unfavorable for intellectual and scholarly work. Furthermore, active support for administrative studies was taken as an indication of a person's stance on a central question, and the readiness to provide such an indication, which could easily be misunderstood politically, waned over time. As Bodo Dennewitz rightly put it in 1944: "Administrative law or administrative science: ever since the seizure of power, this has become once again and with increasing sharpness the central problem of the science of administration."[43] In the midst of "total war" this problem could no longer be genuinely resolved, least of all in a political environment that was dominated by an activism hostile to intellectual work and in which rational structures were increasingly disintegrating.

The reasons inherent in administrative science itself included, first of all, the uncertainty and lack of consensus about the true goal of this new field. In its most modest form it was conceived as an auxiliary science for administrative law, an empirical propaedeutics and accompanying subject that would be able to fill the gap between administrative reality and administrative law with information about the praxis of administration. In its most ambitious form, administrative science opened up the "grand vista . . . of the totality of all spheres of public life."[44] In this version, once the constitutional question had been "settled," administrative science became the central field of work of political science. While proponents of the modest form wanted to work with the simple aids of statistics and observation, advocates of the ambitious version attempted, on the basis of a "cosmological theory of culture," a "comprehensive view of what belongs together in life."[45] In this regard the two sides were not speaking the same language.

An important reason for the failure of the ambitious version was, of course, the fact that the philosophical foundations it called upon were all vague and irrational. Picking up the thread of Stein's ideas meant, if seriously pursued, either the attempt to transpose a "modernized" Hegel into administrative science, or the reverse, to repackage a Stein freed from the Hegelianism of a specific time in history. Both approaches ran into fundamental difficulties.

Very different problems arose for anyone who tried to do administrative science as administrative sociology: to collect information and arrange it into rationally verifiable hypotheses. Not only had the most important representatives of empirical social research been driven out in 1933, this entire approach did not fit into the climate of National Socialism, which was anti-Enlightenment, antirational, and thus hostile to science. The political system would have been deeply suspicious of anyone who had tried to provide a meticulous account of the growing chaos.

Despite these external and internal conditions unfavorable to the development of an administrative science, a central problem remained: how could an administration that had been expanding for decades in every area, was now guided by a dictatorship, and was purpose-oriented continue to function using the instruments of the liberal *Rechtsstaat?* Since the time of Mayer, the complexion of administration, its size and tasks, had changed tremendously—so much so that none of the building blocks of a "general part" of administrative law that had been found at the time could be used unchanged. Only on the surface had the totalitarian state displaced Mayer's liberal *Rechtsstaat.* In reality, a hybrid of state and industry, later called the "state of industrial society," had taken its place. The foundation of this new state's legitimation as it began to take shape in the 1920s was no longer democracy but the system of social security. The current of continuity that is visible here is also a mainstay of the Federal Republic, which is why it is no coincidence that a mere restoration of liberal administrative law after 1945 was not enough. Instead, the efforts noticeable in the writings of Forsthoff[46] and Köttgen[47]—to include the administration of social services, to make the element of purpose in administrative law into a systemic criterion, and to see administration as a whole as dependent on basic political and constitutional decisions—were pursued further. The proposition that administrative law is constitutional law made concrete (Fritz Werner),[48] so often cited under democratic premises, was emphatically advocated also under National Socialism: "Administration and constitution are one. Their ideological and organizational structure is identical."[49] To that extent only the contents of administrative law had changed after 1945, but not the methodological problem of administrative law and administrative science in industrial society. It therefore comes as no surprise that the difficulties inherent in creating an administrative science suited to the conditions of modern administration and translating it into the subject of study were carried over into the Federal Republic.[50]

EIGHT

Administrative
Jurisdiction under
National Socialism

Administrative jurisdiction is the touchstone of the constitutional state. History has shown that in the absence of an enforceable and independent supervisory authority, the rights of citizens and the rules of public law as a whole are constantly in danger of being violated. The underlying premise, that inviolable individual rights ought to exist and that public life should be conducted in accordance with rules of law, is a liberal belief, as is the notion that a court is best suited to act as the supervising authority. It was therefore inevitable that administrative jurisdiction, created at the height of constitutional liberalism (1863–1875),[1] would clash with the Nazi state. For as vague as that state's *Weltanschauung* may have been in other respects, the rejection of the liberal *Rechtsstaat* was one of its fundamental principles.

The question whether traditional administrative jurisdiction could be retained appeared as early as the first half of 1933 in the journals of administrative law, where new editors were at the helm.[2] The general uncertainty during the first phase of the so-called national revolution struck at the very heart of administrative jurisdiction, whose intellectual roots in the spirit of the liberal *Rechtsstaat* were evident to all. A state that rejected the separation of powers, formal guarantees, and basic rights, was suspicious of all distinctions, and abolished all supervisory mechanism could have no other goal but the elimination of administrative jurisdiction. Therefore, administrative jurisdiction had to redefine itself or perish.

This problem was not really resolved before 1945. But shifts took place, legislation made a commitment on certain points, and opponents and advocates of supervision through administrative jurisdiction staked out new positions. Behind the debate over the "future of administrative jurisdiction" stood, right up to the end of the regime, the conflicts between the "normative state" and the "prerogative state," between state and party, between party chancery and Reich Interior Ministry (allied in this fight with the Reich Justice Ministry and the Academy for German Law), between administration and administrative justice. To that extent the issue was typical of the unresolved contradictions in the entire system.

The hard-core champions of revolutionary activism, of the movement "as such," and of an explicitly antibourgeois, military principle of leadership had their sights set on the elimination of all norms and institutions that impeded "action."[3] To them, administrative jurisdiction was at best acceptable as a transition phase, but only if judges were willing to throw the dualism of state and society overboard, to see not subjective-public rights but the objective national order as worthy of protection, and to unconditionally accept as their guiding principle the public interest as defined by the leadership. Since it was an axiom that Führer and followers were united in the national community, all conflicts of interest were "abolished" in this alleged unity.

But this notion was rarely advocated in professional legal publications. For the most part one found the usual rejection of the liberalism of the past, coupled with a "however" when it came to administrative jurisdiction. The liberal origins of administrative jurisdiction, it was argued, were beyond question, but the essential thing was "the intellectual content that is poured into forms that are recognized as useful . . . The new German state, as well, with its tighter organization, wants to remain a *Rechtsstaat*."[4] Administrative jurisdiction was "by no means incompatible with the nature of the authoritarian state and the idea of the Führer."[5] It had always made the public interest real,[6] its purpose was to relieve the burden on the central authorities,[7] and it was all but indispensable for building the "national *Rechtsstaat*,"[8] especially once the long missing capstone, the Reich Administrative Court, was finally put in place.[9]

Soon the defenders of administrative jurisdiction were able to score a few tactical points. For instance, they attentively noted that the draft of a Reich police administration law, which had been prepared at the Academy for German Law but never enacted, continued to provide for proceedings in contentious administrative matters.[10] Likewise, paragraphs 29 and 30 of the German Communal Statute of January 30, 1935, assumed that administrative jurisdiction would continue, even if the official explanation asserted that this was "not meant to anticipate the final decision via a Reich administrative law on the question whether and to what extent there is any room in the present state for proceedings in contentious administrative matters."[11] The same was the case in paragraphs 146 and 147 of the German Civil Servant Law and in the Reich Disciplinary Law (both January 26, 1937).

Under cover of these regulations, which could now be highlighted emphatically as the "Führer's will" become law, a fervent propaganda in favor of administrative jurisdiction began to take shape. The danger that it might be eliminated in the initial action in 1933–1934 was over. Still, the basic question continued to smolder. Those in the Nazi party who were suspicious of administrative jurisdiction gradually changed their approach as they came to realize that administrative judges, too, were tractable. Some of the decisions that administrative courts had handed down in the spirit of National Socialist *Weltanschauung* were accordingly praised.[12] The task of readjusting administrative jurisdiction to the new state could thus be interpreted as a question of personnel changes and "educational work." That this readjustment would take longer than in other courts because administrative jurisdiction was traditionally occupied by representatives of liberal thinking was something one could live with.

But opinions were divided even within the innermost circle of Nazi leaders. While radical representatives of the SS and the Gestapo continued to push for the outright abolition of the "reactionary" administrative courts, the representatives of the Reich Interior and Justice Ministries pursued the opposite course. The latter had on its side Hans Frank and his Academy for German Law, the overwhelming majority of scholarly opinion, and the entire body of administrative judges. At the district meeting *(Gaufachberatertagung)* of administrative jurists on June 29–30, 1935, the Ministerialrat Justus Danckwerts spoke out emphatically in support of this "proven institution."[13] Undersecretary Wilhelm Stuckart joined in and formulated what was now the official line: A distinction had to be made between political leadership, which, needless to say, should not be subject to any controls, and the implementation of acts of leadership by the executive. The interests of the whole dictated that the legal order be preserved in this process of implementation. And in order to unburden the central authorities, it was not the administration itself but the legal courts that should see to the preservation of the legal order. In fact, the jurisdiction of these courts should be expanded to take in cases of compensation for breach of official duty, compensation for expropriated property, and judicatory law. Finally, all this should be cast into a "uniform Reich administrative law."[14] At the Third Annual Meeting of the Academy for German Law, Reich Interior Minister Frick also committed himself to this course.[15] Hans Frank declared in 1939 that every administrative act had to be verifiable, hence, "administrative jurisdiction . . . is indispensable in the National Socialist state."[16]

The defenders of administrative jurisdiction were happy to make use of these official voices. After 1936 they could concentrate on consolidating their position and could renew their calls for a standardization of administrative procedural law and the organization of the courts. In the process, the question of the Reich Administrative Court was brought up with increasing urgency, since this camp was hoping that its establishment would finally give the Führer's blessing to their cause and strengthen its supporters in the Reich Interior Ministry, the Reich Ministry of Justice, and the Academy for German Law.[17] One example of this was the long article on legal policy by the President of the Saxon Administrative High Court, Herbert Schelcher, who used contemporary arguments in an effort to protect the traditional position of administrative jurisdiction, including the independence of its judges.[18]

Still, the situation of administrative jurisdiction was by no means secure. Looking at the legal journals is deceptive, for here the position of the traditionalist representatives of the civil service and of the "national *Rechtsstaat*" prevailed and was able to create a climate favorable to administrative jurisdiction. We can readily see this from the change in editors after 1933.[19] It was therefore quite true when the radical National Socialist Walther Sommer wrote in 1937, in response to Schelcher, that "there have been articles in all professional journals in favor of administrative jurisdiction." He stated further that "there are repeated attempts to prove that administrative jurisdiction is compatible with the current state, indeed, that it is a national political necessity for this state. Contrary views have not yet received a hearing."[20] However, there was another side to the story that was not written about in the journals and that helps explain the many urgent essays on the preservation of administrative jurisdiction: There were constant disturbances in daily practice, disregard for decisions by administrative judges, interference by local party offices or the Gau chiefs, and attacks in the press against "reactionary"—that is, constitutional—decisions.[21] Administrative jurisdiction was considered the refuge for liberals and conservatives who were seeking to preserve at least the core of the *Rechtsstaat*. Sommer saw this very clearly: "The personnel of the administrative courts is, in any case, not as National Socialist as that of the active administration"; administrative judges were "liberal national citizens," paragraph people and file worms with no connection to active administration.[22]

Sommer's crude summary of arguments against administrative jurisdiction represented the view of the Nazi party, which was underrepresented in the professional journals. In brief, it went something like this: Administrative jurisdiction is dead paragraphs disconnected from life; internal administrative supervision is closer to the people and cannot be abused by enemies of the government; administrative courts are slow and expensive; the separation of political leadership and apolitical administration does not exist in National Socialism; administrative jurisdiction can be tolerated at most as an advisory committee within the administration, and as the institution that settles civil service salary claims, matters relating to the liability of officials, and compensation for expropriated property.

The other camp naturally fought against this kind of dangerous devaluation of administrative jurisdiction. Time and again it repeated what was now its fortified fall-back position. For instance, while the discussion over the judicial examination of Gestapo arrests ("protective custody") was fairly intense in the first years after 1933, it was soon discontinued as a pointless exercise.[23] From the beginning it had been a matter of course that acts of political leadership were exempt from supervision by the courts.[24] Writers repeatedly stressed the subordination of individual rights to the public interest, praised as the advantage of administrative jurisdiction that it lightened the burden of the administration and preserved the unity of the law, affirmed that the National Socialist *Weltanschauung* was the obligatory foundation of judicial independence, now filled with new meaning, and even offered to give up the term *jurisdiction* altogether.[25] The Vice President of the Prussian Administrative High Court tried to prove that his court was clearly in line with the course of the regime.[26] Whether he, an "old fighter" and SS major general, really believed that is another question. Still, it became clear that the champions of administrative jurisdiction were willing to go to considerable lengths to defend their position. Administrative jurisdiction cast off its liberal provenance as unnecessary weight, withdrew without a fight from "political" matters, moved—at least verbally—from standing on the side of the citizen to standing on the side of the state, and opposed the "judicial state."[27]

This was a high price to pay. Administrative jurisdiction lost its intellectual contours by disavowing its true task, that of protecting the individual. To be sure, there were opposing voices. However, by accommodating itself to the rules of language and accepting the subordination of law to the purposes defined by the state, it had in essence already lost its ground. The debate over administrative jurisdiction that dragged on almost to the end of the war excluded the fundamental questions.[28] Authors discussed the remaining spheres of jurisdiction,

the establishment of the Reich Administrative Court,[29] the incorpora-
tion of conquered territories, and the shortening of the procedures. It
is characteristic of the situation that the Nazi candidate who eventually
rose to become President of the Reich Administrative Court was the
one who had the least regard for administrative jurisdiction.[30]

The professional discussion over administrative jurisdiction during
National Socialism thus had a paradoxical outcome. Although administrative jurisdiction was able to hold its ground institutionally to the
end of the war, it had been reduced to irrelevance and pushed away
from important questions, and it had changed beyond recognition once
its defenders themselves disavowed its intellectual foundations. By the
time administrative jurisdiction was finally abolished under the pressures of war, it had hardly any practical importance left; at best it had
minor symbolic value as a residue of constitutional thinking.

II. Just as important as the internal distortion of administrative
jurisdiction under the ideological pressure of the regime was
the process that deprived it of official authority through legislation.

1. What the National Socialists encountered in 1933 under the label
"administrative jurisdiction" lacked institutional uniformity, embraced
different kinds of authority, and followed a variety of procedural rules.
In Prussia, Bavaria, Hessia, and Anhalt, administrative jurisdiction had
three tiers; in Saxony, Baden, Oldenburg, Thuringia, Mecklenburg,
Lippe, Bremen, and Hamburg, it had two tiers; in Württemberg, Lübeck, and Braunschweig, one tier. On the lower and middle tiers it
resembled internal administrative supervision more than genuine jurisdiction.[31] Even at the Administrative High Courts, administration was
still strongly involved, at least through lay judges. In Saxony, Württemberg, Thuringia, and Bremen, jurisdiction was determined by the
general clause, and otherwise the principle of enumeration applied.[32]
Prussia had the general clause for police matters, otherwise enumeration. An administrative jurisdiction for the Reich existed only in special
areas.[33] Individual tasks of the Reich Administrative Court, which was
provided for in the Weimar Constitution (Articles 31, section 2; 107;
166), were taken up by the Reich Court (Electoral Court; § 9 IV, Law
for the Protection of the Republic, March 25, 1930).

2. This rather confusing situation of administrative jurisdiction essentially continued after 1933. However, as Danckwerts put it at the
time, "it has been freed from those components that were clearly incompatible with the basic principles of the National Socialist state,
above all the nomination of lay judges through election. The place of
election has been taken by appointment. In addition, many regulations

have been eliminated which pursued the extreme goal of placing the position of administrative authorities on a par with that of national comrades when it comes to procedural law."[34] The elimination of the decisionmaking function on the lower and middle levels in Prussia still seemed to indicate that a genuine administrative jurisdiction was to be preserved.[35] However, the curtailment of jurisdiction in all questions of any political relevance made it very clear where the new state was headed.

There were, in any case, no legal defenses against the elimination of Jews, Social Democrats, Communists, and others from civil service positions.[36] Communities and schools were no longer allowed to file complaints against supervisory agencies.[37] The course was clear: Legal protection was a casualty whenever the new power wanted to have its way politically, when it intimidated its opponents and deprived them of their rights (for example, by stripping them of their citizenship).[38] Legal protection dropped by the wayside especially when it came to the political police, which laid claim to a sphere of action free of the law.[39]

With the outbreak of the war, the fundamental distrust of administrative jurisdiction joined hands with the state of emergency. Reducing administrative jurisdiction to a minimum, something the party had long since wanted, no longer required any legitimation. The Führer's decree concerning the simplification of administration (August 28, 1939) demanded "unceasing effort and quick decisions free of bureaucratic impediments."[40] It replaced the action to rescind before an administrative court with a complaint to the superior agency or supervisory agency (art. IV); the latter, however, could reopen access to the administrative court through "admission." Appeal was possible only if the administrative court explicitly permitted it because of the importance of a case or its special circumstances. The administrative courts of the first instance were abolished, and the presence of laymen on the bench was ended.[41]

Since "admittance" to appeal was the result of a discretionary decision, which was at the time regarded as immune to challenge,[42] the Reich Interior Ministry tried to weigh in on the side of administrative justice. A circular decree on administrative jurisdiction (August 11, 1941) restored judicial review as the normal case. To guarantee legal unity, the decree maintained that it was necessary "to admit the procedures of administrative courts more extensively than before, thus ensuring the possibility that fundamental cases will be uniformly aligned by the Reich Administrative Court."[43] This decree turned the intent of the Führer decree of August 28 virtually on its head. Later it was also openly said that the principle of admittance in the Führer decree had been "merely a temporary phenomenon."[44]

As far as substantive jurisdiction is concerned, there was a "progressive dismantling" (Ch. F. Menger), while new jurisdictions were constantly added, especially during the war.[45] However, it would be wrong to think that losses and gains kept some kind of balance. Essential powers were lost, unimportant ones were added.

This loss of competence was most evident when it came to the police. When decisions had to be rendered on the first measures of "protective custody" taken in accordance with the Reichstag Fire Decree of February 28, 1933, legal writings, and the courts themselves, questioned whether the courts had the competence to do so in light of the general police clause in the Prussian Police Administration Law.[46] However, the Prussian Administrative High Court resisted those notions. It clung to the principle that affairs of the "political police" were open to judicial challenge, and it tried to narrow police powers by restricting the purposes of the Reichstag Fire Decree.[47] But this strictly positivist line of defense inherent in the law had to fail when the legislative branch began to act, for example, by confiscating Communists' assets. When a Communist's motorcycle was seized, the Prussian Administrative High Court had to accept this as an incontestable "act of state sovereignty of a special kind."[48] Where no special laws existed, the Prussian Administrative High Court for some time searched for a compromise with the Gestapo. It granted that Gestapo orders in the central sphere of the "state police" could not be challenged,[49] but maintained that the jurisdiction of the regular police authorities had remained unaffected in the area of the political police.[50] However, this course could not be maintained, least of all with the somewhat helpless argument that merely designating something as "political" was not sufficient to rule out supervision by administrative courts.[51] When the Prussian legislature ended the uncertainty through the Gestapo Law of February 10, 1936,[52] the Prussian Administrative High Court, which had no other option, relented immediately and declared that its previous decisions had been superseded.[53] It retracted its authority of review even further with the decision of November 10, 1938.[54]

The classic field of reviewing administrative acts by the police had now in part slipped from, in part been wrested from, the hands of administrative jurisdiction. After 1938 it was enough to label a matter "political" to block judicial review. Even the question of whether the label was rightly given was no longer justiciable. It appears that the decision by the Administrative Court of Baden on January 11, 1938, which Ernst Fraenkel mentions, was in fact "the last decision by a

German administrative court in a review of political measures by the police."[55]

However, the total victory of the Gestapo in this matter was possible only because the courts were from the beginning willing to accept the broadest interpretation of the word *political*. Political motives were sufficient even to deny a driver's license,[56] a peddler's license,[57] or a work permit for a midwife who was a Jehovah's Witness,[58] or to dissolve a Jewish organization.[59] Underlying this behavior by the courts was not only the willingness of representatives of a "proper state of affairs" to cooperate with the ruthless "auxiliary police" of the SA, with the Gestapo, and with the local party offices that were de facto untouchable. This was also a case of the persistence of an old mindset, one based on the belief that law and judicial supervision must cease where politics starts. "Politics" in this sense is the sphere devoid of the law in which power acts, and those who hold power define the boundaries where they wish to be controlled and where not. Because of an inbred respect for power, administrative judges—in the history of German law more like servants of the state than bearers of a third power legitimized by popular sovereignty—gave up their jurisdictions faster than was necessary.

Between 1935 and 1944 the authority of administrative jurisdiction was expanded in various areas: disciplinary law, compensations for expropriated property and for war damage, civil service law, commercial law, communal law and communal energy supply, self-governing bodies, and a few special fields.[60] If we add to this the allocations of federal law and the situation in the so-called Ostmark,[61] we get the picture of a considerable increase in power. But this picture is deceptive, for if we compare the powers with the cases actually decided by the Administrative High Courts and the Reich Administrative Court, we see that the granting of jurisdictions did not lead to proceedings in these areas. There could be a great many different reasons for this in addition to that of barring the admission of cases. Proceedings were in general initiated much more rarely, since a system of legal protection in which only remnants were still functioning invariably promoted the tendency to pursue out-of-court arrangements. Those seeking a legal remedy were frequently discouraged from turning to the courts. Moreover, the conditions of war forced individuals to quickly accept unfavorable compensation if the alternative was little or nothing. Finally, there is no doubt that many cases were left unfinished in the chaotic final phase of the regime.

On the whole, notwithstanding the rapid allocation of jurisdictions, Menger was correct in saying that there was a "step-by-step dismantling" of the essential tasks. In the end, administrative jurisdiction's traditional function of providing legal protection had been virtually destroyed.

3. The gap between façade and real significance is particularly glaring in the establishment of the Reich Administrative Court. When it was set up by a Führer decree of April 3, 1941,[62] it was celebrated as the fulfillment of a reform wish long entertained and repeatedly frustrated, as "the most important event that the war has produced in the field of German administrative law."[63] Finally it seemed possible to do away with the jumbled court system in the states of the "Altreich," in Austria, and in the conquered territories, by consolidating the many diverse special jurisdictions.[64] Uniform procedural rules came into sight, as did a clear regulation of jurisdictions.

In fact, none of this was accomplished. The main purpose of the establishment of the Reich Administrative Court was from the outset to simplify the administration and achieve the "necessary savings in personnel and administrative costs."[65] The Reich Interior Ministry had been given the authority to reorganize the court system but made no use of it. Procedural rules were as numerous as the senates that had been absorbed into the Reich Administrative Court. The more irrelevant jurisdictions were in actuality, the more they seemed to proliferate. Geographically the effectiveness of the Reich Administrative Court was limited to Prussia, Austria, and the "Sudeten district."[66] W. Scheerbarth recalled that "there were only few cases."[67] The independence of the judges was no longer intact, in spite of the façade of paragraph 1 of the Law on the Constitution of the Courts, and in spite of the emphatic affirmation that binding instructions were not permissible. The seventy-nine regular members could be transferred, the eleven honorary members were all functionaries of the Nazi party, the fifteen special judges held office for a limited time—all in all the court was an emasculated institution. What saved it from complete inner decay was probably the fact that its personnel overlapped with the Prussian Administrative High Court and other administrative courts.[68]

III. An attempt to examine the decisions by the Administrative High Courts to make out lines of development and differentiate between the various courts confronts us with a host of difficulties. The number of published decisions alone is overwhelming,[69] the different starting points in state law make comparison more difficult, and the reported facts of the cases are abbreviated and rendered anonymous (sometimes they are absent). Because there are few specialized studies,

the personnel policy behind some changes in decisionmaking[70] or noticeable deviations from the prevailing line by certain panels remains
elusive at this time. Apparently there is also uncertainty about the criteria of "judgment" in individual cases,[71] as was demonstrated, for instance, in the question of military justice.[72] Scholars ought to agree
that "trans-temporal" standards of constitutionality do not exist or at
least not in universally binding form, and that the standard attained
in the Federal Republic cannot be used retroactively as a historical
yardstick for the 1930s. That said, there was a consensus on what constituted the ideal of a *Rechtsstaat*,[73] a consensus harking back to the
constitutional and administrative praxis of the monarchy and the Weimar period. Evidence of this is the effectiveness of the compromise
formula of the "national *Rechtsstaat*" in the early years of the regime,
as well as the opposition from within the field to Carl Schmitt's attempt
to wrench the traditional concept of the constitutional state out of its
liberal framework.[74] This normative concept of the constitutional state
as it existed at the time (it, too, undoubtedly a construct after the fact)
would have to be defined more precisely and its underlying premises
laid bare before we could use it as a guideline for evaluating the decisions of administrative courts between 1933 and 1945.

1. The various administrative courts have received very different
treatment from legal scholars. Naturally, the Prussian Administrative
High Court has attracted the most attention. Its legal decisions during
the Nazi period have been repeatedly discussed; Helmut R. Külz, in
particular, has done so while carefully weighing its bright and dark
sides.[75] Within the remaining sphere of jurisdiction, and within the
framework of what was possible for a court that was operating in public
view, the Prussian Administrative High Court was in fact able to preserve constitutional positions to a remarkable degree. It did so by cling-
ing steadfastly, sometimes even craftily, to positive law. For example,
the court rebuked meaningless political justifications,[76] determined
after the fact that the banning of a paper had been illegal,[77] invalidated
the political objections to an organization's statutes and articles,[78] and
confirmed the lawfulness of the granting of a peddler's license.[79] Another decision concerning gypsies culminated in sentences that are
worth quoting: "As German citizens, gypsies are not subject to any
special law. While they are subject to the general obligations of the
law, they are also under the protection of the laws. Of course the police
are entitled to counteract the particular threats that arise from the peculiar habits of gypsies and their nomadic lifestyle. However, they cannot chase them from place to place."[80]

Frege has collected many other examples of the administration of justice by the court.[81] However, there are also cases where the court withdrew, with hardly any comment, from situations calling for uncomfortable decisions—for example, by invoking the changed legal situation or changed conception of the law. Only a few decisions have a decidedly National Socialist imprint.[82]

There are various explanations for this court's relative ability to resist pressures from the National Socialists: the continuity in personnel that reached back to the pre–World War I period and is exemplified especially by its President, Bill Drews;[83] the self-confidence of a court that was renowned precisely for its consistently liberal line;[84] the recruitment of judges from within the traditional fields of law, which was hardly interfered with until 1941. These explanations interlink and supplement one another. The overall picture still lacks depth of focus, and we can only hope that an in-depth look at the court will improve this situation in the future.

2. The Administrative Court of Baden shows a similar course of development on a reduced scale. Christian Kirchberg's thorough study has revealed its external and internal condition under National Socialism.[85] Here, too, there was an old liberal tradition,[86] continuity of personnel,[87] and an attempt to preserve constitutionality as long as possible. As Kirchberg has pointed out, all this was compatible with an accommodation to the course set from higher up, "regardless of whether and to what extent it corresponded to prevailing (positive) law . . . The relevant judicature, whether to the benefit or disadvantage of those concerned, agrees precisely with the declared reasons of state at any given time." Loyalty to the law played itself out in areas not threatened by politics.

After September 1939 the court practically ceased to function as an administrative court, as its presiding judge, Ph. I. Kohlmeier, attended above all to disciplinary matters relating to civil service law.

3. As of yet there is no comparable study of the Administrative Court of Württemberg under National Socialism.[88] A look at its decisions available in print (in the *Reichsverwaltungsblatt* up to 1942) reveals hardly any peculiarities. We find echoes of the *Kirchenkampf,*[89] conflicts over old real rights,[90] compensation decisions in the traditional framework,[91] and the continuation of older judicature concerning communal planning sovereignty, which the court maintained was not subject to judicial oversight.[92]

It is noticeable, however, that the Administrative Court of Württemberg voluntarily, in fact preventively, curtailed its powers of oversight, especially in Gestapo matters,[93] and that it considered even preventive police measures against organizations possible on the basis of the Reichstag Fire Decree.[94] And while steadfast opposition to antireligious measures by the regime could be expected—given the court's prior decisions—when the major churches were concerned, it was lacking when it came to smaller religious communities (Salvation Army, Christian Science, Catholic-Apostolic Community).[95]

4. The Administrative Court of Bavaria, too, shows an ambivalent picture, though a final assessment is still outstanding.[96] Here, as elsewhere, we can observe the usual shrinking process in terms of personnel and jurisdiction. In 1939 the Führer-principle caused the assignment of business "to pass into the hands of the President,"[97] though after the retirement of Staatsrat Dr. Schmelzle in 1939, there no longer was a President.

As with the other Administrative High Courts, the basic thrust of the administration of the law was positivist and constitutional, to the extent that the laws permitted and that an adherence to earlier decisions was possible: for instance, in the revoking of a license in case of scab labor.[98] On questions concerning state church law, the Administrative Court adhered to traditional positions when the national churches were involved,[99] but it had this to say about International Bible Students (former name of Jehovah's Witnesses): "This way of thought and its dissemination are subversive, in form because it violates the prohibition of April 13, 1933, in content because it insults the state and the church, alienates nation and state, and renders services to the cause of pacifism, which is irreconcilably opposed to the heroic *Weltanschauung* of current political and national life."[100] The court kept out of conflicts within the Nazi party.[101]

One reason why "political" cases fell outside judicial review to begin with was that no protection from administrative courts against police decrees had existed in Bavaria even before the National Socialists.[102] Where the law did provide a cover, the court tried to protect the rights of Jewish synagogues[103] and Jewish tradesmen.[104] But as soon as the authorities issued concrete directives, the burden of proof was reversed—for example, when it came to the "unreliability" of Jews with respect to commercial law.[105] And the decision to revoke a veterinarian's license because he was homosexual seemed only natural at the time, given that homosexuality was punishable by law.[106]

5. Even stronger tensions are evident in the picture we get of the administration of justice by the Administrative High Court of Saxony. Its development was certainly not as idyllic as Martin Baring has described in his engaging sketch.[107] The system of the general clause with "negative enumeration" that was unique to administrative jurisdiction in Saxony took immediate effect when it came to Gestapo matters,

because the legislative branch had acted as early as 1933.[108] The court did not defend its powers of review through narrow interpretation but referred even "indirect political" matters to the realm outside the law. It yielded to the simple assertion that the Reichstag Fire Decree applied or that the Reich Governor had intervened politically, even if he had no legal basis for doing so.[109] As it was, legal protection from the state of Saxony ended where measures of the Reich authorities were concerned, and there was no equivalent on the level of the Reich.[110]

Even before 1933 the Administrative High Court of Saxony had attained special renown in questions relating to building and land law. It now took the initiative in these area with a leading decision on January 18, 1935, declaring that the liberal notion of a "material building freedom" on the part of the individual had come to an end. Henceforth the highest principle was that "construction must not damage the national community."[111] The ramifications of the decision were widely discussed,[112] and since there was a danger that persons willing to build could be deprived of their rights, the court itself narrowed it down again.[113] In much the same way the court also politicized freedom of trade *(Gewerbefreiheit)*. In particular, it countenanced denying someone the right to engage in commercial activity for political reasons not subject to verification.[114] Communists, International Bible Students, and Jews were therefore not protected when it came to commercial law.[115]

On the whole, the efforts of the Administrative High Court of Saxony to preserve the standards of the *Rechtsstaat*—and it did make such efforts—were limited to formalities and to material questions of less importance. Examples include the necessity to justify decisions on legal redress, respect for a decision on the part of the police, the retracting of preferential administrative acts, the duration of the time limit for legal redress (falsely set too long), and the improper use of a small fee as a "fine."[116] The Administrative High Court of Saxony, like other high courts, was practically shut down by the Führer decree on simplifying the administration. Herbert Schelcher, presiding judge from 1932 on, tried to maintain the traditional course as best he could. But that very proviso, "as best he could," is the crux of the problem.

6. The Administrative High Court of Thuringia, in existence from 1912 to 1948,[117] was among the small Administrative High Courts. It clashed with the National Socialists as early as 1930 because of the National Socialist Minister of the Interior Frick. As a result, its position was from the outset not very strong. The position of presiding judge became vacant in 1934 and was not filled. Decisionmaking came to an end at this court in 1941.[118]

Its best known decision during the period of National Socialism concerned the question of police restrictions on commercial freedom *(Gewerbefreiheit)* outside of § 143 of the Commercial Code.[119] While the Administrative High Court of Prussia preserved the liberal position on this issue,[120] the court in Thuringia bypassed the question of legality by invoking the notion that individual rights were embedded within the larger community, a notion freely drawn from Nazi ideology. On the other hand, in tax law it opposed the abolition of an "absolutely clear regulation" by Nazi ideology as conveyed through § 1 of the Tax Amending Law,[121] rebuffed police interference in the enforcement of decisions,[122] and maintained the tax-exempt status of synagogues as corporations under public law, at least until 1936.[123] If we examine the judicature of this court chronologically, we see here, as elsewhere, first the surrender of the authority of judicial review, followed by a phase of closer identification with the Nazi state (1935–1939) during which corrections were only made at the margins and in less important issues. Since administrative jurisdiction was "crippled" after 1939, there was no opportunity for the court to distance itself clearly from the Nazi state or to carve out an identity.

7. At present there is no specific study of the judicature of the Administrative Court of Hessia (in Darmstadt) between 1933 and 1945.[124] Given that the archival records were destroyed in the war, such a study would be very difficult to undertake. But at least the organizational outlines are discernible. In 1937 the existing Provincial Boards *(Provinzialausschüsse)* became District Administrative Courts, and as late as 1938 a new President was appointed. However, a substantive assessment of the administration of justice, which became increasingly irrelevant in connection with the Nazi system of rule, is not possible.

8. A substantial account of the smaller Administrative High Courts is currently not possible either, without detailed preliminary studies. This is even more true for District Administrative Courts like Lüneburg or Schleswig.[125] However, we do have Martin Sellmann's detailed study of administrative jurisdiction in Oldenburg.[126] It describes the cutback in the Administrative High Court's personnel, the decline in the number of cases, the curtailing of authority by legislation, and the territorial reduction of Oldenburg when the regions of Birkenfeld and Lübeck were ceded in 1937. Here, too, it all ended with the de facto cessation of judicature through the Führer decree of August 28, 1939. The administration of justice that we can trace to 1939 through the *Zeitschrift für Verwaltung und Rechtspflege in Oldenburg* seems to have followed closely that of the Administrative High Court of Prussia.[127]

It is more difficult still to gain an insight into the administrative jurisdiction of Mecklenburg.[128] Established only in 1922, the State Administrative Courts (Schwerin, Neustrelitz) did not have much time to develop their own traditions. Here, too, the published decisions were clearly oriented toward the judicature in Prussia.[129] As in Prussia, the regime in 1937 eliminated the review of Gestapo matters by administrative courts, which may have already ceased in practice in any case.[130] In 1939 administrative jurisdiction was de facto shut down.

Much the same applies to the administrative courts of the Hanse cities,[131] to Braunschweig, Anhalt, and Lippe.[132] The published case material is not very extensive, and it seems difficult to assess, especially with the limited sources available, how much litigious material was eliminated in preliminary proceedings, how frequently the final instance was reached, and what was eventually released to the journals for publication. It is possible that cases the court feared would lead to tensions with the state or the party were not published. Still, this court, too, shows the typical traits we have highlighted so far: the curtailing of the court's authority, a conception of the law that was in principle positivist, combined with a willingness to yield in cases of conflict to pressures from the Gestapo and to "political directives" from above. Within a state governed half by rules and half by authoritative decisions, these courts were thus neither effective bulwarks of civic freedoms nor instruments of terror. Rather, they were quiet guarantors of what the regime defined as "normality" for as long as it deemed it useful to maintain that normality.

IV. From the perspective of the regime, administrative jurisdiction under National Socialism remained to the end an element that was liberal in origins and that slowed down the regime's dynamism. To a high degree it preserved continuity with the judicial tradition of the civic *Rechtsstaat* in terms of personnel and ideas. That is to its credit, and I am not one to detract from it here.

However, this perspective is too simplistic. It prevents us from realizing that the regime stabilized itself in very different ways in its various phases: from the phase of revolution in 1933–1934 to the internal consolidation between 1935 and 1937, to the renewed "revolutionization" in 1938–1939 and wartime rule. The regime was largely dependent on cooperation from traditional civil servants and judges who were nationalistic and conservative but not National Socialist in their thinking. But these groups were willing to cooperate only if the civic façade of a "national *Rechtsstaat*" was preserved. The continued existence of administrative jurisdiction played a major role in doing just that. The Nazis got rid of administrative jurisdiction without further ado whenever it was in the way, as in the regime's repression of its opponents and its anti-Jewish measures; whenever it was inconvenient, as in the supervision of municipalities and schools; and whenever it slowed things down, as during the war. But administrative jurisdiction had a useful function in conveying the impression that the authoritarian Führer-state was adhering strictly to its own rules or was merely helping rightfulness *(Rechtmäßigkeit)* prevail over the obsolete notion of lawfulness *(Gesetzmäßigkeit)*. Administrative jurisdiction did not cost much, and it allowed the bourgeois public to preserve the illusion that the *Rechtsstaat* was continuing to exist, at least in part.

The importance of this function of the courts became clear especially during the war, when the regime sounded out the mood at the "domestic front." "The finding," it was said from official sides, "is favorable to the judges. It states that the judiciary is having an excellent effect on the population. Confidence in regular judges is high among the people. The few lapses are completely negligible, so that one can say that the judges are doing their duty fully in holding up the domestic front . . . We have come to realize that one of the pillars bearing up the domestic front is called legal security."[133]

But administrative justice was also a useful negotiating point within the regime's power centers. Once Himmler had assured the inviolability of the Gestapo through legislation, court decisions, and legal writings, it was easy to concede the continued existence of administrative jurisdiction to Ministers Frick, Gürtner, and Frank, though with the proviso that it not get out of line. The separation of spheres was a division of power, though in the end the Gestapo and SS emerged the winners. The façade of the normative state with its administrative jurisdiction concealed the real strengthening of the "prerogative state" until it was too late for effective countermeasures.

Finally, we must bear in mind that the continuation of administrative jurisdiction and the preservation of constitutional standards must be attributed to the confluence of different circumstances, and no one can take credit for it. The speed with which the National Socialists transformed state and society differed from one sphere to the next. Administrative jurisdiction, once deprived of its ability to protect the individual and obligated to obey the new rulers, could remain for some time untouched in the "slipstream." Moreover, it typically takes several years before upper courts get around to dealing with a given state of affairs. They are thus always a few steps behind, a situation that can later be favorably highlighted as the preservation of tradition. We can never determine how many cases of gross injustice were never brought before the courts or how many cases were ended in the first and second instance and with what outcome. The case material available to us today, which was deliberately selected for publication, does not represent the reality of the Nazi state. It is that reality, with its banal and its terrible aspects, that one must keep in mind if one has to render judgment, in whatever sense, on administrative jurisdiction under National Socialism.

NINE

"Harsh but Just": Military Justice in the Service of National Socialism

Military justice during the Nazi period was hardly discussed in Germany in the first decades after 1945. The interest of the public and of historians was focused on the Holocaust and "normal" criminal law, especially its function as an instrument of political oppression. Military justice remained in the shadows, so to speak.

The history of scholarly work on this topic began in 1959 with a sketch by the Marburg criminal lawyer and former military judge Erich Schwinge.[1] His essay set the tone for a research project planned by the Institute for Contemporary History in Munich, before the project even got off the ground. In 1962 the project director, the former Reichsgerichtsrat and later President of the Federal High Court, Hermann Weinkauff, asked Otto Peter Schweling, a former military judge and then senior public prosecutor at the Federal High Court, to write a history of military justice. The study was to be published as part of a comprehensive series entitled "The German Judicial System and National Socialism." In the end, however, the book was not published in this series.

Weinkauff had written the introductory volume to this series, in collaboration with A. Wagner. In it Weinkauff, an active representative of the "renaissance of natural law,"[2] had anticipated the results of the research project, which was still in its planning stage. Weinkauff combined the dubious advantage of having "been there" with a subjective interpretation that was also based on generational sentiment and his own life experiences. As a result he superimposed upon historical objectivity a pedagogical impulse, his opposition to legal positivism, and the real argument behind his interpretation: namely, that the German legal system was better than its reputation and had been the true victim of National Socialism.

The second volume of the project showed the same tendencies,[3] though it was little more than a collection of material organized according to an anachronistic scheme derived from the Basic Law of the Federal Republic. By contrast, the third volume, W. Wagner's *Der Volksgerichtshof* (The People's Court [1974]), was substantially better. Most of all, Wagner did not impose a hasty interpretation on the richly documented material. That would have been easy to do since an account of the People's Court could not possibly have had any apologetic intent.

The hope that the scholarship of this project would show a growing professionalization and historicization would have been dashed if Schweling's volume had been published as part of the series. It is clear that the institute's decisionmaking process was unusually long and unpleasant for the author. However, it was a positive sign that the institute did not give in to the massive pressure from the editor, Schwinge. Had it published the book, the institute would have destroyed much of the reputation it had built through careful work of impeccable scholarship.

The story of how this book came to be written is bizarre in itself. Members of the Association of Former Military Judges met in Marburg on May 8–9, 1965, to support the project by gathering and coordinating material. Schweling got to work and submitted a first draft in 1966. This version was reworked at the institute, deliberated upon, and eventually put aside. Several reviewers gave their opinions, some positive, some negative. The advisory committee, under the chairmanship of the historian K. D. Erdmann, gathered further information, and after a long time it finally decided not to accept the book as an institute publication. Shortly thereafter the author died, perhaps even as a result of the emotional turmoil caused by this decision. Erich Schwinge, asked by Schweling's widow to represent her late husband's interests, condensed and improved the manuscript and published it in 1977 with a Marburg publishing house.[4]

II. The chief problem of the Schwinge / Schweling book[5] is methodological. It begins by defining the topic "military justice" very narrowly, with the result of excluding the jurisdictions of the SS, the police units, and the Volkssturm (home guard), which were troubling to the overall picture. Although one can justify this in formal terms, it does arouse suspicion that the intent is to shed inconvenient baggage. This suspicion is reinforced when the author proceeds to marginalize the courts-martial. Later in the book (§ 13), Schweling discusses all of four court-martial cases, which he grades as "unobjectionable," "correct," "conscientiously and carefully carried out," "harsh but still justifiable in legal and military terms." He argues that the gloomy cases from the "turbulent" final phase of the war, which he is certainly aware of, must not be "held against Wehrmacht justice," since they were supposedly atypical.[6] Having limited his topic by way of definition, Schweling characterizes German military justice as an institution that, by "its nature and task," was called upon "to serve the law and only the law."[7] Although he does indicate that military interests may have occasionally prevailed over the law, he maintains that, for the most part, "the interplay worked fine."[8]

This already sketches out the crucial positions of the "a priori understanding" the author reveals on nearly every page. Let us follow his argument further: The organization and procedures of military justice were "simple but functional," indeed "exemplary."[9] Material criminal law was "clear and easy to survey and had adequately defined offenses."[10] The traditional reputation was "good" (criticism came mostly "from circles of the political left,"[11] which presumably means it was invalid to begin with). Schweling even maintains that the military justice of World War I was too formalistic and constitutional *(rechtsstaatlich)*, a judgment fully in line with the views of the political right in the Weimar period and under National Socialism. This is underlined by weighty side glances at the British and the French, who supposedly needed a harsher military justice because of their lack of military talent and poorer discipline.

Having laid down this foundation, Schweling proceeds to discuss his actual topic. He begins with a rough sketch of the relationship between National Socialism and the law, on the one hand, and between the Wehrmacht and Wehrmacht justice, on the other. Its upshot is the contention that Wehrmacht justice, as a particularly "clean" and suffering part, stood in latent opposition to National Socialism. Next he inserts brief accounts of Hitler and Göring, and their relationship to Wehrmacht justice. The Wehrmacht jurists he describes by way of contrast, down to the selected—and universally positive—examples of individual Wehrmacht judges, were either not members of the Nazi party or had joined only under pressure. The unequivocal National Socialists who do appear, such as General-Judge Roeder, were "atypical." Here, too, the author's intent is clear as day: The Wehrmacht jurists as a group (individual "lapses" are always readily admitted) are to emerge from the events without a blemish. This is a very understandable view for someone who was there and thinks he has nothing to reproach himself for. But it is not the perspective of the historian, for whom the question whether something or somebody "remained clean" or not is not very meaningful to begin with.

The core of the book is an examination of the files of the military courts. Schweling provides an informative survey of the existing material (about 11,000 files), which he reduces to 1,000 files through an acceptable random-selection process. What follows next, however, is not an analysis of these files but vague speculation: Since the official collections of the Federal Court and the Social Courts contain few decisions involving "miscarriages of justice" from the wartime period, the author infers that there were few miscarriages of justice (again not counting verdicts of courts-martial). This line of reasoning is inadequate, since it ignores some vital questions: What cases were brought before the courts of the Federal Republic, to begin with? What cases came before the Obergerichte (higher courts)? Finally, what was selected for inclusion in the official collections? Schweling supplements this argument with a selective polemic against three authors who criticized Wehrmacht justice (we shall leave aside the question of whether their views were well founded or not).

In discussing individual decisions, first those of the Reich War Court from the official collection, the author proceeds by examining whether a decision should be regarded as having been "influenced by National Socialism." His conclusion is that among the decisions of the official collection before 1939, only one was "National Socialist," while the other 161 showed "hardly a trace of the National Socialist spirit."[12] However, since he does not provide verifiable criteria for determining what makes a decision "National Socialist," his findings have to be taken on faith, at best. Of the decisions of the Reich War Court after 1939, he examines only those that have been previously discussed.[13] Why only these? Apparently because the decisions that have not yet been discussed do not need to be defended. Much discussed, even during the war, were the harsh decisions by the First Senate of the Reich War Court on the concept of "the public" as it related to the offense of "demoralization of the troops." Schweling, who acknowledges that these decisions were a "mistake," emphasizes that they were episodic and of little importance for the jurisdiction over the troops. And in two other questions on which the Reich War Court took a harder line, Schweling states flatly and entirely without substantiation: "There is, in any case, no indication that the view of the Third Senate prevailed at the grassroots." He further maintains that "this controversy in all likelihood had little influence on the rulings of the field courts."[14] Schweling's line of defense is to prove that the Reich War Court administered justice largely in line with the traditional notion of the *Rechtsstaat*. Sometimes he is unable to do so, no matter how hard he might try, even by invoking the "necessities of war" and claiming repeatedly that "the same happens in all civilized states in the world." In indefensible cases he assumes that the lower courts were not influenced by the Reich War Court's "mistakes" and "lapses caused by the circumstances of the times."[15] However, he assumes as a matter of course that maxims of the Reich War Court that adhered to the principles of the *Rechtsstaat* filtered down to the lower courts.

This basic pattern characterizes Schweling's account of proceedings against conscientious objectors (Jehovah's Witnesses) and generals, and the accounts (apparently abridged by Schwinge) of proceedings for spying, committing sabotage, giving aid and comfort to the enemy, and committing economic offenses.

The actual study of field court decisions begins with numerical data without precise reference to the distribution of groups of offenses. This is followed by brief remarks on the punishment of homosexuality and political offenses. These passages contain a host of value judgments that are not verifiable and are always favorable to Wehrmacht justice: Numbers are called "high" or "very low," death sentences are always "rare," sentencing is always "mild," and so on. Problems concerning ratios and the potential manipulation of figures by altering classifications and the number of unreported cases are not addressed. Either the author is unaware of them or he deliberately ignores them because a precise analysis would have weakened the suggestive power he seems to invest in them.

The thrust of the account becomes clearest in the roughly sixty-page chapter on the praxis of sentencing. It opens with the tirelessly repeated statements that tough times require tough measures and that the practice in other countries was equally harsh, if not harsher. At the same time, the author emphasizes that the German praxis during the war was not really harsh; rather, it was in keeping with the principles of the *Rechtsstaat*, and it became increasingly lenient. Trends toward harsher sentencing are strenuously denied; where this is not possible because of the numerical data (for example, a rise in prison sentences and the approximately 10,000 death sentences that were handed down), the causes are shifted away from the court to outside "circumstances." While highlighting anything that points to mild sentencing, Schweling quickly skips over sentences he himself describes as "excessive." The category that he creates based on his subjective feeling and uses most frequently to describe sentences is "harsh but still justifiable."[16] Only 6 of 1,636 sentences struck him as "excessively harsh," whereas he rates 200 as "unusually mild." There would be something pitifully naive about this blind faith in numbers were the subject matter not so horrible and the constant self-righteous comparison with other countries—which is truly unjustified—so revolting.

Given what we have seen so far, it comes as no surprise that the examined files proved to be "generally in order" with respect to procedural law. The independence of the administration of justice was "hardly ever encroached upon,"[17] National Socialists were not favored, and there were, in the author's opinion, no indications that the judiciary was submissive toward military or professional superiors. Only the appointment of defense attorneys was not always "the way one would have hoped."[18] During review proceedings the files were "conscientiously examined, and each case was appreciated not only in legal but also in human terms." As for pretrial detention, "apprehension and arrest . . . were not infrequent, but they always met the legal requirements."[19]

III. The book is written from the perspective of someone who was there and thinks this gives him an advantage in speaking about the events. In reality, a participant is thoroughly unsuited for the role of detached observer. It is unavoidable that personal recollections, pride, anger, shame, and a desire to justify the events to oneself and posterity merge with the findings from a renewed examination of the files. At the same time, the book is written from the perspective of a soldier (whose political views are probably German National). This perspective has shaped the value judgments about military necessities in a dictatorship at war. On this point the book is presumably representative of a large segment of veterans, and the findings, if presented in an abbreviated popular form at veterans' meetings, would presumably receive enthusiastic approval.

Finally, the book was written by a jurist who worked within the judicial system of the Federal Republic. Pension law, restitution law, and penal law have a peculiar way of dividing people into those who are "compromised by National Socialism" and those who are "not compromised." The significance of this for the book is that Schweling takes this division and turns it into a historical yardstick. However, ever since the ill-fated "de-Nazification" by the Allies, we have known that such a division is neither very practical nor informative, given the innumerable gradations, mixtures, and transformations that people underwent, and given the facelessness of what is to be called "National Socialist." This division is not sustainable as a historical and heuristic principle.

The author's (and editor's) threefold bias as participant, soldier, and jurist imparted to the well-intentioned work the distorted structure and disastrous statements that make it unusable as a scholarly study. (Of course, it is a good example of a fairly typical way of coming to terms with the past.) The history of German military justice under National Socialism must therefore be taken up anew. Schweling's book can be no more than a point of departure that has to be abandoned.

No sooner had the book been published than it received high praise from Friedrich Karl Fromme in a review in the *Frankfurter Allgemeine Zeitung* entitled "Wie Militärgerichtsbarkeit wirklich war" (What military justice was really like). My own letter to the editor, which opposed Fromme's verdict, triggered a broad public debate during the second half of 1978. Former military judges, in particular, joined the debate on Schweling's side. This was the time of the Filbinger affair.[20] A second edition of the book appeared in 1978.

A decade later, the military historian Manfred Messerschmidt and the layman Fritz Wüllner published their response to Schweling's study.[21] Its goal was the "destruction of a legend," which had read as follows in the version of Schweling and Schwinge: Military justice was not Nazi justice; its judgments were "harsh but just"—appropriate, in any case, to the pressure it was under. Finally, what it did was no different from what the military justice of other countries also did. This was and is the view of former military judges. It is "normal" in the sense that participants in historical events create a picture they can live with, one in which they are cast in as favorable a light as possible— as they wish to be seen by posterity. A part of this is the attempt to lend authenticity to the picture by invoking their own experiences and by dismissing critical objections with the comment that the critics "weren't there."

It is equally normal, of course, that the perspective of participants is too narrow and cannot be generalized, that participants can offer little more than subjective impressions, and that a particular individual's innocence makes it impossible to see how his own group, beyond the individual level, was involved with the regime. All this is readily apparent in the account of military justice by Schweling and Schwinge. The book by Messerschmidt and Wüllner, for its part, is not the hoped-for objective, comprehensive study of the topic. Instead, driven by a barely concealed outrage, it is a reckoning with Schweling and Schwinge, with the overall apologetic tendency of their work (of which there can be no doubt), and with many details that have proven to be wrong upon closer examination. The number of death sentences imposed by the more than 3,000 military judges was not from 10,000 to

12,000, but about 50,000—that is, more than were imposed by all special courts and the People's Court combined. The number of cases brought was not 70,000, but about 3 million.

But the point here is not to correct the figures, no matter how important this is for an objective historical picture where we already have to expect hecatombs of innocent victims. The essence of the matter is rather to thwart the attempt by a specific, self-contained group of judges to obfuscate their own history with the help of simple arithmetic tricks and arbitrary value judgments ("harsh but just" and "on the whole mild"), using an aura of scholarship and the protection of good political connections to do so. The thinking in the circle of former military judges must have gone something like this: Once someone from "their own ranks" has been put in a position where he can write an official study, and once the basic outline has been drawn and he has been supplied with selected material, it is only the details that need retouching. Inconvenient elements are defined away from the outset (the SS, courts-martial), and the rest is declared "normal," especially in comparison with other countries; obvious crimes become "isolated cases"; contacts with the resistance are gloriously highlighted. In fact, the entire book—in a move of consummate bad taste—was dedicated to the memory of the honorable Nazi victims Dr. Karl Sack and Dr. Rüdiger Schleicher.

To this extent the book by Messerschmidt and Wüllner is indispensable as a counterargument. Its contention is as follows: Military justice was part of the Nazi system; it supported that system right up to the last days of its downfall; its punishment was barbarically harsh, especially in comparison to that in other countries; and it has a still undetermined but very high number of innocent victims on its conscience.

Starting from this basis, which cannot be seriously challenged, given the available material, the subtleties should now be worked out: cases of leniency, which were perhaps not rare; long prison terms to avoid the death penalty; clever delays of proceedings in view of the imminent end of the war; cases of open mutiny and resistance. All these things existed, but Messerschmidt and Wüllner either do not mention them or only hint at them, precisely because Schweling and Schwinge had already used them so blatantly. However, this does not mean that the truth must lie somewhere in between: One must beware of this kind of reconciliation of opposing views. For even though all indications are that Messerschmidt and Wüllner's views are closer to the truth, it is at least conceivable that these authors, too, have underestimated the actual extent of the entire complex of military justice. This uncertainty will remain unless and until the files in the archives are inventoried with a sound and verifiable statistical method and are evaluated with an openly declared catalog of criteria. It is more than doubtful that this will ever happen. The energy it takes to review tens of thousands of files will probably be invested only if there is strong external motivation that will make the necessary research resources available. Once those who were directly involved are no longer alive and no longer provoke political interest in the subject matter (as Hans Filbinger did, for instance), National Socialist military justice and the records it left behind will also gradually be covered by the dust of history. The voices that are still audible today will become only a faint murmuring: As Theodor Adorno said in 1944, "The expression of history in things is nothing other than that of past suffering."

IV. The story continues, however. After the first book (by Schweling and Schwinge), the counter article,[22] and the counter book by Messerschmidt and Wüllner, as well as the response by Schwinge, Fritz Wüllner published another study in 1991, *Die NS-Militärjustiz und das Elend der Geschichtsschreibung. Ein grundlegender Forschungsbericht* (National Socialist military justice and the poverty of historiography: A basic research report). As Hans Wrobel said, this book is an "anti-Schwinge" written "cum ira et studio."[23] And Wrobel gave all the reasons why it is excusable that this book does not live up to the ideals of scholarly detachment and coolness, and that it has clear shortcomings in its presentation. The facts that Wüllner has compiled and has for the most part backed up with documentation are not wrong because the author presents them with moral outrage and has a purpose: namely, to prove that the account of Schweling and Schwinge is wrong. Future research is not finished, but it now has much more material to work with than it had a decade ago. Scholars will reexamine most of the questions, they will look at the 11,000 files in the Archiv Kornelimünster near Aachen, and most of all, they will have to attempt a "verdict in the historical context."

In the meantime the judicial system has been active. The Federal Social Court changed its previous decisions. In the wake of a resolution of the Bundestag on January 25, 1985, it recognized compensation for victims of National Socialist military justice,[24] on the grounds that the verdicts of the nonindependent military courts in a "war that violated international law" constituted "obvious injustice." In rendering its decision, the court drew explicitly on the work of Messerschmidt and Wüllner. It was severely attacked but also emphatically defended for doing so.[25] Though this does not settle any question of legal history, it appears that a change of generations and outlook has taken place in the judiciary, as well. Here, too, the pressures for conformity and collegial solicitude are lessening. Here, too, the view that has long appeared most persuasive to less biased historical observers seems to be gaining ground.

TEN

The White Rose
and Its Judges

The White Rose,[1] a film by Michael Verhoeven and Mario Krebs, came to German theaters in the fall of 1982. Its closing statement led to an outcry in the media: "It is the opinion of the Federal Court that the sentences against the White Rose are legal. They are still in force."[2] Commentators called it "false,"[3] "objectively wrong" and "infamous,"[4] "doubly wrong,"[5] "shocking and wrong,"[6] "aggressive and wrong,"[7] "false and outrageous,"[8] "clearly false and polemical."[9] The President of the Federal Court declared that his court had never reviewed the sentences against members of the White Rose. He carefully indicated that he was distancing himself from the so-called Rehse decision,[10] and raised the question whether the Bundestag might not consider nullifying all sentences handed down by the People's Court.[11]

That triggered another wave of letters to the editor, press releases, and articles in professional journals.[12] The Federal Minister of Justice became involved, and surviving convicted defendants from those trials spoke up.[13] Verhoeven and Krebs wrote a new closing statement, but it was still open to attack.[14] During parliamentary questioning, the federal government argued that a declaration invalidating all sentences was not necessary given the repeal legislation after 1945. Moreover, since the People's Court had acquitted some defendants, such a declaration would go too far.[15] On the fortieth anniversary of the execution of Hans and Sophie Scholl, there were church services, panel discussions, and the laying of wreaths. A letter by the Federal President was read, there were speeches by the Bavarian Minister President (*Bayernkurier,* February 25, 1983), the Minister of Culture, the Lord Mayor of Munich, the President of the University of Munich, theologians, philosophers, and many others. In the midst of all these declarations, warnings, corrections, and even continuing legal debates, the film was shown and became more and more widely known. Teachers went to see it with their students, and the public bought books about the White Rose.[16]

Everything thus seemed to be turning out to the satisfaction of Verhoeven and Krebs. Though they may have fired their broadside a bit off the mark, its impact exceeded expectations. However, the latest act in this drama was bothersome. The Federal Ministry of Justice informed the Foreign Office that the revised trailer of the film was legally indefensible. According to the Foreign Office, the film therefore could not be loaned to foreign Goethe Institutes via Inter Nationes.[17] The attempt to get the director to drop the closing statement failed. Somehow the entire affair did not seem to have a happy ending.

To understand what happened, we must bear two things in mind. First, the film touched on essential elements of prior attempts to come to terms with the Nazi past: the sentencing of Nazi criminals, the rehabilitation of victims, the question about the validity of "right" over "law," and suspicion about the power of the judicial system to clean its own house. Second, the showing of the film coincided with a major publicity campaign on the fiftieth anniversary of the Nazi seizure of power. Here are some examples of what was going on at the time: Shortly after the debate over the White Rose, the forged Hitler diaries were published. With the perpetrator still in pretrial detention, the magazine that fell for his forgery described itself as an "embarrassed" victim, but it wanted to sell its embarrassment for as much as possible. At the same time, the petition for a retrial of the "Reichstag arsonist" Marinus van der Lubbe was finally turned down.[18] The chief of the SS in Lyons, Klaus Barbie (Altmann), ended up in French pretrial detention, and the German judicial system was relieved that it would not have to prosecute this case. In East Berlin, one of the SS murderers of Oradour (June 10, 1944) was sentenced to life in prison on June 7, 1983. According to press reports, Alois Mertens, Secretary of State in Bonn, wanted to get to work "immediately" on winning the release of Rudolf Hess. After the retired Finanzrichter Wilhelm Stäglich published his right-wing book *The Auschwitz Myth* (1979), the University of Göttingen sought to strip him of the Ph.D. it had awarded in 1951, even though the law it invoked has been called a "Nazi law." In mid-1983 former members of the SS divisions SS Bodyguard Regiment Adolf Hitler and Hitler Youth celebrated in Bad Hersfeld what they called their "fiftieth anniversary" *(Dienstjubiläum)*. Finally, prosecutors in West Berlin, following an eleven-year break between 1968 (the Rehse decision of the Federal High Court)[19] and 1979, resumed investigations against former judges and prosecutors of the People's Court and other special courts. Of the 565 people originally in this group,

89 were still alive in 1983. Investigations against 37 of these were dropped. As the year 1985 unfolds, we shall discover what the investigations against the remaining 52 people can yield at this point in time.[20]

If we want to step back somewhat from this background and disentangle the main lines of the discussion, it is best to begin with what is beyond dispute. The uncertainty about the "validity" of the sentences against the White Rose that was caused by the first version of the closing statement has been resolved. The legislative branch has stripped the verdicts of legal force, not only in Bavaria but also in the other former occupation zones.[21] All that remains unclear is whether there are still repercussions of those verdicts worth rescinding (register entries), and whether there are verdicts that still need to be overturned and have remained in force because a postwar petition did not meet some requirement or other. So far there has only been speculation on these two issues.

There are three areas in which one might look for the practical significance of the general annulment of the verdicts of the People's Court that the Bundestag called for: (1) the effect of annulment on what are presumed to be the remaining cases, though in all likelihood this has almost no relevance whatsoever for the people who were affected; (2) easier prosecution of former judges and prosecutors, now that the Bundestag—evidently not only an organ of the political will but also of historiography—has declared that the People's Court was not a court; (3) the effect of nullification as a political symbol (although, since such a symbol was cheap in 1983, it probably would not have been worth very much).

Some have voiced hopes that such a resolution will reveal "whether the continuity constructed by the judicial system can be broken, and whether the legislative branch can bring itself to vindicate the victims of National Socialism in a manner that has legal force."[22] It seems to me, however, that such hopes greatly exaggerate the effect of such a late declaration, which has practically no consequences and was extorted from the members of Parliament by public opinion.

It is striking that those who champion the annulment of the verdicts—which in their eyes are thus "valid," after all—simultaneously maintain that the People's Court was an instrument of terror and as such could not have rendered any legally valid "verdicts." Thus, the goal is to remove merely the appearance of legal validity for the purpose of rehabilitating the victims. Quite apart from the question of whether the victims need this in the first place, since they do not need the Bundestag to affirm their unsullied honor, we have here arrived at the heart of the problem. Were the norms by which Freisler, the notorious chief judge of the People's Court, rendered his judgments "valid law" at the time? Did resistance fighters such as the White Rose "objectively violate laws that were valid at the time"? Were the judges of the People's Court subject to laws?[23]

Verhoeven and Krebs, who have raised these questions, distinguish between "valid law," on the one hand, and "elements of the Nazi terror system," on the other. Valid law to them means nonterroristic, "just," normal law. The criterion for this distinction is a natural-law yardstick that allows one to distinguish between a normal legal order and a system based on injustice. What they are doing is thus in principle no different from what the Allies did after 1945 through the legislation of the Control Council, the legislatures of the occupation zones and the *Länder*, and the Federal Republic: seeking a way to distinguish between "normal" valid law from that period and "law" that should be considered "nonlaw" because it violated elementary notions of justice (natural law, human and civil rights of classic liberal provenance).[24]

A parallel notion has emerged on the institutional level. According to this view, there were institutions in the Nazi state that functioned "normally" and could have been found in any other state. In addition, there were institutions that were elements of the system of terror and as such could produce nothing but "injustice." This distinction is evidently based on the idea that whatever served the Nazi terror was not law (in the sense of being materially "just") and is therefore not "valid." This layman's idea that legal norms and other sovereign acts are invalid if they are felt to be unjust or immoral is widely shared. It is based on an unhistorical understanding of natural law, which holds, for example, that what is unjust today must also have been unjust in the past. This is precisely what Hans Filbinger meant, though from a different perspective, when he said that what was law back then could not be immoral *(Unrecht)* today. This argument confuses or deliberately obfuscates the formal validity of a law and the justice of its content. Those who use it ignore the fact that it is easy to label a legal norm "valid law": All one has to do is show that it was formally enacted in accordance with the written or unwritten constitutional rules and that it was recognized by the legal community at the time. Finally, proponents of this argument overlook the fact that calling a norm "valid law" or a sentence "valid" says nothing about its moral qualification. In other words, legal norms or sentences from the Nazi period could be based on law that was valid at the time and still be in force, while simultaneously being highly unjust in substantive terms and morally reprehensible. The doctrine in the Federal Republic, however, established by Gustav Radbruch and adopted in the administration of justice, has felt the need to temper this point of view by arguing that cases of blatant and obvious violations of justice must be assumed to be invalid. The argument says that legal norms can no longer claim validity "if they are so obviously contradictory to the principles of justice that the judge who wanted to apply them or accept their legal consequences would render injustice instead of justice."[25] I consider this inconsequential, at least for the areas in which Nazi terror and Nazi injustice wrapped themselves in the mantle of the legal order, and I am inclined to let formal legal validity extend as far as the legal form did. Beyond the legal form begins brute force—that is, at that point the problem posed by the legal form ceases to exist. Admittedly difficult are the transitional cases where the legal form has been cracked but not entirely abandoned. There may well be no "clean" theoretical solution for these cases.

However, I will not pursue the problem further in the realm of legal theory. The following question is probably more important: Let us assume it to be possible, using criteria drawn from natural law, to separate ex post facto a legal order of the years 1933–1945 from a Nazi terror system that existed alongside it. The question would arise whether this is what historical reality looked like. Aren't contemporary value judgments being used anachronistically to produce the desired result for criminal justice? Is this not a case where Ernst Fraenkel's idea of the "dual state," a fertile idea in itself, has been taken to absurd lengths?

There is no question that the Nazi system was capable of enacting law. The system emerged during a period of transition from a veiled to an open breach of the constitution, out of a coalition of the political right that was in formal terms legal. It established itself by virtue of prevailing domestically and winning recognition internationally (not least from the Vatican) as the legal Reich government. Thanks to the doctrine of the lawmaking power of a successful revolution, it was able to leave behind its dubious birth (*Entscheidungen des Bundesgerichtshofs in Zivilsachen* 5:96). The new constitutional situation was fluid; in any case, it could no longer be measured against the Weimar Constitution, large parts of which had been repealed. The sovereign acts of this regime were at the time and in the context of the regime valid law. Other countries and the majority of the people recognized and abided by this legal order—notwithstanding all the obvious moral and political objections to the regime. Someone who denies that National Socialism produced "valid law" is either trying to cling to a doctrine of legal validity that is based on natural law and formulated independently of the facts, with a moral condemnation perhaps being projected into law, or else seeking to deny, with apologetic intent, that the broad mass of the German people accepted the regime and its domestic order right up to the end of the war. These are two very different motivations, but they lead to the same result.

That is why it is important to emphasize repeatedly how typical the combination of normality and terror was for the Nazi regime. The regime's ability to function was based on the fact that the traditional elites in the civil service, the judiciary, the military, and the economy could reassure themselves by looking at the partial "normality" and justify to themselves and others their involvement through daily collaboration. Terror could thus appear as a regrettable exception—and surely not approved of by the Führer! Thus law that is considered "normal" and law that is considered terroristic propped each other up. To separate them is to distort legal-historical reality. An equally grave consequence of such a separation would be the exoneration of "normal" justice and the day-to-day administrative oppression brought about by it.

In general, the resistance fighters thus violated valid law. Therein lies their courage and dignity; this can only increase our respect for them. They broke the terrorist legal rules imposed by the Nazi regime out of moral conviction, and they knew it. Internally they did not accept these rules as just, and they had moral contempt for those who implemented them.

They were condemned by an institution of the system that called itself a "court," and which, judged by its record of 5,286 death sentences, was really the "death machine of the Nazi party."[26] But does this mean that the People's Court was therefore not a "court" in the formal sense of § 1 of the GVG, the Law on the Constitution of the Law Courts? Since this question usually stirs up emotions, as though the person who poses it also agrees with the Rehse decision by the Federal High Court, I shall examine the arguments in greater detail.

Some recognize that the Nazi state, on the basis of the Enabling Act, was in a position to enact valid law and that consequently the People's Court, too, was established in a valid way.[27] However, they go on to maintain that it was not an "independent" court.[28] The latter statement is indeed true. The court's dependent status, factually and in terms of personnel, has been confirmed many times by contemporary statements (from Hitler, Freisler, K. Engert, H. Parisius, O. G. Thierack), by the recorded verdicts, by protocols, films, and firsthand accounts.[29] The purpose of the court was to destroy or intimidate the domestic political opposition. The breakdown of procedural forms and the elimination of all constitutional guarantees, Freisler's unpredictability and shouting are perfectly consistent with this purpose. Someone who wants to create terror and fear cannot be seriously bothered by the Code of Criminal Procedure—he must cast off what Thierack called the "crutches of the law." The People's Court was a "dependent" court borne up by Nazi ideology, a situation that seems perfectly natural in a state that from the outset had rejected the "independence of the judge."[30] To that extent the relevant passage in the Rehse decision, which attested that the court was "independent" in the current sense and that the judges were bound "only by conscience," is historically untenable.

Still, it was a court, and "independent" in the sense in which the independence of judges was interpreted between 1933 and 1945. It was a "dependent" court if one wants to measure historical reality, and within it the interpretation of § 1 of the Law on the Constitution of the Law Courts that was in force at the time, with a supra-temporal yardstick of independence and dependence. But the criteria for such a yardstick are problematic.

The sentences passed by this court, on the basis of a law that is morally repugnant but was without question "valid" at the time, were certainly valid sentences, which the legislature was later right in annulling. Likewise, Freisler, Rehse, and all the others who were active as "judges" knew very well what they were doing and were fully aware that if the Nazi state failed, the gallows awaited them. Punishment on the basis of § 336 of the Penal Code would have been entirely possible. The thesis that the People's Court was a court and that its judgments were valid law in the context of the system at the time does not entail the legal consequences the Federal High Court drew in the Rehse decision.

Of course, one can take a more fundamental approach and deny that the Enabling Act was legal. This would allow one to declare all sovereign acts of the Nazi state as nonlaw. By making a clean sweep in this way, one could spare oneself a lot of trouble. Distinctions become superfluous since all are united by the injustice created by all. However, such a "national community" never existed and would not be desirable. Above all, for the sake of their own exoneration, many wouldn't mind hearing that they lived under a regime that was generally incapable of enacting law. The "everyday fascism" in the guise of legal form would thus vanish.

Moreover, faced with such a simplistic thesis, we need to recall that there were practical reasons why a general invalidation of sovereign acts by the Nazi state was not an option after 1945. A uniform annulment of all norms, court decisions, and administrative acts would have created insurmountable problems of retroactive liquidation and, if seriously implemented, would have resulted in chaos.

Anyone who pursues a more limited goal—that of invalidating only the verdicts of the People's Court and of the other special courts set up by the decrees of May 21 and December 31, 1933—must bear in mind that this could be gratefully seized upon as an exoneration for all other courts. However, there is no question that other courts, foremost among them the Reichsgericht, rendered decisions every bit as scandalous as those of the People's Court. Are the judges of these courts to be told by a declaration of the Bundestag that their decisions were in principle different from those of the People's Court? Such a declaration could be easily misread to mean that these decisions were "just" decisions—and some would be only too happy to misread it that way.

III. The second set of issues that has been touched on by the discussion about the White Rose seems to be more important in public awareness. It is also what Verhoeven and Krebs were primarily after. I am talking about the prosecution of Nazi judges by the judicial system of the Federal Republic. It is clear that the Rehse decision on April 30, 1968, brought prosecution to a halt, as prosecutors believed they could not prove the subjective requirement of a "perversion of justice" demanded by the Federal Supreme Court. However, it is misleading to speak of a halt to prosecution, since even by this time nothing much had gotten under way that could have been stopped.

In making the Rehse decision, did the court follow the maxim that "dog does not eat dog,"[31] or were the judges thinking about the future interpretation of § 336 of the Penal Code regardless of the impact on this particular case? This question would at least be open to debate, were it not for the lenient treatment of Nazi judges in the de-Nazification proceedings, as well as a long list of unsuccessful attempts to bring criminal proceedings against judges and prosecutors of the People's Court.[32] If we look at these failed attempts in context, even the friendliest observer invariably gets the impression that "prevailing doctrine" and decisions by the Federal Supreme Court, which prop each other up, have been used to construct defensive bulwarks for former judges. In this case, as was rightly observed in an open letter by forty professors in January 1980, the judge's privilege protects "the most dependent and submissive justice in the history of German law . . . Acknowledging these judges in retrospect as independent and bound only by their conscience surely cannot improve the reputation of the People's Court. It stands before the legal consciousness of the nations bloodstained and despised, no matter how the postwar German judicial system deals with it. However, democratic justice has a reputation to lose if it spreads protective paragraphs over the murderers in the robes of the People's Court and the Special Courts."[33]

Since the publication of this open letter, it has been repeatedly noted that the judicial system of the Federal Republic has failed to deal with Nazi judges on the level of criminal law.[34] Not only did it fail to move resolutely when there was still time, it even placed itself protectively in front of them, by recognizing those who were active at the People's Court as "judges" and by declaring that judges could be prosecuted as perpetrators only if they could be shown to have acted with the intent of perverting justice. Critics further argued that there were too many examples of courts generously declaring defendants unfit to attend trial or endure incarceration; that proceedings had been dragged out, given the advanced age of many defendants; that courts didn't do much to procure files and did not pursue extradition proceedings with vigor.[35] On the whole, this gave rise to the suspicion that the judicial system didn't really want to deal with these matters and was hoping that they would gradually take care of themselves.

There is very little to say against these observations and accusations. The conclusions they reach are correct, even if it seems to me that they pursue the wrong justification by denying that the People's Court was actually a court. The fact that they have by now condensed into an accusatory ritual and that they sometimes—and not unintentionally—underestimate the difficulties of research that is both precise and constitutionally above reproach cannot destroy the core of truth they contain.

If we wanted to indicate the reasons for this state of affairs, we would have to mention, in addition to the social history of the judiciary,[36] the history of how the Nazi past has been dealt with on a psychological level, together with the public opinion that has sustained and enveloped this process. This would lead us into deep layers of collective desire for repression. It would uncover the feelings of solidarity within the judiciary that have been virtually untouched by political upheavals, and in the end we would find that such symbolic punishment of a handful of old men is quite pointless. The dead are not brought back to life by such punishment. The honor of those condemned by the People's Court has, in any case, nothing to do with the fate of the perpetrators. "Retribution" as the purpose of punishment seems harder to justify now, four or five decades after the events, than ever before. What the prosecutors in Berlin may yet bring to light—and what may lead to another guilty verdict—is nothing more than a sop to calm a public that is morally outraged and has every right to be so. But it doesn't really make sense any more. In life, and in the life of a nation, there are some things you can't make up for later once the time has passed when reparation would have been appropriate.

There are more important things than symbolic declarations in the Bundestag or the attempt to get a few more convictions in the race against time: namely, a more thorough historical examination of Nazi law, an answer to the basic problems of legal theory, as well as the creation of a certain minimum standard of political awareness and political ethics in the culture at large.

PART THREE

The Postwar
Aftermath

ELEVEN

The Legal System and Judicial Policy in Germany, 1945–1949

For some time now, the period from 1945 to 1949 has been a separate field of study among German historians. Research institutes and funding have created a new scholarly specialty.[1]

By contrast, the study of the legal history of these years is still in its infancy.[2] There is no comprehensive account of the nullification of Nazi law by the legislation of the military government, the Control Council, the various occupying powers, and later the restored West German Parliament. It was a complex process dependent on many contingencies. A detailed analysis of this process could provide insight into the understanding of the law in this period, and into the prevailing notion of what was considered typically "National Socialist."[3] We also know little about the methodological approach of the judges, who had to operate a superficially "de-Nazified" legal system and render decisions in the new spirit by using traditional methods. Only for the British occupation zone do we now have a study of the reconstruction of the judicial system;[4] local studies are rare.[5] And when it comes to the de-Nazification and reappointment of judges and prosecutors, we have more memoirs and partially substantiated hypotheses than solid studies. The reasons for this may be that it is the most sensitive and darkest issue, and one that can form the starting point for explaining many of the characteristics of the "failure to come to terms with the past."

The reasons why legal history has so far been hesitant in examining this period are varied. Apart from its general reluctance to venture beyond the nineteenth century, legal history left the years 1945–1949 in the dark primarily because they were seen as a "transition" and "prehistory" to the Federal Republic. Naturally, the legal situation of Germany, the creation of the sovereignty of the *Länder*, and the Basic Law attracted the most attention from scholars. Historians were evidently more interested in other issues than the judicial system: for example, Germany's capitulation, the outbreak of the Cold War, the political reconstruction, the economic rebuilding, and the history of the parties, churches, unions, and so on. To this we must add another observation: After the most important Nazi laws had been invalidated by the military government (Law No. 1) and the Control Council (Law No. 1 of September 20, 1945), all subsequent measures affecting the judicial system were enacted before a public of legal professionals but without popular participation. While the public was certainly aware of Nazi crimes, the Nuremberg trials, and de-Nazification as "legal problems," it is only natural that its attention was focused primarily on economic and political problems. It hardly took note of the re-opening of the courts and the appointment of judges or of the profound basic issues (depoliticization of judges, natural law vs. legal positivism). The judiciary was happy to leave it that way, since it had little inclination or cause to openly discuss its problems over methodology and personnel policies.

From 1947 on, when political developments began to focus on the establishment of the Federal Republic, the central methodological questions had already been discussed and the reconstruction of the judicial system had been largely completed. That is why the session on the "legal system" proved relatively easy during constitutional deliberations at Herrenchiemsee and in the Parliamentary Council. The courts were already working and the professional associations were up and running. Still missing, apart from social jurisdiction, was the organizational superstructure provided by a federal jurisdiction and constitutional guarantees of judicial independence, on the one hand, and the basic legal rights of the citizen, on the other. However, there was essentially consensus on these issues in the programmatic declarations by former émigré groups, the parties, the unions, and expert committees.[6] One can indeed say that the creators of the Basic Law "devoted such special care to the judicial power because they were well aware of how the administration of justice had been undermined and perverted by the Nazi regime. The creation of a separate and independent judicial power was thus among the special goals of the creators of the Constitution."[7] Still, compared to the very thorough discussions about other fundamental issues concerning the reconstruction of the state in the Basic Law, there was widespread consensus on which path to take when it came to the judicial system: secure its independence, retain the basic outlines of the existing court system, create a strong constitutional jurisdiction, and assign jurisdiction, except for that of the highest courts, to the Länder.[8]

While it is thus understandable that the subject of the administration of justice and judicial policy from 1945 to 1949 has attracted little attention, there is good reason to change that. For it is evident that the process of grappling with the legal norms left behind by National Socialism, the nearly complete absorption of the old judicial personnel into the new system in the West, and the fundamental rejection of the previous principles in the Soviet occupation zone (later the German Democratic Republic), were extraordinarily important developments of social policy. The current constitution of the courts, the intellectual profile of the entire judicial system of the postwar period, and especially the manner in which Nazi crimes were dealt with by the courts can all be traced back to the events of those years.

The year 1945 did not witness a revolution in the classic sense.[9] However, the capitulation of the Reich and the Allied assumption "of supreme authority with respect to Germany"[10] did produce the most important consequence of a revolution: the destruction of the old legal system and the creation of a new one.

The essential war aim of the Allies was to destroy the Nazi system along with its institutions and the legal system that supported them.[11] The goal of the war was not only military defeat, but also the mental and social remaking of the enemy. From the very outset, the elimination of Nazi law was regarded as the logical consequence of capitulation.[12]

In theory there were several ways in which this could be achieved. The clearest solution would have been to declare all sovereign acts by the Nazi state null and void. According to the traditional notion of when a legal act was invalid, the Hitler state would have to have been a despotic regime without legitimacy, from the outset and in an "obvious" way. Nobody, however, took this position,[13] either because the regime had been legitimated at home by the de facto approval of the majority of the people, or because it had been internationally recognized. Moreover, the unpredictable consequences this position would have had on legal security by invalidating countless sovereign acts during the twelve years of the regime made it impossible to implement.

A less radical solution would have been to declare that henceforth at least the legislative sovereign acts between 1933 and 1945 were invalid. This would have affected not only all of the *Reichsgesetzblatt*, but also unpublished Führer decrees, autonomous statute law, legislative acts by the Nazis, and more. This position, too, proved unrealistic in view of the obvious catastrophic impact this would have on legal security.[14] The only feasible approach appeared to be a middle course that would permit the elimination of obvious Nazi law without posing an excessive threat to legal security. As early as 1943 the American and British planning groups envisaged a return to the "pre-Hitler system of law."[15] To that end they drew up lists of laws and regulations that appeared to be typically National Socialist and, most of all, incompatible with human rights.

However, until these legal norms were actually abrogated, only partial legal systems existed in the chaos at the end of the war. In the West, Eisenhower claimed "the highest legislative, judicial, and executive power" in the territory under his control;[16] the Soviets did the same in the East. Behind the front lines there existed military justice and a makeshift regular jurisdiction that was set up by the Allies in the immediate aftermath and that was dependent on them.[17] Where the power of the German state was still intact, it carried through with the Nazi legal system "to the bitter end." This limbo state, partly already under military control, partly in a state of anarchy, lasted from the fall of 1944 to June 1945. Nazi law had been abrogated at all levels of Allied authority, without coordination and according to the needs of the day. The result was an extraordinary legal fragmentation.

▐▐▐▐ Following the official takeover of the power of the German state by the Allies on June 5, 1945, the American military government repealed a first batch of Nazi laws.[18] It prohibited interpreting the law that remained in force according to Nazi ideology and drawing on decisions and literature from the Nazi period.[19] Decisions should be based on the "clear meaning of the text," though this rule failed precisely in borderline cases. This law constituted the first partial foundation of the new legal system. It reveals the technique the Allies used: removing the ideological core through legislation in the form of open-ended lists that could be expanded at will and steering the judicial personnel, which had not been replaced in its entirety for practical considerations, in the desired direction by committing it to a new system of values. There are several sketches of this system of values, for example, in the military government's Law No. 1,[20] the Potsdam Agreement of August 2, 1945,[21] and the Control Council's Proclamation No. 3 of October 20, 1945.[22] Everything was secured by a vague threat of punishment (Law No. 1 of the Military Government, art. V), which clearly reveals the dilemma of having to implant a liberal system by force as well as the distrust of the German judges.

The Control Council left standing the changes to the legal system that the occupying authorities had made up to August 1945, and it sternly advised the German authorities and courts to adhere to the new legal situation.[23] Its Law No. 1 of September 20, 1945,[24] proceeded to repeal a second, considerably larger batch of Nazi laws, but it, too, included only spectacular fragments of Nazi legislation. Many of the subsequent court battles over the continuing validity of legal norms from the period 1933–1945 go back to the lack of precision in this first measure.

The later supplements to Law No. 1 dealt initially with penal law,[25] so that by mid-1947 the special penal law, which had arisen alongside the Penal Code, had been cut back to where it had been in 1933. Legal norms were also repealed in the field of administrative jurisdiction[26] and especially in marriage law,[27] also in inheritance law,[28] labor law,[29] land law,[30] film law,[31] and state church law.[32] The fact that the occupying powers repealed additional Nazi laws in their respective zones didn't help much to clarify the situation.[33] For example, the American military government and the Control Council did not invalidate § 48, sec. 1 of the Testamentary Law of July 31, 1938, and the Decree on the Regulation of Inheritance Law of October 4, 1944, but the authorities in the British zone did,[34] though it was understood outside the British zone, as well, that this was Nazi law.[35]

Slowly it became clear that ever longer lists of repealed Nazi laws would not be able to solve the problem entirely. Like it or not, the remaining difficulties had to be left to the judicial system. However, since the Allies had different ideas about how to deal with the judiciary and were projecting their own, different legal traditions onto the German situation, there was certainly no uniform solution.

Before we turn to the substantive content of this administration of justice, I will sketch at least the outlines of the organizational rebuilding of the judicial system and the praxis of rehiring judicial personnel, for both factors had significant repercussions on the content itself.

IV. April and May 1945 saw the "cessation of the administration of justice," a scenario hitherto known only in theory (§ 203 of the Civil Code, § 245 of the Code of Civil Procedure). However, away from the front some of the Amtsgerichte and Landesgerichte remained intact. Even the Supreme Court of the Reich was formally "ready for service"[36] until April 20, 1945, when the Americans closed it down and set up a commission to oversee its administration.[37] The commission was subsequently dissolved by the Soviets on October 8, 1945.[38]

Eisenhower's Proclamation No. 1, which he issued as Supreme Commander of the Allied Forces, declared: "All German courts . . . within the occupied territories are closed until further notice. Jurisdiction is revoked throughout the occupied territories from the People's

Court, the Special Courts, the SS Police Courts, and all other extraordinary courts. Resumption of work by the criminal and civil courts . . . will be authorized as soon as circumstances permit."[39] Accordingly, regular and administrative courts in the American zone were shut down, the special courts and party courts were abolished, and the admission of jurists to the practice of law became subject to review.[40] The Soviet Military Administration, the British Control Commission, and the French Chief Military Command took corresponding steps in their respective zones.

These negative measures were soon followed by constructive legislation from the Control Council.[41] Initially this legislation gave the impression of an all-German structure of the judiciary: the Law on the Constitution of the Courts, in the version of March 22, 1924, was taken as the starting point, and the plan called for Amtsgerichte and Landgerichte, as well as Oberlandgerichte. Jurisdictions were to be what they had been before 1933, with an increase in the value in litigation before the Amtsgerichte to 2,000 Reichs marks. Subsequently the foundations were laid for the jurisdiction of labor courts and for administrative jurisdiction.[42] The first Amtsgerichte and Landgerichte resumed work as early as the end of May 1945. The fall of 1945 saw the appointment of the first presidents of Oberlandesgerichte. In the spring of 1946 regular jurisdiction was more or less in working order again. It faced roughly the same problems in all four zones. Unfinished cases had backed up. A much smaller body of judges, some of them underqualified, was overburdened, especially by divorce cases and a rise in crime, to which were added crimes from the Nazi period that had to be dealt with in the courts. Everywhere there was uncertainty about what law should be used, about lines of continuity with the Weimar judicial system, about how to deal with the legislation of the Control Council and the hastily enacted new law. Moreover, all German jurists were subject to the Allied de-Nazification program.[43] In organizational terms nothing was uniform. Still, there were some supraregional organizational centers of judicial administration. The most important, apart from the German Central Administration for the Judicial System in the Soviet zone, were the Central Judicial Office of the British zone, and after July 24, 1948, the Legal Office of the Administration of the Unified Economic Region.[44] The last two institutions became—organizationally and in part also in terms of personnel—the immediate precursors of the first Federal Ministry of Justice.

That essentially covers the elements common to the four zones. As time went on, consensus among the occupying powers increasingly eroded in the field of judicial policy. Developments unique to each zone proved stronger than any consensus. Those developments began early, and their roots definitely reached back to the war years, when plans for the structure of the judicial system were made in émigré groups and among the Allies.

1. This was emphatically the case for the *Soviet zone*. To be sure, the proclamations concerning the judicial system that were issued by the KPD, the SPD, the Christian Democratic Union (CDU), and the Liberal Democratic Party of Germany (LDPD) in the summer of 1945 were largely the same. However, thanks to good preparation and with protection from the advancing Soviet forces, initiative groups of the KPD were able to attend to the judicial system relatively quickly. Depending on the local situation, untainted bourgeois jurists, reactivated retirees, prominent citizens, and members of the KPD were appointed "judges for immediate service" and entrusted with exercising the function of judges in village and city courts, in Amtsgerichte and Kreisgerichte, in Bezirksgerichte and Volksgerichte.[45] Mecklenburg, Mark Brandenburg, and the province of Saxony were under stronger Communist control, while Saxony, Thuringia, and Berlin were at first predominantly in the hands of the noncommunist parties. Order No. 17 of the Soviet Military Administration in Germany (SMAD), issued on July 17, 1945, created an umbrella organization for the judicial departments of the newly formed *Länder* administrations in the German Central Administration for Justice (Deutsche Zentralverwaltung für Justiz). The Socialist Unity Party (SED) (founded on April 21–22, 1946) acquired growing influence in the central administration, though for the sake of appearance it left the respected Weimar politician Eugen Schiffer (1860–1954) at the head of the institution until 1948. Behind him stood the Soviet justice officials of SMAD, whose help is gratefully acknowledged in modern, official East German accounts of the events.[46]

As far as the structure of the courts was concerned, the Soviet authorities, in accord with Control Council Law No. 4 of October 30, 1945, returned to the 1924 Law on the Constitution of the Law Courts,[47] while the approach that was taken in disputes involving labor law and social security marked a departure from tradition.[48] Heated disagreements developed over administrative jurisdiction. The original conception of the Control Council and the Soviets called for its establishment in all *Länder* of the Soviet zone, but in the end it was set up only in Thuringia, Mark Brandenburg, and Mecklenburg.[49]

A direct manifestation of the shift in political power was the gradual restructuring of the body of judges through a deliberate personnel policy on the part of the SED. An initial phase of improvisation was followed by a period when Communists, Social Democrats, and bourgeois elements coexisted. It lasted until the SED felt strong enough to drive out the noncommunists, especially Social Democrats, in systematic purges.

The SED ran into particularly vigorous opposition in Berlin. As Hilde Benjamin has described it, "the president of the reopened Superior Court of Justice for Berlin, Dr. Georg Strucksberg, also resisted every effort to bring new manpower into the Berlin judicial system, even though the number of judges declined to 213 in 1946. Until 1948 reactionary forces in leading positions of the Berlin judicial system succeeded in preventing courses for people's judges (Volksrichterkurse) from being held."[50] A similar situation prevailed in Thuringia, whose "bourgeois" state judicial administration found itself in constant conflict with the central administration. The clashes intensified into a genuine judicial crisis, which was debated in the Thuringian Landtag (state parliament) under the slogans "separation of powers," "independence of judges," and "people's judges."[51] One side advocated that judges be politically tied to the SED (selection of the prosecutors general and the presidents of the Higher Regional Courts by the parliaments), that they be subject to dismissal, that former members of the Nazi party not be used on principle (in keeping with SMAD Order No. 204), and that gaps in personnel be filled by rapidly trained "people's judges." The other side, basing itself on the ideas of the liberal Rechtsstaat and natural law, promoted the model of the apolitical judge immune from dismissal and criticized the sweeping refusal to rehire former members of the Nazi party. The crisis was intensified by a decision of the Administrative High Court of Thuringia, which challenged the contention that graduates of the people's judges courses were qualified to hold judicial office.[52]

The SED, with support from SMAD, pushed through its policies both at the center and, after 1948 at the latest, in the Länder. Graduates from the first courses for people's judges (1946–1948)[53] who were members of the SED went to work for the prosecutor's office. It was not long before the SED also chose lay judges and gave them uniform "schooling." By 1950 the proportion of laymen trained as "people's judges" among judges and prosecutors had grown to 50 percent. Only in the 1950s was the SED able to push through its policies at the law schools in Berlin, Leipzig, Halle, and Jena. This success allowed the party to slowly dispense with the political makeshift of the "people's judges." Private practice also existed for some time as a fall-back for lawyers who did not want to work in the judicial system or were not hired.

2. The administrative concept in the *British zone,* centralist in nature with a clear predominance of the military government, was relatively similar to its Soviet and French counterparts. However, the decision to pursue the reconstruction of the judiciary on the basis of Oberland-gericht (Higher Regional Court) districts steered the development in a special direction. The eight presidents of the Oberlandgerichte were affiliated directly with the Legal Division of the Control Commission for Germany and "functioned practically as Ministers of Justice at the time."[54] They issued legal decrees, had the right to initiate laws, and acted as expert consultants on legislation. After October 1, 1946, the legislative authority of the presidents and some of their authority on matters of personnel—namely, the right to appoint the presiding judges of courts and the heads of prosecutor's offices—was transferred to the Central Office of Justice of the British Zone, which was headed by Wilhelm Kiesselbach.[55] At first this office was significantly more important than the Ministries of Justice of the *Länder,* which did not receive their full authority until 1947.

Initially the presidents themselves tried to smooth out differences in the way the law was administered in the various Oberlandgericht districts. But the call for a Supreme Court grew steadily more urgent.[56] Eventually, once the Reichsgericht had been shut down for good and a bizonal court had failed, the Supreme Court for the British Zone was set up in Cologne. It functioned until September 1950, and it formed, both in its personnel and in the content of its decisions, the most important connecting link between the tradition of the Reichsge-richt and the Federal Supreme Court (Bundesgerichtshof) that was inaugurated on October 8, 1950.[57]

A detailed account of how the various jurisdictions were recon-structed or newly created is not possible within the framework of the present essay.[58] The rebuilding of the bar, including the quarrel over the admission of lawyers from the East to the bar in the British zone,[59] would be a chapter to itself. One topic we cannot skip over, however, is personnel policy in the judicial system of the British zone. Bernhard Diestelkamp, drawing on the study by J. R. Wenzlau, summarized the findings as follows:

As for jurists in the British zone, a change from the initial policy of radical exclusion to a policy of punishment began as early as October of 1945 with the "50:50" or "piggyback rule." It stated that for every jurist with a clean political past, one jurist who was compromised by his past (though at first only formally) could be rehired into the judicial system. Despite this early relaxation of the policy, it was not possible to fill all posts in the judicial system, which by the middle of 1946 was once again thoroughly organized. In mid-June of 1946, the British therefore lifted the 50 percent clause in favor of all those who had been cleared by the de-Nazification procedures. This set in motion the return of growing numbers of judges and prosecutors. By mid-1948, 80–90 percent of Landgerichtsräte and Landgerichtsdirektoren (county court judges and directors) were former party members.[60]

A recent study of Braunschweig has examined this process in concrete detail.[61] The solidarity among jurists and what was referred to as their "outstanding professional qualification" and anticommunist attitude—the only acceptable element of Nazi ideology—proved stronger on the whole than the principle of not rehiring judges with a Nazi past. In addition, the occupying powers themselves did not act in a consistent manner. The process of de-Nazification itself was seen as a burdensome compulsory exercise imposed by the victors. Hence jurists were willing to help colleagues get a job, even without the need to invoke a common background, training, professional membership, and the like. The British tolerated this return of the old judicial personnel, though in part they were also outmaneuvered. As a result, "contrary to the original intent of the British to undertake a particularly radical cleansing of the judicial system, it was here, in particular, that the almost complete restoration of the old personnel structure was completed long before the founding of the Federal Republic."[62]

3. The judicial system in the *American zone* was not rebuilt on the old court districts but via the *Länder* that were created in 1945. Judicial administration culminated in the Ministries of Justice, which in turn came together in the Länderrat for a certain degree of cooperation. Still, there was neither a uniform court system covering the entire U.S. zone nor a common Supreme Court.[63]

De-Nazification of the judicial system[64] was pursued in a broad and bureaucratic manner, and the outcome was as unsatisfactory as it was in other professions. It failed precisely because it was set up as a mass process, and it had to be halted in 1948.[65] As in the British zone, many opportunities were found to rehire as "auxiliary judges" jurists who had been nominal members of the Nazi party, as well as those with a real Nazi past; later they were quietly given permanent positions. Despite an initial shortage of personnel, the judicial system in the American zone was quickly completed in the traditional sense. It also exerted a strong influence on the other zones, especially after the merger into the bi-zone, which also gave rise to an administrative agreement concerning the administration of justice.

4. In judicial policy, as in occupation policy as such, the *French zone* pursued its own path, one strictly concerned with demarcating the

French sphere. When it came to the structure of the system of courts, the French stuck with the pre-1933 Law on the Constitution of the Law Courts, in keeping with the Control Council's Law No 4. Procedural law was uniformly regulated for the *Länder*. All questions concerning the judicial system were handled centrally from Baden-Baden, and important decisions were handed down by the Supreme Military Court in Rastatt.[66]

The style of administration was that of a colonial power, "based neither on ideology nor on morality, but oriented solely toward its usefulness to the French state."[67] After a particularly harsh phase of initial measures, moral cleansing and democratization—goals that were very important to the Americans—no longer seemed to play a special role. Little work has so far been done on de-Nazification and the rehiring of judicial personnel.[68]

5. The situation of the judicial system in *Berlin* was not comparable to that in any of the occupied zones.[69] To begin with, there was a joint judicial administration, which, as I have indicated, ran into problems especially in the Soviet sector. The growing tensions in the Allied Headquarters and the crippling of the Control Council also dragged the judicial system into the Berlin crisis in 1948. The Berlin administration split, and an exodus of judicial personnel to the West began. In 1949 the President of the Superior Court of Justice for Berlin, Dr. Strucksberg, and the prosecutor general, Dr. Neumann, cleared out of their offices in East Berlin. A separate Landgericht and the Superior Court of Justice were set up in the West. In the East, meanwhile, the vacuum was filled relatively quickly in keeping with the SED's ideas.

As one can see, it is difficult to give an overall assessment of the organizational rebuilding of the judicial system in the occupied zones and in Berlin. Even though the starting situation was much the same everywhere, the respective national legal traditions of the occupying powers and the basic political lines of occupation policy led to different results. For instance, the Western zones did not take a coordinated organizational approach, while the Soviets and the Americans essentially pursued similar paths. On the other hand, the Western zones and the Soviet zone took a diametrically opposite position on the rehiring of judges compromised by their political past.

As for the intellectual outlook of judges and the results of their administration of justice, the differences in personnel policy were far more momentous than the organizational differences, which in any case were gradually smoothed out in the Western zones. Personnel policy is indeed the key to the quite conscious and deliberate continuation in the West of the traditions of the Reichsgericht, the Reich Fiscal

Court, the Reich Insurance Office, and the Higher Administrative Courts.

V "The German legal system of today presents itself to the observer as a structure of many components, which for the time being is held together by the pre-Nazi German legal tradition." This is how Walter Lewald aptly characterized the situation that was created between 1945 and 1948.[70] This being so, the judicial system had considerable difficulty determining what should be applied as "valid law" in the first place. These difficulties began with the procuring of texts and continued in questions of whether a regulation was "still," "no longer," or "once again" valid and what the occupying power had said about it. Add to this the grievous absence of uniform guidance by the Higher Courts and a lack of communication among the courts through a reliable publication of decisions. Moreover, jurisprudence was slow to resume its analytic, critical, and descriptive work.

However, the problems of determining what should be regarded as "valid law" and how it should be applied were not primarily technical in nature. Rather, they were intimately connected to the entire political climate, the personnel structure of the judiciary, and the "prior understanding" of the judges. A variety of balances were struck between the justice officials of the occupying powers and the German legal profession, which had remained intact in the West. Respected members of the profession with a clean political record (E. Schiffer, W. Kieselbach, H. Schetter, H. Freiherr von Hodenberg, G. Radbruch, and others) gained considerable influence in the process, because they could act with impeccable professional qualifications and a self-confidence born of a clear conscience. In their dealings with the occupying powers they propagated a judicial system based on the central notion of "depoliticization." This was a catchword with a variety of meanings: It aimed at judicial independence from interference by the occupying powers, a commitment to natural law and supra-temporal spiritual values, and a return to the principles of the civic *Rechtsstaat*. The experience of the massive politicization of the judicial system under National Socialism, together with the widely shared desire not to hear another word about politics, seemed to make the champions of this position nearly unassailable.[71] Only a few scattered voices pointed out that a thoroughly restorationist program could also sail under the flag of depoliticization and that the vaunted apolitical judges before 1933 had in fact been quite political in their thinking and decisionmaking.[72] The good intentions of its advocates notwithstanding, depoliticization was also a shield against pressure from the occupying powers to remove former party members among the judges and against the punishment of colleagues, a task the victors imposed upon a reluctant judicial system.

In the Soviet zone, the Western slogans of "human rights," "basic rights," "judicial independence," "legal security," "the idea of justice," and "depoliticization" were branded as elements of bourgeois ideology. At the same time, however, the Soviets also criticized legal positivism as "formalism" and talked about overcoming it, with the goal of allowing the administration of justice to take sides politically while ignoring all prior law. Criticism of positivism did not die down in the West and the East until the early 1950s, more or less at the same time: in the West with the gradual waning of the renaissance of natural law, in the East with the move to commit the judicial system to "democratic legitimacy."

These few remarks reveal the deep and early ruptures that the division of Germany caused in the judicial system and in judicial policy. In 1946 and 1947 legal journals could still publish reports about the development of the judicial system in all of Germany, East and West could still discuss the application of Control Council legislation (for example, Law No. 10), and all-German legal conferences could still take place. The first two conferences (Bad-Godesberg, June 16–17, 1946, and Wiesbaden, December 3–6, 1947)[73] were unquestionably all-German events. However, at the conference in Konstanz, June 2–5, 1947,[74] there were heated debates especially about the application of Control Council Law No. 10 and the depoliticization of the judicial system. Three months later, at the conference in Bad-Godesberg, September 30–October 1, 1947,[75] the break was obvious: The representatives of the Soviet occupation zone, H. Lange and E. Melsheimer, were no longer allowed to participate.

We have to bear this development in mind as we consider individual court decisions on which legal norms were still "valid law." It becomes clear very quickly how the overall legal-political climate affected these decisions. In the Soviet zone, as in the West, it was initially necessary to regard the bulk of legal norms from the Weimar Republic and the Nazi period as still in force. The first layers of clear Nazi law were then stripped away by the legislation of the Control Council and by the legislative acts of SMAD and the judicial administrations of the various *Länder*.[76] Judicial decisions on the continuing validity of laws enacted after 1933, such as were left, had to deal especially with the following issues:

—the restriction of legal redress in criminal cases by the Emergency Decree of June 14, 1932 (repealed by § 17 of the Decree of September 1, 1939)[77]

—the regulations concerning the forcing of the accusation (§§ 172 ff. of the Code of Criminal Procedure, repealed by § 2 of the Decree of August 13, 1942)[78]
—the continuing validity of § 359 of the Code of Criminal Procedure in the redaction of 1943[79]
—reinstatement of the prohibition of *reformatio in peius*[80]
—the earlier versions of §§ 175 ff., 240, 339 of the Penal Code and the continuing validity of § 170 of the Penal Code[81]
—the powers of the state prosecutor in marital matters according to the Decree of March 18, 1943,[82] and in challenges to a child's legitimacy[83]
—the continuing validity of § 1549 of the Civil Code in the version before 1938[84]
—the legitimation of marriages to soldiers killed in the war[85]
—the invalidity of anti-Jewish administrative acts

The main issues of these decisions were clearly in the area of criminal and family law.

From the outset the prosecution of Nazi crimes and war crimes was vigorously pursued in the Soviet zone, especially when it concerned crimes against "antifascists." The legal basis was above all Control Council Law No. 10. In the Soviet zone, failure to apply this law and delays in applying it because of its incompatibility with the prohibition of retroactive laws were seen and denounced as a sign of "bourgeois legal thinking."[86] This denunciation was aimed especially at the judicial system in Thuringia: eventually, under further pressure from criticism and SMAD Order No. 201, it came around "to a proper application of the law," as Benjamin later described it.[87] This SMAD order in August 1947, which made it possible to focus the trials on the major perpetrators and spare the mass of sympathizers and nominal party members, served to accelerate the trials and, above all, to calm the population, which had to be won over to the new regime.

On the question of what should be regarded as "valid law," there was consensus in the Western zones that the repeal of Nazi laws by the Allies had taken effect ex nunc, from the time of their repeal. The typical justification went like this: "It would lead to massive confusion and legal insecurity to pretend that those Nazi laws that are contrary to current notions were never present and to judge all legal situations arising from them as though these laws had never existed. The consequences would be highly deleterious, especially in the sphere of economic life."[88] However, there was already controversy surrounding the question of whether the repeal of Nazi laws by the Allies was final. While the prevailing position was to keep open the possibility of future repeals by the courts,[89] the Oberlandesgericht Hamburg, concerned to put a stop to the continuing uncertainty about the foundations of the law, declared that the power of judicial review of Nazi laws had come to an end.[90] That view did not prevail.

When courts were called upon to decide on the continuing validity of specific norms from the Nazi period, they drew on the familiar instruments of judicial methodology to explain their decisions. Justices argued from a norm's purpose and how it had come into being, pointed out the consequences of invalidating the norm, or invoked foreign legal systems in which comparable norms existed. Arguments that used "moral law," axioms of natural law, and the principles of the restored *Rechtsstaat* were methodologically the least secure, but could be understood by a broader public.

For example, there was a debate over whether the older version of § 175a, subsection 3 of the Penal Code should be used or the tougher version created by the law of June 28, 1935. Although this law had not been repealed by the Control Council, there were indications that this was a typical Nazi law. Some courts, invoking the legal-historical development of this paragraph, which had seen several attempts to tighten it after 1919, concluded that the expanded version was the result of a legitimate process and its application could continue. However, they conceded that decisions of the Reichsgericht concerning this norm had been influenced by Nazi tendencies and should therefore be disregarded.[91] Parallel problems were discussed in connection with § 218 of the Penal Code.[92] Arguing that the goals of norms from the period after 1933 must be seen as reasonable also under changed circumstances, some courts found, for example, that a Decree on Rights of Timeless Value of November 16, 1940,[93] and § 1595a of the Civil Code[94] were valid. It was rare for positive law to be directly passed over with reference to contrary natural law or, say, "the most elementary principles of the system of criminal law."[95] A comprehensive analysis of the decisions rendered between 1945 and 1949 might show that the practical effects of the so-called renaissance of natural law on decisionmaking and opinions did not run as deep as has sometimes been assumed.

The most important debates were triggered by the question about the validity of administrative acts and judicial decisions from the Nazi period.[96] Could the Nazi state enact "valid law" while at the same time being morally reprehensible? Anyone who answered this question in the affirmative was compelled to make a principled separation between legal and moral judgments.[97] Prevailing opinion after 1945 condemned such a separation nearly as unanimously as had been the case between 1933 and 1945. The opposing position should have followed up by asking if this meant that all sovereign acts by the Nazi state were invalid from the outset. Nobody advocated this position in its extreme version. Instead, prevailing opinion, drawing different lines of distinction and invoking various justifications, sought to do justice to the historical fact that National Socialism could enact valid law in many areas of daily life as well as obvious unjust law that was invalid from the outset.

That is why sovereign acts based on Nazi laws were initially regarded as valid in principle. There were legal exceptions to this—for instance, the possibility of repealing decisions by family courts that were "based entirely or predominantly on racial, political, or religious grounds"[98] or the nullification of sentences handed down on the basis of the so-called *Volksschädlings* Decree (Decree on enemies of the people).[99] Other than that, the invalidation of court decisions and administrative acts was possible only by using the conventional procedural and administrative rules. As examples of judicial grappling with these questions, I will mention the invalidity of the auctioning off of Jewish property,[100] the validity of a deletion in the land registry,[101] and the execution of an immoral legal title.[102] Other cases concerned the question of whether the suspension of criminal prosecutions ordered by the Nazi state was in force.[103] The problems posed by "administrative acts contrary to natural law" emerged very clearly in a case from 1942, in which permission for the sale of land had been denied because the person concerned was considered politically and ideologically unreliable. The courts found that this administrative act had been valid, arguing that a contrary decision would mean "that all administrative acts and many court decisions of the twelve years in question would have to be subjected to a review and many of them declared to be invalid. However, this would throw all legal and economic life into chaos."[104] H. Coing criticized this justification by arguing that sanctioning sovereign acts that are contrary to natural law as lawful for reasons of legal security imposed "the stain of illegality on resistance to these acts."[105]

The punishment of Nazi crimes, which was progressively handed over to the regular courts, got off the ground slowly in the Western zones and was not carried through in a uniform manner. Justices were reluctant to apply Control Council Law No. 10—originally intended for the administration of justice by the Allies—because it left the facts of a case vague and was "retroactive." The Penal Code was preferred as the legal basis for prosecution, especially in the so-called informant trials and the euthanasia trials. On the whole, West German jurists were of the opinion that they were dealing here with a special political jurisdiction that lay outside the regular judicial system and that they should do their best to avoid it by invoking the slogan of "depoliticization."[106]

It is well known that the omissions in this area during the first years have grown into a heavy burden for the German judicial system.[107]

VI. Although there was a common normative starting point in the legislation of the Control Council, the question of how the judicial system developed between 1945 and 1949, and what connecting lines we can draw to other problems of reconstruction, can be answered only separately for the various zones. The Soviet zone, in particular, went its own path, as did the French zone to some extent. The British and American zones preserved certain shared elements, thanks to a joint background of common law and a related Anglo-American conception of politics. The British, however, promoted centralized institutions, while the Americans in general pursued their course through the *Länder*. The British and American zones also conducted de-Nazification in quite different ways, though the results of their efforts were very similar.

The Soviet administration removed the old judicial elite in its zone by a "revolution from above," allowed a new elite loyal to the SED to move into its place, and replaced the old dictatorship by a new one. By contrast, the Western powers in part did not seek a break with tradition in their zones, and in part were unable to implement such a break against opposition from the legal profession. The legal profession, held together by common training, professionalism, and a traditional sense of elitism, remained essentially untouched. The profession dropped only individual jurists who were simply too heavily burdened by their Nazi past to be retained. Jurists used some common phrases, which always contain a nugget of truth but also a lot of self-deception and self-pity, to shield themselves from accountability: "I remained in place to prevent worse from happening," "I held up the ideal of nonpartisan judiciary in difficult times," "I served justice as best I could," and so on. After 1945 not a single judge was punished in West Germany for his activity under National Socialism. Not one of the approximately 2,000 continuing education conferences for judges and prosecutors that have been held since 1949 was devoted to the topic of National Socialist law. These facts shed a revealing light on the underlying attitudes.[108]

Features common to the overall development become visible only on a more abstract level where all political differences between the new directions taken after 1945 are ignored. If we look at the issue from this vantage point, it becomes clear that the methodology used in East and West moved along parallel tracks: In the first phase, Nazi laws that were heavily ideological and considered untenable were repealed by the legislative authority, and an improvised emergency administration of justice was put in place. The second phase saw the repeal of questionable norms by the courts. To help the new system of values take root, the occupying powers prohibited judges from following in the footsteps of the old judicature and judicial literature. They also attempted to guide the administration of justice by setting positive goals and committing it to values transcending positivism—be it the Western system of values or the higher law of the working class. Where there was little confidence that the judicial personnel was amenable to guidance, it was replaced. The third phase saw the enactment of new norms by a legislative power established under the protection of the occupying powers.

This process occurred in postwar Germany in stages between 1945 and 1949. It seems to have been based on a scheme that is always repeated when an old legal system is to be replaced by a new one in the wake of revolution or defeat in war: Highly visible symbols or symbolic figures of the old regime are immediately removed, and the top of the old legal system is cut off. The justice system bridges the gulf in public order until the new legislative power has established itself. The risks of transition this entails are ameliorated in various ways, depending on the circumstances: by ideological training of the judges or the intimidation or radical replacement of the judicial personnel. Once the new legislative authority starts working, the "hour of the judicial system"[109] is over and it returns to its original function, which is primarily supportive. Postwar Germany with its four zones provides a wealth of examples to illustrate all of these phases.

TWELVE

Theodor Maunz:
The Life of a Professor of
Constitutional Law

Theodor Maunz (1901–1993) has undergone a definitive meta-
morphosis: Once the pillar of the German doctrine of constitutional law, he has become its stumbling block and the center of controversy. All the undiscussed and undigested part of the German past
that seemed in part buried, in part paid off and forgiven, is reemerging
in disturbing and unpleasant ways.

The files of the "Maunz case" seemed closed. The obituaries for
the kind and reclusive old man, who died on September 10, 1993, had
been written, and there were no surprises. Most writers followed the
eulogy Peter Lerche had penned in the festschrift *Juristen im Portrait*
(Portraits of jurists [C. H. Beck, 1988]). Lerche took Maunz's Nazi
past, known to a wider public for thirty years, and marginalized it with
a single, skillfully obscuring sentence. That was not pretty, and it was
no testimony to the author's candor. But one could concede that
Maunz was, after all, still alive at the time, and Lerche was not writing
a scholarly study but a contribution to a festschrift.

There were dozens of professors with a Nazi past, though Maunz
was the only one whose past led to his spectacular fall as Minister of
Culture. This had engendered a lot of discussion in 1964, but later it
was all gradually forgotten again. For the younger generation of university students at the time, the "Maunz affair,"[1] triggered by Gerhard
Haney (Jena), Konrad Redeker, and Hildegard Hamm-Brücher, was
a revelation within the halls of academia. Together with the cases of
M. Oberländer, H. Globke, and G. Freiherr von Pölnitz, and the
Auschwitz and Eichmann trials, it was part of the postwar generation's
discovery of its own identity and another piece of ammunition in the
generational conflict. These cases and trials fed the younger generation's distrust of declarations and hush-ups from the official political
establishment and helped set in motion the student movement of 1968.

Maunz appeared tailor-made as an example of it all: His solid, though not exactly inspiring, textbook on German constitutional law seemed an indestructible model of the Federal Republic, like the Volkswagen Beetle—and like the Beetle it had its hidden roots in the Third Reich. The commentary on the Basic Law by Maunz and Günther Dürig became the constitutive oracle, so to speak, for the new state. "Papa Maunz" was a Munich institution, especially when it came to obtaining seminar certificates in public law. He was "an incomparable teacher (and a very lenient examiner)," as Peter Lerche wrote, adding that Maunz "showed almost too much lenience."[2] Kindness, courtesy, unusual diligence and self-discipline, tolerance, an orientation toward praxis, a scholarly freedom from bias: Nobody who ever knew him would deny that he possessed all these qualities. As Lerche put it: "So far hardly anybody has been able to tip his hat to Maunz sooner than Maunz tipped his own."

It is likely that with the passage of time, the conviction will prevail that no truly independent idea can be linked with Maunz's name in the history of constitutional law, despite the extensive bibliography of his publications (running into the many hundreds). Scholars will admit that his contributions to whatever was prevailing law were rarely original or bold. Instead, they can be seen as the embodiment of the middle-of-the-road, conflict-avoiding opinion. As the *Frankfurter Allgemeine Zeitung* put it, his publications are "characterized by a pithiness tinted by positivism and focused on the essential."[3] One could at least mention that "leniency" in grading student papers also had the welcome effect of raising income from enrollments. But apart from this, until recently the unanimous view went something like this: "It is true that Maunz had a Nazi past, there is no denying that, but he had long since transcended it by his active participation in the democratic state and his sincere work in developing the Federal Republic's constitutional and administrative law." If one got a little carried away by pathos, one might actually say, "His name is among the great names in German constitutional theory,"[4] or, "One cannot solemnly praise the jurisprudence of current public law without praising Maunz."[5]

However, a few characteristically puzzling questions remained unanswered. As early as 1934 a reviewer noted that Maunz had swiftly reversed "his position that was so diametrically contrary just last year" and had rushed to embrace Carl Schmitt's concrete-order theory with an "excessively repentant 'pater peccavi.'"[6] The lecturer *(Privatdozent)* Maunz—in 1932 a vehement champion of law and politics, and ardent critic of the "subversion of the legal position of the individual through the erosion and dissolution of existing legal guarantees"[7]—

was now waiting for a chair and emphasizing the political nature of law and the totalitarian nature of the Führer's will. As though to prove his absolute devotion to the party line, Maunz—a student of Hans Nawiasky, whose Jewish background had already embroiled him in one of the largest anti-Jewish hate campaigns[8]—appeared as a speaker in 1936 at the conference on "the Jews in jurisprudence." There he expounded on the "fatal predilection of Jewish theorists of administrative law for the liberal doctrine of the *Rechtsstaat*."[9] In 1935 he received an appointment in Freiburg, and in 1937 he was made full professor. Maunz, who had administrative experience, knew what it meant in practical terms to replace the word *Gesetzmäßigkeit* (conformity to the law) with *Rechtmäßigkeit* (conformity to what is right) in the lecture hall, to declare the "end of subjective-public right," and to pronounce arrests by the Gestapo sovereign acts outside the judicial realm.[10] The fact that he did not break off his ties to the church and attended Sunday mass in a village in the Black Forest, away from the public limelight of Freiburg, proved a farsighted insurance strategy. After the Nazi system had gone down in ruin, Maunz was able to join the Christian-Social camp, become involved in the "battle over the Southwest state" as an expert adviser, participate in the deliberations over the Basic Law, write the textbook *Deutsches Staatsrecht* (German constitutional law), and accept an appointment in Munich in 1952. In Munich he became a "regular member" of the CSU and was soon after appointed Bavarian Minister of Culture. Thus he had returned to where he had begun, with parliamentary democracy and the *Rechtsstaat*.

For a long time, the prevailing interpretation of Maunz's career had therefore gone something like this: While it had contained a good dose of opportunism, the dominant theme was solid professionalism, very hard work, pedagogical talent, and a propensity for a "conservative middle-of-the-road position," accompanied by decades of unquestioned work on behalf of parliamentary democracy. All that changed on September 24 and October 8, 1993, when the *Deutsche National-Zeitung (DNZ)*, the paper of Dr. Gerhard Frey, leader of the right-radical Deutsche Volksunion (DVU),[11] revealed that Maunz had been a "wonderful companion" and "important adviser" for twenty-five years. According to the *DNZ*, Maunz had written hundreds of anonymous articles for the paper, had advised the DVU in drafting its program and bylaws, and had continuously prepared legal opinions on party law and asylum law, on the Maastricht Treaty, on whether the *DNZ* could be mailed through the postal service, and on many other topics. And that was not all: "During the 1970s and for many years thereafter, Professor Maunz and Dr. Frey met weekly (usually on Monday) for several hours to discuss all important political and legal issues" (*DNZ,* September 24, 1993). The television show *Panorama* picked up the matter and asked Rupert Scholz (professor of public law and former minister of defense) and Roman Herzog (former professor of public law and now President of the Federal Republic) for their comments. The large newspapers and magazines responded (*Zeit, Spiegel, Süddeutsche Zeitung;* of course, the *Frankfurter Allgemeine Zeitung* did so only with a brief news agency report in the side column of the page). Nobody has any serious doubts about the essential truth of Dr. Frey's statements. It is obvious what interest Frey had in revealing triumphantly his close relationship with the best known commentator on the Basic Law. The *DNZ* and the DVU became respectable if "Germany's greatest legal scholar" (*DNZ,* September 24, 1993) and a "democrat through and through" (Scholz) had advised and helped them for many years.

This revelation may have been an embarrassment to Maunz's family (among them his son-in-law Franz Klein, the President of the Federal Fiscal Court),[12] to his assistants, to those who obtained *Habilitation* under him, and to his Ph.D. students. That did not bother Dr. Frey. He is not the kind of person who cares about such sensitivities and fears of contact with the political right wing. His intent is to move from the right wing into the conservative middle by systematically blurring the boundaries. Maunz's work was a godsend for this strategy. The neo-Nazis become more reputable if they can show that they have succeeded in penetrating into the very entrance hall, so to speak, of the Association of Constitutional Lawyers.

To date, the interpretations of this symbiotic relationship between Maunz and Frey have fallen into familiar patterns: Maunz "could not say no," and perhaps, Scholz speculated, the old gentleman "may have been somewhat abused." Some have argued that Frey, who has become wealthy from his mail-order business of extreme-right books, records, and videos, probably paid well for all the advice and writing. Moreover, Frey probably soothed Maunz's bruised ego after his fall as Minister of Culture by depicting the whole affair as the machinations of a leftist press campaign.

All these interpretations might be true individually or collectively. It is interesting that so far nobody has claimed that this was a case of uninterrupted continuity of extreme-right thinking since 1933. And in fact, the situation is not that clear-cut. We can probably come closer to understanding the type of person Maunz the jurist was by looking at his activities—right across changing regimes—as those of someone trying to create the best possible circumstances for his life and work.

Maunz was a *Vernunftrepublikaner*[13] and supporter of the *Rechtsstaat* when that was still part of the traditional code of conduct at the end of the Weimar Republic; he was a National Socialist as long as the others were, and a little bit more so and for a little longer; then he was once again a legal positivist with a touch of natural law. It all depended on the time and circumstances, like a chameleon that has the ability to adjust its color and temperature to the environment. Of course, the chameleon can do so only within a certain range. I think we can assume that the articles Maunz wrote for the *DNZ* reflect his real and deepest convictions. He was writing anonymously, and since he had emeritus status there was no pressure to toe anyone's line. The fact that he published his innermost convictions with strict secrecy about authorship reflects not so much a rudimentary consciousness of injustice as a finely honed sense of how much he could expect the public and his colleagues to put up with. His nose for taboos made him shy away from the conflict he knew his views would stir up. Maunz remained true to himself: During the Nazi period he "secretly" went to mass on Sundays, in the Federal Republic he "secretly" went to the right-wing radicals on Mondays. A double life as a strategy of maximizing his options.

Quite apart from the unsavory nature of these activities, wherein lies the moral problem for German constitutional law? In my view it is not with Maunz and his place in the history of his profession. Rather, the problem is with constitutional lawyers and professors as a corporate body. Events like these are not discussed within the Association of Constitutional Lawyers; in fact, they are probably not deemed worthy of discussion. The responsibility of a constitutional lawyer as teacher, scholar, expert witness, and counsel, against the backdrop of what we have learned from cases like that of Maunz—what a topic that would make! But no managing committee of the association has dared to open this Pandora's box. Those who listen closely will merely hear some embarrassed whispering for a while longer. After that, a brooding silence is likely to descend once again on the profession.

When the present essay appeared in a newspaper and in the journal *Kritische Justiz*,[14] it met with a broad response, especially in letters. The events surrounding the Maunz case were intimately linked with current politics.

Roman Herzog, at the time a candidate for the presidency of the Federal Republic, in this affair distanced himself repeatedly and unequivocally from his old teacher.[15] Faced with inquiries in the state parliament, the state government of Bavaria responded that none of its current members had anything to do with the DVU; Maunz had been the second minister in its ranks who had contacts to Frey.[16] Of course, it was soon revealed that there had been contacts between the state government and the so-called Republicans.[17] Frey himself attracted the interest of the media through his support for the surprise winner of the elections in Russia in December 1993, Vladimir Zhirinovsky. The latter thanked him and declared after the elections, "I send greetings to my friend Dr. Gerhard Frey and the Deutsche Volksunion, with whom we shall continue to work together very closely."[18] This cooperation was publicly demonstrated on several occasions, for instance, when Zhirinovsky openly adopted the Führer-principle within his party in the spring of 1994. Finally, several student organizations asked the publishing house of C. H. Beck to strike Maunz's name from its list of publications.[19] That request is surely a very problematic one and merely makes Maunz disappear from view. It is not a posthumous ostracism of Maunz that we are after, but critical understanding.

Several political lines thus intersect here. Frey received the media attention long denied him precisely because the public as such—and not merely the "left," as was foolishly claimed—was concerned about him and the general rise of right-wing extremism. This concern is reflected in all the public declarations, demonstrations, candlelight chains, and other symbolic acts of the last years concerning right-wing extremism and hatred of foreigners, as well as by the vast majority of statements about Maunz's dubious entanglements.

At the same time, a few individual members of the Association of Constitutional Lawyers reacted with visible anger to my article,[20] in one instance in a defamatory outburst beyond the bounds of civilized discourse.[21] There are probably two main reasons for this reaction: unlike earlier statements,[22] my voice of criticism came from within the ranks of the profession and was published in a daily paper. Such broad exposure seemed more difficult to accept than statements in books and professional journals that were read only by specialists. For example, what Alexander Hollerbach had written about Maunz's role in the National Socialist state had not drawn any comments:

> From the very beginning, Maunz stood with the National Socialist revolution and turned his attention especially to administrative law . . . Maunz turned Freiburg into a center of German administrative jurisprudence with a National Socialist bent . . . For all that, Maunz was neither a fanatical ideologue nor an ideological warrior. Rather, he embodied the type of the versatile legal expert with practical experience and concern for practical issues, whose basic positivist-technical attitude

leads him to spell out the political and constitutional givens in conformity with the system, and who sees to it that they become "operational" in the administrative reality of a state that was becoming increasingly totalitarian.[23]

A few constitutional lawyers were particularly incensed that the controversy spread to the Association of Constitutional Lawyers. Certainly it would have been more agreeable if one could have isolated the Maunz affair and seen it as the regrettable lapse of a colleague whom one had to treat with leniency because of his age and his undeniable services in other ways. In that case the whole thing could have been taken care of with a minor correction to his lifelong accomplishments in the obituary. But why this indulgence from an association that otherwise kept a close watch to make sure no "radicals" were admitted into its ranks? And in light of the freedom of research, scholarship, and teaching guaranteed in Article 5, section 3 of the Basic Law, the question of whether a constitutional lawyer who teaches the liberal-democratic order in the classroom is permitted to spend his leisure hours drafting legal opinions for extremist parties on the left or right is at least worth discussing within the profession. That same passage of the Basic Law declares that "freedom of teaching shall not absolve from loyalty to the Constitution." Can there be any possible interpretation of this clause that would allow a professor who appears loyal to the constitution in the classroom to devote his time outside the classroom to writing articles and offering advice to enemies of the Constitution? What is the association's general view on advice and expert opinions requested by those at the fringes of democratic consensus?

My own position on these question is easily summed up: In this area it is not possible to find a truly convincing line of distinction between professional advice and substantive support. The interpretation of normative statements is not value-neutral or free of value judgments. Equally unconvincing is a fictitious separation of the roles of scholar, legal adviser, and professor. Expert opinions are usually not secret information but are intended for public presentation in legal disputes of every kind. They are often published, as they should be; their author stands by them. If it is therefore true to say that for reasons of professional ethics there needs to be an inner coherence to the roles of professor, scholar, and adviser when it comes to the expression of professional opinions, it is also legitimate to ask how far the core of this inner coherence may be allowed to drift from what is at the heart of the liberal and democratic order. Still worth pondering are the words Gerhard Anschütz wrote in his application for emeritus status: "The task of the professor of constitutional law is not merely to transmit to students a knowledge of German constitutional law, but also to educate students in the meaning and spirit of the prevailing system of government. This requires that a professor possess a high degree of inner commitment to the system of government."[24] To be sure, these words provide no protection if they are not linked to a system of political values. But if we embed them in the context clearly outlined by the Basic Law, it is clear that expert opinions or even anonymous writings in the world of extremist antidemocratic parties are reprehensible politically and from the standpoint of professional ethics.

For now we can merely say that this is a classic didactic drama about the professional and political condition of the Federal Republic: The revelations come through the way in which the public, the academic world, jurists, and civil servants reacted and *failed* to react to National Socialism. Maunz was a jurist of constitutional and administrative law, an expert witness and commentator, but most of all a teacher whose success was unparalleled. He was a minister whose skill in exercising this office was widely acknowledged. Erasing his name cannot change any of this. His abilities took him far—too far, in the view of a critical public. He held many offices, but he was also brought down by public pressure. He was successful, but he had to pay for the revelations after his death with a shadow that will forever hang over his name. Of course, how much of a shadow depends on the kind of consensus achieved in political and professional ethics that committed work for National Socialists and their modern-day intellectual successors cannot be silently accepted.[25] This consensus has sustained the Federal Republic until now. Should it disappear, the basis on which the essays in this volume implicitly rest would also be destroyed.

NOTES

Cross-references in notes refer to notes within the same chapter.

GENERAL INTRODUCTION

1. Here "nonlaw" includes legal infractions as well as all norms that do not possess the quality of law—that is to say, customs and mores.

2. This presupposes that the factual acceptance on the part of those subject to a norm is irrelevant to its validity, a point that is certainly open to debate.

3. Here is Fraenkel's definition of these two states: "By the Prerogative State we mean that governmental system which exercises unlimited arbitrariness and violence unchecked by any legal guarantees, and by the Normative State an administrative body endowed with elaborate powers for safeguarding the legal order as expressed in statutes, decisions of the courts, and activities of the administrative agencies" (*The Dual State*, translated by E. A. Shils [New York, 1969], xiii).

4. H. Schorn, *Der Richter im Dritten Reich* (1959); Schorn, *Die Gesetzgebung des Nationalsozialismus als Mittel der Machtpolitik* (1963).

5. Revised version of my article "Nationalsozialistisches Recht," in A. Erler and E. Kaufmann, eds., *Handwörterbuch zur Deutschen Rechtsgeschichte*, part 20 (1981), cols. 873–892.

6. M. Etzel, *Die Aufhebung von nationalsozialistischen Gesetzen durch den Alliierten Kontrollrat (1945–1948)* (1992), with additional references.

7. *Entscheidungen des Bundesverfassungsgerichts* 3:58, 4:115, 6:132, 23:98.

8. *Entscheidungen des Bundesverfassungsgerichts* 23:98, 106.

9. The most important document of this kind is probably the book by E. Kogon, *Der SS-Staat. Das System der deutschen Konzentrationslager* (1946); English translation by Heinz Norden, *The Theory and Practice of Hell: The German Concentration Camps and the System behind Them* (New York, 1953). This category also included A. Mitscherlich and F. Mielke, *Das Diktat der Menschenverachtung* (1947).

10. E. Linsmayer, "Das Naturrecht in der deutschen Rechtsprechung der Nachkriegszeit," diss., Munich, 1963; F. Wieacker, *Zum heutigen Stand der Naturrechtsdiskussion* (1965); H. D. Schelauske, *Naturrechtsdiskussion in Deutschland* (1968); W. Rosenbaum, *Naturrecht und positives Recht* (1972).

11. F. v. Hippel, *Die nationalsozialistische Herrschaftsordnung als Warnung und Lehre* (1946); Hippel, *Die Perversion von Rechtsordnungen* (1955).

12. See, for example, F. Kindler, *Der Rechtspositivismus. Der erste Kriegsverbrecher und seine Überwindung* (Linz: Katholische Schriftenmission, 1947). A representative

example from the opposing camp is H. Coing, *Die obersten Grundsätze des Rechts* (1947).

13. *Entscheidungen des Bundesverfassungsgerichts* 7:198.

14. W. Wippermann, *Faschismustheorien*, 3d ed. (1976).

15. *Braunbuch: Kriegs- und Naziverbrecher in der Bundesrepublik und in Westberlin*, 3d ed. (Berlin: Staatsverlag der DDR, 1968); *Graubuch: Expansionspolitik und Neonazismus in Westdeutschland*, 2d ed. (Berlin: Staatsverlag der DDR, 1967).

16. Munich: "Die deutsche Universität im Dritten Reich" (1966); Tübingen: A. Flitner, ed., *Deutsches Geistesleben und Nationalsozialismus* (1965); Berlin: "Nationalsozialismus und Deutsche Universität" (1966); Gießen: "Kritische Justiz" (1968–1969). A second series of courses began two decades later, for example, in Münster: P. Salje, ed., *Recht und Unrecht im Nationalsozialismus* (1985); in Frankfurt: B. Diestelkamp and M. Stolleis, eds., *Justizalltag im Dritten Reich* (1988); in Göttingen: R. Dreier and W. Sellert, eds., *Recht und Justiz im "Dritten Reich"* (1989); in Kiel: F. J. Säcker, ed., *Recht und Rechtslehre im Nationalsozialismus* (1992).

17. Critique in W. F. Haug, *Der hilflose Antifaschismus* (1967).

18. H. Mommsen, *Beamtentum im Dritten Reich* (1966); H. Jäger, *Verbrechen unter totalitärer Herrschaft*, 2d ed. (1982); P. Thoss, *Das subjektive Recht in der gliedschaftlichen Bindung* (1968); B. Rüthers, *Die unbegrenzte Auslegung* (1968); P. Diehl-Thiele, *Partei und Staat im Dritten Reich* (1969); M. Broszat, *Der Staat Hitlers* (1969; English translation by John W. Hiden, *The Hitler State* [London, 1981]); H. Matzerath, *Nationalsozialismus und kommunale Selbstverwaltung* (1970); U. Hientzsch, *Arbeitsrechtslehren im Dritten Reich und ihre historische Vorbereitung* (1970); F. Kaul, *Geschichte des Reichsgerichts 1933–1945*, vol. 4 (1971); D. Kirschenmann, *"Gesetz" im Staatsrecht und in der Staatsrechtslehre des Nationalsozialismus* (1970); L. Gruchmann, "Euthanasie und Justiz im Dritten Reich," *Vierteljahreshefte für Zeitgeschichte* 20 (1972): 255 ff.; H. Kiesewetter, *Von Hegel zu Hitler* (1974). For the literature during the two decades from 1974 to 1994, which has long since become impossible to keep track of, the reader is referred to the ongoing reviews in the journal *Vierteljahreshefte für Zeitgeschichte*.

19. An exemplary work is that of E. John et al., eds., *Die Freiburger Universität in der Zeit des Nationalsozialismus* (1991), with an essay by A. Hollerbach, 91–113.

20. The contributions of legal history at the law faculties in Berlin, Halle, Jena, and Leipzig on this topic were extremely sparse. Scholars took no interest in a differentiated account of "Fascism" as defined by the party, and the similarities with their own system were obvious. To this we must add as exacerbating factors the general marginalization of legal history and scarcity of materials.

21. D. Majer, *"Fremdvölkische" im Dritten Reich. Ein Beitrag zur nationalsozialistischen Rechtssetzung und Rechtspraxis in Verwaltung und Justiz unter besonderer Berücksichtigung der eingegliederten Ostgebiete und des Generalgouvernements* (1981); and *Grundlagen des nationalsozialistischen Rechtssystems. Führerprinzip, Sonderrecht, Einheitspartei* (1987). On criminal law, see most recently G. Werle, *Justiz-Strafrecht und politische Verbrechensbekämpfung im Dritten Reich* (1989).

22. J. v. Kruedener, "Zielkonflikt in der nationalsozialistischen Agrarpolitik," *Zeitschrift für Wirtschafts- und Sozialwissenschaften* 94 (1974): 335–361.

23. J. H. Kumpf, "Die Finanzgerichtsbarkeit im Dritten Reich," in B. Diestelkamp and M. Stolleis, eds., *Justizalltag im Dritten Reich* (1988), 81 ff.; Kumpf, "Der

Reichsfinanzhof im 'Dritten Reich'," *Deutsche Steuer-Zeitung* 82 (1994): 65–68; Kumpf, "Der Reichsfinanzhof 1933 bis 1944," *Steuer und Wirtschaft* (1994): 15–25; Tanzer, "Steuerrecht im nationalsozialistischen Staat," in Davy et al., eds., *Nationalsozialismus und Recht* (Vienna, 1990), 331–346; Mehl, *Das Reichsfinanzministerium und die Verfolgung der Deutschen Juden 1933–1945* (1990); S. Werner, *Wirtschaftsordnung und Wirtschaftsstrafrecht im Nationalsozialismus* (1991).

24. P. Schwerdtner, *Fürsorgetheorie und Entgelttheorie im Recht der Arbeitsbedingungen* (1970); Hientzsch (see note 18, above); T. W. Mason, *Sozialpolitik im Dritten Reich: Arbeiterklasse und Volksgemeinschaft* (1977); U. Reifner, ed., *Das Recht des Unrechtsstaates. Arbeitsrecht und Staatsrechtswissenschaften im Faschismus* (1981); A. Kranig, *Lockung und Zwang. Zur Arbeitsverfassung im Dritten Reich* (1983); Kranig, "Das Gesetz zur Ordnung der nationalen Arbeit," in H. Steindl, ed., *Wege zur Arbeitsrechtsgeschichte* (1984); also numerous articles by Th. Mayer-Maly, Th. Ramm, and B. Rüthers.

25. M. Sunnus, *Der NS-Rechtswahrerbund (1928–1945)* (1990); H.-R. Pichinot, "Die Akademie für Deutsches Recht," law diss., Kiel, 1981.

26. W. Kohl, *Das Reichsverwaltungsgericht* (1991); U. Reifner and B.-R. Sonnen, eds., *Strafjustiz und Polizei im Dritten Reich* (1984); U. Schumacher, *Staatsanwaltschaft und Gericht im Dritten Reich* (1985); G. Riehle, "Die rechtsstaatliche Bedeutung der Staatsanwaltschaft unter besonderer Berücksichtigung ihrer Rolle in der nationalsozialistischen Zeit," law diss., Frankfurt, 1985; L. Gruchmann, *Justiz im Dritten Reich, 1933–1940. Anpassung und Unterwerfung in der Ära Gürtner* (1987); on this last, see also my review in *Historische Zeitschrift* 249 (1989): 105–112.

27. B. Diestelkamp and M. Stolleis, ed., *Justizalltag im Dritten Reich* (1988).

28. R. Schröder, *". . . Aber im Zivilrecht sind die Richter standhaft geblieben!" Die Urteile des OLG Celle aus dem Dritten Reich* (1988).

29. H. Wrobel, *Strafjustiz im totalen Krieg. Aus den Akten des Sondergerichts Bremen 1940 bis 1945* (1991).

30. U.-D. Oppitz, *Strafverfahren und Strafvollstreckung bei NS-Gewaltverbrechen. Dargestellt an Hand von 319 rechtskräftigen Urteilen deutscher Gerichte aus der Zeit von 1946–1965* (1976).

31. T. Krach, *Jüdische Rechtsanwälte in Preußen. Bedeutung und Zerstörung der freien Advokatur* (1991); E. Douma, "Organ der Rechtspflege oder Garant der Freiheit? Die deutschen Rechtsanwälte 1933–1955," diss., Bielefeld, 1994; also H. Siegrist, *Advokat, Bürger und Staat: Sozialgeschichte der Rechtsanwälte in Deutschland, Italien und der Schweiz (18.–20. Jh.),* 2 vols. (Frankfurt, 1996).

32. "Verordnung des Reichspräsidenten zum Schutz von Volk und Staat vom 28.2.1933," *Reichsgesetzblatt* 1 (1933): 83; E. Matthias and R. Morsey, eds., *Das Ende der Parteien 1933* (1960).

33. "Gesetz gegen die Neubildung von Parteien vom 14.7.1933," *Reichsgesetzblatt* 1 (1933): 479.

34. "Gesetz zur Sicherung der Einheit von Partei und Staat vom 1.12.1933," *Reichsgesetzblatt* 1 (1933): 1016.

35. "Gesetz zur Wiederherstellung des Berufsbeamtentums vom 7. April 1933," *Reichsgesetzblatt* 1 (1933): 175; "Deutsches Beamtengesetz vom 26.1.1937," *Reichsgesetzblatt* 1 (1933): 39.

36. The German word *Gleichschaltung* literally means "putting into the same gear" (generally translated as "coordination") and refers to the Nazi efforts to force all institutions and activities into line with the party's policies.—Trans.

37. "Gesetz über den Neuaufbau des Reichs vom 30.1.1934," *Reichsgesetzblatt* 1 (1934): 75.

38. "Gesetz über die Aufhebung des Reichsrats vom 14.2.1934," *Reichsgesetzblatt* 1 (1934): 89.

39. "Gesetz zur Behebung der Not von Volk und Reich (Ermächtigungsgesetz) vom 24.3.1933," *Reichsgesetzblatt* 1 (1933): 141.

40. "Gesetz über Volksabstimmung vom 14.7.1933," *Reichsgesetzblatt* 1 (1933): 479.

41. "Gesetz über das Staatsoberhaupt des Deutschen Reichs vom 1.8.1934," *Reichsgesetzblatt* 1 (1934): 747.

42. "Schriftleitergesetz vom 4. Oktober 1933," *Reichsgesetzblatt* 1 (1933): 713.

43. A. Hitler, *Mein Kampf*, 328th ed. (1938), 93; English translation by Ralph Manheim (Boston, 1943), 95; on this see also J. Wulf, *Presse und Funk im Dritten Reich* (1964).

44. On this see chapter 4, below.

45. P. Hüttenberger, "Nationalsozialistische Polykratie," *Geschichte und Gesellschaft* 2 (1976): 417–442.

46. E. R. Huber, *Verfassungsrecht des Großdeutschen Reiches* (1939), 55–56.

47. See note 3, above.

48. J. Meinck, *Weimarer Staatslehre und Nationalsozialismus. Eine Studie zum Problem der Kontinuität im staatsrechtlichen Denken in Deutschland 1928 bis 1936* (1978); E. W. Böckenförde, ed., *Staatsrecht und Staatsrechtslehre im Dritten Reich* (1985). See also chapter 5.

49. B. Limperg, "Personelle Veränderungen in der Staatsrechtslehre und ihre neue Situation nach der Machtergreifung," in E. W. Böckenförde, ed., *Staatsrecht und Staatsrechtslehre im Dritten Reich* (1985), 44 ff.

50. "Gesetz über den Widerruf von Einbürgerungen und die Aberkennung der deutschen Staatsangehörigkeit vom 14. Juli 1933," *Reichsgesetzblatt* 1 (1933): 480.

51. "Reichsbürgergesetz vom 15. September 1935," *Reichsgesetzblatt* 1 (1935): 1146; "Gesetz zum Schutze des deutschen Blutes und der deutschen Ehre vom 15. September 1935," *Reichsgesetzblatt* 1 (1935): 1146. On the Roma and Sinti, see J. S. Hohmann, *Geschichte der Zigeunerverfolgung in Deutschland* (1981); Hohmann, *Zigeuner und Zigeunerwissenschaft. Ein Beitrag zur Grundlagenforschung und Dokumentation des Völkermordes im "Dritten Reich"* (1980); D. Kenrick and G. Puxon, *Sinti und Roma— die Vernichtung eines Volkes im NS-Staat* (1981); M. Krausnick, ed., *"Da wollten wir frei sein!"* (1985).

52. B. Blau, *Das Ausnahmerecht für die Juden in Deutschland 1933–1945*, 3d ed. (1965); D. Majer, *"Fremdvölkische" im Dritten Reich* (1980); H. Hofmann, "Die deutsche Rechtswissenschaft im Kampf gegen den jüdischen Geist," in K. Müller and K. Wittstadt, eds., *Geschichte und Kultur des Judentums* (1988), 223–240; K. Henning and J. Kestler, "Die Rechtsstellung der Juden," in E. W. Böckenförde, ed., *Staatsrecht und Staatsrechtslehre im Dritten Reich* (1985), 191 ff.

53. "Bäuerliches Erbhofrecht vom 15. Mai 1933," *Preußische Gesetzessammlung* (1933): 165; "Reichserbhofgesetz vom 29. September 1933," *Reichsgesetzblatt* 1 (1933): 685; "Gesetz über den vorläufigen Aufbau des Reichsnährstandes vom 13. September 1933," *Reichsgesetzblatt* 1 (1933): 626; as well as numerous other decrees. On the concept itself, see J. v. Kruedener, "Zielkonflikt in der nationalsozialistischen Agrarpolitik," *Zeitschrift für Wirtschafts- und Sozialwissenschaften* 94 (1974): 335–361.

54. C. Schmitt, "Neue Leitsätze für die Rechtspraxis," *Juristische Wochenschrift* 62 (1933): 2793–2794.

55. In *Deutsche Rechtswissenschaft* 1 (1936): 123–124; *Deutsche Juristenzeitung* 41 (1936): 179–180.

56. H. Boberach, ed., *Richterbriefe: Dokumente zur Beinflussung der deutschen Rechtsprechung 1942–1944* (1975).

57. H. K. J. Ridder, "Vom Grund des Grundgesetzes," *Juristenzeitung* 13 (1958): 323–324.

58. E. Franssen, "Positivismus als juristische Strategie," *Juristenzeitung* 24 (1969): 766–775.

59. F. K. Kübler, "Der deutsche Richter und das demokratische Gesetz," *Archiv für civilistische Praxis* 162 (1963): 104–128.

60. D. Simon, *Die Unabhängigkeit des Richters* (1975), 54.

61. H. Matzerath, *Nationalsozialismus und kommunale Selbstverwaltung* (1970).

62. P. Hüttenberger, *Die Gauleiter* (1969); P. Diehl-Thiele, *Partie und Staat im Dritten Reich* (1969).

63. Examples: M. Broszat, *Nationalsozialistische Polenpolitik 1939–1945* (1961); D. Rebentisch and A. Raab, *Neu-Isenburg zwischen Anpassung und Widerstand* (1978).

64. See, for example, the slogans of the Nazi functionary and, for a short time, President of the Reich Administrative Court, Walther Sommer (1893–1946): "A healthy administration does not have the least bit to do with paragraphs" (W. Sommer, "Die Verwaltungsgerichtsbarkeit," *Deutsches Verwaltungsblatt* 85 [1937]: 425–430, quotation on 427).

65. As an example see, for instance, Ch. Kirchberg, *Der Badische Verwaltungsgerichtshof im Dritten Reich* (1980).

66. W. Kohl, *Das Reichsverwaltungsgericht* (1991).

67. M. Stolleis, "Die Verwaltungsgerichtsbarkeit im Nationalsozialismus"; see chapter 8, below.

68. An instructive example (as a now detached voice) is H. Lange, *Die Entwicklung der Wissenschaft vom bürgerlichen Recht seit 1933* (1941). W. Grunsky provided a first, brief overview: "Gesetzesauslegung durch die Zivilgerichte im Dritten Reich," *Kritische Justiz* 2 (1969): 146–162. See now also G. Otte, "Die zivilrechtliche Gesetzgebung im 'Dritten Reich,'" *Neue juristische Wochenschrift* (1988): 2836–2842.

69. J. W. Hedemann, *Die Flucht in die Generalklauseln* (1933).

70. In retrospect see F. Wieacker, "'Wandlungen der Eigentumsverfassung' Revisited," *Quaderni fiorentini* 5–6 (1976–1977): 703–721; and H. Rittstieg, "Die juristische Eigentumslehre in der Zeit des Nationalsozialismus," *Quaderni fiorentini* 5–6 (1976–1977): 841–859. The most important legal prescriptions have been compiled in E. Brahm Garcia, *Eigentum und Enteignung im Dritten Reich* (1985). On the commitment to duties, see P. Thoss, *Das subjektive Reicht in der gliedschaftlichen Bindung* (1968).

71. M. Stolleis, "Volksgesetzbuch," in A. Erler and E. Kaufmann, eds., *Handwörterbuch zur Deutschen Rechtsgeschichte*, vol. 5, part 36 (1993), cols. 990–992, with additional references.

72. In *Mein Kampf* (1926, 275–276), Hitler had proclaimed "the increase and preservation of the species and the race" as the goal of marriage. See the English translation by Ralph Manheim (1943), 252.

73. See § 35 of the Law on the Organization of National Labor (AOG). See also P. Schwerdtner, *Fürsorgetheorie und Entgelttheorie im Recht der Arbeitsbedingungen*

(1970); Th. Ramm, "Nationalsozialismus und Arbeitsrecht," *Kritische Justiz* 1 (1968): 108–120; U. Hientzsch, *Arbeitsrechtslehren im Dritten Reich und ihre historische Vorbereitung* (1970).

74. "Kraft durch Freude" was a National Socialist recreational organization designed to boost morale among workers.

75. T. Mason, *Sozialpolitik im Dritten Reich* (1977).

76. "Aktiengesetz vom 30.1.1937," *Reichsgesetzblatt* 1 (1937): 107.

77. "Gesetz über Errichtung von Zwangskartellen vom 15.7.1933," *Reichsgesetzblatt* 1 (1933): 488.

78. On the history of cartel law, see now K. W. Nörr, *Leiden des Privatrechts* (1994).

79. On this see Kumpf (note 23, above) with additional references, as well as E. Hoffmann and M. Janssen, *Die Wahrheit über die Ordensdevisenprozesse 1935/1936* (1967); U. v. Hehl, ed., *Walter Adolph. Geheime Aufzeichnungen aus dem nationalsozialistischen Kirchenkampf 1935–1943* (1979).

80. "Gesetz gegen Wirtschaftssabotage vom 1.12.1936," *Reichsgesetzblatt* 1 (1936): 999; "Verordnung über Strafen und Strafverfahren bei Zuwiderhandlungen gegen Preisvorschriften vom 3.6.1939," *Reichsgesetzblatt* 1 (1939): 1762; "Verbrauchsregelungsstrafverordnung vom 6.4.1940," *Reichsgesetzblatt* 1 (1940): 610. See references in Werner (note 23, above).

81. This was done especially by suppressing charitable collections devoted to causes that were remote from the state's goals. See M. Stolleis, "Sammlungswesen," in E. Friesenhahn and U. Scheuner, eds., *Handbuch des Staatskirchenrechts der Bundesrepublik,* vol. 2 (1975), 437–451.

82. "Gesetz über den Ausbau der Rentenversicherung vom 21.12.1937," *Reichsgesetzblatt* 1 (1937): 1393.

83. "Gesetz über die Altersversorgung für das Deutsche Handwerk vom 21.12.1938," *Reichsgesetzblatt* 1 (1938): 1900.

84. "Gesetz über den Aufbau der Sozialversicherung vom 5.7.1934," *Reichsgesetzblatt* 1 (1934): 577; "Verordnung über die Anlegung des Vermögens der Träger der Reichsversicherung vom 14.4.1938," *Reichsgesetzblatt* 1 (1938): 398.

85. See note 23, above.

86. K. Marxen, *Der Kampf gegen das liberale Strafrecht. Eine Studie zum Antiliberalismus in der Strafrechtswissenschaft der 20er und 30er Jahre* (1975).

87. "Gesetz über Verhängung und Vollzug der Todesstrafe ("Lex van der Lubbe") vom 29.3.1933," *Reichsgesetzblatt* 1 (1933): 151; "Gesetz gegen heimtückische Angriffe auf Staat und Partei . . . vom 20.12.1934," *Reichsgesetzblatt* 1 (1934): 1269; "Kriegssonderstrafrechtsverordnung vom 17.8.1938," *Reichsgesetzblatt* 1 (1938): 1455; "Verordnung über ausserordentliche Rundfunkmaßnahmen vom 1.9.1939," *Reichsgesetzblatt* 1 (1939): 1683; "Verordnung gegen Volksschädlinge vom 5.9.1939," *Reichsgesetzblatt* 1 (1939): 1679.

88. "Verordnung über die Strafrechtspflege gegen Polen und Juden vom 4.12.1941," *Reichsgesetzblatt* 1 (1941): 759. Shortly thereafter, Jews were entirely excluded from the application of this law.

89. A. Wagner, *Die Umgestaltung der Gerichtsverfassung und des Verfahrens- und Richterrechts im nationalsozialistischen Staat* (1968); M. Broszat, *Nationalsozialistische Polenpolitik* (1961); Broszat, *The Hitler State,* translated by John W. Hiden (1981).

90. See also G. Gribbohm, "Nationalsozialismus und Strafrechtspraxis—Versuche einer Bilanz," *Neue juristische Wochenschrift* (1988): 2842–2849.

91. "Einführung der Maßregeln der Sicherung und Besserung durch Gesetz vom 24.11.1933," *Reichsgesetzblatt* 1 (1933): 995; the introduction of "Jugendarrest durch Reichsjugendgerichtsgesetz vom 6.11.1943," *Reichsgesetzblatt* 1 (1943): 637; as well as the differentiation of guilt in murder and manslaughter, cases involving several perpetrators, and accessoriness in instigating and abetting in the principal offense. See G. Werle, "Zur Reform des Strafrechts in der NS-Zeit: Der Entwurf eines Deutschen Strafgesetzbuchs 1936," *Neue juristische Wochenschrift* (1988): 2865–2867.

92. "Gesetz zur Änderung des Strafgesetzbuchs vom 28.6.1935," *Reichsgesetzblatt* 1 (1935): 839.

93. "Gesetz über Verhängung und Vollzug der Todesstrafe vom 29.3.1933," *Reichsgesetzblatt* 1 (1933): 151; "Gesetz gegen erpresserischen Kindesraub vom 22.6.1936," *Reichsgesetzblatt* 1 (1936): 493; "Gesetz gegen Straßenraub mittels Autofallen vom 22.6.1938," *Reichsgesetzblatt* 1 (1938): 651; "Verordnung gegen Gewaltverbrecher vom 5.12.1939," *Reichsgesetzblatt* 1 (1939): 2378; "Verordnung zum Schutz gegen jugendliche Schwerverbrecher vom 4.10.1939," *Reichsgesetzblatt* 1 (1939): 2000.

94. S. König, *Vom Dienst am Recht. Rechtsanwälte als Strafverteidiger im Nationalsozialismus* (1987); T. Krach, *Jüdische Rechtsanwälte in Preußen. Über die Bedeutung der freien Advokatur und ihre Zerstörung durch den Nationalsozialismus* (1991).

95. H. Wrobel, ed., *Strafjustiz im totalen Krieg*, vol. 1 (1991).

96. "Gesetz zur Änderung der Vorschriften des Strafrechts und des Strafverfahrens vom 24.4.1934," *Reichsgesetzblatt* 1 (1934): 341; see the comprehensive work by W. Wagner, *Der Volksgerichtshof im nationalsozialistischen Staat* (1974).

97. "Verordnung zur weiteren Anpassung der Strafrechtspflege an die Erfordernisse des totalen Krieges vom 13.13.1944," *Reichsgesetzblatt* 1 (1944): 339.

98. An overview is given by E. Schmidt, *Einführung in die Geschichte der deutschem Strafrechtspflege* (1965), pars. 345 ff.

99. E. Schwinge, "Die deutsche Militärgerichtsbarkeit im Zweiten Weltkrieg," *Deutsche Richterzeitung* (1959): 350–352; O. P. Schweling, *Die deutsche Militärjustiz in der Zeit des Nationalsozialismus* (1977).

100. M. Messerschmidt and F. Wüllner, *Die Wehrmachtjustiz im Dienste des Nationalsozialismus* (1987). See chapter 9.

101. B. Rüthers, *Die unbegrenzte Auslegung* (1968); H. Kiesewetter, *Von Hegel zu Hitler* (1974); K. Anderbrügge, *Völkisches Rechtsdenken. Zur Rechtslehre in der Zeit des Nationalsozialismus* (1978); H. Rottleuthner, ed., *Recht, Rechtsphilosophie und Nationalsozialismus*, Beiheft zum Archiv für Rechts- und Sozialphilosophie 18 (1983).

102. K. F. Werner, *Das nationalsozialistische Geschichtsbild und die deutschen Geschichtswissenschaften* (1967); H. Heier, *Walter Frank und sein Reichsinstitut für Geschichte des neuen Deutschland* (1966); F. Graus, "Geschichtsschreibung und Nationalsozialismus," *Vierteljahreshefte für Zeitgeschichte* 17 (1969): 87–95; G. G. Iggers, *The German Conception of History* (1971).

103. D. Schwab, "Zum Selbstverständnis der historischen Rechtswissenschaften im Dritten Reich," *Kritische Justiz* 2 (1969): 59–70; R. Wahsner, "Die deutsche Rechtsgeschichte und der Faschismus," *Kritische Justiz* 6 (1973): 172–181; M. Stolleis, *Gemeinwohlformeln im nationalsozialistischen Recht* (1974), 12 ff.; M. Stolleis and D. Simon, eds., *Rechtsgeschichte im Nationalsozialismus* (1988).

104. On this see now S. Gagnér, *Zur Methodik neuerer rechtsgeschichtlicher Untersuchungen. I. Eine Bestandsaufnahme aus den sechziger Jahren* (1993), 9 ff.

105. D. Simon, "Die deutsche Wissenschaft vom römischen Recht nach 1933,"

in M. Stolleis and D. Simon, eds., *Rechtsgeschichte im Nationalsozialismus* (1988); see also chapter 3.

106. P. Koschaker, *Die Krise des römischen Rechts und die romanistische Rechtswissenschaft* (1938); Koschaker, *Europa und das römische Recht* (1947), chap. 17.

107. B. Rüthers, *Entartetes Recht. Rechtslehren und Kronjuristen im Dritten Reich* (1988); on this work see M. Stolleis, "Lehren aus der Rechtsgeschichte? Zur Auseinandersetzung mit den Thesen von Bernd Rüthers," in R. Eisfeld and I. Müller, eds., *Gegen Barbarei. Essays Robert M. W. Kempner zu Ehren* (1989), 385–395. See also Rottleuthner (note 101, above).

108. See the skeptical review by W. Naucke in *Neue juristische Wochenschrift* (1988): 2873. The book was translated into English by Deborah Lucas Schneider under the title *Hitler's Justice: The Courts of the Third Reich* (Cambridge, Mass.: Harvard University Press, 1991).

109. The most important texts of this controversy have been collected in the volume entitled *Historikerstreit* (Munich, 1987); English translation by James Knowlton and Truett Cates, *Forever in the Shadow of Hitler? Original Documents of the "Historikerstreit," the Controversy concerning the Singularity of the Holocaust* (Atlantic Highlands, N.J.: Humanities Press, 1993). See also H. U. Wehler, *Entsorgung der deutschen Vergangenheit? Ein polemischer Essay zum "Historikerstreit"* (1988). [English readers can consult the book by Charles S. Maier, *The Unmasterable Past: History, Holocaust, and German National Identity* (Cambridge, Mass.: Harvard University Press, 1988).]

CHAPTER ONE

1. U. Wesel, "Zur Methode der Rechtsgeschichte," *Kritische Justiz* (1974): 339. On legal history after 1945, see Regina Ogovek's contribution, in D. Simon, ed. *Geschichte der Rechtswissenschaft in der Bonner Republik* (Frankfurt, 1994).

2. P. Koschaker, *Die Krise des römischen Rechts und die romanistische Rechtswissenschaft* (1938); Koschaker, "Probleme der heutigen romanistischen Rechtswissenschaft," *Deutsche Rechtswissenschaft* (1940): 110 ff.; H. Kreller, "Die Bedeutung des römischen Rechts in neuen deutschen Hochschulunterricht," *Zeitschrift der Akademie für deutsches Recht* 3 (1936): 409 ff.; J. v. Kempski, "Krise des römischen Rechts oder Grundlagenkrise der Rechtswisenschaft," *Archiv für Rechts- und Sozialphilosophie* 32 (1938–1939): 404 ff.; E. Schönbauer, "Zur Krise des römischen Rechts," in *Festschrift Koschaker*, vol. 2 (1939), 385; M. Kaser, "Die deutsche Wissenschaft vom römischen Recht seit 1933," *Forschung und Fortschritte* 15 (1939): 205 ff.; F. Wieacker, "Der Standort der römischen Rechtsgeschichte in der deutschen Gegenwart," *Deutsches Recht* (1942): 49.

3. F. Meinecke, *Die deutsche Katastrophe: Betrachtungen und Erinnerungen* (1946). For a thorough discussion of this work, see M. Erbe's contribution, in *Friedrich Meinecke heute. Kolloquium zum 25. Todestag* (1981). The quote is from Meinecke, *Kausalitäten und Werte in der Geschichte* (= *Werke*, vol. 4 [1959]), 68.

4. G. Dulckeit, *Philosophie der Rechtsgeschichte* (1950). Compare on this the very differently nuanced responses by W. Kunkel and K. Larenz, in *Gerhard Dulckeit als Rechtshistoriker, Rechtsphilosoph und Rechtsdogmatiker* (1955).

5. H. Mitteis, *Vom Lebenswert der Rechtsgeschichte* (1947).

6. H. Mitteis, *Die Rechtsidee in der Geschichte* (1957).

7. H. Mitteis, *Vom Lebenswert der Rechtsgeschichte* (1947), 8; also Mitteis, "Rechtsgeschichte und Gegenwart," *Neue Justiz* 2 (1947).

8. Important insights are offered by the catalog of the German Literature Archive in the Schiller-Nationalmuseum, Marbach a.N., *Als der Krieg zu Ende war* (1973). See also G. Hay, "Wiederkehr und Aufbruch in der Literatur," in *Westdeutschlands Weg zur Bundesrepublik* (1976); R. Opitz, "Politische Ideologiekonzeptionen im Vorfeld der Gründung der Bundesrepublik," in Albrecht et al., eds., *Geschichte der Bundesrepublik* (1979); A. Diller, "Kultur nach dem Ungeist. Auf der Suche nach einem neuen Standort," in J. Weber, ed., *Das Entscheidungsjahr 1948* (1979).

9. H. Glaser, *Als die Republik geboren wurde*, Frankfurter Hefte 9 (1978).

10. K. S. Bader, *Aufgaben und Methoden des Rechtshistorikers* (1951); H. Coing, *Grundzüge der Rechtsphilosophie* (1950); P. Koschaker, *Europa und das römische Recht* (1947); H. Thieme, "Ideengeschichte und Rechtsgeschichte," in *Festschrift J. v. Gierke* (1950); Th. Viehweg, *Topik und Jurisprudenz* (1953); F. Wieacker, *Privatrechtsgeschichte der Neuzeit* (1952).

11. V. Klemperer, *Lingua tertii imperii* (1946); H. Dölle, *Vom Stil der Rechtssprache* (1949).

12. F. Wieacker, *Notizen zur rechtshistorischen Hermeneutik*, Nachrichten der Akademie der Wissenschaften in Göttingen, Philosophisch-historische Klasse (1963); Wieacker, "Der gegenwärtige Stand der Disziplin der neueren Privatrechtsgeschichte," in *Eranion Maridakis*, vol. 1 (1963), 339–366; Wieacker, "Zur Methodik der Rechtsgeschichte," in *Festschrift Schwind* (1978), 355; Wieacker, "Methode der Rechtsgeschichte," in A. Erler and E. Kaufmann, eds., *Handwörterbuch zur Deutschen Rechtsgeschichte*, part 19 (1980), cols. 518–526; Wieacker, "Besprechung von H. Coing, *Aufgaben des Rechthistorikers 1976*," *Zeitschrift für historische Forschung* (1978): 81–86; Wieacker, "Vorbedingungen und aktuelle Grundfragen einer rechtshistorischen Methodik," *Archiv für Rechts- und Sozialphilosophie* (1980): 2–15.

13. Mitteis, *Vom Lebenswert der Rechtsgechichte* (1947), 7.

14. H. Lau, "Möglichkeiten einer emanzipatorischen Rechtsgeschichte," in C. U. Schminck-Gustavus, ed., *Bericht über ein Rechtshistorikersymposium an der Universität Bremen* (1976).

15. U. Wesel (see note 1, above).

16. U. Wesel (see note 1, above), 346. Compare on this J. Rückert, "Zur Erkenntnisproblematik materialistischer Positionen in der rechtshistorischen Methodendiskussion," *Zeitschrift für historische Forschung* (1978): 257.

17. See note 12, above, for Wieacker's discussion of H. Coing's *Aufgaben des Rechtshistorikers* (1976); see also P. Landau, "Bemerkungen zur Methode der Rechtsgeschichte," *Zeitschrift für neuere Rechtsgeschichte* (1980): 117–131.

18. The *Zeitschrift für neuere Rechtsgeschichte* is edited by W. Brauneder, P. Caroni, B. Diestelkamp, C. Schott, and D. Willoweit, and published by Manz'sche Verlags- und Universitätsbuchhandlung Vienna. On the state of legal scholarship on National Socialism, see M. Stolleis, "Nationalsozialistisches Recht," in A. Erler and E. Kaufmann, eds., *Handwörterbuch zur Deutschen Rechtsgeschichte*, vol. 3, part 20 (1981), cols. 873–892.

19. H. Schorn, *Der Richter im Dritten Reich* (1959); H. Weinkauff, *Die deutsche Justiz und der Nationalsozialismus* (1968); O. P. Schweling, *Die deutsche Militärjustiz in der Zeit des Nationalsozialismus* (Marburg, 1977).

20. F. K. Fromme, "Wie Militärgerichtsbarkeit wirklich war," *Frankfurter Allgemeine Zeitung*, July 10, 1978; M. Broszat, "Der Streit um die Wehrmachtsgerichtsbarkeit," *Frankfurter Allgemeine Zeitung*, October 30, 1978; A. C., "Deutsche Militärjustiz

im Prüfstand. Ein fragwürdiger Rechtfertigungsversuch," *Neue Zürcher Zeitung*, September 19, 1978; M. Stolleis, review of Schweling's *Die deutsche Militärjustiz in der Zeit des Nationalsozialismus, Geschichte in Wissenschaft und Unterricht* (1978): 650–654; K. D. Erdmann, "Zeitgeschichte, Militärjustiz und Völkerrecht," *Geschichte in Wissenschaft und Unterricht* (1979): 129–139. On the sociolegal meaning of the death penalties handed down by Nazi courts-martial, see the decision of the Federal Social Court *(Bundessozialgericht)* on September 11, 1991 *(Entscheidungen des Bundessozialgerichts* 69:211), as well as the responses by W. Stoecker *(Sozialgerichtsbarkeit* [1993]: 352) and O. Gritschneder *(Sozialgerichtsbarkeit* [1993]: 603), with additional references.

21. Munich: "Die deutsche Universität im Dritten Reich" (1966); Tübingen: A. Flitner, ed., *Deutsches Geistesleben und Nationalsozialismus* (1965); Berlin: "Nationalsozialismus und Deutsche Universität" (1966). The lectures at the University of Gießen can be found in *Kritische Justiz* (1968): 108; (1969): 58, 146, 221, 367. See also S. Harbordt, ed., *Wissenschaft im Nationalsozialismus* (Berlin, 1983).

22. G. Dahm, *Deutsches Recht* (1951), 332; compare also his *Deutsches Recht* (1944), §§ 9, 10, 18 ff., and the broad account of National Socialist law that can be found there.

23. Th. Rasehorn, review of Anderbrügge, *Völkisches Rechtsdenken* (1978), *Recht und Politik* (1978): 234.

24. H. Hattenhauer, *Die geistesgeschichtlichen Grundlagen des deutschen Rechts*, 2d ed. (1980), 298. In the first edition (1971), the passage read: "When it comes to rendering judgment on this period in history, everybody is an interested party and compelled to take a partisan *[parteiliche]* position." On the word *parteilich*, which is here obviously used in a neutral way, see H. Rumpler and J. Kocka, in Koselleck, Mommsen, and Rüsen, *Objektivität und Parteilichkeit* (1977).

25. G. Dahm, *Deutsches Recht* (1951), 332–333 (emphasis added).

26. R. Scheyhing, *Deutsche Verfassungsgeschichte der Neuzeit* (1968), 10.

27. Along these lines, for example, H. Weinkauff, *Juristenzeitung* (1970): 54; E. Schwinge, in Schweling (see note 19, above), 152; as well as the debate in letters to the editor over military justice: A. Tilmann, "Die Verhältnisse vor und im '3.Reich' können nur von denen beurteilt werden, die sie selbst miterlebt und durchgestanden haben," *Frankfurter Allgemeine Zeitung*, March 17, 1980.

28. F. P. Kahlenberg, "Archivalische Quellen zur Verwaltungsgeschichte," in R. Morsey, ed., *Verwaltungsgeschichte* (1977); P. Hüttenberger, "Gegenwärtige Forschungsansätze der Zeitgeschichte," *Der Archivar* 32 (1979): 23 ff.

29. *Die deutsche Justiz und der Nationalsozialismus*, vol. 1 (1968), introduction.

30. See on this D. Simon, "Rechtsgeschichte," in A. Görlitz, ed., *Handlexikon zur Rechtswissenschaft* (1972); and Simon's discussion in *NS-Recht in historischer Perspektive* (1982): 33 ff.

31. R. Echterhölter, *Das öffentliche Recht im nationalsozialistischen Staat* (= *Die deutsche Justiz und der Nationalsozialismus*, vol. 2 [1970]), 12.

32. For a detailed discussion, see my review (note 20, above).

33. Echterhölter (see note 31, above), 11.

34. Rasehorn (see note 23, above), 234 (emphasis added).

35. Used in this sense by Rasehorn, for instance.

36. Hattenhauer (see note 24, above), 298.

37. Hattenhauer (see note 24, above), 298.

38. See note 9, above.

39. W. Abendroth, in D. Döring and E. O. Kempen, eds., *Sozialistengesetz, Arbeiterbewegung und Demokratie* (1979), 13.

40. K. D. Bracher, *The German Dictatorship*, translated by Jean Steinberg (New York, 1970), 493.

41. R. Koselleck, "Historia Magistra Vitae. Über die Auflösung des Topos im Horizont neuzeitlich bewegter Geschichte," in *Natur und Geschichte: Karl Löwith zum 70. Geburtstag* (1967), 196–219; D. Junker, "Über die Legitimität von Werturteilen in den Sozialwissenschaften und der Geschichtswissenschaft," *Historische Zeitschrift* 211 (1970): 1; K. Acham, *Analytische Geschichtsphilosophie* (1974); H. Lübbe, *Geschichtsbegriff und Geschichtsinteresse* (1977).

42. For a discussion of Habermas, see K. G. Faber, *Theorie der Geschichtswissenschaft*, 4th ed. (1978), 183 ff., with additional references.

43. J. R. Searle, "How to Derive 'Ought' from 'Is'," *Philosophical Review* 73 (1965): 43; N. Hoerster, "Zum Problem der Ableitung eines Sollens aus einem Sein in der analytischen Moralphilosophie," *Archiv für Rechts- und Sozialphilosophie* 55 (1969): 11; Winkler, "Sein und Sollen," *Rechtstheorie* (1979): 257.

44. F. Wieacker, *Vom römischen Recht* (1944), 280; see also his essay in *Zeitschrift für Rechtsgeschichte, Romanistische Abteilung* 69 (1952): 342; Wieacker, *Textstufen klassischer Juristen* (1960), 10 ff. Wieacker, *Privatrechtsgeschichte der Neuzeit*, 2d ed. (1967), 16: "legal history's task of understanding is, like that of any other field of history, not based on the pregiven material of individual dates and facts and their usefulness for the present." Similarly expressed in his essay in *Eranion Maridakis* (see note 12, above), 339, where he describes the "emancipation of scholarship from a relationship to its historical sources that is authority-bound" as the prerequisite for a "reflective legal history."

45. F. Wieacker, *Privatrechtsgeschichte der Neuzeit*, 2d ed. (1967), 16.

46. K. R. Popper, *The Open Society and Its Enemies*, vol. 2 (London, 1945), 255.

47. R. Wittram, *Das Interesse an der Geschichte*, 3d ed. (1968); Wittram, *Anspruch und Fragwürdigkeit der Geschichte* (1969).

CHAPTER TWO

1. K. F. Werner, *Das NS-Geschichtsbild und die deutsche Geschichtswissenschaft* (1967); F. Graus, "Geschichtsschreibung und Nationalsozialismus," *Vierteljahreshefte für Zeitgeschichte* 17 (1969): 87 ff.; G. Iggers, *Deutsche Geschichtswissenschaft* (1971), 318 ff.

2. J. Rückert, "Das 'gesunde Volksempfinden'—eine Erbschaft Savignys?" *Zeitschrift für Rechtsgeschichte, Germanistische Abteilung* 103 (1986): 199–247.

3. The speakers were Hans Hattenhauer (Kiel), Wolfgang Naucke (Frankfurt a. M.), Siegbert Lammel (Bielefeld), and Detlev F. Vagts (Harvard).

4. Guido Kisch, professor in Halle, was one exception.

5. D. Klippel, *Juristische Zeitgeschichte. Die Bedeutung der Rechtsgeschichte für die Zivilrechtswissenschaft* (1985), departs knowingly from the usage of the term *Zeitgeschichte* in history. The subtitle of his work describes precisely what he means. See my review in *Zeitschrift für Rechtsgeschichte, Romanistische Abteilung* 104 (1987): 813–816.

6. G. Dahm, *Deutsches Recht* (1951), 332. There is no indication that this was a revised edition. Compare G. Dahm, *Deutsches Recht* (1944), pars. 9, 10, 18 ff.

7. R. Scheyhing, *Deutsche Verfassungsgeschichte der Neuzeit* (1968), 10.

8. K. Kröger, *Einführung in die jüngere deutsche Verfassungsgeschichte (1806–1933).* *Ein Grundriß ihrer Entwicklungslinien* (1988).

9. K. W. Nörr, *Zwischen den Mühlsteinen. Eine Privatrechtsgeschichte der Weimarer Zeit* (1988), 244.

10. H. Mitteis, *Vom Lebenswert der Rechtsgeschichte* (1947).

11. G. Dulckeit, *Philosophie der Rechtsgeschichte. Die Grundgestalten des Rechtsbegriffs in seiner historischen Entwicklung* (1950).

12. K. S. Bader, *Aufgaben und Methoden des Rechtshistorikers* (1951); H. Coing, *Die obersten Grundsätze des Rechts. Ein Versuch zur Neugründung des Naturrechts* (1947); Coing, *Grundzüge der Rechtsphilosophie* (1950); H. Thieme, "Ideengeschichte und Rechtsgeschichte," in *Festschrift J. Gierke* (1950); Thieme, *Das Naturrecht und die europäische Privatrechtsgeschichte* (1947); F. Wieacker, *Privatrechtsgeschichte der Neuzeit*, 1st ed. (1952).

13. P. Koschaker, *Europa und das römische Recht* (1947). See now S. Gagnér, *Zur Methodik neuerer rechtshistorischer Untersuchungen* (1993).

14. A. Flitner, ed., *Deutsches Geistesleben und Nationalsozialismus* (1965); *Nationalsozialismus und Deutsche Universität* (1966); *Die deutsche Universität im Dritten Reich* (1966). See most recently, for example, S. Harbordt, ed., *Wissenschaft und Nationalsozialismus* (Technische Universität Berlin, 1983); P. Salje, ed., *Recht und Unrecht im Nationalsozialismus* (1985); P. Lundgreen, ed., *Wissenschaft im Dritten Reich* (1985).

15. D. Schwab, "Zum Selbstverständnis der historischen Rechtswissenschaft im Dritten Reich," *Kritische Justiz* (1969): 58 ff.

16. R. Wahsner, "Die Deutsche Rechtsgeschichte und der Faschismus," *Kritische Justiz* (1973): 172 ff.

17. A. Kranig, *Lockung und Zwang. Zur Arbeitsverfassung im Dritten Reich* (1983).

18. P. Schiera, *Il laboratorio borghese* (Bologna, 1986).

19. F. Wieacker, *Römische Rechtsgeschichte*, part 1 (1988), 47 ff., with additional references.

20. H. Planitz, *Germanische Rechtsgeschichte*, 2d ed. (1941), 1.

21. For this and additional references, see M. Stolleis, *Gemeinwohlformeln im nationalsozialistischen Recht* (1974), 12–30; and M. Stolleis and D. Simon, "Vorurteile und Werturteile der rechtshistorischen Forschung zum Nationalsozialismus," in *NS-Recht in historischer Perspektive*, Kolloquien des Instituts für Zeitgeschichte (1981), 13–51.

22. C. v. Schwerin, "Rechtsgeschichte und Rechtserneuerung," in J. W. Hedemann et al., *Zur Erneuerung des bürgerlichen Rechts* (1938), 39.

23. W. Merk, "Rechtserneuerung," *Volk und Werden* 2 (1933): 8.

24. Rückert (see note 2, above), with additional references.

25. Scholarship is still in need of a study of the Gierke renaissance under National Socialism. A few remarks must therefore suffice here: because of his cooperative law and his criticism of the Civil Code and of Labandian positivism, the "model German" Gierke seemed especially well suited to be the leading figure in legal thought under National Socialism (see the revealing nuances in the two editions of E. Wolf, *Große Rechtsdenker* [1939], 562–563, and 2d ed. [1944], 637 ff.); on the other hand, his ties to the "individualism" of the nineteenth century bothered the Nazi activists. R. Höhn, *Der individualistische Staatsbegriff und die juristische Staatsperson* (1935). On this see H. Helfritz, "Otto von Gierke und die neueste Lehre von der juristischen Staatsperson," *Reichsverwaltungsblatt* (1935): 485–490; R. Höhn, *Otto von Gierkes Staatslehre und un-*

sere Zeit (1936), reviewed by K. G. Hugelmann, "Zur Gierke-Renaissance im National-sozialismus," *Braune Wirtschaftspost* 5 (1936–1937): 990 ff.; H. Krupa, "Genos-senschaftslehre und soziologischer Pluralismus. Ein Beitrag zur Staatslehre Otto von Gierkes," *Archiv des öffentlichen Rechts Neue Folge* 32 (1940): 97–114; and Krupa, *Otto von Gierke und die Probleme der Rechtsphilosophie* (1940)).

26. References for Nicolai, Freisler, Elster, Bechert, Rust and others are in Rückert (see note 2, above), 200. For Hans Frank, who was particularly susceptible to popularized legal history, see the essay by Willoweit in *Rechtsgeschichte im Nationalsozialismus* (1989), 25 ff.

27. J. W. Hedemann, *Das Volksgesetzbuch des Deutschen* (1941); Hedemann, "Arbeit am Volksgesetzbuch," *Deutsches Recht* (1941): 1913 ff.; Hedemann, "Wert der Entwürfe. Arbeit am Volksgesetzbuch," *Zeitschrift der Akademie für Deutsches Recht* (1943): 3 ff.; Hedemann, Lehmann, and Siebert, *Volksgesetzbuch* (1941); R. Freisler, "Von der Arbeit am Volksgesetzbuch," *Zeitschrift der Akademie für Deutsches Recht* (1941): 10; H. Lange, "Wesen und Gestalt des Volksgesetzbuches," *Zeitschrift für die gesamten Staatswissenschaften* 103 (1943): 208 ff. Compare H. Hattenhauer, "Das NS-Volksgesetzbuch," in *Festschrift für R. Gmür* (1983); M. Stolleis, "Volksgesetzbuch," in A. Erler and E. Kaufmann, eds., *Handwörterbuch zur Deutschen Rechtsgeschichte,* vol. 5 (1993), cols. 990–992. On Hedemann see H. Mohnhaupt, in *Rechtsgeschichte im Nationalsozialismus* (1989), 107 ff.

28. M. Frisch, *Andorra*, 12. Bild, used as a motto by B. Rüthers in *Die unbegrenzte Auslegung* (1968).

29. See chapter 3.

30. H. Mohnhaupt, "Beobachtungen zur Rechtsgeschichte in der DDR im Spiegel der Zeitschrift 'Staat und Recht,'" *Ius Commune* 12 (1984): 253–285.

31. H. Mitteis, *Vom Lebenswert der Rechtsgeschichte* (1947).

32. H. Thieme, "Hundert Jahre Zeitschrift für Rechtsgeschichte," *Zeitschrift für Rechtsgeschichte, Germanistische Abteilung* 78 (1961): xv; in a similar vein, Thieme, "Zum Erscheinen von Band 100 der Savigny-Zeitschrift für Rechtsgeschichte," *Zeitschrift für Rechtsgeschichte, Germanistische Abteilung* 100 (1983): 1–8.

33. A. Erler, in Erler and E. Kaufmann, eds., *Handwörterbuch zur Deutschen Rechtsgeschichte,* vol. 4 (1990), col. 1325.

CHAPTER THREE

1. D. Schoenbaum, *Hitler's Social Revolution: Class and Status in Nazi Germany 1933–1939* (New York, 1966); R. Dahrendorf, *Society and Democracy in Germany* (Garden City, N.Y.: Doubleday, 1967), 402 ff.; H. Matzerath and H. Volkmann, "Modernisierungstheorie und Nationalsozialismus," in J. Kocka, ed., *Theorie in der Praxis des Historikers. Forschungsbeispiele und ihre Diskussion* (1977), 86–102; W. D. Narr, "Der Stellenwert der Auseinandersetzung mit dem Nationalsozialismus in der gesellschaftlichen Diskussion heute," *Niemandsland. Zeitschrift zwischen den Kulturen* 1 (1987): 26–44, especially 41: "National Socialism not only demonstrates the 'modernity' in the political reaction; it likewise reveals the reaction in 'modernity'." On the corresponding discussion in Italy, see I. Staff, "Italien und der Faschismus. Ein Beitrag zu Hermann Hellers Faschismus-Interpretation," in Ch. Müller and I. Staff, eds., *Der soziale Rechtsstaat* (1984), 443–444, with additional references.

2. Matzerath and Volkmann (see note 1, above), 99 ff.

3. H. Seier, in K. Schwabe, ed., *Deutsche Hochschullehrer als Elite 1815–1945,*

Deutsche Führungsschichten in der Neuzeit 17 (1988); on the prior history, see F. Ringer, *The Decline of the German Mandarins: The German Academic Community 1890–1933* (Cambridge, Mass.: Harvard University Press, 1969).

4. W. Kunkel, "Der Professor im Dritten Reich," in *Die deutsche Universität im Dritten Reich. Eine Vortragsreihe der Universität München* (1966), 112–113. For the biography of Kunkel, see D. Nörr in *Gedächnisschrift für Wolfgang Kunkel* (1984), 9–24.

5. On this see P. Landau in *Rechtsgeschichte im Nationalsozialismus* (1989), 11 ff.

6. H. Nehlsen, "Karl August Eckhardt, Nachruf," *Zeitschrift für Rechtsgeschichte, Germanistische Abteilung* 104 (1987): 497–536.

7. *Reichsgesetzblatt* 1 (1934): 727. On this see M. Wagner, *Justizausbildungsordnung des Neuen Reiches* (1934). Remarkable are the critical statements by Julius Binder, "Zur Neugestaltung des Rechtsunterrichts," *Deutsche Rechtswissenschaft* 2 (1937): 188–189, on the difficulties created by the "irruption of the Eckhardtian curriculum reform into our teaching routine."

8. A *Referendar* is a candidate for higher civil service who has passed the first state examination—Trans.

9. M. Sunnus, *Der NS-Rechtswahrerbund 1928–1945* (1990).

10. H. Kreller, "Die Bedeutung des römischen Rechts im neuen deutschen Hochschulunterricht," *Zeitschrift der Akademie für Deutsches Recht* (1936): 409–411. See also his comments in his 1945 work *Römische Rechtsgeschichte*, 2d expanded ed. (Tübingen, 1948), 3–6, on "contemporary Romanistic teaching at the university."

11. K. A. Eckhardt, "Das Studium der Rechtswissenschaft, 1935" (= *Der deutsche Staat der Gegenwart*, published by C. Schmitt, issue 11), 2d ed. (1940). For a detailed discussion of this talk, see Nehlsen (note 6, above), 504–505.

12. Palandt and Richter, *Die Justizausbildungsordnung des Reiches nebst Durchführungsbestimmungen* (1934). On Palandt, see H. Wrobel, "Otto Palandt zum Gedächtnis," *Kritische Justiz* 15 (1982): 1–17.

13. A. Hitler, *Mein Kampf*, translated by Ralph Manheim (Boston, 1943), 423. These words were gratefully picked up by Kreller (see note 9, above) and F. Wieacker, "Die Stellung der römischen Rechtsgeschichte in der heutigen Rechtsausbildung," *Zeitschrift der Akademie für Deutsches Recht* (1939): 403, 406.

14. On this see now D. Klippel, "Entstehung und heutige Aufgaben der 'Privatrechtsgeschichte der Neuzeit,'" in G. Köbler, ed., *Wege europäischer Rechtsgeschichte. K. Kroschell zum 60. Geburtstag* (1987), 145–167, with additional references.

15. P. Koschaker, however, made no such tactical concessions in his book *Die Krise des römischen Rechts und die romanistische Rechtswissenschaft* (1938), when he pleaded for the reintroduction of a course on Roman private law. Very instructive on this is the detailed review by Cl. v. Schwerin, *Deutsche Rechtswissenschaft* 4 (1939): 182–190.

16. Kunkel (see note 4, above), 126.

17. Kunkel (see note 4, above), 118: "In my field, eight of the ten or eleven internationally recognized scholars from the generation born around 1880 left."

18. P. Koschaker, "Probleme der heutigen romanistischen Rechtswissenschaft," *Deutsche Rechtswissenschaft* 5 (1940): 110, 113, speaks of the collapse of Romanistic courses, after 1938 also in Austria. Plans still called for one course on Roman law limited to a maximum of five hours.

19. A. Rosenberg, *Das Parteiprogramm. Wesen, Grundsätze und Ziele der NSDAP*, 25th ed. (1943), 49.

20. H. Frank, "Neugestaltung des deutschen Rechts," *Deutsches Recht* (1935): 470: "We demand above all that *foreign* law, which serves a materialist world view, be replaced by German common law." For a catalog of the supposed characteristics of Roman and German law, see K. Luig, "Die sozialethischen Werte des römischen und germanischen Rechts . . . ," in the Kroeschell festschrift (note 13, above), 218 ff., especially 286.

21. W. Merk, *Vom Werden und Wesen des deutschen Rechts*, 3d ed. (1935), 35.

22. Klippel (see note 14, above), 145 ff.

23. Similar images about the "conquests of new fields" in Germanic law are in Cl. v. Schwerin, *Zeitschrift der Akademie für Deutsches Recht* (1938), 15. For ancient legal history, see Martin David's inaugural lecture in Leiden, *Der Rechtshistoriker und seine Aufgabe* (Leiden, 1937), which, as far as I know, remained completely unknown to German scholars.

24. F. Wieacker, "Die Stellung der römischen Rechtsgeschichte in der heutigen Rechtsausbildung," *Zeitschrift der Akademie für Deutsches Recht* (1939): 403–406.

25. Ibid.

26. See note 15, above.

27. Koschacker (see note 18, above).

28. According to the report by D. S., *Zeitschrift der Akademie für Deutsches Recht* (1938): 24.

29. F. Wieacker, "Über 'Aktualisierung' der Ausbildung im römischen Recht," in *Gedenkschrift Koschacker* (1953), 519; Wieacker, "Der gegenwärtige Stand der Disziplin der neueren Privatrechtsgeschichte," in *Eranion Maridakis*, vol. 1 (Athens, 1963), 339–366.

30. G. Dilcher, "Vom Beitrag der Rechtsgeschichte zu einer zeitgemäßen Zivilrechtswissenschaft," *Archiv für civilistische Praxis* 184 (1984): 247–288; on this see the brief remarks by D. Simon, *Rechtshistorisches Journal* 4 (1985): 272–273; D. Klippel, *Juristische Zeitgeschichte. Die Bedeutung der Rechtsgeschichte für die Zivilrechtswissenschaft* (1985); and see my review of Klippel, *Zeitschrift für Rechtsgeschichte, Germanistische Abteilung* (1987): 813–816.

31. D. Simon, "Memorandum zur Forschungsplanung und Forschungsorganisation," unpublished manuscript, 1987, at the Max Planck Institute for European Legal History, Frankfurt.

32. J. v. Kempski, "Krise des römischen Rechts oder Grundlagenkrise der Rechtswissenschaft," *Archiv für Rechts- und Sozialphilosophie* 32 (1938–1939): 404; E. Schönbauer, "Zur Krise des römischen Rechts," in *Festschrift Koschaker*, vol. 2 (1939), 385–410. Dissenting: Koschaker, "Probleme" (see note 18, above), 114; M. Kaser, "Die deutsche Wissenschaft vom römischen Recht seit 1933," *Forschungen und Fortschritte* 15 (1939): 205; F. Wieacker, "Der Standort der römischen Rechtsgeschichte in der deutschen Gegenwart," *Deutsches Recht* (1942): 40–55; E. Genzmer, "Was heißt und zu welchem Ende sutdiert man antike Rechtsgeschichte?" *Zeitschrift der Akademie für Deutsches Recht* 3 (1936): 403–408; R. Köstler, "Was heißt und zu welchem Zweck studiert man Rechtsgeschichte?," *Zeitschrift der Akademie für Deutsches Recht* 7 (1940: 194–195).

33. H. Kreller, "Die Bedeutung" (see note 10, above).

34. The Italian Minister of Justice, Arrigo Solmi, spoke about the "exaggerated suggestion" to eliminate Roman law (*Deutsches Recht* [1938]: 176) and expressed the hope that the new Germany, too, would recognize the "incomparable and irreplaceable

value of Roman law." See also the Frankfurt lecture by Emilio Betti, "Grund und Wert einer Lehre der 'Antiken Rechtsgeschichte' mit vorwiegender Berücksichtigung des römischen Rechts," edited by G. Crifó, in *Estudios de Derecho Romano en Honor de Alvaro d'Ors* (Pamplona, 1987), 381–400. For the same reason the Romanists also liked to cite in their footnotes the publications of Italian colleagues on Roman law. For a typical example, see B. v. Bonin, *Vom nordischen Blut im römischen Recht* (1935).

35. Kreller, "Die Bedeutung" (see note 10, above).

36. Ibid.

37. H. Lange, "Deutsche Romanistik?" *Deusche Juristenzeitung* (1934): 1493–1494.

38. E. Schönbauer (see note 32, above), with references to his older works. See also the obituary by A. Lhotsky, *Almanach der Österreichischen Akademie der Wissenschaft* 116 (1967): 295–300.

39. Along these lines, for example, O. Palandt, *Kommentar zum BGB*, 3d ed., p. xxxix; also in *Deutsche Justiz* (1939): 532.

40. F. Schulz, *Prinzipien des römischen Rechts* (1934).

41. W. Kunkel, "Fides als schöpferisches Element im römischen Schuldrecht," in *Festschrift Koschaker*, vol. 2 (1939), 1–15.

42. See note 37, above.

43. Schulz (see note 40, above), 161.

44. Ibid., 107.

45. Lange (see note 37, above), 1495.

46. Schulz (see note 40, above), 172.

47. The meeting was held October 12–15, 1936, and opened with a speech by Hans Frank. Reports on the meeting were written by H. Conrad and G. Dulckeit, in *Zeitschrift für Rechtsgeschichte, Germanistische Abteilung* 57 (1937): 767, and *Zeitschrift für Rechtsgeschichte, Romanistische Abteilung* 57 (1937): 534, 539 ff. See also the documentation by B. Sutter, *Fünfundzwanzig Deutsche Rechtshistorikertage, Heidelberg 1927–Graz 1984* (Heidelberg, 1984).

48. Dulckeit (see note 47, above), 540.

49. B. v. Bonin (see note 34, above).

50. Cl. v. Schwerin, "Rechtsgeschichte und Rechtserneuerung," in J. W. Hedemann et al., *Zur Erneuerung des bürgerlichen Rechts* (1938), 42.

51. Tübingen, 1939 (= Recht und Staat in Geschichte und Gegenwart 126).

52. Ibid., 7.

53. Ibid., 31.

54. Ibid., 36.

55. Ibid., 41. See also his article in *Zeitschrift für Rechtsgeschichte, Romanistische Abteilung* 60 (1940): 95 ff.; as well as F. Wieacker, "Das antike römische Recht und der neuzeitliche Individualismus," *Zeitschrift für die gesamten Staatswissenschaften* 101 (1941): 167–171.

56. In the same vein, see Wieacker (note 55 above).

57. M. Bullinger, *Öffentliches Recht und Privatrecht. Studien über Sinn und Funktion der Unterscheidung* (1968); S. Gagnér, "Über Voraussetzungen einer Verwendung der Sprachformel 'Öffentliches Recht und Privatrecht' im kanonistischen Bereich," in *Deutsche Landesreferate zum VII. Internationalen Kongreß für Rechtsvergleichung in Uppsala 1966* (1967), 21–55; D. Grimm, "Zur politischen Funktion der Trennung von

öffentlichem und privatem Recht in Deutschland," in *Recht und Staat der bürgerlichen Gesellschaft* (1987), 84–103.

58. M. Stolleis, "Die Entstehung des Interventionsstaates und das öffentliche Recht," *Zeitschrift für neuere Rechtsgeschichte* (1989): 129–147.

59. Waldmann, "Öffentliches und privates Recht in nationalsozialistischer Weltanschauung," *Reichsverwaltungblatt* (1934): 733; E. Swoboda, "Die gegenseitige Durchdringung des öffentlichen und privaten Rechts," *Archiv für Rechts- und Sozialphilosophie* 28 (1934): 184; "Die aktuellen Tendenzen im öffentlichen Recht und im Privatrecht," in R. Höhn, Th. Maunz, and E. Swoboda, *Grundfragen der Rechtsauffassung* (1938), 89; U. Scheuner, "Die Bedeutung der Unterscheidung zwischen öffentlichem und privatem Recht, insbesondere für die Gerichtsverfassung," *Deutsche Juristenzeitung* (1935): 1462; G. A. Walz, "Der Gegensatz von öffentlichem und privatem Recht," *Zeitschrift der Akademie für Deutsches Recht* 98 (1938): 581; E. R. Huber, "Einheit und Gliederung des völkischen Rechts. Ein Beitrag zur Überwindung des Gegensatzes von öffentlichem und privatem Recht," *Zeitschrift für die gesamten Staatswissenschaften* 98 (1938): 310; H. Kummer, "Öffentliches und privates Recht in der politischen Grundordnung," *Zeitschrift für die gesamten Staatswissenschaften* 104 (1944): 29.

60. H. Meyer, "Öffentliches und Privates Recht nach germanischer Anschauung," *Zeitschrift der Akademie für Deutsches Recht* (1935): 49.

61. G. Dulckeit, "Öffentliches Recht und Privatrecht im römischen Recht," *Zeitschrift der Akademie für Deutsches Recht* (1936): 277.

62. On this, see A. Steinwenter, "Utilitas publica—utilitas singulorum," in *Festschrift Koschacker*, vol. 1 (1939), 85.

63. P. Bender, *Die Rezeption des römischen Rechts im Urteil der deutschen Rechtswissenschaft* (1979), with a foreword by H. Thieme. The dissertation was completed in 1955. A summary of the current state of the discussion can now be found in H. Kiefner, "Rezeption (privatrechtlich)," in A. Erler and E. Kaufmann, eds., *Handwörterbuch zur Deutschen Rechtsgeschichte*, vol. 4 (1990), cols. 970–984.

64. H. Ch. Caro, *Der Fortschritt des Deutschen Rechts unter Kaiser Wilhelm II* (1913), 11.

65. Koschaker criticized Spengler's amateurish ideas on Roman law; see *Deutsche Rechtswissenschaft* 5 (1940): 110 (115).

66. R. Schlette, "Houston Steward Chamberlain als Wegbereiter nationalsozialistischer Weltanschauung," *Publik* 42 (1970): 21, and 43 (1971): 28; G. Field, *Evangelist of Race: The Germanic Vision of Houston Steward Chamberlain* (1981).

67. K. Sontheimer, *Antidemokratisches Denken in der Weimarer Republik* (1962, study edition 1968), 237–241.

68. F. Wieacker, *Das antike römische Recht* (see note 55, above), 167.

69. W. Engelmann, *Die Wiedergeburt der Rechtskultur in Italien durch die wissenschaftliche Lehre. Eine Darlegung der Entfaltung des gemeinen italienischen Rechts und seiner Justizkultur im Mittelalter unter dem Einfluß der herrschenden Lehre der Gutachterpraxis der Rechtsgelehrten und der Verantwortung der Richter im Sindikatsprozeß* (1938); H. Coing, *Die Rezeption des römischen Rechts in Frankfurt* (1939). F. Schaffstein, "Die Carolina in ihrer Bedeutung für die strafrechtliche Begriffsbildung" (1932); Schaffstein, "Tiberius Decianus und seine Bedeutung für die Entstehung des Allgemeinen Teils im Gemeinen deutschen Strafrecht" (1938); both essays now in *Abhandlungen zur Strafrechtsgeschichte und zur Wissenschaftsgeschichte* (1986). Also K.

Michaelis, "Wandlungen des deutschen Rechtsdenkens seit dem Eindringen des fremden Rechts," in G. Dahm et al., *Grundfragen der neuen Rechtswissenschaft* (1935), 9–61.

70. G. Dahm, "Zur Rezeption des römisch-italienischen Rechts," *Historische Zeitschrift* 167 (1942; reprinted 1955): 50.

71. F. Wieacker, "Corpus iuris," *Zeitschrift für die gesamten Staatswissenschaften* 102 (1942): 444; Wieacker, "Der Standort der römischen Rechtsgeschichte in der deutschen Gegenwart," *Deutsches Recht* (1942): 49–55; Wieacker, "Ratio scripta. Das römische Recht und die abendländische Rechtswissenschaft," in *Vom römischen Recht, Wirklichkeit und Überlieferung* (1944), 195 ff.; Wieacker, *Das römische Recht und das deutsche Rechtsbewußtsein* (1945); Wieacker, *Privatrechtsgeschichte der Neuzeit* (1952).

72. Wieacker, *Vom römischen Recht* (see note 71, above), 222.

73. Ibid., 246.

74. On this, see H. Schultze-v. Lasaulx's review of Wieacker, *Privatrechtsgeschichte, Zeitschrift für ausländisches und internationales Privatrecht* 20 (1955): 536; and Wieacker's review of Koschaker, *Gnomon* 21 (1949): 187. Summary overview in Wieacker, *Privatrechtsgeschichte der Neuzeit*, 2d ed. (1967), 124 ff.; and Kiefner (see note 63, above).

75. Wieacker, "Der Standort der römischen Rechtsgeschichte" (see note 71, above).

76. Revealing in this regard is the talk entitled "The State of European Jurisprudence" that Carl Schmitt gave in 1943 and 1944 in Bucharest, Budapest, Madrid, Coimbra, Barcelona, and Leipzig. For a more detailed discussion, see M. Stolleis, "Carl Schmitt," in M. J. Sattler, ed., *Staat und Recht. Die deutsche Staatslehre im 19. und 20. Jahrhundert* (1972), 123–146 (144–145).

77. D. Schwab, "Zum Selbstverständnis der historischen Rechtswissenschaft im Dritten Reich," *Kritische Justiz* (1969): 58–70; R. Wahsner, "Die Deutsche Rechtsgeschichte und der Faschismus," *Kritische Justiz* (1973): 172 ff.; M. Senn, *Rechtshistorisches Selbstverständnis im Wandel* (1982); Nehlsen (see note 6, above).

78. Informative on this point are, for example, the essays by Adalbert Erler in the magazine *Der Ring* (edited by H. von Gleichen), 1928–1930.

79. On this, see especially the following works by K. von See: *Deutsche Germanen-Ideologie vom Humanismus bis zur Gegenwart* (1970); *Die Ideen von 1789 und die Ideen von 1914* (1975); and "Kulturkritik und Germanenforschung zwischen den Weltkriegen," *Historische Zeitschrift* 245 (1987): 343–362, with further references.

80. H. Hattenhauer, ed., *Rechtswissenschaft im NS-Staat. Der Fall Eugen Wohlhaupter* (1987), 16. See, for instance, H. Meyer, *Das Wesen des Führertums in der germanischen Verfassungsgeschichte* (1938). Parallel phenomensuggested on the occasion of Werner Jaeger's one hundredth birthday (U. Hölscher, "Angestrengtes Griechentum," *Frankfurter Allgemeine Zeitung*, July 30, 1988, 19).

81. H. Thieme, "Ideengeschichte und Rechtsgeschichte," in *Festschrift J. von Gierke* (1950), 267; now in Thieme, *Gesammelte Schriften*, vol. 1 (1987), 5.

82. Thieme, *Gesammelte Schriften* (see note 81, above), 4.

83. Likewise D. Klippel (see note 14, above), 158–159.

84. See, for instance, G. Lenz, "Die Erneuerung unseres Verfahrensrechts aus dem germanischen Rechtsdenken," *Deutsche Rechtswissenschaft* 2 (1937): 325–365.

85. R. Bechert, "Der sittliche Ehebruch," *Zeitschrift der Akademie für Deutsches Recht* (1939): 444. Critical response by K. G. Hugelmann, "Rechtsgeschichte und Ge-

setzgebung," *Zeitschrift der Akademie für Deutsches Recht* (1939): 674–677. On Hugel-mann, see, on the one hand, the obituary by E. Schönbauer, *Almanach der Öster-reichischen Akademie der Wissenschaften* 110 (1961): 377–390; and, on the other, G. Oberkofler and E. Rabofsky, eds., *Juristen-Romanistik im NS-Staat, Pflicht der Ver-nunft. Festschrift für Manfred Buhr* (East Berlin, 1987), 44–60 (54–55).

86. The transmission of this saying, which may even have been invented by Rauschning, is uncertain. In Rauschning's book *Gespräche mit Hitler* (Vienna, 1973), 52, we read: "these professors and obscurantists, who are making up their Nordic religions, are merely spoiling everything for me." Still, it expresses perfectly Hitler's well-attested hostility to scholarship.

87. Nehlsen (see note 6, above), with additional references.

88. H. Mitteis, *Vom Lebenswert der Rechtsgeschichte* (1947), 7.

89. Confirmed by Cl. v. Schwerin, *Deutsche Rechtswissenschaft* 4 (1939): 182–190 (188).

90. This statement must be qualified at least with regard to Heinrich Mitteis, *Der Staat des hohen Mittelalters* (1940). See P. Landau, H. Nehlsen, and D. Willoweit, eds., *Heinrich Mitteis nach hundert Jahren (1889–1989)* (1991), with additional references.

91. O. Brunner, *Land und Herrschaft. Grundfragen der territorialen Verfassungs-geschichte Österreichs im Mittelalter* (1939), 3d ed. (1943), 5th ed. (1965).

CHAPTER FOUR

1. In a review of O. Koellreuter, *Der deutsche Führerstaat, Juristische Wochenschrift* (1934): 538.

2. This is not the place to address the difficulties inherent in the term *ideology*. Here it means the values that form the basis of political action and (legal) argumenta-tion. An overview of the state of the discussion on the problem of ideology can be found in the collection of essays entitled *Ideologie*, edited by K. Lenk (Neuwied, 1961); E. Topitsch, *Sozialphilosophie zwischen Ideologie und Wissenschaft* (Neuwied, 1961); E. Topitsch, "Ideologie," in *Staatslexikon der Görresgesellschaft*, 6th ed. (1959).

3. P. Schwerdtner, *Fürsorgetheorie und Entgelttheorie im Recht der Arbeitsbedin-gungen, ein Beitrag zum Gemeinschafts- und Vertragsdenken im Individualarbeitsrecht und allgemeinen Zivilrecht* (1970); Schwerdtner, "Gemeinschaft, Treue, Fürsorge—oder: die Himmelfahrt des Wortes," *Zeitschrift für Rechtspolitik* (1970): 62–63, with addi-tional references. See also Th. Ramm, "Die Rechtswirkung der Anfechtung des Ar-beitsvertrages," *Arbeit und Recht* (1963): 97 ff., who points to the continuity between National Socialist and current doctrines of labor law.

4. *Entscheidungen des Bundesverwaltungsgerichts* 2:85 (87); 2:295 (300); 4:167 (171). This formulation was rejected in particular by the Federal Constitutional Court (Bun-desverfassungsgericht), *Entscheidungen des Bundesverfassungsgerichts* 7:377 (411). See also O. Bachof, in *Juristenzeitung* (1957): 337; K. Hesse, *Grundzüge des Verfassungs-rechts der Bundesrepublik Deutschland*, 4th ed. (Karlsruhe, 1969), 129n.6.

5. *Entscheidungen des Bundesverwaltungsgerichts* 1:159 (162); *Juristenzeitung* (1954): 757.

6. Hamann and Lenz, *Das Grundgesetz*, 3d ed. (Neuwied-Berlin, 1970).

7. A detailed discussion is in B. Rüthers, *Die unbegrenzte Auslegung* (Tübingen, 1968), 91 ff.

8. Ibid.

9. Cornelia Berning, *Vom "Abstammungsnachweis" zum "Zuchtwart"* (Berlin, 1964);

Siegfried Bork, *Mißbrauch der Sprache. Tendenzen nationalsozialistisher Sprachregelung* (Bern, 1970); Sigrid Frind, "Die Sprache als Propagandainstrument in der Publizistik des Dritten Reiches," Ph.D. diss., Berlin, 1964; E. Seidl and I. Seidl-Zlotty, *Sprachwandel im Dritten Reich* (Halle an der Saale, 1961).

10. G. Radbruch, *Kulturlehre des Sozialismus*, 2d ed. (Berlin, 1927), 22.

11. K. Sontheimer, *Antidemokratisches Denken in der Weimarer Republik* (Munich, 1962), quotation from the 1968 study edition, 251.

12. Radbruch (see note 10, above), 11.

13. Eberhard Welty, *Gemeinschaft und Einzelmensch* (Salzburg and Leipzig, 1935), with additional references to the communal concept in Catholic social doctrine.

14. Hans Gerber, *Die Idee des Staates in der neueren evangelisch-theologischen Ethik* (Berlin, 1930), 22 ff.

15. Ferdinand Tönnies, *Gemeinschaft und Gesellschaft*, 1st ed. (1887; reprint, Darmstadt, 1963); H. Plessner, *Grenzen der Gemeinschaft* (Bonn, 1924); F. Sander, *Allgemeine Gemeinschaftslehre* (Jena, 1930).

16. In a speech at the Nuremberg party congress in 1934, in *Deutsche Juristenzeitung* (1934): cols. 1169 ff. (1172).

17. A list of examples: Bilfinger, "Der Gemeinschaftsgedanke im geltenden Recht," *Juristische Wochenschrift* (1933): 2550; E. Langen-Eupen, "Der Gemeinschaftsgedanke im geltenden Recht," *Deutsche Justiz* 34 (1934): 160; Allardt, *Das deutsche Volk als Gemeinschaft* (Berlin, 1935); Höhn, *Vom Wesen der Gemeinschaft* (Berlin, 1934); *Rechtsgemeinschaft und Volksgemeinschaft* (Hamburg, 1935); Roquette, "Das Mietrecht im Lichte des Gedankens der Volksgemeinschaft," *Juristische Wochenschrift* (1935): 1670; Stoll, "Gemeinschaftsgedanke und Schuldvertrag," *Deutsche Juristenzeitung* (1936): 414; Schieck, "Boden und Gemeinschaft," *Deutsche Justiz* (1936): 807; Siebert, "Arbeit und Gemeinschaft," *Deutsche Justiz* (1936): 808; Freiherr von Steinäcker, "Rechtsprechung und Gemeinschaft," *Deutsche Justiz* (1936): 808; Graf von der Goltz, "Ehre und Gemeinschaft," *Deutsche Justiz* (1936): 809; Larenz, "Gemeinschaft und Rechtsstellung," *Deutsche Rechtswissenschaft* (1936): 31; Rothe, "Schadensersatzanspruch und Gemeinschaftsgedanke," *Juristische Wochenschrift* (1937): 1449; Freisler, "Gemeinschaft und Recht," *Deutsche Justiz* (1938): 1867; Hoffmann, "Der einzelne und die Gemeinschaft," *Juristische Wochenschrift* (1938): 2581; Oppermann, "Das Arbeitsverhältnis als Gemeinschaftsverhältnis," *Juristische Wochenschrift* (1938): 2509; Kaser, *Römisches Recht als Gemeinschaftsordnung* (Tübingen, 1939); Stöwer, "Der Richter und die Ordnung der Gemeinschaft," *Deutsche Justiz* (1942): 763.

18. According to the material I have analyzed (*Reichsgesetzblatt* 1 [1933–1945]), the term *common weal (Gemeinwohl)* was used in legislation about one hundred times, *common welfare (gemeines Wohl)* about twenty times, *common interest (Gemeinnutz)* and *welfare of the people (Wohl der Allgemeinheit)* about ten times each, *common benefit (gemeiner Nutzen)* five times, and *the best for all (gemeines Bestes)* twice. Such an analysis says little without an examination of the contexts in which the terms appear. Still, it is worth thinking about why, within a group of synonyms, certain words and phrases were preferred while others disappeared. See M. Stolleis, *Gemeinwohlformeln im nationalsozialistischen Recht* (1974).

19. In the material mentioned in note 18, above, the term was used more than a hundred times.

20. See, for example, W. Dyckmans, *Das mittelalterliche Gemeinschaftsdenken unter*

dem Gesichtspunkt der Totalität (Paderborn, 1937); J. Eichinger, "Individuum und Gemeinschaft bei Aegidius Romanus," *Divus Thomas* 13 (1935): 160 ff.; Th. Eschmann, "Gemeinschaft und Einzelmensch," *Bulletin thomiste* 4 (1936): 708 ff.; J. Tonneau, "Personne et individu," *Bulletin thomiste* 5 (1937–1939): 467 ff.; E. Kurz, *Individuum und Gemeinschaft beim hl. Thomas von Aquin* (Munich, 1933).

21. E. R. Huber, *Verfassung* (Hamburg, 1937), 243.

22. C. H. Ule, "Herrschaft und Führung im nationalsozialistischen Reich," *Verwaltungsarchiv* 46 (1941): 51n.75.

23. Emge, "Über die Beziehungen der nationalsozialistischen Bewegung zu Rechtswissenschaft und Recht," *Deutsches Recht* (1934): 33.

24. H. Helfritz, "Rechtsstaat und nationalsozialistischer Staat," *Deutsche Juristenzeitung* (1934): 427.

25. W. Siebert, "Das Wesen der Rechtsfähigkeit privatrechtlicher Personenverbände," *Deutsche Juristenzeitung* (1935): 713.

26. On the distinction between abstract-general and concrete-general concepts, see K. Larenz, "Gemeinschaft und Rechtsstellung," *Deutsche Rechtswissenschaft* 36: 31–32; Larenz, "Zur Logik des konkreten Begriffs—eine Voruntersuchung zur Rechtsphilosophie," *Deutsche Rechtswissenschaft* 40: 279; Larenz, *Methodenlehre der Rechtswissenschaft*, 2d ed. (1969), chap. 5. Rüthers (see note 7, above), 302–303, gives many additional references.

27. *Reichsgesetzblatt* 1 (1933): 1058; expanded in *Reichsgesetzblatt* 1 (1935): 1247 to business serving the health of the *Volk*. See Grund, "Das Gesetz über die Beschränkung der Nachbarrechte," *Juristische Wochenschrift* (1934): 203; Neubert, "Nachbarrecht und Gemeinwohl," *Deutsche Justiz* (1934): 1240; Klausing, "Immissionsrecht und Industrialisierung," *Juristische Wochenschrift* (1937): 68 ff.

28. A good overview is given by F. Wieacker, "Die Enteignung," in Frank, *Deutsches Verwaltungsrecht*, § 23; and Weber, "Das Problem der öffentlich-rechtlichen Entschädigung," in *Deutsches Verwaltungsrecht*, § 24; the latter with a compilation of forty-eight compensation clauses. See also Walther Merk, *Das Eigentum im Wandel der Zeiten* (1934); and F. Wieacker, *Wandlungen der Eigentumsverfassung* (1935).

29. W. Herschel, "Wiederkehrschuldverhältnis, Sukzessivlieferungsvertrag und Gemeinschaft," *Juristische Wochenschrift* (1936): 633.

30. H. Stoll, "Gemeinschaft und Schuldvertrag," *Deutsche Juristenzeitung* (1936): 414; Stoll, *Die Lehre von den Leistungsstörungen* (1936). See also W. Arnold, "Die Eingliederung in die Gemeinschaft als Verpflichtungsgrund im künftigen Schuldrecht," law diss., Gießen, 1937.

31. Two jurists who did so were H. Dölle, "Vom alten zum neuen Schuldrecht," *Deutsche Juristenzeitung* (1934): 1016 (1018); and H. Lange, *Vom alten zum neuen Schuldrecht* (Hamburg, 1934).

32. Rothe, "Schadensersatzanspruch und Gemeinschaftsgedanke," *Juristische Wochenschrift* (1937): 1451.

33. Roquette, "Das Mietrecht im Lichte des Gedankens der Volksgemeinschaft," *Juristische Wochenschrift* (1935): 1670.

34. *Reichsgesetzblatt* 1 (1934): 45.

35. See especially W. Siebert, *Das Arbeitsverhältnis in der Ordnung der nationalen Arbeit* (1935); and Dersch and Nipperdey, in *Zeitschrift der Akademie für deutsches Recht* (1935): 371, 911.

36. "Urteil des sozialen Ehrengerichts, Treuhänder Bez. Brandenburg, vom

18.12.34," *Juristische Wochenschrift* (1935): col. 1299. The effects of the idea of community in labor law are described in Ulf Hientsch, *Arbeitsrechtslehren im Dritten Reich* (1970); Rüthers (see note 7, above), 379–400; Rüthers, "Die Betriebsverfassung im Nationalsozialismus," *Arbeit und Recht* (1970): 97 ff.; O. Radke, "Die Auswirkungen des 'Gesetzes zur Ordnung der nationalen Arbeit,'" *Arbeit und Recht* (1965): 302–308; Th. Ramm (see note 3, above).

37. E. R. Huber, in *Juristische Wochenschrift* (1934): 1019; similar statement in his article "Betriebsgemeinschaft und Arbeitsverhältnis," *Juristische Wochenschrift* (1937): 1111.

38. Kalberlah, among many others, in *Deutsche Justiz* (1941): 331.

39. Deneke, "Die soziale Ehrengerichtsbarkeit," *Juristische Wochenschrift* (1934): 1010.

40. Hitler, *Mein Kampf,* translated by Ralph Manheim (Boston, 1943), 252.

41. H. Lange, "Nationalsozialismus und bürgerliches Recht," in Frank, *NS-Handbuch* (1935), col. 954.

42. B. Rüthers, *Institutionelles Rechtsdenken im Wandel der Verfassungsepochen* (Bad Homburg v. d. H., 1970), 23–24.

43. Ibid., 25.

44. Ibid., 27.

45. Hamm, "Recht und Wirtschaft," *Deutsche Juristenzeitung* (1933): 1402; Merkel, "Von der Gewerbefreiheit zur geordneten Wirtschaft," *Deutsche Justiz* (1936): 800; Merkel, "Beispiele zur Neubildung des Gemeinschaftsrechts," *Deutsche Juristenzeitung* (1936): 228; G. W. Heinemann, "Die Verfassung der gewerblichen Wirtschaft," *Juristische Wochenschrift* (1935): 1057–1058.

Darge, "Das Energiewirtschaftsgesetz," *Deutsche Juristenzeitung* (1936): 26; Fr. List, *Energierecht* (Berlin, 1938); H. Müller, *Gesetz zur Förderung der Energiewirtschaft* (Berlin, 1936).

Danielcik, "Umbruch im Kartellwesen und Kartellrecht," *Juristische Wochenschrift* (1935): 3593; Müllensiefen and Dörinkel, *Das neue Kartell-, Zwangskartell- und Preisüberwachungsrecht,* 2d ed. (Berlin, 1934); O. Klug, "Wandlungen des Kartellrechts," *Juristische Wochenschrift* (1934): 2369.

46. W. Hoffmann, "Der einzelne und die Allgemeinheit im Urheberrecht und im gewerblichen Rechtsschutz," *Juristische Wochenschrift* (1936): 153; Waldmann, "Nationalsozialistische Forderungen an das kommende Patentgesetz," *Deutsche Juristenzeitung* (1935): 790; Klauer, "Die Neugestaltung des deutschen Patentrechts," *Juristische Wochenschrift* (1936): 1489; Hedemann, "Deutschlands neues Patentgesetz," *Deutsche Juristenzeitung* (1936): 657; Harmsen, "Das neue Gebrauchsmustergesetz," *Juristische Wochenschrift* (1936): 1494; Hueck, "Sammelbericht über neues Patentrecht," *Kritische Vierteljahresschrift für Gesetzgebung und Rechtswissenschaft* 24 (1938): 292; Kisch, "Der soziale Gehalt des Patentrechts," *Deutsche Juristenzeitung* (1935): 655.

47. F. Wieacker, *Privatrechtsgeschichte der Neuzeit,* 2d ed. (Göttingen, 1967), 551–552. Parallel tendencies are described by C. F. Menger, *Moderner Staat und Rechtsprechung* (Tübingen, 1968), 18, in economic administrative law; and by P. Badura, *Das Verwaltungsmonopol* (Berlin, 1963), 135 and passim.

48. Siegert, "Die gemeinschaftsbildende Kraft des Strafrechts," *Deutsche Juristenzeitung* (1936): 476.

49. Gerland, "Neues Strafrecht," *Deutsche Juristenzeitung* (1933): 857.

50. For instance, the call for a "protection of the community's honor": see Freisler,

in *Deutsche Justiz* (1936): 1458; W. Tepper, "Die Gemeinschaftsehre," law diss., Cologne, 1937.

51. Dahm, *Gemeinschaft und Strafrecht* (Hamburg, 1935). A sketchy attempt also by Nicolai, *Die rassengesetzliche Rechtslehre*, 3d ed. (Munich, 1934), 44–45.

52. Dahm, "Verrat und Verbrechen," *Zeitschrift für die gesamten Staatswissenschaften* 95 (1935): 284.

53. E. R. Huber, "Die deutsche Staatswissenschaft," *Zeitschrift für die gesamten Staatswissenschaften* 95 (1935): 58–59. Administrative law cannot be addressed in the present framework. A summary of the most important voices is found in Frank, *Deutsches Verwaltungsrecht* (Munich, 1937). See also H. R. Külz, "Verwaltungskontrolle unter dem Nationalsozialismus," *Kritische Justiz* (1969): 367.

54. Sontheimer (see note 11, above), chap. 4, provides a summary overview.

55. For instance, Th. Maunz noted that it was a basic question "whether the legal norm continues to be at the center and community forms merely an intepretive aid or a general clause in the administration's application of the norms; or whether the actual communities with their concrete orders will be placed at the center and constitute the law itself" (in Frank, *Deutsches Verwaltungsrecht*, § 2, p. 34).

56. See Klaus Hornung, *Der Jungdeutsche Orden* (Düsseldorf, 1958), 80–81.

57. Höhn, *Der bürgerliche Rechtsstaat und die neue Front* (Berlin, 1929).

58. O. v. Gierke, *Das Wesen der menschlichen Verbände*, reprint (Darmstadt, 1954), 10.

59. Hans Frank, speech in Berlin on June 18, 1938, in *Juristische Wochenschrift* (1938): 1799.

60. Höhn, "Die staatsrechtliche Lage," *Volk im Werden* (1934–1935): 286.

61. Ibid., 284.

62. Maunz, "Das Verwaltungsrecht des nationalsozialistischen Staates," in Frank, *Deutsches Verwaltungsrecht*, § 2; Maunz, "Das Ende des subjektiven öffentlichen Rechts," *Zeitschrift für die gesamten Staatswissenschaften* 96 (1936): 71; Jerusalem, *Gemeinschaft und Staat* (Tübingen, 1930); Jerusalem, *Der Staat* (Jena, 1934); more recently again in Jerusalem, *Die Zersetzung im Rechtsdenken* (Tübingen, 1968). Also G. Küchenhoff, *Nationaler Gemeinschaftsstaat, Volksrecht und Volksrechtsprechung* (Berlin and Leipzig, 1934).

63. Höhn, *Der individualistische Staatsbegriff und die juristische Staatsperson* (Berlin, 1935).

64. Ibid., 15.

65. Overview in Sontheimer (see note 11, above), 348–349.

66. Lange, "Deutsche Romanistik?" *Deutsche Juristenzeitung* (1934): 1493.

67. Compare Walz, *Der Begriff der Verfassung* (Berlin, 1942), 63: "Now that the new state has been permeated by *volkisch*–National Socialist principles, there is no reason to maintain the old opposition between *Volk* and state."

68. Hitler, *Mein Kampf*, translated by Ralph Manheim (Boston, 1943), 393.

69. E. R. Huber, "Die Einheit der Staatsgewalt," *Deutsche Juristenzeitung* (1934): 955.

70. See note 19, above.

71. *Reichsgesetzblatt* 1 (1934): 48.

72. *Reichsgesetzblatt* 1 (1933): 540.

73. *Reichsgesetzblatt* 1 (1936): 993.

74. *Reichsgesetzblatt* 1 (1937): 192.

75. *Reichsgesetzblatt* 1 (1941): 383.

76. *Reichsgesetzblatt* 1 (1940): 485 (violation of the honor of the "community of the Reich Labor Service," corrosion of the "community in the Reich Labor Service").

77. *Reichsgesetzblatt* 1 (1937): 1180.

78. Freisler, "Gemeinschaft und Recht," *Deutsche Justiz* (1938): 1867; Höhn, *Volk und Verfassung* (Hamburg, 1937).

79. W. Merk, *Der Staatsgedanke im Dritten Reich* (Stuttgart, 1935); Höhn, in *Zeitschrift für die gesamten Staatswissenschaften* 95 (1935): 656.

80. Reuß, in *Juristische Wochenschrift* (1936): 2205, also used the argument of inter-state relations to preserve the concept of the state.

81. Helfritz, in *Reichsverwaltungsblatt* (1935): 485; Reuß, in *Juristische Wochenschrift* (1938): 1308; Jerusalem, *Der Staat* (Jena, 1934), 311n.1; Neesze, in *Zeitschrift für die gesamten Staatswissenschaften* 96 (1936): 395. Merk's work was vigorously criticized by Franzen, in *Archiv des öffentlichen Rechts NF* 28 (1937): 110–111; Münch, in *Zeitschrift für die gesamten Staatswissenschaften* 97 (1937): 558; and Seydel, in *Deutsches Recht* (1936): 48, to which Merk responded in *Archiv des öffentlichen Rechts NF* 29 (1938): 99.

82. Koellreutter, "Japans Staatserneuerung," *Volk und Reich* (1941): 304; Koellreutter, "Das faschistische Staatsrecht," *Reichsverwaltungsblatt* (1942): 161.

83. Koellreutter, "Führung und Verwaltung," in *Festschrift für Hedemann* (Jena, 1938), 95; see also his article in *Archiv des öffentlichen Rechts NF* 27 (1936): 118–119, 238–239.

84. Huber, "Die deutsche Staatswissenschaft," *Zeitschrift für die gesamten Staatswissenschaften* 95 (1935): 32n.1.

85. Huber, *Verfassungsrecht des Großdeutschen Reiches* (Hamburg, 1939), 163, 166–167. The same suggestion had been made earlier by Reuß, "Partei und Staat im Dritten Reich," *Juristische Wochenschrift* (1935): 2314; and Linge, in *Deutsches Recht* (1936): 28.

86. Huber, "Öffentliches Recht und Neugestaltung des Bürgerlichen Rechts," in *Zur Erneuerung des bürgerlichen Rechts* (Munich and Berlin, 1938), 55.

87. Huber, "Bau und Gefüge des Reiches," in *Idee und Ordnung des Reiches* (Hamburg, 1941), 13.

88. V. Rüfner, *Gemeinschaft, Staat und Recht* (Bonn, 1937), 157.

89. A. Köttgen, "Das Beamtenurteil des Bundesverfassungsgerichts," *Archiv des öffentlichen Rechts* 79 (1953–1954): 354.

90. *Entscheidungen des Bundesverfassungsgerichts* 3:58 ff., *Juristenzeitung* (1954): 76 ff.; "Vorlagebeschluß des BGH v. 20.5.1954," *Juristenzeitung* (1954): 489 ff.; "BVerfG v. 19.2.1957," *Juristenzeitung* (1957): 250. A summary of the various voices can be found in the excellent essay by H. Peters, "Der Streit um die 131er-Entscheidungen des BVerfG," *Juristenzeitung* (1954): 589 ff.

91. However, Herbert Lemmel's *Habilitation* thesis at the University of Berlin, *Die Volksgemeinschaft, ihre Erfassung im werdenden Recht* (Stuttgart and Berlin, 1941), tried as late as 1939 to "ground" the coming communal law from the race-breeding perspective of the SS.

92. Koellreutter against Heckel, *Verwaltungsarchiv* 47 (1942): 230; Koellreutter against Best, *Die deutsche Polizei* (Darmstadt, 1940), 15.

93. Koellreutter against Heckel (see note 92, above).

94. Quoted by M. Broszat, *Der Staat Hitlers* (Munich, 1969), 357. English translation by John Hiden, *The Hitler State* (New York, 1981), 293.

95. Ritterbusch, "Der Führer und Reichskanzler, des Deutschen Volkes Staatsoberhaupt," *Juristische Wochenschrift* (1934): 2193–2194.

96. Höhn, *Vom Wesen der Gemeinschaft* (Berlin, 1934), 15.

97. Dernedde, "Staatslehre als Wirklichkeitswissenschaft," *Juristische Wochenschrift* (1934): 2516.

98. Larenz, *Rechts- und Staatsphilosophie der Gegenwart*, 2d ed. (Berlin, 1935), 104.

99. E. Topitsch, *Die Sozialphilosophie Hegels als Heilslehre und Herrschaftsideologie* (Neuwied-Berlin, 1967), 24, 63–64.

100. A. Pfennig, "Gemeinschaft und Staatswissenschaft," *Zeitschrift für die gesamten Staatswissenschaften* 96 (1936): 313.

101. Representative for administrative law is Scheuner, "Die Rechtsstellung der Persönlichkeit in der Gemeinschaft," in Frank, *Deutsches Verwaltungsrecht* (Munich, 1937), 82–98. In the area of civil law, Rüthers (see note 7, above), 340, gives many references. Compare on this also P. Thoss, *Das subjektive Recht in der gliedschaftlichen Bindung* (Frankfurt, 1968).

102. Höhn, in Frank, *Deutsches Verwaltungsrecht*, 79–80.

103. Freisler, "Gemeinschaft und Recht," *Deutsche Justiz* (1938): 1870–1871.

104. Cases in which the term *community* corresponded to real shared characteritics, which of course do exist, are not meant here; for example, if the sources speak of *Erbengemeinschaft* (community of heirs), *Gesamthandgemeinschaft* (joint ownership association), *Gütergemeinschaft* (community of property), and so on.

CHAPTER FIVE

1. The original German title speaks of *Staatsrechtslehre*, which poses some difficulty of translation. German legal theory knows both *Staatsrecht* (positive law of the state) and *Verfassungsrecht* (constitutional law). English does not, and *Staatsrecht* is usually rendered into English as constitutional law.—Trans.

2. On what follows see R. Smend, "Die Vereinigung der Deutschen Staatsrechtslehrer und der Richtungsstreit," in *Festschrift Scheuner* (1973), 575 ff.; M. Friedrich, "Der Methoden- und Richtungsstreit. Zur Grundlagendiskussion der Weimarer Staatsrechtslehre," *Archiv des öffentlichen Rechts* 102 (1977): 161 ff.; K. Rennert, *Die 'geisteswissenschaftliche Richtung' in der Staatsrechtslehre der Weimarer Republik* (1987); W. Heun, "Der staatsrechtliche Positivismus in der Weimarer Republik. Eine Konzeption im Widerstreit," *Der Staat* 28 (1989): 377 ff.

3. Smend (see note 2, above), 579.

4. E. Kaufmann, "Die Gleichheit vor dem Gesetz im Sinne des Art. 109 der Reichsverfassung," *Veröffentlichungen der Vereinigung der Deutschen Staatsrechtslehrer* 3 (1927): 2 ff.

5. Smend (see note 2, above), 579.

6. On Heller, see W. Schluchter, *Entscheidung für den sozialen Rechtsstaat*, 2d ed. (1983); and I. Staff, "Hermann Heller," in B. Diestelkamp and M. Stolleis, eds., *Juristen an der Universität Frankfurt a. M.* (1989), 187 ff.

7. On this and the following, see D. Grimm, "Die 'Neue Rechtswissenschaft'— über Funktion und Formation nationalsozialistischer Jurisprudenz," in *Recht und Staat der bürgerlichen Gesellschaft* (1987), 373–395; J. Meinck, *Weimarer Staatslehre und Na-*

tionalsozialismus (1978); D. Schefold, in *Justiz und Nationalsozialismus—kein Thema für deutsche Richter?* Schriftenreihe des Gustav-Stresemann-Instituts 1 (1984), 64–82; M. Stolleis, in S. Harbordt, ed., *Wissenschaft im Nationalsozialismus. Zur Stellung der Staatsrechtslehre, Staatsphilosophie, Psychologie, Naturwissenschaft und Universität zum Nationalsozialismus*, Veröffentlichungen der Universitätsbibliothek Berlin (1983), 21 ff.

8. O. Koellreutter, *Parteien und Verfassung im heutigen Deutschland* (1932); *Der Nationale Rechtsstaat* (1932); *Vom Sinn und Wesen der nationalen Revolution* (1932). On Koellreutter see Meinck (note 7, above), 103 ff.; and M. Stolleis, "Otto Koellreutter," *Neue Deutsche Biographie* 12 (1980): 324.

9. E. Tatarin-Tarnheyden, *Volksstaat oder Parteienstaat?* (1932); Tatarin-Tarnheyden, *Werdendes Staatsrecht. Gedanken zu einem organischen und deutschen Verfassungsneubau* (Berlin, 1934).

10. H. Herrfahrdt, *Der Aufbau des neuen Staates* (Berlin, 1932); Herrfahrdt, *Werden und Gestalt des Dritten Reiches* (1933).

11. J. Binder, *Der deutsche Volksstaat* (1934).

12. H. Gerber, *Staatsrechtliche Grundlinien des neuen Reiches* (1933).

13. K. Larenz, *Deutsche Rechtserneuerung und Rechtsphilosophie* (1934).

14. E. R. Huber, *Die Gestalt des deutschen Sozialismus* (1945); Huber, "Die Totalität des völkischen Staates," *Die Tat* (1934): 30 ff.; Huber, "Die Einheit der Staatsgewalt," *Deutsche Juristen-Zeitung* (1934): cols. 950 ff.; Huber, "Die deutsche Staatswissenschaft," *Zeitschrift für die gesamten Staatswissenschaften* (1935): 1–2.

15. E. Forsthoff (alias Friedrich Grüter), "Der Rechtsstaat in der Krise," *Deutsches Volkstum* (1932): 260 ff.; Forsthoff, *Der totale Staat* (1933).

16. R. Höhn, *Die Wandlung im staatsrechtlichen Denken* (1934); Höhn, "Das Gesetz als Akt der Führung," *Deutsches Recht* 4 (1934): 443 ff.

17. See B. Rüthers, *Entartetes Recht. Rechtslehrer und Kronjuristen im Dritten Reich*, 2d ed. (1989), 101 ff.; Rüthers, *Carl Schmitt im Dritten Reich*, 2d ed. (1990).

18. On Hermann Heller, see note 6, above.

19. M. Stolleis, *Gemeinwohlformeln im nationalsozialistischen Recht* (1974), 198 ff.

20. See most recently W. Heun, "Der staatsrechtliche Positivismus in der Weimarer Republik," *Der Staat* 28 (1989): 390 ff.

21. *Reichsgesetzblatt* 1 (1934): 529.

22. H. Kelsen, "Verteidigung der Demokratie," *Blätter der Staatspartei* (1932): 90–98, reprinted in Kelsen, *Demokratie und Sozialismus* (Vienna, 1967), 60 ff.

23. By the so-called "Decree for the Protection of *Volk* and State" (Reichstag Fire Decree) of February 28, 1933, *Reichsgesetzblatt* 1 (1933): 83.

24. Called the "Law to Remove the Distress of *Volk* and State," March 23, 1933, *Reichsgesetzblatt* 1 (1933): 173.

25. See the summary in E. R. Huber, *Verfassungsrecht des Großdeutschen Reiches*, 2d ed. (1939), 46–52.

26. U. Scheuner, *Archiv für Rechts- und Sozialphilosophie* 28 (1934): 163.

27. W. Sommer, "Die NSDAP als Verwaltungsträger," in H. Frank, ed., *Deutsches Verwaltungsrecht* (1937), 175.

28. For details, see Limperg, "Personelle Veränderungen in der Staatsrechtslehre und ihre neue Situation nach der Machtergreifung," in E.-W. Böckenförde, ed., *Staatsrecht und Staatsrechtslehre im Dritten Reich* (1985), 49 ff. See also H. Pross in *Nationalsozialismus und die deutsche Universität* (1966), 143 ff.; H. Göppinger, *Die Ver-*

folgung der Juristen jüdischer Abstammung durch den Nationalsozialismus (1963), 2d expanded ed. (1990).

29. See especially C. Schmitt, *Staat, Bewegung, Volk* (1933); Schmitt, "Ein Jahr nationalsozialistischer Verfassungsstaat," *Deutsches Recht* (1934): 27 ff.; Schmitt, "Nationalsozialistisches Rechtsdenken," *Deutsches Recht* (1934): 225 ff.; Schmitt, *Über die drei Arten des rechtswissenschaftlichen Denkens* (1934).

30. *Deutsche Juristen-Zeitung* (1934): cols. 945 ff. On this see Rüthers (note 17, above) (1989), 120 ff.; and L. Gruchmann, *Justiz im Dritten Reich 1933–1940* (1988), 453.

31. On Schmitt in general, see P. Schneider, *Ausnahmezustand und Norm. Ein Studie zur Rechtslehre von Carl Schmitt* (1957); H. Hofmann, *Legitimität gegen Legalität. Der Weg der politischen Philosophie Carl Schmitts,* 2d ed. (1993); M. Stolleis, "Carl Schmitt," in Sattler, ed., *Staat und Recht. Die deutsche Staatslehre im 19. und 20 Jahrhundert* (1972), 123 ff.; I. Maus, "Zur 'Zäsur' von 1933 in der Theorie Carl Schmitts," *Kritische Justiz* (1969): 113 ff.; Maus, *Bürgerliche Rechtstheorie und Faschismus. Zur sozialen Funktion und aktuellen Wirkung der Theorie Carl Schmitts,* 2d ed. (1980); J. Bendersky, *Carl Schmitt, Theorist for the Reich* (Princeton, 1983); Rüthers (see note 17, above); H. Quaritsch, ed., *Complexio Oppositorum. Über Carl Schmitt. Vorträge und Diskussionsbeiträge des 28. Sonderseminars 1986 der Hochschule für Verwaltungswissenschaften in Speyer* (1988).

32. O. Koellreutter, *Grundriß der allgemeinen Staatslehre* (1933); Koellreutter, *Deutsches Verfassungsrecht* (1935); Koellreutter, *Deutsches Verwaltungsrecht. Ein Grundriß* (1936).

33. E. R. Huber (see note 14, above); and Huber, *Verfassungsrecht des Großdeutschen Reiches,* 2d ed. (1939).

34. Forsthoff (see note 15, above).

35. G. A. Walz, "Autoritärer Staat, nationaler Rechtsstaat oder völkischer Führungsstaat," *Deutsche Juristenzeitung* (1933): cols. 1334 ff.; Walz, *Das Ende der Zwischenverfassung* (1933).

36. H. Krüger, "Die Absage an den Westen," *Volk im Werden* 1 (1933): 81 ff.; Krüger, "Die Aufgabe der Staatsrechtswissenschaft," *Jugend und Recht* (1935): 150 ff.

37. T. Maunz, *Neue Grundlagen des Verwaltungsrechts* (1934); Maunz, "Das Ende des subjektiven öffentlichen Rechts," *Zeitschrift für die gesamten Staatswissenschaften* 96 (1936): 71 ff.; Maunz, "Das Verwaltungsrecht des nationalsozialistischen Staates," in H. Frank, ed., *Deutsches Verwaltungsrecht* (1937), 27 ff. See chapter 12, below.

38. U. Scheuner, "Die nationale Revolution," *Archiv des öffentlichen Rechts* n.f. 24 (1934): 166 ff. and 261 ff.

39. P. Ritterbusch, "Die Volksgemeinschaft als Grundlage der deutschen Verfassung," *Deutsches Recht* (1936): 349 ff.

40. Höhn (see note 16, above), as well as Höhn, *Der individualistische Staatsbegriff und die juristische Staatsperson* (1935); Höhn, "Der Führerbegriff im Staatsrecht," *Deutsches Recht* (1935): 296 ff.; Höhn, "Führung und Verwaltung," in H. Frank, ed., *Deutsches Verwaltungsrecht* (1937), 67 ff.

41. On Nicolai, see D. Rebentisch, in Jeserich, Pohl, and v. Unruh, eds., *Deutsche Verwaltungsgeschichte,* vol. 4 (1985), 741n.25.

42. For the level of constitutional and administrative reality, see now the superb study by D. Rebentisch, *Führerstaat und Verwaltung im Zweiten Weltkrieg. Verfassungs-*

entwicklung und Verwaltungspolitik 1939–1945 (1989). See my review in *Der Staat* 28 (1989): 630–633.

43. H. Gerber, *Staatsrechtliche Grundlinien des neuen Reiches* (1933); H. Herrfahrdt, *Werden und Gestalt des Dritten Reiches* (1933); E. R. Huber, "Das Ende des Parteienbundesstaates," *Juristische Wochenschrift* (1934): 193; O. Koellreutter, "Der nationale Rechtsstaat," *Deutsche Juristenzeitung* (1933): col. 517; Medicus, *Programm der Reichsregierung und Ermächtigungsgesetz* (1933); E. Menzel, *Grundlagen des neuen Staatsdenkens* (1934); U. Scheuner (see note 37, above); Scheuner, "Die staatsrechtliche Bedeutung des Gesetzes zur Behebung der Not von Volk und Reich," *Leipziger Zeitschrift für Deutsches Recht* (1933): col. 899; C. Schmitt, "Das Gesetz zur Behebung der Not von Volk und Reich," *Deutsche Juristenzeitung* (1933): col. 455; Steinbrink, *Die Revolution Adolf Hitlers. Eine staatsrechtliche und politische Betrachtung der Machtergreifung des Nationalsozialismus* (1933); E. Tatarin-Tarnheyden, *Werdendes Staatsrecht* (1934); H. Triepel, "Die nationale Revolution und die deutsche Verfassung," *Allgemeine Zeitung* 157, April 2, 1933, p. 1; G. A. Walz, *Das Ende der Zwischenverfassung* (1933); Walz, "Autoritärer Staat, nationaler Rechtsstat oder völkischer Führerstaat?" *Deutsche Juristenzeitung* (1933): col. 1334; H. J. Wolff, *Die neue Regierungsform des Deutschen Reiches* (1933).

44. A Gau chief was the head of a Gau, the main territorial unit in the Nazi party structure. After the annexation of Austria and the Sudetenland, there were forty-two Gaue.—Trans.

45. In somewhat greater detail, W. Kohl and M. Stolleis, "Im Bauch des Leviathan. Zur Staats- und Verwaltungsrechtslehre im Nationalsozialismus," *Neue juristische Wochenschrift* (1988): 2849, 2851 ff.

46. See on this I. Müller, *Hitler's Justice: The Courts of the Third Reich*, translated by Deborah Lucas Schneider (Cambridge: Harvard University Press, 1991); H. Wrobel, *Zur Demokratie verurteilt. Justizpolitik 1945–1949* (1989).

47. *Veröffentlichungen der Vereinigung der Deutschen Staatsrechtslehrer* 8 (1950): 1.

48. *Entscheidungen des Bundesverfassungsgerichts* 3:58.

CHAPTER SIX

1. "MilchG v. 31. Juli 1930," *Reichsgesetzblatt* 1 (1930): 421; "VO des Reichspräs. zur Behebung finanzieller, wirtschaftlicher und sozialer Notstände v. 26. Juli 1930," *Reichsgesetzblatt* 1 (1930): 311; "NotVO v. 1. Dez. 1930," *Reichsgesetzblatt* 1 (1930): 517; "VOen zum Zusammenschluß der Zucker- u. Stärkeindustrien v. 27. März 1931," *Reichsgesetzblatt* 1 (1931); "v. 12. Juni 1931," *Reichsgesetzblatt* 1 (1931): 339; "u. v. 30. April 1932," *Reichsgesetzblatt* 1 (1932): 188; "VO des Reichspräs. zur Sicherung von Wirtschaft und Finanzen v. 8. Dez. 1931," *Reichsgesetzblatt* 1 (1931): 699; "VO des Reichspräs. über Maßnahmen auf den Gebieten der Rechtspflege und Verwaltung v. 14. Juni 1932," *Reichsgesetzblatt* 1 (1932): 285.

2. Josef and Ruth Becker, eds., *Hitlers Machtergreifung, Dokumente* (Munich, 1983).

3. Helge Pross, "Die geistige Enthauptung Deutschlands: Verluste durch Emigration," in *Nationalsozialismus und die deutsche Universität* (Berlin, 1966), 143 ff. We can mention, among others, Hans Kelsen, Hermann Heller, Erich Kaufmann, Gerhard Leibholz, Karl Loewenstein, Hans Nawiasky, Karl Strupp (List of Displaced German Scholars, London, 1936).

4. Gerhard Anschütz, Willibalt Apelt, Richard Thoma, Heinrich Triepel, Hans-Julius Wolff.

5. Hatto G. Bölling, "Die neue Verwaltungsrechtslehre," *Deutsche Verwaltung* (1934): 42; Hans Fabricius, "Die Bewegung und der Verwaltungsjurist," *Deutsche Verwaltung* (1934): 33; Ernst Forsthoff, "Das neue Gesicht der Verwaltung und die Verwaltungswissenschaft," *Deutsches Recht* (1935): 331; Forsthoff, "Von den Aufgaben der Verwaltungsrechtswissenschaft," *Deutsches Recht* (1935): 398; Franz Wilhelm Jerusalem, "Das Verwaltungsrecht und der neue Staat," in *Festschrift für Hübner* (Jena, 1935); Otto Koellreutter, "Das Verwaltungsrecht im nationalsozialistischen Staat," *Deutsche Juristenzeitung* (1934): 627; Herbert Krüger, "Das neue Rechtsdenken," *Reichsverwaltungsblatt* (1935): 1012; Klaus Lauer, "Die Bedeutung der nationalsozialistischen Revolution für das Verwaltungsrecht," *Reichs- und Preußisches Verwaltungsblatt* (1934): 706; Theodor Maunz, *Neue Grundlagen des Verwaltungsrechts* (Hamburg, 1934); Maunz, "Zum Neubau des deutschen Verwaltungsrechts," *Deutsche Juristenzeitung* (1934): 1046; Maunz, "Neues Rechtsdenken in der Verwaltung," *Deutsche Verwaltung* (1935): 65; Karl Parthe, "Revolution und Verwaltung," *Deutsches Recht* (1934): 35; Eberhard von Scheurl, "Zum Neubau der deutschen Verwaltung," *Deutsche Verwaltung* (1935): 199; Edgar Tatarin-Tarnheyden, "Grundlagen des Verwaltungsrechts in neuen Staat," *Archiv des öffentlichen Rechts* n.f. 24 (1934): 345.

6. Michael Stolleis, "Gemeinschaft und Volksgemeinschaft. Zur juristischen Terminologie im Nationalsozalismus," *Vierteljahresheft für Zeitgeschichte* (1972): 16–38, especially 19n.17. See chapter 4, p. 64, above.

7. A hope strongly held by Otto Koellreutter, who also voiced his disappointment after 1939. See Carl Hermann Ule, *Verwaltungsarchiv* 63 (1972): 109–111.

8. H. Frank, *Deutsche Verwaltung* (1934): 93.

9. Hans Helfritz, "Rechtsstaat und nationalsozialistischer Staat," *Deutsche Juristenzeitung* (1934): 426; Otto Koellreutter, "Der nationalsozialistische Rechtsstaat," *Verwaltungsarchiv* 1 (1934): 16; Günter Krauß and Otto von Schweinichen, *Disputation über den Rechtsstaat* (Hamburg, 1935); Carl Schmitt, "Nationalsozialismus und Rechtsstaat," *Deutsche Verwaltung* (1934): 35; Schmitt, "Was bedeutet der Streit um den Rechtsstaat?" *Zeitschrift für die gesamten Staatswissenschaften* 95 (1935): 189; Schmitt, "Der Rechtsstaat," in *NS-Handbuch für Recht und Gesetzgebung*, 2d ed. (Munich, 1935), 24 ff.

10. Compare the revealing statement by Theodor Maunz, "Das Verwaltungsrecht des nationalsozialistischen Staates," in Hans Frank, ed., *Deutsches Verwaltungsrecht* (Munich, 1937), 27: "If anyone in the administrative law of the present day intended to make his stand on the ground of individualism, in a time whose every effort is aimed at transcending the individualistic principle of the law, or if someone merely wanted to stabilize the state of administrative law of the transition period, developments would soon pass them by."

11. For example, Eberhard Scheurl, "Grundsätze deutscher Verwaltung," *Deutsches Recht* (1934): 35, who advised "not to abandon the line of the past." Similarly, Hans Helfritz, *Deutsche Juristenzeitung* (1934): 426 ff.

12. Maunz (see note 10, above), 27.

13. Hermann Göring, *Die Rechtssicherheit als Grundlage der Volksgemeinschaft* (Hamburg, 1935).

14. Maunz (see note 10, above), 63.

15. On this, see notes 41–45, below.

16. Reinhard Höhn, *Der individualistische Staatsbegriff und die juristiche Staatspserson* (Berlin, 1935); Höhn, *Die Wandlung im staatsrechtlichen Denken* (Hamburg, 1934). On the debate about the concept of the state as a legal person that Höhn set in motion with Wilhelm Merk and Otto Koellreutter, see *Vierteljahresheft für Zeitgeschichte* (1972): 28–35.

17. P. Diehl-Thiele, *Partei und Staat im Dritten Reich* (1969); Peter Hüttenberger, *Die Gauleiter* (Stuttgart, 1969); Hüttenberger, "Interessenvertretung und Lobbyismus im Dritten Reich," in Hirschfeld and Kettenacker, eds., *"Der Führerstaat." Mythos und Realität* (Stuttgart, 1981).

18. Ernst Fraenkel, *The Dual State* (New York, 1969).

19. For discussion of the phenomena described by these terms, see M. Broszat, *Der Staat Hitlers* (Munich, 1969); English translation by John Hiden, *The Hitler State* (New York, 1981). See also the literature listed in note 17, above. A juxtaposition of the ideal types *Ordofaschismus* and *Anarchofaschismus* (Reifner) promises more as a global formula than it yields when applied to historical realities; already the classification of leading National Socialists into one camp or the other poses the greatest difficulties (a critical view in this direction by Günter Bertram, "Der Jurist und die 'Rutenbündel des Faschismus,'" *Zeitschrift für Rechtspolitik* [1983]: 81–86). It is, however, indisputable, as Udo Reifner has emphasized ("Juristen im Nationalsozialismus," *Zeitschrift für Rechtspolitik* [1983]: 19), that the functioning of the "normal" administration and judicial system was indispensable for the regime and, in a sense, formed the foundation that made possible the crimes of the regime to begin with. Therein lies a certain element of tragedy for administrative officials and judges who acted correctly and with personal integrity in such a system. The sensitive ones among them certainly felt this tragedy.

20. Ludwig von Köhler, *Grundlagen des deutschen Verwaltungsrechts* (Stuttgart and Berlin, 1935); Otto Koellreutter, *Deutsches Verwaltungsrecht* (Berlin, 1936; 2d ed. Berlin, 1938); Arnold Köttgen, *Deutsche Verwaltung* (Berlin, 1935; 2d ed., Berlin, 1937; 3d ed., Berlin, 1944); Wilhelm Laforet, *Deutsches Verwaltungsrecht* (Munich, 1937); Theodor Maunz, *Verwaltung* (Hamburg, 1937); Frank (see note 10, above). See also the shorter works listed in note 71, below.

21. Helmut Nicolai, J.D. (1895–1955); for biographical data see Rebentisch, in Jeserich, Pohl, and v. Unruh, eds., *Deutsche Verwaltungsgeschichte*, vol. 4 (1985), 741.

22. Carl Herrmann Ule, "Vom Preußischen Verwaltungs-Blatt zum Deutschen Verwaltungsblatt," *Deutsches Verwaltungsblatt* (1985): 9–21.

23. Ottmar Kollmann (1886–1969), J.D., after 1912 served in the Bavarian civil service, refounded the *Bayerische Verwaltungsblätter* in 1925, served as Staatsrat, left the Bavarian Interior Ministry in 1934, served as President of the Bavarian Chamber of Insurance in 1937–1943, after 1946 returned to the Interior Ministry, participated in the constitutional convention of Herrenchiemsee, and served as President of the Bavarian Administrative Court in 1950–1954. See the notices in *Bayerische Verwaltungsblätter* (1956): 177; (1961): 146; (1969): 237.

24. Walther Sommer (1893–1946); biographical data in Rebentisch (see note 21, above), § 2n.16.

25. Wilhelm Stuckart (1902–1953); biographical data in Rebentisch (see note 21, above).

26. *Reich-Volksordnung-Lebensraum. Zeitschrift für völkische Verfassung und Verwaltung* 1–6 (1941–1943). This journal was published at Darmstadt (Wittich) and edited

by Wilhelm Stuckart, Werner Best, Gerhard Klopfer, Rudolf Lehmann, and Reinhard Höhn.

27. K. Anderbrügge, "Verwaltungsrechtliche Aspekte der volksgenössischen Rechtsstellung," *Archiv für Rechts- und Sozialphilosophie* 18 (1983): 128–139.

28. Frank (see note 10, above), introduction.

29. Parthe (see note 5, above), 35 (36).

30. Walther Sommer, "Die Verwaltungsgerichtsbarkeit," *Deutsches Verwaltungsblatt* 85 (1937): 425 (427).

31. Forsthoff always pointed out the necessity of formal structures in the "total state." See his essay "Von den Aufgaben der Verwaltungsrechtswissenschaft," *Deutsches Recht* 5 (1935): 399. Of course, there was still room for the "creative administration" that operated without legal rules. See Wolfgang Luthardt, "Unrechtsstaat oder Doppelstaat?" *Archiv für Rechts- und Sozialphilosophie* 18 (1983): 197 ff.

32. The literature on the "lawfulness" *(Gesetzmäßigkeit)* or "legality" *(Rechtmäßigkeit)* of administration is extensive, one reason being that many contributions to the discussion avoid generalizations and take the more cautious form of partial examinations (police law, building law, commercial law, right of eminent domain). See the overview by T. Maunz, "Die Rechtmäßigkeit der Verwaltung," in Frank (see note 10, above), 51 ff.

33. Forsthoff (see note 31, above), 398 (399).

34. On the positivist thesis, by now thoroughly discussed, see Hubert Rottleutner, "Substantieller Dezisionismus—Zur Funktion der Rechtsphilosophie im Nationalsozialismus," *Archiv für Rechts- und Sozialphilosophie* 18 (1983): 20–35, especially the references in notes 1–7.

35. For a parallel, see Rüping, "'Auflockerung' im Strafverfahrensrecht. Grundsätzliche Entwicklungen zwischen Liberalismus, 'Deutschem Gemeinrecht' und Naturrecht," *Archiv für Rechts- und Sozialphilosophie* 18 (1983): 65 ff.

36. Alfons Rehkopp, "Die Generalklauseln im Verwaltungsrecht," *Deutsche Verwaltung* (1937): 118–119; Curt Rothenberger, "Die Rechtsquellen im neuen Staat," *Deutsche Juristenzeitung* (1936): 22; Helmut Seydel, "Treu und Glauben," *Deutsches Recht* (1935): 454; Theodor Steimle, "Über Wesen und Bedeutung verwaltungsrechtlicher Generalklauseln," *Deutsche Verwaltung* (1940): 293.

37. Wilhelm Hofacker, "Die subjektiven öffentlichen Rechte," *Deutsche Juristenzeitung* (1935): 723; Eberhard Kraiss, "Das klagbare subjektive öffentliche Recht im deutschen Führerstaat," diss., Tübingen, 1935; Herbert Krüger, "Volksgemeinschaft statt subjektiver Rechte," *Deutsche Verwaltung* (1935): 37; Karl Larenz, *Rechtsperson und subjektives Recht* (Berlin, 1935); Maunz (see note 10, above), 27 ff., especially 35 ff.; Maunz, "Das Ende des subjektiven öffentlichen Rechts," *Zeitschrift für die gesamten Staatswissenschaften* 96 (1936): 71 ff.; essays by Karl August Eckhardt, Reinhard Höhn, Karl Larenz, Wolfgang Siebert, and Hans Würdinger, *Deutsche Rechtswissenschaft* 1 (1936); Gerhard Brings, "Das subjektiv öffentliche Recht und die Verwaltungsgerichtsbarkeit in ihrer Bedeutung für den nationalsozialistischen Staat," diss., Würzburg, 1938; Erich Jung, *Subjektives und objektives Recht—die neue Rechtsquellenlehre* (Marburg, 1939); Ulrich Scheuner, "Die Rechtsstellung der Persönlichkeit in der Gemeinschaft," in Frank (see note 10, above), 82 ff.; Walter Schönfeld, "Der Kampf wider das subjektive Recht," *Zeitschrift der Akademie für Deutsches Recht* (1937): 107; Peter Schwerdtner, "Person, Persönlichkeitsschutz und Rechtsfähigkeit im Nationalsozialismus," *Archiv für Rechts- und Sozialphilosophie* 18 (1983): 82 ff., with additional

references; Peter Thoss, *Das subjektive Recht in der gliedschaftlichen Bindung* (Frankfurt, 1968).

38. Maunz (see note 10, above), 35–36.

39. Scheuner (see note 37, above), 82 ff. (95–96).

40. Maunz, "Neubau" (see note 5, above), 1050.

41. Bahmann, "Das Verhältnis des Verwaltungsstreitverfahrens zu den tragenden Gedanken des neuen Staates," *Deutsche Verwaltung* (1934): 51; Justus Danckwerts, "Die Verwaltungsgerichtsbarkeit im nationalsozialistischen Staat," in Frank (see note 10, above), 99; Wilhelm Frick, "Die Verwaltungsgerichtsbarkeit im nationalsozialistischen Staat," *Deutsche Verwaltung* (1936): 332; Frick, "Probleme des neuen Verwaltungsrechts," *Deutsche Verwaltung* (1936): 329 ff.; Dietrich Holtz, "Das Problem der Verwaltungsgerichtsbarkeit," *Deutsche Verwaltung* (1934): 290; Rudolf Knauth, "Die Verwaltungsgerichtsbarkeit im neuen Reich," *Reichsverwaltungsblatt* (1933): 885; Otto Koellreutter, "Grundsätzliches zur Frage der Verwaltungsgerichtsbarkeit," *Reichsverwaltungsblatt* (1936): 885; Theodor Maunz, "Die Zukunft der Verwaltungsgerichtsbarkeit," *Deutsches Recht* (1936): 478; Hermann Reuß, "Die Verwaltungsgerichtsbarkeit im neuen Reich," *Juristische Wochenschrift* (1935): 2025; Herbert Rößiger, *Führertum und Verwaltungsgerichtsbarkeit* (Leipzig, 1936); Herbert Schelcher, "Um die Verwaltungsrechtspflege des Dritten Reiches," *Reichsverwaltungsblatt* (1937): 569; Scheuner (see note 37, above), 95–96; Karl Schneider, "Verwaltungsgerichtsbarkeit im neuen Reich," *Deutsches Recht* (1935): 458; Franz Scholz, *Die Verwaltungsgerichtsbarkeit im Dritten Reich* (Cologne, 1936); Wilhelm Stuckart, "Nationalsozialistischer Staat und Verwaltungsgerichtsbarkeit," *Deutsche Verwaltung* (1935): 161. Aggressively National Socialist in tone are the following works: Heinrich Herrfahrdt, "Zum Streit um die Verwaltungsgerichtsbarkeit," *Deutsche Verwaltung* (1938): 611; Alfred von Keil, "Zur Frage der Verwaltungsgerichtsbarkeit," *Deutsche Verwaltung* (1937): 298, 334; Georg Schmidt, "'Rechtswahrung in der Verwaltung' anstelle von 'Verwaltungsgerichtsbarkeit'," *Deutsche Verwaltung* (1938): 229; Rudolf Sievers, "Die geistigen Grundlagen der Verwaltungsgerichtsbarkeit," *Deutsche Verwaltung* (1938): 77; Walther Sommer, "Die Verwaltungsgerichtsbarkeit," *Deutsche Verwaltung* (1937): 425.

42. Ludwig Frege, "Der Status des Preußischen Oberverwaltungsgerichts und die Standhaftigkeit seiner Rechtsprechung auf politischem Gebiet," in Helmut R. Külz and Richard Naumann, eds., *Staatsbürger und Staatsgewalt*, vol. 1 (Karlsruhe, 1963), 131 ff.; Walter Scheerbarth, "Das Schicksal der Verwaltungsgerichtsbarkeit unter dem Nationalsozialismus," *Deutsche Verwaltung* (1963): 729–732. To be sure, one should read as a counterpoint to this how persuasively the Vice President of the Prussian Higher Administrative Court could demonstrate that his administration of justice had been consciously oriented toward National Socialist ideology: Bach, "Die Rechtsprechung des preußischen Oberverwaltungsgerichts im Lichte der nationalsozialistischen Weltanschauung und Rechtsauffassung," *Deutsche Verwaltung* (1938): 199. On this see also H. R. Külz, "Verwaltungskontrolle unter dem Nationalsozialismus," *Kritische Justiz* (1969): 367–378; as well as Carl Hermann Ule, "Über das Wirken des Präsidenten des Preußischen Oberverwaltungsgerichts Professor Dr. h. c. B. Drews in der Zeit nach 1933," in Dieter Wilke, ed., *Festschrift zum 125 jährigen Bestehen der Juristischen Gesellschaft zu Berlin* (1984), 803 ff.

43. Rudolf Knauth, "Die Neuordnung der Verwaltungsgerichtsbarkeit im Reich," *Deutsche Verwaltung* (1942): 361; Hermann Reuß, "Der Krieg und die Verwaltungsgerichtsbarkeit," *Zeitschrift der Akademie für Deutsches Recht* (1940): 10; Reuß, "Zustän-

digkeit und Verfahren der Verwaltungsgerichte," *Deutsches Recht* (1942): 1345; Helfried Pfeifer, "Zur Neuordnung der Verwaltungsgerichtsbarkeit im Reich," *Zeitschrift der Akademie für Deutsches Recht* (1943): 185; Johannes Poppitz, "Die Verwaltungsgerichtsbarkeit im Kriege," in Ernst Rudolf Huber, ed., *Idee und Ordnung des Reiches,* vol. 1 (Hamburg, 1941); Poppitz, "Die Anfänge der Verwaltungsgerichtsbarkeit," *Archiv des öffentlichen Rechts* n.f. 33 (1943): 158; 34 (1944): 3; Werner Weber, "Zuständigkeit und Zukunft der Verwaltungsgerichte," *Zeitschrift für die gesamten Staatswissenschaften* 104 (1944): 424 ff.

44. On Article 2, sections 2, 107, 166 of the Weimar Constitution, see Gerhard Anschütz, *Kommentar zur Reichsverfassung,* 14th ed. (Berlin, 1933), 499; Gerhard Marohn, "Das Reichsverwaltungsgericht," *Verwaltungsarchiv* 32 (1927): 382–408. One of the first voices to call for the Reich Administrative Court after 1933 was that of Hartmann, "Zur Reform des deutschen Rechts," *Deutsches Recht* (1934): 37. The Reich Administrative Court was eventually established by a decree of the Führer dated April 3, 1941 (*Reichsgesetzblatt* 1 [1941]: 201), "to simplify the administration of the highest administrative courts, and at the same time to achieve in this way the savings in personnel and administrative costs that are called for, especially in wartime." On this see chapter 8, below; and Wolfgang Kohl, "Reichsverwaltungsgericht," in A. Erler and E. Kaufmann, eds., *Handwörterbuch zur Deutschen Rechtsgeschichte,* vol. 4 (Berlin, 1990); and Kohl's comprehensive work *Das Reichsverwaltungsgericht* (1991).

45. Walther Sommer, "Verwaltungsstreitverfahren oder Verwaltungsrechtspflege?" *Deutsche Verwaltung* (1941): 245.

46. Günter Stratenwerth, "Faschismus als Krise des Liberalismus?" *Archiv für Rechts- und Sozialphilosophie* 18 (1983): 36–44.

47. As rightly pointed out by Meyer-Hesemann, *Methodenwandel in der Verwaltungsrechtswissenschaft* (1981), 101.

48. Forsthoff (see note 31, above), 398 (399).

49. Karl Jaspers, *Die geistige Situation der Zeit* (Berlin, 1931). For example, see in the 5th (partly revised) ed. (1933) "Massenordnung in Daseinsfürsorge" (p. 25), "Leistungsapparat" (p. 27), "Massenversorgung durch Technik," "Riesenapparat der Daseinsfürsorge" (p. 44); the state "nimmt den Gedanken des Wohlfahrtsstaates als der ökonomischen Daseinsordnung in sich auf" (p. 73). See also Georg Weipert, *Daseinsgestaltung* (Leipzig, 1938).

50. Ernst Forsthoff, *Die Verwaltung als Leistungsträger* (Stuttgart and Berlin, 1938). A detailed discussion of this in Meyer-Hesemann (see note 47, above), 86 ff., 102 ff.; Storost, *Staat und Verfasung bei Ernst Forsthoff* (1979), 80 ff. For the older roots of the concept, see Ernst Rudolf Huber, "Vorsorge für das Dasein. Ein Grundbegriff der Staatslehre Hegels und Lorenz von Steins," *Festschrift Ernst Forsthoff* (Munich, 1972), 139–163.

51. The term *Daseinsvorsorge* was not adopted until the 1950s, primarily through Forsthoff's *Lehrbuch* (1950). An interim assessment by Erich Becker, *Veröffentlichungen der Vereinigung der Deutschen Staatsrechtslehrer* 14 (1956): 98 ff. The reactions between 1938 and 1945 remained weak. See Wilhelm Hofacker, *Deutsche Verwaltung* (1938): 416; Ernst Rudolf Huber, *Zeitschrift für die gesamten Staatswissenschaften* 101 (1941): 411–412; Otto Koellreutter, "Die Verwaltung als Leistungsträger," *Reichsverwaltungsblatt* 62 (1941): 649–651; Arnold Köttgen, *Deutsche Verwaltung,* 3d ed. (Berlin, 1944), 171 ff.; Karl Lohmann, *Zeitschrift der Akademie für Deutsches Recht* (1938): 860; Otto Naß, "Die Philosophie der Verwaltung als Grundlage der Verwaltungswis-

senschaft. Kritische Betrachtungen über den Begriff der Verwaltung als Daseinsvorsorge," *Reichsverwaltungsblatt* (1942): 345.

52. Ernst Forsthoff, "Erledigung der Verfassungsfrage," *Deutsches Recht* (1935): 332.

53. Unmistakable in Forsthoff (see note 31, above), 399–400. See on this Storost, "Die Verwaltungsrechtslehre Ernst Forsthoffs," in Heyen, ed., *Wissenschaft und Recht der Verwaltung seit dem Ancien Régime* (Frankfurt, 1984), 163–188.

54. Meyer-Hesemann, "Modernisierungstendenzen in der nationalsozialistischen Verwaltungsrechtswissenschaft," *Archiv für Rechts- und Sozialphilosophie* 18 (1983): 145 ff.

55. Reinhard Höhn, "Führung und Verwaltung," in Frank (see note 10, above), 74.

56. See, for instance, Roderich Ungern-Sternberg, "Wesen und Struktur der Planwirtschaft," *Kartellrundschau* (1933): 313.

57. On the connection between planning *(Planung)* and guidance *(Lenkung)*, see especially Köttgen (note 51, above), 159 ff.

58. Max Imboden and Klaus Obermayer, "Der Plan als verwaltungsrechtliches Institut," *Veröffentlichungen der Vereinigung der Deutschen Staatsrechtslehrer* 18 (1960): 113 ff., without explicit reference, and with Obermayer even denying a "theoretical past" of the plan (p. 145).

59. Peter Badura, *Verwaltungsrecht im liberalen und im sozialen Rechtsstaat* (Tübingen, 1966), 22; Badura, "Die Daseinsvorsorge als Verwaltungszweck der Leistungsverwaltung und der soziale Rechtsstaat," *Die öffentliche Verwaltung* (1966): 624.

60. Theodor Maunz, "Die Rechtmäßigkeit der Verwaltung," in Frank (see note 10, above), 65.

61. Carl Schmitt, *Über die drei Arten des rechtswissenschaftlichen Denkens* (Hamburg, 1934).

62. See Anderbrügge, *Völkisches Rechtsdenken* (1978), 109; Meyer-Heseman, *Methodenwandel*, 115.

63. See especially Wilhelm Frick, "Probleme des neuen Verwaltungsrechts," *Deutsche Verwaltung* (1936): 329–339 (where he also calls for a general "Reich administration law"); Frick, "Gestalt und Aufbau des 3. Reiches," *Deutsche Verwaltung* (1937): 34–40; Frick, "Der Oberpräsident als Organ der Zentralgewalt des Reiches," *Deutsche Verwaltung* (1941): 133.

64. As Otto Naß repeatedly urged, for instance, in "Verwaltungsrecht als Universitätsfach," *Deutsche Verwaltung* (1941): 418.

65. Walther Sommer, "Verwaltungsstreitverfahren oder Verwaltungsrechtspflege," *Deutsche Verwaltung* (1941): 245.

66. Von Köhler (see note 20, above). See the review by Otto Koellreutter, *Archiv des öffentlichen Rechts* 66 (1936): 118; and Hermann Reuß, *Juristische Wochenschrift* (1935): 2346.

67. Laforet (see note 20, above); see the reviews by Hermann Reuß, *Juristische Wochenschrift* (1937): 2182; Carl Hermann Ule, *Archiv des öffentlichen Rechts* 69 (1939): 111; obituary notice in *Bayerische Verwaltungsblätter* (1959): 374.

68. This can also be said of Jerusalem (see note 5, above). Jerusalem's former assistant, who was by this time the guardian of the "progressive" SS line in constitutional and administrative law, sharply rejected this essay oriented toward "the old world of thinking" (Reinhard Höhn, *Deutsches Recht* [1935]: 379–380).

69. Bodo Dennewitz, *Verwaltung und Verwaltungsrecht* (Vienna, 1944).

70. Dennewitz, *Die Systeme des Verwaltungsrechts* (1948), 145: "that here the theory of administrative practice is not only given an impulse, rather is already being guided."

71. Johann von Leers and Willy Becker, *Nationalsozialistische Staatskunde*, Selbstunterrichtsbriefe (Potsdam and Leipzig, 1939). Otto Meißner and Günter Kaisenberg, *Staats- und Verwaltungsrecht im Dritten Reich* (Berlin, 1935); but see on this Reuß (note 66, above), 2416: merely "satisfies the need for practical orientation." Hans Georg Rahn, *Staatsrecht und Verwaltungsaufbau*, 7th ed. (Berlin, 1943); Alfons Rehkopp, *Staats- und Verwaltungskunde* (Berlin, 1941); Wilhelm Stuckart and Walter Scheerbarth, *Verwaltungsrecht* (Leipzig, 1937); later Wilhem Stuckart and Harry von Rosen–von Hoewel, *Verwaltungsrecht*, 8th ed. (Leipzig, 1944).

72. Michael Stolleis, "Otto Koellreutter," *Neue Deutsche Biographie* 12 (1980): 324–325, with further references. See also Fritz Giese, *Juristische Wochenschrift* (1936): 2207, who states that "long years of experience on the highest administrative court and an early grasp of National Socialist *Weltanschauung* made the Munich professor of constitutional and administrative law seem eminently qualified to supplement his well-known work on constitutional law with an outline of administrative law that was brief but exhaustive of the essence and coherent in its basic approach."

73. Otto Koellreutter, *Deutsches Verwaltungsrecht* (Berlin, 1936), 1.

74. Ibid., 26.

75. Theodor Maunz, *Verwaltung* (Hamburg, 1937). Lengthy review by Kurt Münch, "Neues Verwaltungsrecht, eine kritische Auseinandersetzung mit den Lehrbüchern von Maunz und Koettgen," *Zeitschrift für die gesamten Staatswissenschaften* 99 (1939): 359–374.

76. Maunz, *Neue Grundlagen* (see note 5, above); Maunz, "Die Entwicklung des deutschen Verwaltungsrechts seit dem Jahre 1933," *Zeitschrift für die gesamten Staatswissenschaften* 95 (1935): 311; Maunz, "Der Führergedanke in der Verwaltung," *Deutsches Recht* (1935): 219; Maunz, "Neues Rechtsdenken" (see note 5, above), 65; Maunz, "Staatsbegriff und Verwaltung," *Deutsches Recht* (1935), 393; Maunz, "Das Verwaltungsrecht des nationalsozialistischen Staates" (see note 10, above), 27–48; and Maunz, "Die Rechtmäßigkeit der Verwaltung" (see note 10, above), 51–66.

77. Reuß (see note 67, above), 2263.

78. Köttgen (see note 51, above), 17.

79. Maunz (see note 75, above), 11.

80. Reuß (see note 67, above), 2263 (2264); similarly Ule (see note 67, above), 111 (114).

81. Frank (see note 10, above), with introductory articles by Maunz, §§ 2, 3.

82. In this context we must dispense with an analysis of the individual essays in the anthology. See especially §§ 4 (Höhn), 5 (Scheuner), 7 (Stuckart), 10 (Forsthoff), 16 and 17 (Schack und Schüle on *Verwaltungsakt*, "administrative act," and *Verwaltungsermessen*, "administrative discretion"), 19 (Hamel on police), and 21 (Best on the Gestapo).

83. Köttgen (see note 20, above); among the reviews see especially von Bohlen, *Juristische Wochenschrift* (1937): 2507.

84. See also Arnold Köttgen, "Wissenschaft und Verwaltung," *Deutsche Verwaltung* (1938): 37.

85. From 1943 to 1945 Köttgen worked in the civil administration of Kattowitz *(Regierungspräsidium)*, that is, in immediate proximity to Auschwitz. On the adminis-

tration of Upper Silesia, see Martin Broszat, *Nationalsozialistische Polenpolitik 1939–1945* (Frankfurt, 1965), 55n.17, 55n.18; as well as D. Majer, *"Fremdvölkische" im Dritten Reich* (1980), 992, s.v. "Kattowitz."

86. See especially the sections "Der Sinn des Verwaltungsrechts" and "Die Verbindlichkeit des Verwaltungsrechts," in Köttgen (see note 51, above), 12 ff.

87. Peter Badura, obituary notice in *Juristenzeitung* (1967): 420.

88. Köttgen (see note 51, above): 15.

CHAPTER SEVEN

1. K. Wenger, "Lorenz von Stein und die Entwicklung der Verwaltungswissenschaft in Österreich," in R. Schnur, ed., *Staat und Gesellschaft. Studien über Lorenz von Stein* (1978), 479 ff.

2. K. Th. v. Inama-Sternegg, *Verwaltungslehre in Umrissen* (Innsbruck, 1870); Inama-Sternegg, "Die Entwicklung der Verwaltungslehre und des Verwaltungsrechts seit dem Tode von Lorenz von Stein," *Zeitschrift für Volkswirtschaft, Sozialpolitik und Verwaltung* 11 (1902): 137 ff.; L. Gumplowicz, *Verwaltungslehre mit besonderer Berücksichtigung des österreichischen Verwaltungsrechts* (Innsbruck, 1882). Additional references in M. Stolleis, *Geschichte des öffentlichen Rechts in Deutschland 1800–1914* (Munich, 1992). An English translation will be published in 1997 by Berghan Books, Providence, Rhode Island.

3. "Über die Bedeutung der Verwaltungslehre als selbständiger Wissenschaft," *Zeitschrift für die gesamten Staatswissenschaften* 65 (1909): 193 ff. (194).

4. E. V. Heyen, "Positivistische Staatslehre und politische Philosophie. Zur philosophischen Bildung Otto Mayers," *Quaderni fiorentini* 8 (1979): 275 ff.; Heyen, *Otto Mayer. Studien zu den geistigen Grundlagen seiner Verwaltungsrechtswissenschaft* (1981), especially 155 ff.; A. Hueber, *Otto Mayer. Die 'juristische Methode' im Verwaltungsrecht* (1982).

5. S. Gargas, "Verwaltungslehre und Verwaltungsrecht," *Zeitschrift für die gesamten Staatswissenschaften* 59 (1903): 426 ff.; I. Jastrow, *Sozialpolitik und Verwaltungswissenschaft* (1902); Jastrow, "Das Studium der Verwaltungwissenschaft nach dem Kriege," *Archiv für Sozialwissenschaft und Sozialpolitik* 42 (1916–17): 958 ff.; F. Stier-Somolo, "Die Zukunft der Verwaltungswissenschaft," *Verwaltungsarchiv* 25 (1917): 89 ff.; F. Schmid, *Eine deutsche Zentralstelle zur Pflege der Verwaltungswissenschaft und Verwaltungspraxis* (1916); Schmid, "Zur Förderung der Verwaltungswissenschaft," *Verwaltungsarchiv* 26 (1918): 288 ff.

6. I. Jastrow, "Verwaltungswissenschaft," in Jastrow, ed., *Die Reform der staatswissenschaftlichen Studien. Fünfzig Gutachten*, Schriften des Vereins für Sozialpolitik 160 (1920), 313: "The science of administration displays the rare case of a science gone missing. One would have good reason to report it to the lost and found."

7. The "central establishment" *(Zentralstelle)* called for by Schmid (see note 5, above) was not set up. Equally unsuccessful was the attempt to establish a seminar for administrative studies at the University of Leipzig; see O. Nass, "Verwaltungsrecht als Universitätsfach," *Deutsche Verwaltung* (1941): 418 ff. (422). W. Norden's initiative to make administrative studies the focal point of the Kommunalwissenschaftliches Institut in Berlin (K. Jeserich, *Das Kommunalwissenschaftliche Insitut an der Universität Berlin* [1936]) met with success only in the final phase of the Weimar Republic.

8. W. Jellinek, *Verwaltungsrecht*, 3d ed. (1931), 100.

9. W. Norden, *Was bedeutet und wozu studiert man Verwaltungswissenschaft?* (1933), 1.

10. E. Walz, "Kommunalverwaltungslehre," in F. Giese et al., eds., *Die Beamten-Hochschule*, vol. 4 (1930), 671 ff.; and in the same work, E. v. Scheurl, "Staatsverwaltungslehre," 859 ff. Also O. Bühler and A. Ley, "Raum und Verwaltung," in H. Aubin, O. Bühler et al., eds., *Der Raum Westfalen* (1931), 125 ff.; H. Peters, *Zentralisation und Dezentralisation. Zugleich ein Beitrag zur Kommunalpolitik im Rahmen der Staats- und Verwaltungslehre* (1928); G. Lassar, "Reichseigene Verwaltung," *Jahrbuch des öffentlichen Rechts der Gegenwart* 14 (1926): 1 ff.; H. B. Storck, *"Großkreise" und industrielle Siedlungsform* (1925).

11. See note 9, above.

12. O. Koellreutter, "Vorbemerkungen der Schriftleitung," *Verwaltungsarchiv* 38, no. 3 (1933): 305; Koellreutter, "Die Bedeutung des Verwaltungslehre im neuen Staat," *Reichsverwaltungsblatt und Preußisches Verwaltungsblatt* (1933): 741 ff.

13. E. Forsthoff, "Von den Aufgaben der Verwaltungsrechtswissenschaft," *Deutsches Recht* 5 (1935): 398 ff.

14. See K. A. Eckhardt, *Das Studium der Rechtswissenschaft* (1935); J. Heckel, "Staats-, Verwaltungs- und Kirchenrecht im Dritten Reich," in Heckel, G. A. Walz, and K. Larenz, *Berichte über die Lage und das Studium des öffentlichen Rechts* (1935).

15. A. Köttgen, *Deutsche Verwaltung* (1935), 2d ed. (1937), 3d ed. (1944); Th. Maunz, *Verwaltung* (1937). H. Frank's anthology *Deutsches Verwaltungsrecht*, published in 1937, did not go along with the renaming and had no section on administrative science.

16. Nass, "Über verwaltungsrechtliche und verwaltungswissenschaftliche Begriffe," *Verwaltungsarchiv* 46 (1941): 65 ff.; Nass, "Staatskunst und Verwaltung. Zugleich ein Beitrag zur Quellenlehre der Verwaltungswissenschaft und zur Neuordnung des Polizeibegriffs," *Reich und Länder* (1937): 233 ff.; Nass, "Verwaltungserfahrung und Verwaltungsrecht," *Reichsverwaltungsblatt* (1936): 760 ff.; Nass, "Ministerialakten als Quelle der Verwaltungswissenschaft," *Deutsche Verwaltung* (1938): 213 ff.; Nass, "Der Begriff der Verwaltung und die Vorbildung der Verwaltungsbeamten," *Reichsverwaltungsblatt* (1939): 613 ff.; Nass, "Die Geschichte der Vorbildung der Verwaltungsbeamten und ihre Lehren für die Gegenwart," *Reichverwaltungsblatt* (1941): 479 ff.; Nass, "Die Philosophie der Verwaltung als Grundlage der Verwaltungswissenschaft," *Reichsverwaltungsblatt* (1942): 345 ff.; Nass, "Über die Bedeutung verwaltungsgeschichtlicher Forschungen und verwaltungsrechtlicher Übungen für die Vorbereitung der Verwalter," *Zeitschrift der Akademie für deutsches Recht* (1942): 149 ff. After the war Nass continued to publish in much the same vein, for example, in his book *Verwaltungsreform durch Erneuerung der Verwaltungswissenschaft* (1950). In a review of the book, O. Bachof graciously said that the legitimate core of Nass's concern "should not be overlooked because of the infelicitous form of the work, whose effectiveness is largely nullified by exaggerations and resentments"; see Bachof, "Das Verwaltungsrecht im Spiegel der Rechtslehre. Eine Betrachtung zu den neuen Lehrbüchern des Verwaltungsrechts," *Juristenzeitung* (1951): 538 ff. (539). See also O. Nass, *Staatsberedsamkeit. Ein staats- und verwaltungswissenschaftlicher Versuch* (1972).

17. Koellreutter (see note 12, above); Forsthoff (see note 13, above); Forsthoff, "Das neue Gesicht der Verwaltung und die Verwaltungsrechtswissenschaft," *Deutsches Recht* (1935): 331 ff.; Th. Maunz, *Neue Grundlagen des Verwaltungsrechts* (1934); Maunz, "Zum Neubau des deutschen Verwaltungsrechts," *Deutsche Juristen-Zeitung* (1934): cols. 1046 ff.; Maunz, "Neues Rechtsdenken in der Verwaltung," *Deutsche*

Verwaltung (1935): 65 ff.; F. W. Jerusalem, "Das Verwaltungsrecht und der neue Staat," in *Festschrift für Hübner* (1935), 124 ff.; E. Tatarin-Tarnheyden, "Grundlagen des Verwaltungsrechts im neuen Staat," *Archiv des öffentlichen Rechts* 63 (1934): 345 ff.

18. P. Badura, *Die Methoden des Neueren Allgemeinen Staatslehre* (1959), especially 184 ff.; W. Bauer, *Wertrelativismus und Wertbestimmtheit im Kampf um die Weimarer Demokratie* (1968); M. Friedrich, "Die Grundlagendiskussion in der Weimarer Staatsrechtslehre," *Politische Vierteljahresschrift* 13 (1972): 582 ff.; Friedrich, "Der Methoden- und Richtungsstreit. Zur Grundlagendiskussion der Weimarer Staatsrechtslehre," *Archiv des öffentlichen Rechts* 102 (1977): 161 ff.

19. P. Laband, *Das Staatsrecht des Deutschen Reiches,* 2d ed. (Freibur, 1888), xi (foreword).

20. Very obvious from the time of Erich Kaufmann's talk on the principle of equality *(Gleichheitssatz)* given at the 1926 Meeting of Constitutional Lawyers, *Veröffentlichungen der Vereinigung der Deutschen Staatsrechtslehrer* 3 (1927): 2 ff.

21. *Reichsverwaltungsblatt* (1933): 481 ff.

22. Forsthoff (see note 13, above).

23. Nass, "Verwaltungserfahrung" (see note 16, above); Nass, "Ministerialakten" (see note 16, above).

24. *Die Praxis der öffentlichen Verwaltung* (1936), 250. Harnack was sentenced to death by the Volksgerichtshof on February 1, 1945, and executed.

25. H. Peters, "Universitätsausbildung der Verwaltungsbeamten," *Völkischer Beobachter,* December 15, 1936, supplement: Der Beamte im Dritten Reich 69, refuting A. Köttgen, *Die Bedeutung der Universität für die Ausbildung des Verwaltungsbeamten in Reich und Ländern* (1936).

26. A. Köttgen, "Wissenschaft und Verwaltung," *Deutsche Verwaltung* (1938): 37 ff.

27. A. Köttgen, "Aufgaben und Methoden der verwaltungsrechtlichen Forschung," *Jahrbuch für Kommunalwissenschaft* 5 (1938): 210 ff.

28. Jäger, "Der VI. Internationale Kongreß für Verwaltungswissenschaft," *Deutsche Verwaltung* (1936): 237 ff.

29. Reported in *Deutsche Verwaltung* (1937): 156. The members of this section included J. Heckel, R. Höhn, K. Jeserich, O. Kollmann, P. Ritterbusch, and W. Sommer.

30. R. Höhn, *Das ausländische Verwaltungsrecht der Gegenwart* (1940).

31. H. R. Pichinot, "Die Akademie für Deutsches Recht," diss., Kiel, 1981.

32. H. Frank, "Technik des Staates," *Zeitschrift der Akademie für Deutsches Recht* (1941): 2 ff.; Frank, *Die Technik des Staates* (1942); A. Dresler, "Das Münchner 'Institut für die Technik des Staates,'" *Deutsche Verwaltung* (1942): 44–45; O. Müller-Haccius, "Verwaltung und Technik," *Deutsche Verwaltung* (1942): 2 ff.

33. "Der Stand der deutschen Verwaltungwissenschaft," *Beamten-Jahrbuch* (1939): 144 ff.

34. Ibid., 151.

35. *Lehrbuch der Verwaltung* (1949), 14 ff.

36. G. Wacke, "Zur Arbeit an der Verwaltungswissenschaft," *Zeitschrift der Akademie für Deutsches Recht* (1942): 83 ff.; Wacke, "Der Gegenstand der Verwaltungslehre," *Verwaltungsarchiv* 47 (1942): 169 ff.

37. Wacke, "Verwaltungswissenschaft" (see note 36, above), 83.

38. R. Thoma, "Zur Reform des Verwaltungsstudiums," *Reichsverwaltungsblatt* (1941): 709 ff.

39. *Deutsche Verwaltung* (1942), with contributions by G. Schmidt (61 ff.), G. Kasper (67 ff.), G. Wacke (125 ff.), K. H. Seifert (164 ff.), K. Hahn (168 ff.), H. Beuster (235 ff.), O. Nass (249 ff.), F. Klausing (335 ff.), and J. Gaedke (338 ff.).

40. W. Taeuber, "Verwaltungswissenschaft, Verwaltungsrecht, Heeresverwaltung," *Zeitschrift für die gesamten Staatswissenschaften* 102 (1942): 338 ff. (352).

41. Wacke, "Verwaltungswissenschaft" (see note 36, above), 83.

42. B. Dennewitz, *Verwaltung und Verwaltungsrecht* (1944), 20.

43. Ibid., 32.

44. Taeuber (see note 40, above), 355.

45. Ibid., 363.

46. See note 13, above; also *Die Verwaltung als Leistungsträger* (1938).

47. See notes 15, 26, 27, above.

48. F. Werner, "Verwaltungsrecht als konkretisiertes Verfassungrecht," *Deutsches Verwaltungsblatt* (1959): 527 ff.

49. Heckel (see note 14, above), 26.

50. G. Püttner, *Verwaltungslehre* (1982), 1 ff.

CHAPTER EIGHT

1. M. Sellmann, "Der Weg zur neuzeitlichen Verwaltungsgerichtsbarkeit, ihre Vorstufen und dogmatischen Grundlagen," in H. R. Külz and R. Naumann, eds., *Staatsbürger und Staatsgewalt*, vol. 1 (Karlsruhe, 1963), 25–86; see also, in the same volume, the essays by Rapp, Knoll, Klinger, Kuntzmann-Auert, Frege, and Walz. M. Baring, *Aus 100 Jahren Verwaltungsgerichtsbarkeit*, 2d ed. (Cologne, 1964); W. Rüfner, "Die Entwicklung der Verwaltungsgerichtsbarkeit," in K. G. A. Jeserich et al., eds., *Deutsche Verwaltungsgeschichte*, vol. 1 (Stuttgart, 1984), 909 ff.

2. M. Stolleis and I. Schmitt, "Zur Entstehung der Zeitschriften des Öffentlichen Rechts seit 1848," *Quaderni fiorentini* 13 (1984): 747–761 (757–758). See also chapter 7, above.

3. Bahmann, "Das Verhältnis des Verwaltungsstreitverfahrens zu den tragenden Gedanken des neuen Staates," *Deutsche Verwaltung* (1934): 51–54; R. Höhn, "Das subjektive öffentliche Recht und der neue Staat," *Deutsche Rechtswissenschaft* 1 (1936): 39; W. Sommer, "Die Verwaltungsgerichtsbarkeit," *Deutsches Verwaltungsblatt* (1937): 425–430. Also J. Kölble, *Behördenfeindliche Verwaltungsjustiz* (Berlin, 1937); with critical responses by v. Bohlen, *Juristische Wochenschrift* (1938): 489; and H. P. Ipsen, *Zeitschrift der Akademie für Deutsches Recht* (1938): 285.

4. Voltz, "Nationalsozialismus und Verwaltungsgerichtsbarkeit," *Der Städtetag* (1933): 499–500.

5. R. Knauth, "Die Verwaltungsgerichtsbarkeit im neuen Reich," *Reichsverwaltungsblatt* (1933): 885 (886).

6. Schneider, "Verwaltungsgerichtsbarkeit im neuen Reich," *Deutsches Recht* (1935): 458–461.

7. D. Holtz, "Das Problem der Verwaltungsgerichtsbarkeit," *Deutsche Verwaltung* (1934): 290 (291).

8. O. Koellreutter, "Das Wesen des Politischen in der öffentlichen Verwaltung," *Reichsverwaltungsblatt* (1933): 483.

9. R. Knauth (see note 5, above), 888.

10. R. Knauth, "Die heutige Lage der Verwaltungsgerichtsbarkeit," *Deutsche Juristenzeitung* (1934): 1120.

11. R. Knauth, "Die Deutsche Gemeindeordnung und die Verwaltungsgerichtsbarkeit," *Deutsches Verwaltungsblatt* (1935): 105–108; Schneider (see note 6, above); the official explanation is in M. Schattenfroh, *Die Deutsche Gemeindeordnung* (Munich, 1935), § 29.

12. Administrative High Court of Saxony, January 18, 1935, *Jahrbuch des Sächsischen Oberverwaltungsgerichts* 39, no. 1: 6–7, on *Baufreiheit*. See Felsch, "Baufreiheit," *Reichsverwaltungsblatt* (1935): 329; Th. Maunz, "Neues Rechtsdenken in der Verwaltung," *Deutsche Verwaltung* (1935): 65; Krüger, "Die neue Rechtsprechung des SächsOVG," *Verwaltungsarchiv* 41 (1936): 177; Scheller, "Verwaltungsgerichtsbarkeit und Baurecht . . . ," *Reichsverwaltungsblatt* (1937): 149, with a response by Hofacker, *Reichsverwaltungsblatt* (1937): 319; Rehkopp, "Die Baupolizei im Spiegel der neuen Rechtsprechung," *Reichsverwaltungsblatt* (1937): 633; A. Hofacker, "Zum Umschwung der Rechtsprechung des Sächsischen Oberverwaltungsgerichts," *Württembergische Zeitschrift für Verwaltung und Verwaltungsrechtspflege* 29 (1937): 161 ff. The court later backed away from this course. Administrative High Court of Saxony, October 23, 1936, *Reichsverwaltungsblatt* (1937): 181, on prohibiting the carrying on of business. See H. Krause, "Die Untersagung von Unternehmungen," *Zeitschrift der Akademie für Deutsches Recht* (1938): 660; F. Schack, "Die Untersagung von Gewerbebetrieben im Lichte der neueren Rechtsprechung," *Reichsverwaltungsblatt* (1939): 323.

13. Report in H. Reuß, "Die Verwaltungsgerichtsbarkeit im neuen Reich," *Juristische Wochenschrift* (1935): 2025–2028. This essay is a prime example of veiled argumentation. Supervision by administrative courts, legal security, subjective-public rights, and the function of the legal profession are defended by invoking Nazi authorities. Unfortunately, the account by P. v. Feldmann, *Kritische Justiz* (1983): 57–63, neglects this aspect, which can also be found in the numerous reviews that Reuß wrote, especially for the *Juristische Wochenschrift*.

14. W. Stuckart, "Nationalsozialistischer Staat und Verwaltungsgerichtsbarkeit," *Deutsche Verwaltung* (1935): 161–164.

15. W. Frick, "Die Verwaltungsgerichtsbarkeit im nationalsozialistischen Staat," *Deutsche Verwaltung* (1936): 329, continued in *Zeitschrift der Akademie für Deutsches Recht* (1936): 160 ff.

16. H. Frank, *Recht und Verwaltung* (Munich, 1939).

17. F. Scholz, *Die Verwaltungsgerichtsbarkeit im Dritten Reich, nebst Entwurf einer Reichsverwaltungsgerichtsordnung* (Cologne, 1936). Scholz moved from the Reich Interior Ministry to the Prussian Administrative High Court on January 1, 1937. Agreement came especially from F. Giese, "Reformfragen der Verwaltungsgerichtsbarkeit," *Deutsches Verwaltungsblatt* (1936): 508–513; as well as O. Koellreutter, "Grundsätzliches zur Frage der Verwaltungsgerichtsbarkeit," *Reichsverwaltungsblatt* 57 (1936): 885–887.

18. H. Schelcher, "Um die Verwaltungsrechtspflege des Dritten Reiches," *Reichsverwaltungsblatt* (1937): 569–581.

19. See note 2, above.

20. W. Sommer (see note 3, above).

21. See, for example, Bernhard Scheer, "Staatspolitik, Polizei und Verwaltungsgerichte," *Völkischer Beobachter*, March 1, 1936, supplement: Der Beamte im Dritten Reich. Scheer emphatically opposed any supervision of "state-political measures by

the police"—and thus not only of the Gestapo—by administrative courts, although he wanted to "essentially retain" administrative jurisdiction.

22. Sommer (see note 3, above), 427. Dissenting opinion by O. Koellreutter, "Verfassungsschutz. Zum Wesen der deutschen völkischen Verfassung," *Reichsverwaltungsblatt* 59 (1938): 302 ff.

23. See, for instance, Lüdtke, "Die Schutzhaft gemäß der Verordnung vom 28. Februar 1933," *Juristische Wochenschrift* (1933): 2241; R. Neubert, "Die Schranken richterlichen Prüfungsrechts bei staatspolitischen Handlungen der Verwaltung," *Juristische Wochenschrift* (1933): 2426; Boehr, "Nochmals: Die Schutzhaft gemäß der Verordnung vom 28. Februar 1933," *Juristische Wochenschrift* (1933): 2499; Hoche, "Schutzhaft nach der VO v. 28. Februar 1933," *Deutsche Juristenzeitung* (1933): 1490; R. Berger, "Sind politische Maßnahmen, insbesondere Schutzhaftbefehle der richterlichen Nachprüfung unterzogen?" *Juristische Wochenschrift* (1934): 14; H. Schwabe, "Unzulässigkeit des Rechtsweges gegenüber politischen Entscheidungen," *Juristische Wochenschrift* (1934): 1616; Schoetzau, "Maßnahmen der politischen Leiter unterliegen nicht der Nachprüfung durch die Gerichte," *Juristische Wochenschrift* (1935): 3210; F. Schack, "Die richterliche Kontrolle von Staatsakten im neuen Staat," *Reichsverwaltungsblatt* (1934): 592; Schack, "Die richterliche Prüfung von Gesetz und Verordnung," *Reichsverwaltungsblatt* (1937): 68; U. Scheuner, "Die Gerichte und die Prüfung politischer Staatshandlungen," *Reichsverwaltungsblatt* (1936): 437; Scheuner, "Paßpolizei und Verwaltungsgerichte," *Reichsverwaltungsblatt* (1937): 129; H. Schelcher, "'In der Regel ohne Angabe von Gründen,'" *Reichsverwaltungsblatt* (1936): 913; Schelcher, "Zur Frage der Paßpolizei und Verwaltungsgerichte," *Reichsverwaltungsblatt* (1937): 135.

24. G. Schmidt, "'Rechtswahrung in der Verwaltung' anstelle von Verwaltungsgerichtsbarkeit," *Deutsche Verwaltung* (1938): 229 (230); likewise H. Schelcher (see note 18, above), 571; U. Scheuner, "Die Rechtsstellung der Persönlichkeit in der Gemeinschaft," in H. Frank, ed., *Deutsches Verwaltungsrecht* (Munich, 1937), 82 ff. See also Scheuner's review of H. P. Ipsen's *Politik und Justiz* (Hamburg, 1937), in *Archiv des öffentlichen Rechts* n.f. 30 (1939): 363; S. Grundmann, "Die richterliche Nachprüfung von politischen Führungsakten nach geltendem deutschen Verfassungsrecht," *Zeitschrift für die gesamten Staatswissenschaften* 100 (1940): 511.

25. Schmidt (see note 24, above): 233, with *Reichsverwaltungshof* instead of *Reichsverwaltungsgericht*, *Spruch* instead of *Urteil*, *Verwaltungsrechtspflege* instead of *Verwaltungsgerichtsbarkeit*, and so on.

26. Bach, "Die Rechtsprechung des Preußischen Oberverwaltungsgerichts im Lichte der nationalsozialistischen Weltanschauung und Rechtsauffassung," *Deutsche Verwaltung* (1938): 199–205.

27. R. Sievers, "Die geistigen Grundlagen der Verwaltungsgerichtsbarkeit," *Deutsche Verwaltung* (1938): 77 (81).

28. H. Reuß, "Der Krieg und die Verwaltungsgerichtsbarkeit," *Zeitschrift der Akademie für Deutsches Recht* (1940): 10; Reuß, "Zuständigkeit und Verfahren der Verwaltungsgerichte," *Deutsches Recht* (1942): 1345; Reuß, "Die Verwaltungsrechtspflege im Kriege," *Verwaltungsarchiv* 45 (1940): 154 ff.; G. Schmidt, "Die Rechtsmittel in der Verwaltung," *Deutsche Verwaltung* (1940): 1; Schmidt, "Die Vereinfachung des Rechtsmittelwesens in der Verwaltung," *Deutsche Verwaltung* (1941): 13; W. Herold, "Die Bedeutung der Verwaltungsgerichtsbarkeit im Dritten Reich," law diss., Gießen, 1940; W. Sommer, "Verwaltungsstreitverfahren oder Verwaltungsrechtspflege?"

Deutsche Verwaltung (1941): 245; Sommer, "Für die Verwaltungsgerichtsbarkeit," *Reichsverwaltungsblatt* (1941): 549; H. P. Ipsen, "Zur Lage der Verwaltungsgerichtsbarkeit," *Nationalsozialistische Beamtenzeitung, Der deutsche Verwaltungsbeamte* (1943): 23 ff.; R. Knauth, "Die Neuordnung der Verwaltungsgerichtsbarkeit im Kriege," in E. R. Huber, ed., *Idee und Ordnung des Reiches*, vol. 1 (Hamburg, 1941); H. Pfeifer, "Zur Neuordnung der Verwaltungsgerichtsbarkeit im Reich," *Zeitschrift der Akademie für Deutsches Recht* (1943): 185; W. Weber, "Zuständigkeit und Zukunft der Verwaltungsgerichte," *Zeitschrift für die gesamten Staatswissenschaften* 104 (1944): 424 ff.

29. W. Stuckart, "Das Reichsverwaltungsgericht," *Deutsches Recht* (1941): 189; Th. Maunz, "Ein Jahr Rechtsprechung des Reichsverwaltungsgerichts," *Deutsches Recht* (1943): 1127; R. Freisler, "Reichsverwaltungsgericht und Reichsuniversität Posen," *Deutsche Justiz* (1941): 537; H. Reuß, "Das Reichsverwaltungsgericht," *Verwaltungsarchiv* 47 (1942): 28.

30. W. Sommer (1893–1946), head of the central office in the staff of the deputy of the Führer, Ministerial Director. For biographical data, see D. Rebentisch, in *Deutsche Verwaltungsgeschichte*, vol. 4, part 2 (note 1, above). He lost his position in September 1942 because of a personal affair. At Göring's intervention, Dr. Franz Hueber (1894–1979), former Austrian Minister of Justice (March 11–May 24, 1938) and at the time Undersecretary of State in the Reich Justice Ministry, was appointed his successor. Hueber's plea for the independence of judges and "respect for private rights," for legal security and consideration for the irritable public mood is remarkable, and his references to interference by "high-ranking officials" are unequivocal (*Deutsche Verwaltung* [1942]: 5–9). Of course, Hueber could afford to make such comments, given his past services to the regime and the fact that he was Göring's brother-in-law. See H. Slapnicka, *Die Oberösterreichische politische Führungsschicht* (Linz, 1976), 136–137. I am grateful to Dieter Rebentisch, Frankfurt, for kindly providing me with information from the files of the Reich Chancellery.

31. An overview of the legal basis, the structure, and the procedures of administrative jurisdiction as of December 31, 1935, in J. Danckwerts, "Die Verwaltungsgerichtsbarkeit im nationalsozialistischen Staate," in H. Frank, ed., *Deutsches Verwaltungsrecht* (Munich, 1937), 99 (121–125).

32. F. Genzmer, "Die Verwaltungsgerichtsbarkeit," in G. Anschütz and R. Thoma, eds., *Handbuch des Deutschen Staatsrechts*, vol. 2 (Tübingen, 1932), § 97, 506–523.

33. Genzmer (see note 32, above), 522; M. Kuntzmann-Auert, "Verwaltungsgerichte des Reiches außerhalb des Bereichs der Sozialleistungen und des Reichswirtschaftsgerichts," in Külz and Naumann (see note 1, above), 117–130.

34. Danckwerts (see note 31, above), 100.

35. "Preußisches Gesetz über die Anpassung der Landesverwaltung an die Grundsätze des nationalsozialistischen Staats v. 15. Dezember 1933," *Preußische Gesetzessammlung:* 479; E. Nedden, *Die Zuständigkeit der Verwaltungsbehörden und Verwaltungsgerichte in Preußen* (Wesermünde, 1935); Ch. F. Menger, "Zur Geschichte der Verwaltungsgerichtsbarkeit in Deutschland," *Die öffentliche Verwaltung* (1963): 726–729, now in his *Verfassung und Verwaltung in Geschichte und Gegenwart* (Heidelberg, 1982), 286 (292).

36. Par. 7, sec. 1, "Gesetz zur Wiederherstellung des Berufsbeamtentums v. 7. April 1933," *Reichsgesetzblatt* 1 (1933): 175.

37. Par. 11, sec. 1, "Anpassungsgesetz" (see note 35, above).

38. "Gesetz über Reichsverweisungen vom 23. März 1934," *Reichsgesetzblatt* 1 (1934): 213. On this see M. Stolleis, *Gemeinwohlformeln im nationalsozialistichen Recht* (Berlin, 1974), 225–226.

39. The legal basis, outside of the general clause concerning the police (§ 14 PVG), was the so-called Reichstag Fire Decree of February 28, 1933. The states acted with varying speed in eliminating legal protection against Gestapo orders; Prussia did so through § 7 of the Gestapo Law of February 10, 1936, PrGS, p. 21.

40. "Erlaß des Führers und Reichskanzlers über die Vereinfachung der Verwaltung vom 28. August 1939," *Reichsgesetzblatt* 1 (1939): 1535.

41. Art. 1, §§ 1 and 2 of the second Decree on the Simplification of Administration, November 6, 1939, *Reichsgesetzblatt* 1 (1939): 2168. Detailed information on this in J. Poppitz, *Die Verwaltungsgerichtsbarkeit im Kriege* (Hamburg, 1941), 9 ff. (Führer decree), 12 ff., 46 (admittance), 24 (composition of the courts), 35 (Reich Administrative Court).

42. Reich Administrative Law of December 8, 1941, *Entscheidungen des Reichsverwaltungsgerichts* 1:149 (151).

43. Decree of August 11, 1941, *Reichsministerialblatt* 5 (1941): 1475.

44. W. Weber (see note 28, above), 440.

45. Weber (see note 28, above); H. Pfeifer, "Rechtsvereinheitlichung und Verwaltungsvereinfachung im Großdeutschen Reich," in E. R. Huber, *Idee und Ordnung des Reiches*, vol. 11 (Hamburg, 1943), especially 80 ff.

46. *Entscheidungen des Preußischen Oberverwaltungsgerichts* 94 (1935): 134.

47. *Entscheidungen des Preußischen Oberverwaltungsgerichts* 95 (1935): 131, which states that "the police banning of a paper, intended as a general punitive and educational measure, cannot base itself on § 1 of the Decree of February 28, 1933."

48. *Entscheidungen des Preußischen Oberverwaltungsgerichts* 94 (1935): 140, with reference to the Law on the Confiscation of Communist Assets of May 26, 1933, *Reichsgesetzblatt* 1 (1933): 291.

49. *Entscheidungen des Preußischen Oberverwaltungsgerichts* 96 (1936): 83.

50. Ibid., 77.

51. Ibid., 87.

52. See note 39, above.

53. *Entscheidungen des Preußischen Oberverwaltungsgerichts* 97 (1936): 103.

54. *Entscheidungen des Preußischen Oberverwaltungsgerichts* of November 10, 1938, *Juristische Wochenschrift* (1939): 382. On this decision see E. Fraenkel, *The Dual State* (London, 1969), 28.

55. Baden Administrative Court of January 11, 1938, *Badische Verwaltungszeitschrift* (1938): 96–100; Fraenkel (see note 54, above), 58 ff.

56. Fraenkel (see note 54, above), 43.

57. Administrative Court of Bavaria, May 1936, in *Entscheidungen der Gerichte und Verwaltungsbehörden aus dem Gebiete des . . . Verwaltungs- und Polizeistrafsrechts, begr. v. Reger* (1881–   ), 56:533.

58. Prussian Administrative High Court of December 4, 1936, *Juristische Wochenschrift* (1937): 1368.

59. Hamburg Administrative High Court of October 7, 1935, *Reichsverwaltungsblatt* (1936): 1045.

60. Weber (see note 28, above); Poppitz (see note 41, above), with additional references.

61. H. Spanner, *Die Eingliederung der Ostmark ins Reich* (Hamburg, 1941); Pfeifer (see note 45, above); B. Dennewitz, *Verwaltung und Verwaltungsrecht* (Vienna, 1944), 116–118.

62. *Reichsgesetzblatt* 1 (1941): 201.

63. H. Reuß, "Zuständigkeit und Verfahren der Verwaltungsgerichte," *Deutsches Recht* (1942): 1345; also Pfeifer (see note 45, above), 90. See also W. Fischer, "Der Streit um die Verwaltungsgerichtsbarkeit unter bes. Berücksichtigung der Verfahrensgestaltung," diss., Düsseldorf, 1940.

64. Consolidated were the Prussian Administrative High Court, the Reichsdienststrafhof (Reich Disciplinary Court), the Reichswirtschaftsgericht (Reich Economic Court), the Administrative Court Vienna, the court of arbitration for real estate, the highest tribunal for water and land associations, the compensation court, and the Reich Office for War Damage to Property.

65. Führer decree (see note 62, above); and *Durchführungsverordnung* (implementing decree) of April 29, 1941, *Reichsgesetzblatt* 1 (1941): 224.

66. On the jurisdiction of the Reich Administrative Court, see the finding of the Second Outer Senate Vienna of June 19, 1941, *Entscheidungen des Reichsverwaltungsgerichts* 1:246; decision of the Second Outer Senate Vienna of July 30, 1941, *Entscheidungen des Reichsverwaltungsgerichts* 1:254.

67. "Das Schicksal der Verwaltungsgerichtsbarkeit unter dem Nationalsozialismus," *Die öffentliche Verwaltung* (1963): 729 (732).

68. Chr. Kirchberg, *Der badische Verwaltungsgerichtshof im Dritten Reich* (Berlin, 1982), 113–118, with additional references. On the Reich Administrative Court, see W. Kohl, *Das Reichsverwaltungsgericht* (1991).

69. The list included the collections of decisions by the Prussian Administrative High Court (vols. 90–105), the Administrative Court of Baden, the Administrative Court of Bavaria, the Administrative High Court of Saxony, the Administrative Court of Württemberg, the Administrative High Court of Jena, the Administrative Court of Hessen, the Administrative High Court of Hamburg, the Administrative Court of Braunschweig, the Administrative High Court of Oldenburg, the State Administrative Court of Schwerin, the State Administrative Court of Neustrelitz, the Administrative Court/Administrative High Court of Bremen, the Administrative Court of Lübeck, the Administrative High Court of Detmold, the Administrative High Court of Dessau, and, in addition, the two volumes of decisions by the Reich Administrative Court (1942–1943). Outside of these collections one can find reprints of decisions in the journals. To all this we must add a significant number of unpublished decisions, for example, those of the Reich Administrative Court in the Federal Archives in Koblenz.

70. This holds true, for example, for the much noted changes in the decisions rendered by the Administrative High Courts of Saxony and Thuringia. See note 12, above.

71. Herein lies the unresolved, basic methodological problem of the useful book by R. Echterhölter, *Das öffentliche Recht im nationalsozialistischen Staat* (Stuttgart, 1970). Echterhölter arranged the material according to contemporary "constitutional values and principles," even where "corresponding principles are not yet found in the Weimar Constitution" (p. 12). On the criteria, see M. Stolleis and D. Simon, "Vorurteile und Werturteile der rechtshistorischen Forschung zum Nationalsozialismus," in *NS-Recht in historischer Perspektive* (Munich and Vienna, 1981), 13–51.

72. O. P. Schweling, *Die deutsche Militärjustiz in der Zeit des Nationalsozialismus*

(Marburg, 1977). See also my review in *Geschichte in Wissenschaft und Unterricht* (1978), 650–654.

73. For a representative view, see J. Jellinek, *Verwaltungsrecht*, 3d ed. (Berlin, 1931), 88 ff.

74. C. Schmitt, "Nationalsozialismus und Rechtsstaat," *Juristische Wochenschrift* (1934): 713–718; "Was bedeutet der Streit um den 'Rechtsstaat'?" *Zeitschrift für die gesamten Staatswissenschaften* 95 (1935): 189–201; "Der Rechtsstaat," in H. Frank, ed., *Handbuch für Recht und Gesetzgebung* (Munich, 1935), 3–10.

75. Fraenkel (see note 54, above), 37 ff.; L. Frege, "Der Status des Preußischen Oberverwaltungsgerichts und die Standhaftigkeit seiner Rechtsprechung auf politischem Gebiet," in Külz-Naumann (see note 1, above), 131–155; H. R. Külz, "Verwaltungskontrolle unter dem Nationalsozialismus," *Kritische Justiz* (1969): 367–378; Echterhölter (see note 71, above), passim; W. Hempfer, *Die nationalsozialistische Staatsauffassung in der Rechtsprechung des Preußischen Oberverwaltungsgerichts* (Berlin, 1974).

76. *Entscheidungen des Preußischen Oberverwaltungsgerichts* 94:134.

77. *Entscheidungen des Preußischen Oberverwaltungsgerichts* 96:77.

78. *Entscheidungen des Preußischen Oberverwaltungsgerichts* 95:99.

79. *Entscheidungen des Preußischen Oberverwaltungsgerichts* 97:205.

80. Ibid., 117.

81. Frege (see note 75, above), 146 ff.

82. Külz (see note 75, above), 367 ff.

83. H. Egidi, "Die Präsidenten des Preußischen Oberverwaltungsgerichts im ersten Drittel des 20. Jahrhunderts," *Deutsches Verwaltungsblatt* (1963): 459, 470; L. Frege, "Nochmals: Die Präsidenten des Preußischen Oberverwaltungsgerichts," *Deutsches Verwaltungsblatt* (1964): 134; C. H. Ule, "Bill Drews," in *Männer der deutschen Verwaltung* (Cologne and Berlin, 1963); Ule, "Über das Wirken des Präsidenten des Preußischen Oberverwaltungsgerichts Prof. Dr. Dr. h. c. Bill Drews in der Zeit nach 1933," in D. Wilke, ed., *Festschrift zum 125 jährigen Bestehen der Juristischen Gesellschaft zu Berlin* (Berlin and New York, 1984), 803–819.

84. H. J. Wichardt, "Die Rechtsprechung des Königlich Preußischen Oberverwaltungsgerichts zur Vereins- und Versammlungsfreiheit von 1875 bis 1914," diss., Kiel, 1976; W. Schultze, "Öffentliches Vereinigungsrecht im Kaiserreich 1881 bis 1918," diss., Frankfurt, 1973; U. Stump, *Preußische Verwaltungsgerichtsbarkeit 1875–1914* (Berlin, 1980); W. Rüfner (see note 1, above), 922 ff.

85. Chr. Kirchberg (see note 68, above).

86. E. Walz, "Verwaltungsrechtspflege in Karlsruhe," in *Festschrift zur Eröffnung des BGH in Karlsruhe* (1950); Walz, "100 Jahre Verwaltungsgerichtsbarkeit in Baden—Randbemerkungen zu einem Jubiläum," in M. Baring (see note 1, above), 102–123; M. Rapp, "100 Jahre Badischer Verwaltungsgerichtshof," in Külz and Naumann (see note 1, above), 1–24.

87. Chr. Kirchberg, "Der Badische Verwaltungsgerichtshof im Dritten Reich," *Verwaltungsblätter für Baden-Württemberg* (1981): 370 (373–374).

88. The older literature in Rüfner (see note 1, above), 909, 916. The essay by H. W. Zinser in Baring (see note 1, above) passes over in silence the period after 1933. On this see Rupp, "Die Rechtsprechung des württembergischen Verwaltungsgerichtshofs seit 1933," *Verwaltungsarchiv* 44 (1939): 204; and the material incorporated in R. Nebinger, *Verwaltungsrecht* (Stuttgart, 1946); and Echterhölter (see note 71, above).

89. "WürttVGH v. 21. Juli 1937," *Deutsche Verwaltung* (1938): 126 (confessional *Volksschule*); "WürttVGH v. 22. Dezember 1937," *Reichsverwaltungsblatt* (1939): 14 (real right in favor of a pastorate); "WürttVGH v. 19. Oktober 1938," *Reichsverwaltungsblatt* (1939): 607 (kindergarten law); "WürttVGH v. 13. Dezember 1939," *Reichsverwaltungsblatt* (1941): 474 (confessional *Volksschule*); "WürttVGH v. 5. April 1940," *Deutsche Verwaltung* (1942): 38 (confessional kindergarten).

90. "WürttVGH v. 22. Dezember 1937" (see note 89, above); "WürttVGH v. 11. Oktober 1939," *Reichsverwaltungsblatt* (1940): 136.

91. "WürttVGH v. 5. Mai 1938," *Deutsche Verwaltung* (1938): 412; "WürttVGH v. 19. April 1939," *Reichsverwaltungsblatt* (1941): 223; "WürttVGH v. 17. Mai 1940," *Reichsverwaltungsblatt* (1941): 489.

92. "WürttVGH v. 25. November 1938," *Reichsverwaltungsblatt* (1941): 224; "WürttVGH v. 22. Oktober 1937," *Reichsverwaltungsblatt* (1939): 15; "WürttVGH v. 25. Juni 1941," *Reichsverwaltungsblatt* (1941): 602.

93. "WürttVGH v. 17. Juni 1936," *Deutsche Verwaltung* (1937): 31; "WürttVGH v. 21. Juli 1937," *Deutsche Verwaltung* (1938): 125 (see R. Nebinger, "Zur Handhabung der Polizeigewalt," *Deutsche Verwaltung* [1938]: 292). See also "WürttVGH v. 17. Juni 1936," *Deutsche Verwaltung* (1937): 31 (Jewish healers *[Heilpraktiker]* are prohibited from engaging in their profession).

94. "WürttVGH v. 9. September 1936," *Deutsche Verwaltung* (1936): 385.

95. *Württembergische Zeitschrift für Verwaltungsrechtspflege* (1937): 126, 175, 190.

96. J. Widtmann, "Verwaltungsrechtspflege in Bayern von 1863 bis 1963," in Baring (see note 1, above), 41–64 (57–59). The festschrift for the Administrative Court of Bavaria that was edited by Theodor Maunz (Munich, 1979) avoided the topic of National Socialism. On the latter see, for example, Stritzke, "NS-Weltanschauung und die Rechtsprechung des Bayerischen Verwaltungsgerichtshofs," *Deutsche Verwaltung* (1939): 430.

97. "Gesetz vom 4. März 1939," *Gesetz- und Verordnungsblatt* (1939): 41.

98. *Entscheidungen des Bayerischen Verwaltungsgerichtshofs* 58:25, 58:10, 60:17; "BayVGH v. 30 Juni 1939," *Reichsverwaltungsblatt* (1940): 111. In connection with this, see also *Entscheidungen des Bayerischen Verwaltungsgerichtshofs* 61:34–35, on the continued validity of the Weimar Constitution.

99. See, for example, "Bayerischer Verwaltungsgerichtshof v. 5. Juni 1936," *Reichsverwaltungsblatt* (1938): 17; *Entscheidungen des Bayerischen Verwaltungsgerichtshofs* 59:114 (118). Particularly impressive is the law-abiding defense of the exemption of synagogues from paying the house tax, *Entscheidungen des Bayerischen Verwaltungsgerichtshofs* 58:77 (also reported in Echterhölter [see note 17, above], 127, 137–138).

100. *Entscheidungen des Bayerischen Verwaltungsgerichtshofs* 57:208.

101. *Entscheidungen des Bayerischen Verwaltungsgerichtshofs* 61:15–16.

102. "BayVGH v. 4. Oktober 1933," *Deutsches Verwaltungsblatt* (1934): 144. See also *Entscheidungen der Gerichte und Verwaltungsbehörden* 54:75, on the political actions taken against organizations.

103. *Entscheidungen des Bayerischen Verwaltungsgerichtshofs* 58:77 (see note 99, above).

104. *Entscheidungen des Bayerischen Verwaltungsgerichtshofs* 58:17, 59:76 (79), 108–109. "BayVGH v. 26. Februar 1937," *DeutschesVerwaltungsblatt* (1937): 354, shows that non-Jews, too, who were considered "unreliable" in purchasing goods from Jews

had to be protected. Summary by K. Müller, "Die neue Rechtsprechung des BayVGH," *Verwaltungsarchiv* 43 (1938): 421.

105. *Entscheidungen des Bayerischen Verwaltungsgerichtshofs* 58:17.

106. *Entscheidungen des Bayerischen Verwaltungsgerichtshofs* 59:110–111; "BayVGH v. 1. Dezember 1939," *Reichsverwaltungsblatt* (1940): 303.

107. M. Baring, "Dem Sächsischen Oberverwaltungsgericht zum Gedächtnis!" *Deutsches Verwaltungsblatt* (1951): 649; Baring, "Die Verwaltungsrechtspflege in Sachsen. Ereignisse und Gestalten," in Baring (see note 1, above), 65–93. See also Rüfner (note 1, above), 920–921; on Baring himself, see G. Korbmacher, *Juristenzeitung* (1984): 981.

108. § 75, sec. 1, no. 20 of the Law on Administrative Jurisdiction of July 19, 1900, and later that of December 14, 1933, removed from administrative jurisdiction police decrees issued on the basis of the Reichstag Fire Decree or its implementing regulations.

109. *Jahrbuch des Sächsischen Oberverwaltungsgerichts* 38:277, 39:63, 39:165, 41:203; "E v. 9. Oktober 1937," *Deutsche Verwaltung* (1938): 60; *Entscheidungen der Gerichte und Verwaltungsbehörden* 60:539–540.

110. *Jahrbuch des Sächsischen Oberverwaltungsgerichts* 39:312; *FischersZ* 73:89.

111. *Jahrbuch des Sächsischen Oberverwaltungsgerichts* 39:1 (6–7); *Fischers Zeitschrift für Verwaltungsrecht* 73:135; decision of November 8, 1935, *Deutsche Verwaltung* (1936): 98.

112. See note 12, above; M. Stolleis (note 38, above), 252, with additional references.

113. *Jahrbuch des Sächsischen Oberverwaltungsgerichts* 39:332–333.

114. *Jahrbuch des Sächsischen Oberverwaltungsgerichts* 40:180. For the contrast to Prussia, see Echterhölter (note 71, above), 109, with additional references; M. Stolleis (see note 38, above), 256–257.

115. *Jahrbuch des Sächsischen Oberverwaltungsgerichts* 40:212, 41:317; *Entscheidungen der Gerichte und Verwaltungsbehörden* 58:472; *Gewerbearchiv* 35:207 (closing of a business for "desecration of the race"). See also *Jahrbuch des Sächsischen Oberverwaltungsgerichts* 40:104 (a Jewish *Volksschule* club does not have nonprofit status).

116. *Reichsverwaltungsblatt* 60 (1939): 102; *Jahrbuch des Sächsischen Oberverwaltungsgerichts* 41:202, 39:279; *Deutsche Verwaltung* (1936): 351; *FischersZ* 73:69–70, 73:308; *Entscheidungen der Gerichte und Verwaltungsbehörden* 61:166.

117. H. Loening, "36 Jahre Thüringisches Oberverwaltungsgericht (1912–1948)," in M. Baring (see note 1, above), 153–169; Rüfner (see note 1, above), 930.

118. The last seven decisions can be found in *Reichsverwaltungsblatt* 62 (1941): 374–375.

119. *Jahrbuch der Entscheidungen des Thüringischen Oberverwaltungsgerichts* 17:74.

120. *Entscheidungen des Preußischen Oberverwaltungsgerichts* 101:203 ff., with additional references. The final decision in line with the Administrative High Court of Thuringia by the Reich Administrative Court, "Urteil v. 1. Oktober 1942," *Zeitschrift der Akademie für Deutsches Recht* (1943): 157, with note by R. Reinhardt.

121. "ThürOVG, Urt. v. 21. Oktober 1936," *Deutsches Verwaltungsblatt* (1937): 356; on the exceptions to this, see the decision of April 13, 1938, *Deutsche Verwaltung* (1938): 411.

122. "Entscheidung v. 12. Januar 1938," *Deutsche Verwaltung* (1938): 158.

123. *Jahrbuch der Entscheidungen des Thüringischen Oberverwaltungsgerichts* 17:81.

124. G. Edelmann, "100 Jahre Hessische Verwaltungsgerichtsbarkeit—Entstehung und Entwicklung in Hessen-Darmstadt," *Der Gemeindetag* (1976): 129–138; J. Weitzel, "100 Jahre Verwaltungsgerichtsbarkeit in Hessen," *Deutsches Verwaltungsblatt* (1975): 869–873, with additional references.

125. On Lüneburg, see H. C. Sarnighausen, in *25 Jahre Oberverwaltungsgericht Lüneburg 1949–1974* (Hannover, 1974), 44 ff. On Schleswig, see H. Sander, 90 ff. (104–105).

126. M. Sellmann, *Entwicklung und Geschichte der Verwaltungsgerichtsbarkeit in Oldenburg* (Oldenburg, 1957), 83 ff.; Sellmann, in *Deutsches Verwaltungsblatt* (1956): 845; and Sellmann, in Baring (see note 1, above), 124 ff.

127. References in Echterhölter (see note 71, above).

128. Evidence for the State Administrative Court in Schwerin in Echterhölter (see note 71, above).

129. As demonstrated in the *Mecklenburgische Zeitschrift für Rechtspflege, Rechtswissenschaft, Verwaltung* (the title after 1925–1926).

130. "Gesetz v. 6. Dezember 1937," *Reichsgesetzblatt* (1937): 309.

131. The Administrative High Court of Bremen was established by the Law on Administrative Jurisdiction, as promulgated on September 21, 1933 (*Gesetzblatt* [1933]: 351). The two-tier system thus did not exist before National Socialism. See J. Peters, "Geschichte, Entstehung und Entwicklung der Verwaltungsgerichtsbarkeit in Bremen," law diss., Kiel, 1981 (Düsseldorf, 1981), 114 ff., 122–131, limited to organizational questions; W. Giesges, *Die Verwaltungsgerichtsbarkeit in Hamburg. Unter Einschluß der VO Nr. 141* (Hamburg, 1941); G. Quast, "Die Entstehungsgeschichte der hamburgischen Verwaltungsgerichtsbarkeit," law diss., Hamburg, 1974.

132. H. G. Figge, "Die Entwicklung der Verwaltungsrechtspflege im Bezirk des Verwaltungsgerichts Braunschweig," in *25 Jahre Oberverwaltungsgericht* (see note 125, above), 36 (41–43).

133. F. Hueber, "Justiz im Führerstaat," *Deutsche Justiz* 1942: 5 (9). See note 30, above.

CHAPTER NINE

1. E. Schwinge, "Die deutsche Militärgerichtsbarkeit im Zweiten Weltkrieg," *Deutsche Richterzeitung* (1959): 350–352.

2. See on this the debate between Weinkauff and E. Franssen, *Juristenzeitung* (1969): 766; (1970): 54.

3. R. Echterhölter, *Das öffentliche Recht im nationalsozialistischen Staat* (1970).

4. K. D. Erdmann, "Zeitgeschichte, Militärjustiz und Völkerrecht," *Geschichte in Wissenschaft und Unterricht* (1979): 129–139; M. Broszat, "Der Streit um die Wehrmachtsgerichtsbarkeit," *Frankfurter Allgemeine Zeitung*, October 10, 1978.

5. O. P. Schweling, *Die deutsche Militärjustiz in der Zeit des Nationalsozialismus* (Marburg, 1977).

6. Ibid., 6.

7. Ibid., 14.

8. Ibid., 8.

9. Ibid., 26.

10. Ibid., 28.

11. Ibid., 30.

12. Ibid., 169.

13. Ibid., 173.

14. Ibid., 188–189.

15. Ibid., 211.

16. Ibid., 252 ff.

17. Ibid., 322.

18. Ibid., 329.

19. Ibid., 336–337.

20. Hans Karl Filbinger was a former navy judge who rose to become premier of the state of Baden-Württemberg. Revelations about his Nazi past ended his political career.—Trans.

21. M. Messerschmidt and F. Wüllner, *Die Wehrmachtjustiz im Dienste des Nationalsozialismus* (Baden-Baden, 1987). This is countered, for example, by the retired Major General J. Schreiber, *Soldat im Volk* 37, no. 3 (1988); and by E. Schwinge, *Verfälschung und Wahrheit. Das Bild der Wehrmachtgerichtsbarkeit* (Tübingen, Zurich, and Paris, 1988).

22. M. Messerschmidt, "Deutsche Militärgerichtsbarkeit im Zweiten Weltkrieg," in *Festschrift für Martin Hirsch* (Baden-Baden, 1981), 11–141.

23. H. Wrobel, "Cum ira et studio," *Rechtshistorisches Journal* 10 (1991): 99–101.

24. Decision of September 11, 1991, *Entscheidungen des Bundessozialgerichts* 69:211.

25. See, on the one side, E. Schwinge, *Neue juristische Wochenschrift* (1993): 369; and W. Stoecker, *Sozialgerichtsbarkeit* (1993): 352; on the other, O. Gritschneder, *Sozialgerichtsbarkeit* (1993): 603.

CHAPTER TEN

1. The White Rose (Weiße Rose) was a student anti-Nazi resistance group that was formed at the University of Munich in 1942 at the initiative of Hans and Sophie Scholl. Six members of the group were arrested in mid-February 1943. After a hasty trial before the People's Court, the Scholls were sentenced to death and executed on February 22, 1943. Kurt Huber, a professor of philosophy at the university, was executed on July 13.—Trans.

2. I would like to express my sincere thanks to Diederich Behrend and Günter Frankenberg for their help in gathering the material for this essay.

3. D. Strothmann, "Die Dornen der 'Weißen Rose'," *Die Zeit*, November 26, 1982; Strothmann, "Unter dem Fallbeil der Zeit," *Die Zeit*, January 7, 1983.

4. fr (= F. K. Fromme), "Infam," *Frankfurter Allgemeine Zeitung*, January 18, 1982; similarly, H. Heigert, "Wie Moral zur Verleumdung verdirbt," *Süddeutsche Zeitung*, January 22, 1982. Opposing view by M. Krebs, "Juristische Haarspalterei zum Schutz von Nazi-Richtern," *Süddeutsche Zeitung*, December 11–12, 1982.

5. H. Weber and Chr. Engel, "Der Film 'Die Weiße Rose' und die Rechtslage bei Urteilen des Volksgerichtshofs," *Juristenzeitung* (1983): 192.

6. W. Fikentscher, *Frankfurter Allgemeine Zeitung*, October 16, 1982.

7. H. Heigert, "Eine unsichere Nation," *Süddeutsche Zeitung*, December 11, 1982.

8. President of the Federal Court Pfeiffer, press release in *Frankfurter Allgemeine Zeitung* and *Frankfurter Rundschau*, November 18, 1982.

9. Letter by the deputy press spokesman of the Federal Court to Hans Hirzel (a member of the White Rose), dated November 25, 1982.

10. *Neue juristische Wochenschrift* (1968): 1339.

11. See note 7, above.

12. References in Weber and Engel (see note 5, above), and in H. Hillermeier, "Vom Versagen der Richter gestern und heute," *Kritische Justiz* (1984): 54–57; G. Frankenberg and F. J. Müller, "Verdrängt, vergessen oder ausgeheilt? Die Bewältigung der Vergangenheit durch den Bundesgerichtshof," *Kritische Justiz* (1983); G. Offczors, "Strafrechtliche Wiedergutmachung nationalsozialistischen Unrechts am Beispiel des Widerstandskämpfers Fiete Schulze," *Demokratie und Recht* (1983): 174–182.

13. *Frankfurter Rundschau*, December 13, 1982.

14. The new closing statement read as follows: "1. It is the view of the Federal Court that the paragraphs under which the resistance fighters of the White Rose were sentenced were not part of the Nazi terror system but valid law.

"2. It is the view of the Federal Court that resistance fighters like the White Rose objectively violated laws that were valid at the time.

"3. It is the view of the Federal Court that a judge at the People's Court who sentenced resistance fighters like the White Rose was subject to these laws that were valid at the time.

"4. It is the view of the Federal Court that resistance fighters like the White Rose could, nevertheless, not be criminally charged if they violated valid laws with the intent of helping their country.

"5. It is the view of the Federal Court, however, that a judge who considered a resistance fighter to have been proven guilty in a proper trial cannot be reproached, in terms of criminal law, if he believed, given the laws at the time, that he had to sentence him to death.

"6. So far no government and no Bundestag could bring themselves to annul all sentences of the People's Court by law" (press release, November 25, 1982).

15. Protocol of the 128th and 131st sessions of the Bundestag, November 12, 1982, and November 26, 1982, respectively (responses of Parliamentary State Secretary H. H. Klein).

16. Inge Scholl, *Die Weiße Rose*, reprint (Fischer, 1982); R. Hanser, *"Deutschland zuliebe." Leben und Sterben der Geschwister Scholl* (dtv, 1982); M. Verhoeven and M. Krebs, *Die weiße Rose. Der Widerstand Münchner Studenten gegen Hitler* (Fischer, 1982); H. Vinke, *Das kurze Leben der Sophie Scholl* (O. Maier, 1980).

17. *Frankfurter Rundschau*, June 3, 1982.

18. *Frankfurter Rundschau*, February 25, 1983 (the Superior Court of Justice for Berlin rejected it as inadmissible on December 20, 1982); on the rejection by the Federal High Court, see *Frankfurter Allgemeine Zeitung*, May 31, 1983. The events leading up to this are described in Deiseroth, *Demokratie und Recht* (1980), 63.

19. Hans-Joachim Rehse was, after Roland Freisler, the most incriminated judge at the People's Court. He was acquitted of all charges in 1968. The decision was widely regarded as scandalous.—Trans.

20. The cases ended without any spectacular results, mainly through the death of those under investigation or the prosecution's decision not to indict for lack of evidence.—Trans.

21. W. Fikentscher and R. Koch, "Strafrechtliche Wiedergutmachung nationalsozialistischen Unrechts," *Neue juristische Wochenschrift* (1983): 12–15; Weber and Engel (see note 5, above), with additional references; Offczors (see note 12, above), 174–175.

22. Frankenberg and Müller (see note 12, above).

23. See statements 1–3 of the revised trailer (note 14, above).

24. Compare *Entscheidungen des Bundesgerichtshofs in Zivilsachen* 5:76 (96); *Entscheidungen des Bundesgerichtshofs in Strafsachen* 3:110 (113), 4:66 (68), 9:302 (305).

25. *Entscheidungen des Bundesverfassungsgerichts* 3:58 ff., 6:132 ff.; the quotation is in *Entscheidungen des Bundesverfassungsgerichts* 23:98 (106). Here I can only begin to touch on the debate about the relationship between law and morality and about the validity of immoral legal norms. See especially N. Hoerster, "Zum begrifflichen Verhältnis von Recht und Moral," *Neue Hefte für Philosophie* 17 (1979): 77–88; R. Dreier, "Recht und Moral," in *Recht-Moral-Ideologie* (Frankfurt, 1981), 180–216; H. Hofmann, *Legitimität und Rechtsgeltung* (Berlin, 1977).

26. Claus Arndt, *Süddeutsche Zeitung,* November 6–7, 1982.

27. Art. 3 of "Gesetz zur Änderung von Vorschriften des Strafrechts und des Strafverfahrens v. 24.4.1934," *Reichsgesetzblatt* 1 (1934): 341. On the establishment of the People's Court, see the detailed account by W. Wagner, *Der Volksgerichtshof im nationalsozialistischen Staat* (Stuttgart, 1974), 13 ff.

28. Thus the press statement of nine members of the White Rose sentenced by the court (Bollinger, Grimminger, Guter, Hirzel, Zeller-Hirzel, Jud, F. J. Müller, Th. Müller, Suhr), *Frankfurter Rundschau,* December 13, 1983. Thus also the Social Democratic Party (SPD) *Fraktion* (parliamentary group) in a petition to the federal government on December 7, 1982, on the grounds that the court was "an instrument of political terror to oppress, persecute, neutralize, and destroy the enemies of the Hitler dictatorship."

29. G. Buchheit, *Richter in roter Robe. Freisler, Präsident des Volksgerichtshofs* (Munich, 1968); W. Wagner (see note 25, above), 29 ff.; H. Hillermeier, ed., *"Im Namen des Deutschen Volkes." Todesurteile des Volksgerichtshofes* (Darmstadt und Neuwied, 1980).

30. On the dependent status of the judge under National Socialism, see D. Simon, *Die Unabhängigkeit des Richters* (Darmstadt, 1975), 53 ff.

31. This was the general opinion. See, for instance, Deiseroth (note 18, above), 58 ff.; Strothmann (note 3, above).

32. Documentation in Deiseroth (see note 18, above), 107 ff.; and in W. H. Seiter and A. Kahn, *Hitlers Blutjustiz. Ein noch zu bewältigendes Kapitel deutscher Vergangenheit* (Frankfurt, 1981).

33. Open letter by forty professors to the Justizsenator of Berlin and the prosecutor general, January 1980. *Frankfurter Rundschau,* January 12, 1980.

34. For a discussion of how the historical course was set, see M. Broszat, "Siegerjustiz oder strafrechtliche 'Selbstreinigung'," *Vierteljahreshefte für Zeitgeschichte* (1981): 477. A good summary is in A. Rückerl, *Die Strafverfolgung von NS-Verbrechen 1945–1978* (Heidelberg and Karlsruhe, 1978); Rückerl, *NS-Verbrechen vor Gericht* (Stuttgart, 1982).

35. According to a report in the *Süddeutsche Zeitung,* February 7, 1983, the German authorities declared that they were not interested in the extradition of Barbie, "among other reasons because of the impending parliamentary elections." Reference in Frankenberg and Müller (see note 12, above).

36. J. Feest, "Die Bundesrichter—Herkunft, Karriere und Auswahl der juristischen Elite," in W. Zap, ed., *Beiträge zur Analyse der deutschen Oberschicht,* 2d ed.

(Munich, 1965), 95 ff.; U. Reifner, "Juristen im Nationalsozialismus," *Zeitschrift für Rechtspolitik* (1983): 13–19.

CHAPTER ELEVEN

1. References especially in J. Becker, Th. Stammen, P. Waldmann, *Vorgeschichte der Bundesrepublik Deutschland* (1979); H. A. Winkler, *Politische Weichenstellungen im Nachkriegsdeutschland 1945–1949* (1979); A. Grosser, *Geschichte Deutschlands seit 1945,* 6th ed. (1978); W. Abelshauser, *Wirtschaft in Deutschland 1945–1948* (1975); *West-deutschlands Weg zur Bundesrepublik 1945–1949,* Beiträge von Mitarbeitern des Instituts für Zeitgeschichte (1976); E. U. Huster et al., *Determinanten der westdeutschen Restauration 1945–1949,* 6th ed. (1979).

2. B. Diestelkamp, "Rechts- und verfassungsgeschichtliche Probleme zur Früh-geschichte der Bundesrepublik Deutschland," *Juristische Schulung* (1980): 401–405, 481–485, 790–796; (1981): 96–102, 409–413, 488–494, with extensive references.

3. Readers can now consult the work of M. Etzel, *Die Aufhebung von nationalsozia-listischen Gesetzen durch den Alliierten Kontrollrat (1945–1948)* (1992).

4. J. R. Wenzlau, *Der Wiederaufbau der Justiz in Nordwestdeutschland, 1945–1949* (1979).

5. H. Kramer, ed., *Braunschweig unterm Hakenkreuz* (1981).

6. W. Benz, ed., *Bewegt von der Hoffnung aller Deutschen. Zur Geschichte des Grund-gesetzes: Entwürfe und Diskussionen 1941–1949* (1979); Wenzlau (see note 4, above), 27 ff.

7. *Entscheidungen des Bundesverfassungsgerichts* 22:75.

8. One of the most important documents on this is the memorandum by W. Strauss, *Die Oberste Bundesgerichtsbarkeit* (1949). See also the references in *Jahrbuch des öffentlichen Rechts* n.f. 1 (1951).

9. K. Griewank, *Der neuzeitliche Revolutionsbegriff* (1969).

10. Berlin declaration of the Allies, June 5, 1945, in I. v. Münch, *Dokumente des geteilten Deutschland,* vol. 1 (1976), 19–20.

11. J. Gimbel, *Amerikanische Besatzungspolitik in Deutschland 1945–1949* (1971).

12. Proclamation of Allied Commander in Chief Eisenhower, No. 1, sec. 1: "We will destroy National Socialism in the German territories occupied by military forces under my command, remove the NSDAP from power, and abolish the cruel, harsh, and unjust laws and institutions put in place by the NSDAP."

13. Wenzlau (see note 4, above), 9–10, has also stated this.

14. Ch. F. Menger, *Verfassungsgeschichte der Neuzeit,* 3d ed. (1981), 195.

15. Burke Shartel and H. J. Wolff, "Civil Justice in Germany," *Michigan Law Review* 42 (1943): 864.

16. R. Hansen, *Das Ende des Dritten Reiches* (1966), 205.

17. H. Benjamin et al., *Zur Geschichte der Rechtspflege der DDR 1945–1949* (1976), 44, on the situation in the East.

18. Military Administration Law No. 1, *Amtsblatt der Militärregierung* 1:11. The following laws were repealed: Law for the Protection of National Symbols of May 19, 1933; Law against the New Formation of Parties of July 14, 1933; Law to Secure the Unity of Party and State of December 1, 1933; Law against Treacherous Attacks . . . of December 20, 1934; Reich Flag Law of September 15, 1935; Law on the Hitler Youth of December 1, 1936; Law for the Protection of German Blood and Honor of

September 15, 1935; Decree of the Führer concerning the Legal Status of the NSDAP of December 12, 1942; Reich Citizenship Law of September 15, 1935, as well as thirty-five other norms that were supplementary in nature. Finally, this was followed by a list of anti-Jewish laws, which was explicitly described as not exhaustive.

19. We could add this example to the long tradition of prohibitions against interpreting and commenting on the law. See H. J. Becker, "Kommentier- und Auslegungsverbot," in A. Erler and E. Kaufmann, eds., *Handwörterbuch zur Deutschen Rechtsgeschichte*, vol. 2 (1978), cols. 963 ff.

20. See note 18, above: "In order to eradicate the principles and doctrines of the National Socialist German Workers' Party from German law and the administration within the occupied territories, to restore law and justice to the German people, and to reintroduce the principle of equality before the law . . ."

21. Potsdam Agreement, sec. A, IV, 4: "All Nazi laws which provided the basis of the Hitler regime or established discrimination on grounds of race, creed, or political opinion shall be abolished. No such discriminations, whether legal, administrative, or otherwise, shall be tolerated." A, IV, 8: "The judicial system will be reorganized in accordance with the principles of democracy, of justice under law, and of equal rights for all citizens without distinction of race, nationality or religion."

22. Prologue: "an administration of justice . . . based on the accomplishments of democracy, civilization, and justice."

23. Control Council, Proclamation No. 1 of August 30, 1945, sec. III, xi.

24. v. Münch (see note 10, above), 52–54.

25. Control Council Law No. 11 of January 30, 1946, and Law No. 55 of June 20, 1947. See the survey "Zur Auswirkung der Gesetzgebung der Besatzungsmächte auf das deutsche Strafgesetzbuch," *Süddeutsche Juristenzeitung* (1946): 121.

26. Control Council Law No. 36 of October 10, 1946, art. V.

27. Control Council Law No. 16 of Feburary 20, 1946.

28. Control Council Law No. 37 of October 30, 1946.

29. Control Council Law No. 22 (*Betriebsräte* Law) of April 10, 1946; Law No. 35 of August 20, 1946; Law No. 40 of November 30, 1946; Law No. 56 of June 30, 1947.

30. Control Council Law No. 44 of January 10, 1947; Law No. 45 of February 20, 1947 (repeal of the Reich's Hereditary Farm Law). On this see Wöhrmann, *Monatsschrift des Deutschen Rechts* (1947): 6.

31. Control Council Law No. 60 of December 19, 1947.

32. Control Council Law No. 49 of March 20, 1947 (Repeal of the Law on the Constitution of the German Protestant Church of July 14, 1933); Law No. 62 of February 20, 1948.

33. Examples: Orders of the Sowjetische Militäradministration No. 2 of June 10, 1945; No. 66 of September 17, 1945; No. 79 of September 29, 1945. Further details are in K. H. Schöneburg et al., *Vom Werden unseres Staates*, vol. 1 (1966), 80–81; Thuringian Law on the Repeal of Nazi Law of August 20, 1945, *Gesetzessammlung* (1945): 10.

34. Decree of the President of the Hanseatic Higher Regional Court of December 18, 1945, with the President of the Higher Regional Courts of Düsseldorf, Hamm, and Braunschweig following suit in the course of 1946.

35. O. Küster, *Süddeutsche Juristenzeitung* (1946): 31; W. Meiss, *Süddeutsche Juristenzeitung* (1946): 65.

36. Benjamin et al. (see note 17, above), 16.

37. Wenzlau (see note 4, above), 53; Benjamin et al. (see note 17, above), 323; F. Hartung, *Jurist unter vier Reichen* (1971), 136–138. In August 1945 the Soviets arrested about forty judges of the Supreme Court, eventually taking them to the Buchenwald concentration camp until 1950. Only four are said to have survived. See D. Kolbe, *Reichsgerichtspräsident Dr. Erwin Bumke* (1975), 402.

38. Benjamin et al. (see note 17, above), 323–324.

39. There is a second Proclamation No. 1 from Eisenhower as Supreme Commander of U.S. Forces, dated July 14, 1945.

40. Military Administration Law No. 2, *Amtsblatt der Militärregierung* 3:4.

41. Control Council Proclamation No. 3 of October 20, 1945; Control Council Law No. 4 of October 30, 1945.

42. Control Council Law No. 21 of March 30, 1946, and No. 36 of October 10, 1946.

43. Control Council Directives No. 24 of January 12, 1946, subpars. 87–89; No. 38 of October 12, 1946, app. A, sec. I, lit. N. and sec. II, lit. N.

44. Decree No. 126 of the British military government; Proclamation No. 7 of the U.S. military government; Law on the Legal Office of the Unified Economic Region of July 24, 1948, *Gesetz- und Verordnungsblatt für das Vereinigte Wirtschaftsgebiet*, 77. Dr. Walter Strauss, State Secretary in the Federal Ministry of Justice from 1949 to 1963, was appointed head of the Legal Office.

45. Benjamin et al. (see note 17, above), 46.

46. Ibid., 21.

47. Sowjetische Militäradministration Order No. 49 of September 4, 1945.

48. Sowjetische Militäradministration Order No. 28 and the Decree concerning Obligatory Social Insurance of January 28, 1947, in *Arbeit und Sozialfürsorge* (1947): 249.

49. H. Loening, "Der Kampf um den Rechtsstaat in Thüringen," *Archiv des öffentlichen Rechts* 75 (1949): 56–102, with a response by M. Draht, *Archiv des öffentlichen Rechts* 75 (1949): 124; U. v. Dassel, "Die neue Verwaltungsgerichtsbarkeit," *Neue Justiz* (1948): 27–31; S. Mampel, "Die Entwicklung der Verfassungsordnung in der sowjetisch besetzten Zone Deutschlands von 1945–1963," *Jahrbuch des öffentlichen Rechts* n.f. 13 (1964): 506; K. Sieveking, *Die Entwicklung des sozialistischen Rechtsstaatsbegriffs in der DDR* (1975), 29.

50. Benjamin et al. (see note 17, above), 73.

51. Thuringian Landtag, 4th sess., December 19, 1946, protocol, 6, 10 ff.; sess. of October 10, 1947, protocol, 651 ff.; 29th sess. of November 6, 1947, protocol, 713 ff.; sess. of October 7, 1948, protocol, 1346–1347. See K. A. Bettermann, "Rechtsstaat ohne unabhängige Richter?" *Neue Justiz* (1947–48): 217–220; E. Schiffer, "Der mißverstandene Montesquieu," *Der Morgen*, December 25, 1948, 1–2; E. Melsheimer, "Vom politischen und vom unpolitischen Richter," *Neue Justiz* (1950): 70–73; H. Loening, "Ansprache zur Wiedereröffnung des Thüring. OVG in Jena," *Archiv des öffentlichen Rechts* 74 (1948): 45 ff.

52. *Jahrbuch der Entscheidungen des Thüringischen Oberverwaltungsgerichts* 18 (1946–47): 220 ff.

53. The following figures are drawn from the speech by Thuringian Minister of Justice Külz on October 10, 1947 (Thuringian Landtag, protocol, 659):

	SED	LDPD	CDU	Without Party Affiliation
First course (9 graduates)	—	—	—	—
Second course (23 graduates)	19	8	2	3
Third course (80 graduates)	55	18	8	—

A programmatic statement on the purpose of the course can be found in M. Fechner, *Die soziale Aufgabe der Volksrichter* (1946); as well as in Benjamin et al. (see note 17, above), 90 ff.; also Benjamin, "Der Volksrichter in der Sowjetzone," *Neue Justiz* (1947); Hartwig, "Zur Ausbildung der Volksrichter," *Neue Justiz* (1947).

54. J. Wolffram and A. Klein, *Recht und Rechtspflege in den Rheinlanden* (1969), 247.

55. Military Administration Decree No. 41, *Amtsblatt der Militärregierung*, 299.

56. Wenzlau (see note 4, above), 297 ff.; Diestelkamp (see note 2, above), (1981): 412n.52.

57. R. Zimmermann, "Der OGH und die Fortbildung des Bürgerlichen Rechts," *Zeitschrift für neuere Rechtsgeschichte* (1981), with additional references.

58. Wenzlau (see note 4, above), passim; E. Girndt-Hassenpflug, *Zentralismus in der Britschen Zone*, diss., Bonn, 1971.

59. W. Fischer, "Die Rechtsanwaltschaft in der britischen Zone," *Deutsche Rechtszeitschrift* (1946): 124; Fischer, "Aufbau und Ordnung der Anwaltschaft in der Britischen Zone," *Monatsschrift des Deutschen Rechts* (1947): 180; Bartelmann, "Zur Zulassung von Ostanwälten in der britischen Zone," *Deutsche Rechtszeitschrift* (1947): 95, with a response by Fischer; E. Natter, "Der Wiederaufbau der Rechtsanwaltschaft," *Deutsche Rechtszeitschrift* (1946): 46; W. Kimmig, "Der Wiederaufbau der Rechtsanwaltschaft," *Deutsche Rechtszeitschrift* (1946): 170.

60. Diestelkamp (see note 2, above), (1981): 492.

61. Kramer (see note 5, above), especially 45 ff.

62. Diestelkamp (see note 2, above), (1981): 492.

63. Steidle, "Der Plan für den Aufbau des Rechtspflegewesens in der US-Zone," *Süddeutsche Juristenzeitung* (1946).

64. On the people affected, see "Gesetz zur Befreiung von Nationalsozialismus und Militarismus," March 5, 1946, App. sec. A, lit. N. An interesting discussion of the reception of the law by B. Reifenberg, "Befreiung durch Gesetz," *Die Gegenwart* 1 (1946): 11; H. Ehard, "Das Gesetz zur Befreiung von Nationalsozialimus und Militarismus," *Süddeutsche Juristenzeitung* (1946): 7.

65. O. Bachof, "Die 'Entnazifizierung'," in A. Flitner, ed., *Deutsches Geistesleben und Nationalsozialismus* (1965), 195 ff.; J. Fürstenau, *Entnazifizierung. Ein Kapitel deutscher Nachkriegspolitik* (1969); L. Niethammer, *Entnazifizierung in Bayern* (1972); V. Dotterweich, "Die 'Entnazifizierung'," in Becker et al. (see note 1, above), 123 ff.

66. The most spectacular case was that of the Erzberger assassin, Heinrich Tillessen. In 1933 he had been the beneficiary of an amnesty that Hitler had decreed on March 21, 1933. Now he was brought to justice (Decision of the Landesgericht Konstanz of February 28, 1947, on the basis of Control Council Law No. 10, *Deutsche Rechtszeitschrift* [1947]: 267–270, repeat of the decision of the Supreme Military Court of Rastatt of January 6, 1947, *Journal officiel* 61 [1947]: 605–636; finally, decision of the Higher Regional Court of Tübingen of April 17, 1947, *Deutsche Rechtszeitschrift*

[1948]: 141–142). The case attracted wide attention. See G. Radbruch, *Süddeutsche Juristenzeitung* (1947): 343; K. Geiler, "Legalität und Legitimität," *Die Gegenwart,* February 28, 1947, 15; H. C. Goldscheider, "Heinrich Tillessen und seine Welt," *Frankfurter Hefte* 2 (1947): 349; K. S. Bader, "Der Fall Tillessen in europäischer Beleuchtung," *Neues Europa* (1947). More recently, C. Gebhardt, *Der Fall des Erzberger-Mörders Heinrich Tillessen,* diss., Frankfurt am Main, 1994.

67. Diestelkamp (see note 2, above), (1981): 490 and 410.

68. Wenzlau (see note 4, above), 143, with additional references.

69. Clausnitzer, "Die Organisation der Rechtspflege in Groß-Berlin," *Deutsche Rechtszeitschrift* (1947): 221; Strucksberg, "Das Gerichtswesen in Groß-Berlin," *Haus und Wohnung* (1947); H. Schneider, "Die Verwaltungsgerichtsbarkeit in Berlin," *Archiv des öffentlichen Rechts* 74 (1948): 239, with additional references.

70. W. Lewald, *Grundlagen der neuen Rechtsordnung Deutschlands* (1948), 31.

71. These were some of the contributions to the discussion: K. S. Bader, "Die deutschen Juristen," *Deutsche Rechtszeitschrift* (1946): 33; Rotberg, "Entpolitisierung der Rechtspflege," *Deutsche Rechtszeitschrift* (1947): 107; E. Schmidt, "Der Richter," *Die Sammlung* (1946): 277; Schmidt, "Montesquieus *Esprit des lois* und die Problematik der Gegenwart von Recht und Justiz," in *Festgabe W. Kiesselbach* (1947); Erdsiek, "Politische Kontrolle oder Selbstkontrolle der Justiz," *Monatsschrift des Deutschen Rechts* (1948): 398.

72. K. Oppler, "Justiz und Politik," *Deutsche Rechtszeitschrift* (1947): 323; W. Dirks, "Die Beamten," *Frankfurter Hefte* 1 (1946): 697; G. Willms, "Der 'unpolitische' Richter," *Frankfurter Hefte* 3 (1948): 105; E. Melsheimer, "Vom politischen und vom unpolitischen Richter," *Neue Justiz* (1950): 71.

73. See the report in *Deutsche Rechtszeitschrift* (1947): 27.

74. Report in *Deutsche Rechtszeitschrift* (1947): 231; Klaas, "Der Konstanzer Juristentag," *Zentralblatt für die Britische Zone* (1947).

75. Compare the report in *Deutsche Rechtszeitschrift* (1947): 373.

76. Examples of the latter: Thuringia: "Gesetz zur Beseitigung nationalsozialistischen Rechts v. 20.8.1945" (*Gesetzessammlung* [1945]: 10). Sachsen-Anhalt: "Dritte Verordnung über die Neuordnung des Gerichtswesens v. 3.12.1945," *Verordnungsblatt* (1945); "Verordnung v. 6.2.1946," 306. Mark Brandenburg: "Runderlass v. 5.12.1945," *Verordnungsblatt* (1946): 59; "Runderlass v. 11.11.1945," *Verordnungsblatt* (1945): 81.

77. Oberlandesgericht Halle, *Neue Justiz* (1947): 17, with note by Weiss; Oberlandesgericht Gera, August 10, 1949, *Neue Justiz* (1949): 262. On restrictions on legal redress in criminal cases by the decrees of August 13, 1942, and December 13, 1944, see Oberlandesgericht Gera, May 2, 1946, *Neue Justiz* (1947): 104.

78. Kammergericht, February 27, 1946, *Neue Justiz* (1947): 42.

79. Oberlandesgericht Dresden, *Neue Justiz* (1947): 43.

80. Oberlandesgericht Gera, May 2, 1946, *Neue Justiz* (1947): 104.

81. Oberlandesgericht Halle, October 20, 1948, *Neue Justiz* (1949): 143; Kammergericht, June 2, 1949, *Neue Justiz* (1949): 147; Kammergericht, July 10, 1946, *Neue Justiz* (1947): 40.

82. Landgericht Halle, November 5, 1947, *Neue Justiz* (1948): 114.

83. Oberlandesgericht Gera, November 30, 1946, *Neue Justiz* (1947): 63; Kammergericht, August 1, 1947, *Neue Justiz* (1948): 50.

84. Oberlandesgericht Halle, September 20, 1948, *Neue Justiz* (1949): 143.

85. Kammergericht, May 9, 1947, *Neue Justiz* (1948): 52; Oberlandesgericht Dresden, January 27, 1949, *Neue Justiz* (1949): 53.

86. E. Melsheimer, "Der Kampf der deutschen Justiz gegen die Naziverbrecher," *Neue Justiz-Sonderheft* (1948): 128. The number of guilty verdicts up to 1949 has been given as 8,055. See Benjamin et al. (note 17, above), 232. On this see A. Rückerl, *Die Strafverfolgung von NS-Verbrechen 1945–1978. Eine Dokumentation* (1979), 31.

87. Benjamin et al. (see note 17, above), 350, with additional references; Benjamin, "Zum SMAD-Befehl Nr. 201," *Neue Justiz* (1947).

88. Landgericht Hagen, March 1, 1947, *Monatsschrift des Deutschen Rechts* (1947): 29.

89. Oberlandesgericht Freiburg, September 12, 1946, *Deutsche Rechtszeitschrift* (1947): 65; Oberlandesgericht Braunschweig, February 6, 1946, *Justizblatt Braunschweig* (1946): 71; Oberlandesgericht Celle, December 20, 1946, *Hann. Rechtspflege* (1947): 14; Oberlandesgericht Tübingen, February 24, 1947, *Deutsche Rechtszeitschrift* (1947): 164.

90. Oberlandesgericht Hamburg, March 20, 1947, *Monatsschrift des Deutschen Rechts* (1947): 137; Oberlandesgericht Braunschweig, June 7, 1946, *Süddeutsche Juristenzeitung* (1946): 119; Oberlandesgericht Celle, December 12, 1946, *Neue Justiz* (1947): 32; Oberlandesgericht Hamburg, January 22, 1947, *Monatsschrift des Deutschen Rechts* (1947): 75; Oberlandesgericht Kiel, January 22, 1947, *Deutsche Rechtszeitschrift* (1947): 198.

91. See H. Labin, *Monatsschrift des Deutschen Rechts* (1948): 60, with additional references.

92. Oberlandesgericht Hamburg, January 22, 1947, *Monatsschrift des Deutschen Rechts* (1947): 75; Oberlandesgericht Hamburg, July 30, 1947, *Monatsschrift des Deutschen Rechts* (1948): 26.

93. For example, the Oberlandesgericht Cologne, May 7, 1947, *Monatsschrift des Deutschen Rechts* (1947): 91.

94. Erdsiek, *Deutsche Rechtszeitschrift* (1946): 84; Clemens, *Monatsschrift des Deutschen Rechts* (1947): 221. On the interpretation of this norm under National Socialism, see M. Stolleis, *Gemeinwohlformeln im nationalsozialistischen Recht* (1974), 98n.25.

95. Oberlandesgericht Hamburg, March 26, 1947, *Monatsschrift des Deutschen Rechts* (1947): 137, and July 9, 1947, *Monatsschrift des Deutschen Rechts* (1948): 368; Oberlandesgericht Cologne, July 6, 1948, *Monatsschrift des Deutschen Rechts* (1948): 427.

96. Pappe, "On the Validity of Judicial Decisions in the Nazi Era," *Modern Law Review* 23 (1960): 274.

97. Waldow, "Rechtspositivismus oder Naturrecht?" *Monatsschrift des Deutschen Rechts* (1948): 338.

98. The so-called suit for the mitigation of hardship *(Härtemilderungsklage)*, in accord with § 77 of the Marriage Law of 1946, Control Council Law No. 16 of February 20, 1946.

99. Control Council Law No. 11, art. II, sec. I, subsec. I. See also R. Schwab, *Süddeutsche Juristenzeitung* (1946): 240.

100. Amtsgericht Wiesbaden, November 13, 1945, *Süddeutsche Juristenzeitung* (1946): 36.

101. Landgericht Berlin, May 24, 1946, *Neue juristische Wochenschrift* (1947–48): 230.

102. Amtsgericht Kandel, February 7, 1947, *Deutsche Rechtszeitschrift* (1947): 340.

103. Oberlandesgericht Hamburg, March 17, 1948, *Monatsschrift des Deutschen Rechts* (1948): 428; as well as the cases of Garbe (Oberlandesgericht Kiel, March 26, 1947, *Monatsschrift des Deutschen Rechts* [1947]: 69; *Süddeutsche Juristenzeitung* [1947]: 323, with note by A. Arndt) and Tillessen (see note 66, above).

104. Oberlandesgericht Saarbrücken, May 21, 1947, *Deutsche Rechtszeitschrift* (1947): 341, with note by H. Coing.

105. Coing (see note 104, above), also A. Arndt (see note 103, above); see also Coing, "Zur Frage der strafrechtlichen Haftung der Richter für die Anwendung naturrechtswidriger Gesetze," *Süddeutsche Juristenzeitung* (1947): 61–64; "Das Grundrecht der Menschenwürde, der strafrechtliche Schutz der Menschlichkeit und das Persönlichkeitsrecht des bürgerlichen Rechts," *Süddeutsche Juristenzeitung* (1947): 641–645.

106. On Control Council Law No. 10, see R. H. Graveson, "Der Grundsatz 'nulla poena sine lege' und KontrollratG Nr. 10," *Monatsschrift des Deutschen Rechts* (1947): 278; W. Kiesselbach, "Zwei Probleme aus dem Gesetz Nr. 10 des Kontrollrats," *Monatsschrift des Deutschen Rechts* (1947): 2; Meyer, "Das Kontrollratgesetz Nr. 10 in der Praxis der deutschen Strafgerichte," *Monatsschrift des Deutschen Rechts* (1947): 110; Strucksberg, "Zur Anwendung des Kontrollratsgesetzes Nr. 10," *Deutsche Rechtszeitschrift* (1947): 277; C. Citron, "Das Kontrollratsgesetz Nr. 10," *Die Gegenwart*, April 30, 1947: 23. Important decisions: Obergerichtshof Cologne, June 22, 1948, and May 20, 1948, *Monatsschrift des Deutschen Rechts* (1948): 303; Oberlandesgericht Hamburg, June 18, 1947, *Monatsschrift des Deutschen Rechts* (1947): 241; Oberlandesgericht Hamm, June 21, 1947, *Monatsschrift des Deutschen Rechts* (1947): 203; Kammergericht, May 17, 1947, *Deutsche Rechtszeitschrift* (1947): 308. On the so-called euthanasia trials, see especially Oberlandesgericht Frankfurt, August 12, 1947, *Süddeutsche Juristenzeitung* (1947): 633, with note by Radbruch; as well as Kammergericht, August 24, 1946, *Deutsche Rechtszeitschrift* (1947): 198, with note by R. Lange.

107. A. Rückerl (see note 86, above), with extensive references; M. Güde, *Justiz im Schatten von Gestern* (1959); H. Jäger, *Verbrechen unter totalitärer Herrschaft* (1967); M. Ratz, "Zur Verfolgung von NS-Verbrechen," *Demokratie und Recht* (1974): 351; D. Deiseroth, "NS-Justiz auf der Anklagebank," *Demokratie und Recht* (1980): 58.

108. H. Kramer (see note 5, above), 50–51.

109. E. Kern, "Die Stunde der Justiz," *Deutsche Rechtszeitschrift* (1947): 105.

CHAPTER TWELVE

1. G. Haney, *Theodor Maunz—im Dienste des Faschismus und der CSU* (Jena, 1964); K. Redeker, "Bewältigung der Vergangenheit als Aufgabe der Justiz," *Neue juristische Wochenschrift* (1964): 1097–1100.

2. P. Lerche, "Theodor Maunz," in *Juristen im Portrait* (Munich, 1988), 556.

3. F. K. Fromme, "Theodor Maunz gestorben," *Frankfurter Allgemeine Zeitung*, September 11, 1993.

4. Ibid.

5. Lerche (see note 2, above), 560.

6. H. Reuß on Th. Maunz, "Neue Grundlagen des Verwaltungsrechts (Hamburg, 1934)," *Juristische Wochenschrift* (1935): 469–470.

7. Th. Maunz, *Hauptprobleme des öffentlichen Sachenrechts* (1933), 316.

8. H. Zacher, "Hans Nawiasky," in Heinrichs et al., eds., *Deutsche Juristen jüdischer Herkunft* (1993), 677–692.

9. *Deutsche Juristenzeitung* (1936): col. 1230.

10. Th. Maunz, *Gestalt und Recht der Polizei* (1943). Among his earlier works, see especially *Neue Grundlagen des Verwaltungsrechts* (Hamburg, 1934); "Die Zukunft der Verwaltungsgerichtsbarkeit," *Deutsches Recht* (1935): 478; *Die Enteignung im Wandel der Staatsauffassung* (Freiburg, 1936); "Das Ende des subjektiv-öffentlichen Rechts," *Zeitschrift für die gesamten Staatswissenschaften* 96 (1936): 71 ff.; *Verwaltung* (Hamburg, 1937).

11. On the case brought against Frey in accordance with Article 18 of the Basic Law, see *Entscheidungen des Bundesverfassungsgerichts* 38:23–25 (decision of July 2, 1974).

12. The statements by Prof. Dr. Franz Klein in the discussion about the seventy-fifth anniversary of the Reich Fiscal Court/Federal Fiscal Court in the *Panorama* show on September 9, 1993, were not very felicitous. They deserve to be quoted: "We are the ones who are, for example, carrying out the continuity of the Reich, that is what the controversy was about, whether the Federal Republic had continuity with the Reich." Further, "I have no qualms about celebrating this, as well. For it was a great time also during National Socialism, when justice was professionally rendered. And there are also verdicts that are sinister and have been called sinister, and which have been called sinister also by me." Still further, "I am looking forward to my cele-bration, and even those who think, because they have not been invited, will not spoil it *[sic]*. And those who are today leveling charges probably also wore the uniform of the Hitler youth." On this see G. Felix, "Der Reichsfinanzhof im Dritten Reich, die jüdischen Deutschen und die unbegrenzte Auslegung," *Betriebsberater* (1993): 1297–1303; K. Tipke, "Über die Juden-Rechtsprechung des RFH," *Betriebberater* (1993): 1813 ff.; J. H. Kumpf, "Der Reichsfinanzhof 1933 bis 1945. Eine Nachbetrachtung zur 75-Jahr-Feier des obersten deutschen Steuergerichts im Herbst 1993," *Steuer und Wirtschaft* 1 (1994): 15–25, with additional references.

13. A term used to describe those who accepted the Weimar Republic not out of conviction but because it was the sensible thing to do.

14. *Frankfurter Allgemeine Zeitung*, December 21, 1993; *Kritische Justiz* (1993): 393–396.

15. For instance, in the program *Panorama* on October 7, 1993; in *Die Zeit*, January 14, 1994; and in the *Frankfurter Allgemeine Sonntagszeitung*, February 6, 1994.

16. *Süddeutsche Zeitung*, December 10, 1993. Earlier, the Bavarian Minister of the Interior Alfred Seidl (CSU) had acted as a legal and political adviser to Frey.

17. News about the meeting between Max Streibl, former Minister President of Bavaria, and Schönhuber, chairman of the Republikaner, was lost in February 1994 in the tumult of other affairs. The statement issued to the press, that "politics had not been discussed at this meeting," was surely not meant to be taken seriously. (The Republicans are a small party on the right of the political spectrum. It is active mostly on a local basis.—Trans.)

18. *Frankfurter Allgemeine Zeitung*, December 16, 1993. A short time later, Zhiri-novsky was expelled from Bulgaria, and the German government refused to let him enter the country.

19. H. Kühnert, "Maunz raus?" *Die Zeit*, February 10, 1994, 66; A. Gorkow, "Die braune Seite des Theodor Maunz," *Süddeutsche Zeitung*, February 12–13, 1994. The

December 1993 foreword to the twenty-ninth edition of Maunz and Zippelius, *Deutsches Staatsrecht* (Munich, 1994), did not mention either Maunz's death or the events described here.

20. I will not discuss the private letters addressed to me, which were, of course, also sent to colleague friends as circular letters. Public statements came from Klaus Vogel in a letter to the editor (*Frankfurter Allgemeine Zeitung*, January 5, 1994). His doubts that there were "hundreds of articles by Maunz" are certainly justified, but they touch only a marginal issue: After all, there were articles by Maunz, as has now been confirmed by reprints (for instance in the *National-Zeitung*, February 18, 1994). Moreover, Maunz's work as an expert adviser over a period of about two decades had been sufficiently proved through facsimiles of his handwritten reports.

21. J. H. Kaiser, "Steine von links auf ein Staatsrechtler-Grab," *Frankfurter Allgemeine Zeitung*, January 29, 1994.

22. W. Roth, "Anonyme Beiträge für Extremisten. Enger Kontakt zwischen CSU-Mitglied Maunz und DNV-Chef Frey," *Süddeutsche Zeitung*, October 9-10, 1993; O. Gritschneder, "Die unbedarften Freunde des Staatsrechtlers Theodor Maunz," commentary on cultural affairs in *Bayerischer Rundfunk*, October 24, 1993; G. Mauz in *Der Spiegel* 42 (1993): 33-34.

23. A. Hollerbach, "Juristische Lehre und Forschung in Freiburg in der Zeit des Nationalsozialismus," in E. John et al., eds., *Die Freiburger Universität in der Zeit des Nationalsozialismus* (1991), 104.

24. G. Anschütz, *Aus meinem Leben*, edited with introduction by W. Pauly (1993), 328-329.

25. The popular counter question—what about committed work of constitutional lawyers for left-wing extremism and for the regime of the former East Germany?—remains a theoretical one, given the lack of examples. So far there is no information about support from constitutional lawyers for the Communist Party of Germany (KPD), German Communist Party (DKP), Communist League of West Germany (KBW), or Red Army Faction (RAF, a left-wing terrorist group) and, with few exceptions, the jurists of constitutional and international law in the GDR have by now been dismissed or sent into retirement.

INDEX

Abendroth, Wolfgang, 100
Academy for German Law, 7, 11, 52, 67, 97, 121, 128–30
Adenauer, Konrad, xii, xiii, 3
Adenauer era, 10, 42
Administrative Courts and Administrative High Courts, 132, 135; of Baden, 134–35, 138; of Bavaria, 139; of Bremen, 240n.131; decisions, 136–42; of Hessia, 141; of Oldenburg, 141; of Prussia, 131, 134, 136, 137–38, 141; of Saxony, 130, 139–40; of Thuringia, 140–41, 174; of Württemberg, 138–39. *See also* Reich Administrative Court; Verwaltungsgerichte
administrative jurisdiction, 2, 3, 16–17, 103, 107–8, 127–44, 171, 173
administrative law, 78, 98–100, 221n.10; and administrative studies, 115–16, 124; journals, 104–5; judges, 129; under National Socialism, 16, 102–14; textbooks, 111–14; theory of, 87–88
administrative planning, 109
administrative studies, 115–26, 228n.7; international congresses, 121
Adorno, Theodor, 153
agrarian law and policy, 11, 14
Ahnenerbe, 62
Allied occupation, xii, 3, 9, 167–84; judicial personnel policies, 167–68, 171–72, 174–78, 183–84; law under the military government, 9, 170–78. *See also* zones of occupation
Altmann. *See* Barbie
Amira, K. von, 61
Amtsgerichte, 171–72; defined, 1
Anhalt, 142

Anschütz, Gerhard, 13, 75, 90, 96, 191–92
anti-Bolshevism, 10, 45
antipositivism, 90–92
antirepublicanism, 92
anti-Semitism, 45, 49, 58, 90, 97, 180. *See also* Jews
AOG. *See* Law on the Organization of National Labor
Arbeitsordnung, 17
arbitrary measures, 13. *See also* state: prerogative
Archiv des öffentlichen Rechts, 104
Archiv Kornelimünster, 153
arrests, 95
art: government control, 13
Association of Constitutional Lawyers, 88, 90, 99, 100, 188; avoidance of moral issues, 189; and Maunz case, 190–91
Association of Former Military Judges, 27–28, 146
Augustine, 6
Augustus, 55
Auschwitz trial, 42, 185
Austria, 135, 136, 206n.18; administrative studies in, 115

Bader, Karl Siegfried, 26, 42
Badura, Peter, 110
Barbie, Klaus, 156, 243n.35
Baring, Martin, 139
Basic Law, 34, 65, 88, 100, 146; community clause, 65; creation, 167–68; Maunz/Dürig commentary, 186
Bavaria, 111; government links to DVU, 189–90
Bayerische Verwaltungsblätter, 104
Beck, C. H. (publisher), 190